Piety's Wisdom

Piety's Wisdom

A Summary of Calvin's Institutes
with Study Questions

J. Mark Beach

Reformation Heritage Books
Grand Rapids, Michigan

Piety's Wisdom
© 2010 by J. Mark Beach

Published by
REFORMATION HERITAGE BOOKS
2965 Leonard St., NE
Grand Rapids, MI 49525
616-977-0599 / Fax 616-285-3246
e-mail: orders@heritagebooks.org
website: www.heritagebooks.org

Library of Congress Cataloging-in-Publication Data

Beach, J. Mark (James Mark)
  Piety's wisdom : a summary of Calvin's Institutes with study questions / J. Mark Beach.
    p. cm.
  Includes bibliographical references (p.   ).
  ISBN 978-1-60178-082-9 (pbk. : alk. paper) 1. Calvin, Jean, 1509-1564. Institutio Christianae religionis. 2.
  Reformed Church—Doctrines. 3. Theology, Doctrinal. I. Title.
  BX9420.I69B43 2010
  230'.42—dc22
                              2010001988

To my wife, Sheryl,

with whom I first ventured
a study of Calvin.
I love you.

Contents

BOOK FOUR: *The External Means or Aids by Which God Invites Us Into the Society of Christ and Holds Us Therein*

Preface

Why another book on Calvin and his book, the *Institutes of the Christian Religion*? The answer is simple; many people will never attempt to read Calvin's classic work. They are intimidated because of its daunting size and detail.

Some years ago when I was serving as pastor to a congregation of believers in Pella, Iowa, I proposed to the adult study group that we study Calvin's *Institutes*. I was encouraged by how many were interested in the project. But I also saw furrowed brows. Some asked, "You're not expecting us to read all the way through the *Institutes*, are you?" At that moment I tasked myself with writing a synopsis of Calvin's two big volumes.

The plan was clear. I set out to write summaries of each of Calvin's chapters, trying to capture Calvin's method of presentation and the tenor of his discussion. People in the study group who wanted to tackle assigned sections of the *Institutes of the Christian Religion* were encouraged to do so, but those who simply wanted to read the synopsis that I provided were free to do only that. Since this was to be an adult study of Christian doctrine—particularly of Reformed doctrine—I ended each chapter synopsis with questions for discussion so we might apply Calvin's thinking to some of the issues we face today as believers. Some of these questions directed readers to look more carefully at Scripture, while other questions addressed controversial matters that needed clarity or correction. The goal, however, was to introduce readers to the rudiments of Reformed doctrine, and in so doing to deepen their understanding of the Christian faith, which was the very goal of Calvin in writing the *Institutes*.

Thus this book came to life more than fifteen years ago, but it is now twice the size of the original draft, covering all of Calvin's two volumes.

One might still ask, why write another book on Calvin and the *Institutes*? I offer two reasons for such a project. First, Calvin remains an outstanding teacher of the church. Though the *Institutes* show the marks of age (the weaknesses of sixteenth-century polemics, as well as a certain lopsidedness in treating some topics in disproportionate detail), nonetheless, these two volumes are still winsome, thought-provoking, spiritually inspiring, and heart-searching summations of Christian truth. Thus a modern summary of this work still serves the church today.

Second, though a number of works either offer an analysis of Calvin's views or serve as a guide to his *Institutes*, none shares the pedagogical aim of this book. This summary of Calvin's *Institutes*, keeping to the form, shape, and tenor of Calvin's own work, is offered to busy pastors, seminarians, college students, and laypersons who want a book that presents Calvin on his own terms and does not press an agenda. Thus this summary can be used as an introduction to the Christian faith, as a primer for the study of Calvin, or a combination of each. It can also be used individually or jointly in an adult study group.

I also want to offer a few comments about what this summary does not aim to do. This book does not aim to be a book for Calvin scholars. I am not trying to present a fresh vision on Calvin or his works. Nor am I seeking to commandeer Calvin to win some modern, theological fight. The goal of this synopsis is more modest in the academic sense but no less important in the churchly sense, namely, to present Calvin as a teacher of biblical truth and thus to instruct believers today in the faith they profess. This book therefore is directed to all persons who want to read Calvin's theology but find themselves short on time and too overwhelmed to study the bulky volumes that comprise the *Institutes*. Many such persons, I suspect, still want to learn from Calvin; they want to deepen their knowledge of the Reformed faith beyond a conventional verse-by-verse study of the Bible, and they want to mature in their devotion and trust in the Lord. This book, then, is written for them.

In this connection, here are a few comments on how to use this book. As a summary of Calvin's book, it stands on its own. If readers wish to read Calvin's *Institutes* as well, I certainly encourage this. But that isn't the intention of this synopsis. The summary can be read as a basic manual in Reformed doctrine or as a synoptic guide to Calvin's book (or both). It can be used as a book of doctrine in an adult study group setting, in which the study questions can be explored with other believers. Some chapters will be more challenging than others, some of more current interest than others, but every chapter aims to present Calvin fairly and accurately. I have used Calvin's own words as much as possible. Even when I am not directly quoting Calvin, I have tried to capture the texture and tenor of his words. I have not skipped the bulky polemical sections of Calvin's *Institutes,* but neither have I tried to present all the details of Calvin's heated disputations with others. We must remember that, for all its merits, the *Institutes,* like any book, is a product of its time. It still serves us very well, but there are new ideas and errors that need new answers and replies. In any case, this summary is offered in hopes that Calvin's rich contribution to Christian theology, especially to Reformed theology, may serve a new generation of believers.

I thank the publisher for interest in this project and for the patience shown me as I met with many unforeseen providences that delayed the completion of this work. I also express my heartfelt gratitude to Abby Schaaf, Secretary to the Faculty at Mid-America Reformed Seminary, and to student, Matt Van Dyken, for their assistance in the preparation of this book for publication. I thank my colleague at Mid-America, Dr. Cornelis P. Venema, whose interest in and love for Calvin's theology surpasses my own, and who, as a conversation partner on Calvin through the years, has significantly enriched my own knowledge of the great Genevan. In addition, in this year celebrating the 500th anniversary of Calvin's birth, I want to mention three professors—Dr. James A. De Jong, Dr. Richard C. Gamble, and Dr. Richard A. Muller—under whom I studied Calvin over the years. Each, in his own way, has contributed to my understanding of and appreciation for Calvin and his work. Finally, I thank my wife, Sheryl, for her wise counsel concerning this book. Her warm presence encouraged me through the entire writing process. It is only fitting that this project is completed on her birthday!

—J. Mark Beach
November 24, 2009

Calvin's Institutes in Context

JOHN CALVIN'S *Institutes of the Christian Religion* is one of the magnificent classics of Christian literature. As we embark upon a study of this work our aim is threefold: (1) to become familiar with one of the great theologians of the Christian church; (2) to gain an appreciation of the Reformed Protestant tradition—Calvin, though he is not the single representative of Reformed thinking, is arguably that tradition's most influential theologian; and (3) to cultivate in ourselves, in Calvin-like concern, a genuine life of piety.

Theological Stakes and Issues
In order to appreciate Calvin's achievement as a theologian and church leader, we need to orient ourselves to the times in which Calvin lived and labored. One place to begin is by looking at the "Prefatory Address to King Francis I of France," which served as a prologue to the numerous editions of Calvin's *Institutes*. In this address Calvin states explicitly why he wrote the *Institutes* and what he hoped to achieve.

> My purpose was solely to transmit certain rudiments by which those who are touched with any zeal for religion might be shaped to true godliness. And I undertook this labor especially for our French countrymen, very many of whom I knew to be hungering and thirsting for Christ; but I saw very few who had been duly imbued with even a slight knowledge of him.[1]

Calvin maintains that his aim is to bring instruction to the ignorant souls of France, as well as to offer, by means of this work, a confession of the Protestant faith which is so hated and persecuted by its opponents. In fact, in the

---

1. "Prefatory Address to King Francis I of France" in Calvin's *Institutes of the Christian Religion*, vol. 1, ed. John T. McNeill and trans. Ford Lewis Battles (Philadelphia: Westminster Press, 1960), p. 9. Note: all quotations from the *Institutes* will be taken from this work, unless otherwise noted.

Author's Preface to his Psalms commentary, Calvin offers a more extended
explanation why he was moved to publish the *Institutes*. While at Basel, Calvin learned that "many faithful and holy people were burnt alive in France."
To justify such pitiless treatment, the French court produced and circulated
pamphlets which argued that only those guilty of the most seditious errors
and heretical blunders, thereby overthrowing true religion altogether, came
to such capital justice. This slander against the French Protestants who were
of sound and sober doctrine, so stirred Calvin that he felt he would be guilty
of gross cowardice and mean treachery if he remained silent and failed to oppose this tyranny. "This was the consideration which induced me to publish
my Institutes of the Christian Religion."[2] In that connection he also explains
the aim he had in mind in bringing this work to press.

> My objects were, first, to prove that these reports were false and calum-
> nious, and thus to vindicate my brethren, whose death was precious in
> the sight of the Lord; and next, that as the same cruelties might very
> soon after be exercised against many unhappy individuals, foreign na-
> tions might be touched with at least some compassion towards them
> and solicitude about them (p. xlii).

Thus both in the Prefatory Address to King Francis I and the Author's
Preface to his Psalms commentary we see the peril that the Reformed movement faced in French-speaking lands, especially those under the province
of the French crown. We do not know whether King Francis ever actually
read the *Institutes* or Calvin's address to him, but Calvin issued the work as
an appeal against unjust slander. "For ungodly men have so far prevailed that
Christ's truth, even if it is not driven away scattered and destroyed, still lies
hidden, buried and inglorious. The poor little church has either been wasted
with cruel slaughter or banished into exile, or so overwhelmed by threats and
fears that it dare not even open its mouth.... Meanwhile no one comes forward to defend the church against such furies" (Prefatory Address, p. 11).

Calvin asks the French king to consider the sufferings of the Protestants, who have set their hope on the living God (1 Tim. 4:10). "For the sake
of this hope some of us are shackled with irons, some beaten with rods, some
led about as laughingstocks, some proscribed, some most savagely tortured,

---

2. John Calvin, "The Author's Preface," in *Commentary on the Book of Psalms*, First volume, trans. James Anderson, Calvin Translation Society (repr., Grand Rapids: Baker Book
House, 2003), xli–xlii.

some forced to flee. All of us are oppressed by poverty, cursed with dire execrations, wounded by slanders, and treated in most shameful ways" (p. 14).

Calvin argues that the Protestant cause is neither new, nor unknown or uncertain. It is the faith of the Apostles, and seems unfamiliar only because it has long been buried through human impiety. In support of this claim Calvin seeks to demonstrate that the church fathers prove hostile to many Roman Catholic practices; therefore, it is illegitimate to appeal to them as antagonists to the Protestant faith. He also contends against Rome's appeal to "custom" or what we would call "tradition." Truth must prevail over custom, and believers must yield to truth over custom. "To sum up, evil custom is nothing but a kind of public pestilence in which men do not perish the less though they fall with the multitude" (p. 23).

Calvin also maintains that Rome errs about the nature of the church itself. Arguing against those he calls the Papists (proponents of the Roman papacy), Calvin clarifies the Protestant position:

> Our controversy turns on these hinges: first, they contend that the form of the church is always apparent and observable. Second, they set this form in the see [office] of the Roman Church and its hierarchy. We, on the contrary, affirm that the church can exist without any visible appearance, and that its appearance is not contained within that outward magnificence which they foolishly admire. Rather, it has quite another mark, namely the pure preaching of God's Word and the lawful administration of the sacraments. They rage if the church cannot always be pointed to with the finger. But among the Jewish people how often was it so deformed that no semblance of it remained? (pp. 24–25).

Calvin is not here arguing that the church should not be expected to come to visible manifestation, but he is jealous to demonstrate that the church is a corruptible institution. He points to the fact that in the course of history God has repeatedly punished the unfaithful by a temporary obliteration of the visible image of the true church, yet his children are preserved from extinction.

In reply to the charge by Roman opponents that Protestant preaching was inciting so many appalling disturbances, tumults, and contentions, Calvin contends that Satan, not the gospel, disturbs and disrupts the church. The devil has taken radicals and other "monstrous rascals" into his army "in order to obscure and at last extinguish the truth." Besides, the same things were said about Elijah (you troubler of Israel), Christ (the charge of sedition), and the Apostles (cf. Acts 24:5ff) (pp. 27–30).

In addressing the French monarch Calvin pleads for a fair hearing of Christ's cause, reminding Francis that the persecuted Protestants seek the King's success as they strive to be good citizens and live exemplary lives of godliness (pp. 30–31).

****

From the above we are able to discern the threatening environment in which Calvin, with his fellow Protestants, lived and labored. The stakes were high. One professed the Protestant faith under threat of death.

In order to grasp the *theological* tenor of the times, we do well to examine another early writing of Calvin, specifically, his defense of the Protestant faith against Jacopo Cardinal Sadoleto, Bishop of Carpentras in southern France. Sadoleto wrote a letter to the citizens of Geneva, urging them to return to the Roman Catholic fold. His letter, written in a conciliatory and winsome manner, stated that the Protestant Reformers were heretical innovators and that their ideas were without theological standing, of suspect pedigree, and harmful to the rich heritage of the truth deposited to the church's care.

The Genevan authorities were troubled by Sadoleto's letter—they knew they were unable to provide an articulate and persuasive reply to him. Consequently, they solicited Calvin's help. Calvin, barely thirty years of age, responded in a masterful fashion. His *Reply to Sadoleto* is a potent rejoinder.[3]

The flavor of the times in which Calvin lived—especially the *theological* flavor of the times—becomes evident from the Sadoleto-Calvin debate. We note some of the salient features of Sadoleto's letter and Calvin's reply.

For his part, Sadoleto fairly and clearly articulated the Catholic position. Here we present some representative statements from Sadoleto's writing to the Genevans. He makes it clear that acceptance before God is not solely grounded in Christ and His work. For example, he states: "Christ was sent that *we, by well-doing*, may through Him, be accepted of God, and that we

---

3. Sadoleto's letter and Calvin's response to it have been published together under the title: *A Reformation Debate: John Calvin and Jacopo Sadoleto* (repr., Grand Rapids: Baker Book House, 1976).

may be built up in Him unto good works…" (p. 36, italics added). He does not deny the importance of faith, but typical of the way in which Roman Catholic theologians defined faith, Sadoleto incorporates the works of faith into the definition of what constitutes faith. "When we say, then, that we can be saved by faith alone in God and Jesus Christ, we hold that in this very faith *love is essentially comprehended as the chief and primary cause of our salvation*" (p. 36, italics added). The key phrase is that love is "essentially comprehended" in what faith is and therefore the works of faith (love) are constitutive of the cause of salvation. Given the failures of our faith, Sadoleto points to the role of the church: "And if, at any time, overcome by frailty and inconstancy, we lapse into sin…, we…rise again in the same faith of the Church; and by whatever expiations, penances, and satisfactions, she tells us that our sin is washed away…" (p. 37).

Sadoleto also appeals to the superiority of the ancient and unified teaching of the Roman Catholic Church against the Protestant innovators. "The point in dispute is whether is it more expedient for your salvation, and whether you think you will do what is more pleasing to God, by believing and following what the Catholic Church throughout the whole world, now for more than fifteen hundred years, or…more than thirteen hundred years approves with general consent; or innovations introduced within these twenty-five years, by crafty or, as they think themselves, acute men; but men certainly who are not themselves the Catholic Church?" (pp. 40–41). In short, Sadoleto's point is simple, namely, that it is much more likely that the church, for its many years of existence, has been imparting the truth versus the untimely and novel labors of a few individuals who have confused the thinking of ordinary believers.

Calvin responded to Sadoleto's position (represented by the remarks quoted above) with his own well-stated arguments. Since the doctrine of justification by faith alone was the principal teaching in dispute, not surprisingly Calvin aims some of his arrows at that target. "This, meanwhile, we constantly maintain, that man is not only justified freely once for all, without any merit of works, but that on this gratuitous justification the salvation of man perpetually depends. Nor is it possible that any work of man can be accepted by God unless it be gratuitously approved. Wherefore, I was amazed when I read your assertion, that love is the first and chief cause of salvation" (p. 69). Calvin is careful to point out that when this doctrine is not understood, this leads to an error about the church as well: "Your ignorance of this doctrine leads you on to the error of teaching that sins are expiated by penances and satisfactions." Of course, the Roman Catholic doctrine of the church and its ministry was in large measure defined by its doctrine of the papacy. Thus Calvin writes: "Let your Pontiff, then, boast as he may of the succession of Peter: even should he make good his title to it, he will establish nothing more than that obedience is due to him from the Christian people, so long as he himself maintains his fidelity to Christ, and deviates not from the purity of the gospel" (p. 77).

As for Sadoleto's appeal to the ancient pedigree of the teaching of Rome, Calvin makes clear that finally there can be only one supreme authority in the church, which is the Word of God. "We hold that the Word of God alone lies beyond the sphere of our judgment, and that Fathers and Councils are of authority only in so far as they accord with the rule of the Word..." (p. 92). This leads Calvin to take up a more sinister and disturbing accusation set at the feet of the Reformers, specifically, that they are destroyers of the church, enemies to its well-being, and akin to the blind leading the blind. Thus he writes: "But the most serious charge of all is that we have attempted to dismember the Spouse of Christ. Were that true, both you and the whole world might well regard us as desperate. But I will not admit the charge, unless you can make out that the Spouse of Christ is dismembered by those who desire to present her as a chaste virgin to Christ—who are animated by a degree of holy zeal to preserve her spotless for Christ—who, seeing her polluted by base seducers, recall her to conjugal fidelity—who unhesitatingly wage war against all the adulterers whom they detect laying snares for her chastity. And what but this have we done? Had not your faction of a Church attempted, nay, violated her chastity, by strange doctrines? Had she not been violently prostituted by your numberless superstitions? Had she not been defiled by that vilest species of adultery, the worship of images? And because, forsooth, we did not suffer you so to insult the sacred chamber of Christ, we are said to have lacerated His Spouse" (pp. 92–93).

****

From the tenor of Sadoleto's and Calvin's remarks it is evident that both believed that the gospel itself was at stake for the Genevans; therefore, the salvation of souls was also at stake. Roman Catholics and Protestants, to this day, continue to debate these sorts of issues.

A Sketch of Calvin's Life

As we engage in this summary survey of Calvin's *Institutes* it is fitting that we know something about his life. Although this is not the setting to present an extended biography of John Calvin, a few aspects of his life and labor should be noted.

Calvin was born on July 10, 1509 in the small town of Noyon in Picardy in northern France. Luther was born in 1483 and Zwingli in 1484. That means that Calvin was eight years old when Luther nailed his "Ninety-five Theses" to the church door in Wittenberg, Germany, October 31, 1517. We need to remember that Calvin stood on the shoulders of the first generation Reformers, but we may fairly state that in erudition he came to surpass them all. With the exception of Luther, no Protestant Reformer in the sixteenth century exercised a more profound influence on the ecclesiastical world, and no other Reformer matched Calvin in the rhetorical power of his work.

Calvin was a Frenchman, but most of his life's labors would take place in Geneva, Switzerland. He received a fine education and had associations with the upper strata of society—Luther was of more humble origins. Calvin was bourgeois, that is, he came from the middle-class, but rubbed elbows with the ranks of the elite.

Calvin was a superior student. Early on he exhibited extraordinary intellectual abilities. Consequently, Calvin's father sent him to the University of Paris where he was first enrolled at the Collége de La Marche in order to study for the priesthood. He spent about one year there, and then he enrolled at the more renowned Collége Montaigu—something like the Harvard or Yale of that day—where he spent five years, 1523 to 1528, earning a master's degree. His father, subsequently, altered plans for his son and determined that Calvin should study law—law would prepare Calvin for a lucrative career. Calvin dutifully obeyed his father. He left Paris and went to Orléans, where he studied law and Greek. Calvin continued his legal studies at Bourges.

When Calvin's father suddenly died in 1531, he felt liberated from the obligation to continue his law studies. He immediately enrolled at the Collége de France in Paris and pursued studies in Greek and Hebrew, and wished to become a great humanist scholar like Erasmus. Calvin had received rigorous training in Latin and rhetoric, and possessed a deep knowledge of the Greek/Latin classics. He also had a firm grasp of philosophy and law. In His providence, God was preparing the vessel of His choosing for a great work.

Wishing to pursue the life of a scholar, his first publication in 1532 was a Latin work, an academic commentary, on Seneca's *De Clementia* (On Clemency). Some scholars believe that this work was published shortly after Calvin's conversion. A stronger case can be made, however, that places his conversion in the year 1533. In any event, somewhere around this timeframe Calvin appears to have undergone a "sudden" conversion experience which marked an irreparable break with the Roman Catholic Church. As Calvin writes:

> And first, since I was too obstinately devoted to the superstitions of Popery to be easily extricated from so profound an abyss of mire, God by a sudden conversion subdued and brought my mind to a teachable frame, which was more hardened in such matters than might have been expected from one at my early period of life. Having thus received some taste and knowledge of true godliness, I was immediately inflamed with so intense a desire to make progress therein, that although I did not altogether leave off other studies, I yet pursued them with less ardour.[4]

Because of his Protestant convictions, he had to flee France. He found refuge in Basel, Switzerland. It was here, in 1535/36, that Calvin produced his first writing for the cause of the Reformation, the first edition of the *Institutes of the Christian Religion*. It was a well-ordered, brief, and synoptic presentation of Reformed teaching. It was a modest work in its first edition, and Calvin sought no notoriety from it. He writes, "When it was then published, it was not that copious and laboured work which it now is, but only a small treatise containing a summary of the principal truths of the Christain religion; and it was published with no other design than that men might know what was the faith held by those whom I saw basely and wickedly defamed by those flagitious and perfidious flatterers" (Author's Preface, xlii). Calvin would expand and revise this institution or instruction manual in the Christian religion many times throughout the remainder of his life.

Subsequently, Calvin made travels to northern Italy in order to visit the Duchess of Ferrara, the sister of the French king, who had given shelter to a number of Reformed refugees. On his return from Italy, journeying to Strasbourg, Germany, Calvin found himself needing to take a detour through Geneva, Switzerland, because of war in the region. He intended to

---

4. John Calvin, "The Author's Preface," in *Commentary on the Book of Psalms*, First volume, trans. James Anderson, Calvin Translation Society (repr., Grand Rapids: Baker Book House, 2003), xl–xli.

stay in Geneva just overnight, but he was pressed into service for the Protestant cause by Guillaume Farel, a man twenty years Calvin's senior. Farel had been laboring for reform in Geneva for some time. He immediately recognized Calvin's talent and enlisted him to serve the Protestant cause in that city. When Calvin informed Farel that he planned to retire to a quiet life of study and writing, Farel uttered down a curse from God—a curse that God would damn his sought-after tranquility! Calvin was so shocked and moved by this imprecation that he relented and joined the reform movement in Geneva in August 1536.

After a brief period of reforming work in Geneva, however, Farel and Calvin were both expelled from the city. Their proposals proved too radical for and not to the taste of the Genevans. Calvin went to Strasbourg, where, under the influence of Martin Bucer, he labored for the French refugee congregation from 1538 to 1541. It was during this period that the city authorities of Geneva solicited Calvin to write a response to Cardinal Sadoleto, the Bishop of Carpentras in southern France. Sadoleto was urging the Genevans back to the Roman Catholic fold. Calvin took up this task with his "Reply to Sadoleto," wherein (as we noted above) he masterfully defended the cause of the Reformation. He not only dismantled the Bishop's winsome case for Roman teaching, but in doing so Calvin exhibited a pastoral passion for souls and a love for the gospel, revealing his personal zeal for Christ. This reply served to open the door for renewed labor among the Genevans, and in 1541 Calvin was invited back to Geneva. The course of Calvin's life was now set, for he ministered in the city for the rest of his years. He died on the twenty-seventh day of May, 1564, about a month and a half before his 55th birthday.

Calvin was a prolific writer—often assisted by secretaries and stenographers. Through his writings he continues to exercise his greatest influence. He wrote either commentaries or expository lectures on most of the books of the Bible. Besides the numerous redactions and increasing bulk of his *Institutes*, Calvin also penned numerous polemical treatises, treating at length topics like providence, predestination, the Lord's Supper, freedom of the will, and various works addressing Libertines, Anabaptists, Lutherans, and especially Roman Catholics in their doctrines and practices. Some of Calvin's writings were directed toward the pastoral work of ministry as seen, for example, in the numerous sermons which were taken down in dictation and later published, the important catechisms he authored, as well as works dealing with visitation to the sick, church polity, liturgical issues, and other aspects of a minister's work.

The Nature of the Institutes

As noted above, the first edition of Calvin's *Institutes* appeared in the year 1536. The aforementioned "Prefatory Address to King Francis I" was written August 23, 1535 when Calvin was only twenty-six years old. Later Latin editions appeared in 1539, 1543, 1550, and 1559; and Calvin's own French translations of the work appeared in 1541, 1545, 1551, and 1560. Calvin expanded the *Institutes* with each edition, and in the final edition thoroughly re-arranged material. The *Institutes* was a work that catapulted Calvin to greatness, though not immediately. He was still relatively unknown after the publication of the first edition. However, after a brief time and with subsequent and expanded editions of the *Institutes,* Calvin was a much sought after teacher and leader. The *Institutes* was to become his life's work.

Calvin originally conceived of the *Institutes* as a kind of handbook, that is, as a tool to assist students of the Bible to delve deeply into the Scriptures with some confidence. He did not offer them in order to replace the Bible, but as a handbook to make Scripture easier to understand and advancement in it less difficult. As the *Institutes* grew in size they obviously ceased to be a "handbook," but they remained an instruction manual in theology "for the reading of the divine Word."[5]

This work, an institution—or instruction book—in the Christian religion was loosely ordered according to the Apostles' Creed. It also shows traits that pattern it after the book of Romans. Specifically, it is divided into four books: Book I—The Knowledge of God the Creator; Book II—The Knowledge of God the Redeemer; Book III—The Way in Which We Receive the Grace of Christ; and Book IV—The External Means or Aids by Which God Invites Us into the Society of Christ. The trinitarian ordering of the work is seen in that the first three books each focus upon the work of the Persons of the Trinity—Father, Son, and Holy Spirit.

Calvin's *Institutes* has had a long life in the English language. It was first translated into English by Thomas Norton in 1561, and reprinted many times thereafter: 1562, 1574, 1578, 1582, 1587, 1599, 1611, 1634, and 1762. It is worth noting that in this publication history there is a considerable gap, spanning more than 125 years from 1634 to 1762. A new and fresh transla-

---

5. "John Calvin to the Reader" in *Institutes of the Christian Religion,* vol. 1, p. 4.

tion of Calvin's *Institutes* into English did not appear until the John Allen translation of 1813; this was followed by Henry Beveridge's translation in 1845, and Ford Lewis Battles' translation in 1960.

Study Helps and Abridgements of the Institutes
Students of Calvin have long had available to them several significant "helps" which make a study of his *Institutes of the Christian Religion* a slightly less daunting task. Ford Lewis Battles's *Analysis of the Institutes of the Christian Religion of John Calvin*, assisted by John Walchenbach (1980), presents a fairly detailed summary of the essential components of each section of Calvin's volumes. Also worthy of note is T.H.L. Parker's *Calvin: An Introduction to His Thought* (1995). This work is essentially an examination of the four books of the *Institutes*, following its chapters and presentation of topics. Two other analytical works worthy of mention are Wilhelm Niesel's *The Theology of Calvin* (1956), and François Wendel's *Calvin: The Origins and Development of His Religious Thought* (1963).

A new study by Anthony N.S. Lane is similar but distinct from each of these prior projects, entitled *A Reader's Guide to Calvin's Institutes* (2009). As a reader's guide to the *Institutes*, Lane's volume is not to be read on its own, i.e., it is not intended to be used independently of Calvin's *Institutes*; rather, it is a volume that assists readers as they make their way through Calvin's work, chapter by chapter, section by section. Moreover, this is a guide to the Battles translation of the *Institutes* in the Library of Christian Classics series, edited by John T. McNeill. Thus Lane will refer readers from time to time to footnotes and references from the Battles/McNeill edition. Another work worthy of mention is the recently published title, *A Theological Guide to Calvin's Institutes* (2008), edited by David W. Hall and Peter A. Lillback.

For readers who may not wish to tackle a secondary source on Calvin, but know that the sheer bulk of the *Institutes* constitutes too tall an order for their time or ambition, they might consider a compendium of the work instead, such as Hugh T. Kerr's *Calvin's Institutes: A New Compend* (1989), or Donald K. McKim's abridgement of the *Institutes* (2000). Finally, a slender compendium of the *Institutes* which has the unique feature of being mildly re-written for the modern reader—i.e., rendering Calvin's prose more accessible to a general reading public—is a title edited by Tony Lane and re-written by Hilary Osborne, *John Calvin: The Institutes of the Christian Religion* (1987).

For Study Groups

For those who wish to use this summary of Calvin's *Institutes* in a study group, many of its chapters can be tackled in one session. Some chapters, perhaps, are better handled in two or more sessions, partly because of their length, and partly because the subject matter they treat is detailed or heavy in content. Like everything else in life, diligent effort, coupled with patient reflection and willingness to learn from others, combined with a prayerful dependency upon the Lord, will reap benefits beyond what is sown. I urge readers, in working through this book, to go slow when necessary, to write down questions if material is not immediately clear or understandable, to meditate on and consider the many ways Calvin's presentation of the Christian religion applies to the Christian life, and to heed Calvin's exhortation to take the things of God and use them for edification. These sorts of goals fit with Calvin's aim in writing his instruction manual in the Christian faith, namely that we gain a true knowledge of God and of ourselves which issues forth into a life of piety to God's glory.

Questions for Reflection and Discussion

1. How does Calvin's aim in writing the *Institutes* differ from the reason or aim in many serious works on theology today?

2. What do we learn about the situation of the Protestant cause in France from Calvin's Prefatory Address to King Francis I, the Author's Preface of his Psalms commentary, and his reply to Sadoleto?

3. Inasmuch as Calvin is concerned to defend the legitimacy of affirming the invisibility of the church against the Roman Catholic Church, what do we learn from the life of Elijah? (cf. 1 Kings 19:9–18), Micaiah? (cf. 1 Kings 22:5–28), Jeremiah? (cf. Jeremiah 18), Christ? (cf. John 18:12ff., 19ff.; Luke 22:66–23:1). How do these examples serve to illustrate Calvin's point about the church's invisibility?

4. About whom may Calvin have been speaking when he talks about "monstrous rascals"? Who, besides the Lutherans and the Reformed, were, according to Rome, stirring up trouble? And what characterized the life and teaching of "these rascals"?

5. What key doctrinal issues emerge from the Sadoleto/Calvin debate? (Think of the Protestant *solas*).

6. What were the advantages for the Protestant cause and for Calvin that he was educated and trained in law, languages, and especially the new learning of the Renaissance? Why is an educated clergy necessary for the health of the church today?

Institutes of the Christian Religion

Book One

The Knowledge of God the Creator

∞ 2 ∞

Knowing God

Eph 4 - 17

Chapter One: The Knowledge of God and That of Ourselves Are Connected, and How They Are Interrelated

Orientation

WISDOM AND KNOWLEDGE—those are the concepts that Calvin takes up in the first chapter of Book One of the *Institutes*. Wisdom and knowledge are also what the remainder of Calvin's work will seek to impart to its readers. Christian truth is about God, His creation, and their relation—especially the relation God has with human beings. Thus the opening chapters of Book One treat that which is most basic for humans—the knowledge of God. Although quite brief, chapters one through four take up a number of important issues. Chapter one treats the interrelationship between the knowledge of God and the knowledge of ourselves; chapter two defines the knowledge of God; chapter three considers what it means that God has implanted a knowledge of Himself in the human mind, while chapter four demonstrates how sin and corruption have obscured and stifled but not obliterated this knowledge. Then in chapter five Calvin offers an extended discussion of the revelation of God in creation and divine providence. These chapters are foundational to Calvin's vision and should not be underestimated in their importance for his theological project.

The Sum of True Wisdom

The *Institutes* opens with a discussion of one of the fundamental problems of human existence: how can we know God? Calvin's answer to that question begins with the observation that the knowledge of God is intertwined with the knowledge of ourselves; indeed, they are inseparably interconnected. Without a true knowledge of God, we cannot know ourselves; and, without a true knowledge of ourselves, we cannot know God. True wisdom consists of this interwoven knowledge, for the creature is dependent on the Creator.

> Nearly all the wisdom we possess, that is to say, true and sound wisdom, consists of two parts: the knowledge of God and of ourselves. But, while joined by many bonds, which one precedes and brings forth the other is not easy to discern. In the first place, no one can look upon himself without immediately turning his thoughts to the contemplation of God, in whom he 'lives and moves' [Acts 17:28]. For, quite clearly, the mighty gifts with which we are endowed are hardly from ourselves; indeed, our very being is nothing but subsistence in the one God. Then, by these benefits shed like dew from heaven upon us, we are led as by rivulets to the spring itself (1.1.1).

Calvin argues that God's infinite benefits accentuate our poverty of nature—meaning our wickedness and weakness. Our ruin compels us to look upward, for a "veritable world of miseries" afflicts the human race, and its "shameful nakedness exposes a teeming horde of infamies" (1.1.1). Consequently, "from the feeling of our own ignorance, vanity, poverty, infirmity, and—what is more—depravity and corruption, we recognize that the true light of wisdom, sound virtue, full abundance of every good, and purity of righteousness rest in the Lord alone" (1.1.1).

Knowledge of Self is unto Knowledge of God

This means that we become truly dissatisfied with ourselves when we contemplate God in His perfection. In this way we begin to grasp the extent of our misery and ruin. "Again, it is certain that man never achieves a clear knowledge of himself unless he has first looked upon God's face, and then descends from contemplating him to scrutinize himself" (1.1.2).

Because of our innate pride, we flatter ourselves most highly and praise our uprightness and virtue. With our minds confined to the arena of human corruption we congratulate ourselves most sweetly. We are content with ourselves. But God is "the straightedge to which we must be shaped." When we lift our thoughts to Him the consequences for ourselves soon follow: "what masquerading earlier as righteousness was pleasing in us will soon grow filthy in its consummate wickedness. What wonderfully impressed us under the name of wisdom will stink in its very foolishness" (1.1.2). Thus, whether we contemplate our natural endowments or our wretchedness, human self-knowledge bears with it the knowledge of God.

Humans in God's Presence

Meanwhile, given God's perfection we sense our ugliness and waywardness —thus that "dread and wonder" that even the saints feel in God's presence. The book of Job demonstrates this truth, for "in its description of God's wisdom, power, and purity," we are presented "a powerful argument that overwhelms men with the realization of their own stupidity, impotence, and corruption [Job 38:381ff.]" (1.1.3). Calvin cites numerous biblical examples of this sort. We never know ourselves until we contemplate ourselves in comparison with God's majesty. The knowledge of God requires a knowledge of self; in truly knowing ourselves, we come to know God. So how does Calvin propose to proceed? He writes: "However the knowledge of God and of ourselves may be mutually connected, the order of right teaching requires that we discuss the former first, then proceed afterward to treat the latter" (1.1.3). So Calvin will first take up a discussion of God and our knowledge of Him before he treats the knowledge we must have of ourselves as His creatures.

Chapter Two: What It Is to Know God, and to What Purpose the Knowledge of Him Tends

Knowledge of God Defined

What is the knowledge of God? That is, what is it to know God? Calvin's answer is more than intellectual or theoretical: "Now, the knowledge of God, as I understand it, is that by which we not only conceive that there is a God but also grasp what befits us and is proper to his glory, in fine, what is to our advantage to know of him" (1.2.1). The testimony of the creation calls us to recognize God as our Creator. For God yet sustains and governs the universe He has made, as He yet watches over the human race and is the source of all blessing and truth. Thus, God's providential care and forbearing mercy surround His creatures and serve to teach piety, from which religion springs. Knowledge of God, then, is found in "religion" and "piety." And with "piety" we fix our gaze upon the centerpiece of Calvin's thought.

For Calvin, "piety" is not pietism or being pious in a hypocritical sense. Rather, he defines piety as that reverence joined with love of God which the knowledge of his benefits induces. For until men recognize that they owe everything to God, that they are nourished by his fatherly care, that he is the Author of their every good, that they should seek nothing beyond him—they will never yield him willing service. Nay, unless they establish their complete happiness in him, they will never give themselves truly and sincerely to him (1.2.1).

The Religious Purpose of Knowledge of God

Calvin rebels against idle speculation. He wants to be a scriptural theologian, not a philosopher! Hence to ask: What is God?—is foolishness. Our knowledge of God isn't to satisfy a curiosity. "Rather, our knowledge should serve first to teach us fear and reverence; secondly, with it as our guide and teacher, we should learn to seek every good from him, and, having received it, to credit it to his account" (1.2.2). For Calvin, pure and real religion is "faith so joined with an earnest fear of God that this fear also embraces willing reverence, and carries with it such legitimate worship as is prescribed in the law. And we ought to note this fact even more diligently: all men have a vague general veneration for God, but very few really reverence him; and wherever there is great ostentation in ceremonies, sincerity of heart is rare indeed" (1.2.2).

Chapter Three: The Knowledge of God Has Been Naturally Implanted in the Minds of Men

The Sense of Divinity Implanted in Us

Calvin argues that there is a general knowledge of God as Creator and Sovereign Ruler of the world. This knowledge of God may be discerned throughout His creation—in humanity, in the natural order, and in the historical process itself. Drawing on the apostle Paul's argument in the first two chapters of Romans (though he doesn't quote Romans directly), Calvin demonstrates the universal character of God's testimony in the human heart. For all people have a "sense of divinity" or, what Calvin also calls, a "seed of religion." This seed, implanted in the human mind, accounts for our natural religious instinct, "an awareness of divinity" (1.3.1). This awareness of God leaves all people without excuse.

The Corruption of the Sense of Divinity

Calvin maintains that all humans perceive that God exists and that He is their Maker. All tribes and peoples manifest a deep-seated conviction that there is a God. Calvin will have nothing to do with the claim that religion is an intervention of a few to control the many. Indeed, every idolatry proves otherwise! Consequently, it is vain to argue that religion is a human invention. Idolatry flourishes only because all people instinctively know God is real. People's minds are "imbued with a firm conviction about God, from which the inclination toward religion springs as from a seed" (1.3.2). More specifically, the inclination toward religion springs from this seed of divinity. Humans do not naturally humble themselves to something outside themselves. Yet even atheists turn to God under great distress or fear. They may try to eradicate an awareness of God, but they do so in vain. The very effort to vanquish this awareness testifies to its inborn presence. This is why atheists from time to time "feel an inkling" toward faith in God. But atheism is nothing other than a subterfuge, an ungodly attempt to hide from God and to efface His presence from view, to erase Him from the human mind. In fact, atheists do not escape "anxiety of conscience." In this way, says Calvin, those without piety or fear of God "exemplify the fact that some conception of God is ever alive in all men's minds" (1.3.2).

The Sense of Divinity Not Wholly Extinguished

Again, "a sense of divinity which can never be effaced is engraved upon men's minds" (1.3.3). Thus, those who mock religion and heavenly judgment do so with "sardonic laughter, for the worm of conscience, sharper than any cauterizing iron, gnaws away within" (1.3.3). To be sure, people try to cast away all knowledge of God and corrupt the worship of Him. But this cannot be sustained. Writes Calvin, "I only say that though the stupid harshness in their minds, which the impious eagerly conjure up to reject God, wastes away, yet the sense of divinity, which they greatly wished to be extinguished, thrives and presently burgeons." Then Calvin notes, "From this we conclude that it is not a doctrine that must first be learned in school, but one which each of us is master of from his mother's womb and which nature itself permits no one to forget, although many strive with every nerve to this end" (1.3.3). Knowledge of God in this sense, then, is a law of creation—even pagan philosophers taught that "the highest good of the soul is likeness to God." In fact, without religion, humans degenerate into beasts (but more miserable), wallowing in wickedness, their lives drag out "in ceaseless tumult and disquiet." "Therefore, it is the worship of God alone that renders men higher than the brutes, and through it alone they aspire to immortality" (1.3.3).

Chapter Four: This Knowledge Is Either Smothered or Corrupted, Partly by Ignorance, Partly by Malice

Idolatry and Superstition

Calvin notes that whereas all people have this seed of religion sown within their heart, very few foster it, and in none does it ripen, much less bear good fruit. Because humans either revolt against God or are perversely lost in superstition, "no real piety remains in the world" (1.4.1). People go about blind; but their blindness, says Calvin, "is almost always mixed with proud vanity and obstinacy." Humans devolve from their knowledge of God and turn to false religion, i.e., idolatry, and this exchange is not blameless. It is born of pride and obstinacy, and involves measuring God by the yardstick of one's own carnal stupidity. People are quite conceited and contented in their own imaginings about God. They fashion God into their own image and then worship "a figment and a dream of their own heart." Here Calvin quotes Paul in Romans 1:21–22, where the apostle depicts the fallen man as striving after wisdom but plunging into foolishness, for they had become "futile in their thinking." This darkness—darkness born in the human heart—is stuffed full of "empty haughtiness." "From this it follows that their stupidity is not excusable, since it is caused not only by vain curiosity but by an inordinate desire to know more than is fitting, joined with a false confidence" (1.4.1).

Calvin points us to the Psalms that declare the folly of the fools who deny God (cf. Ps. 14:1; 53:1). In their madness, denying God's existence, they are given over to their depravity. "It is God's just punishment of the wicked that fatness envelops their hearts, so that after they have closed their eyes, in seeing they see not [Matt. 13:14–15; cf. Isa. 6:9–10 and Ps. 17:10]" (1.4.2). Thus, pledged to their atheism, they revolt against the Creator, and attempt to "furiously repel all remembrance of God" (1.4.2). They deny, disregard, and ignore God. "No fear restrains them from rushing violently against God." Calvin notes, "so long as this blind urge grips them, their own oafish forgetfulness of God will hold sway over them" (1.4.2).

False Religion and Religious Hypocrisy
There are many persons, however, who convince themselves that "any zeal for religion, however preposterous, is sufficient." In this way they "gloss over their superstition." They don't grasp that our worship and service of God must be "conformed to God's will as to a universal rule" (1.4.3). God is not worshiped through false religion. He may not be fashioned according to our own whims. False religion is not worship of God but of one's own false ravings (cf. Gal. 4:8; Eph. 2:12) (1.4.3).

A mere veil of devotion is not acceptable either. Some never give God a thought unless compelled to; and they do not draw near to God unless they are dragged as they resist and grumble. "And not even then are they impressed with the voluntary fear that arises out of reverence for the divine majesty, but merely with a slavish, forced fear, which God's judgment extorts from them." They sit in a worship service with dread, even "to the point of loathing." Such devotion is pretense. Worshiping God out of a pretended fear or dread is vain. Such hypocrisy may not be confused with piety. Paltry sacrifices and worthless observances cannot win God's favor. False religion is all rebellion. Its practitioners live in wickedness and shame. Their trust is not in God but in themselves (1.4.4).

Thus, the seed of religion, engraved on human hearts, renders us religious creatures. The seed of religion "can in no wise be uprooted." Yet, because of our stubbornness, "this seed is so corrupted that by itself it produces only the worst fruits." It is prevented from leading us to true religion (cf. 1.4.4). So, indeed, true knowledge of God is either smothered or corrupted, partly by ignorance, partly by malice.

Chapter Five: The Knowledge of God Shines Forth in the Fashioning of the Universe and the Continuing Government of It

God's Works Give Knowledge of Him
Having laid the groundwork for the path to wisdom, Calvin next examines our knowledge of God derived from His creation and providence. Indeed, there is another source, besides our innate sense of divinity, which renders knowledge of God certain (though smothered and corrupted). The certainty it produces renders all human ignorance inexcusable, namely God's self-revelation "in the whole workmanship of the universe" (1.5.1). In this way God

is not without witness to all peoples and nations, tribes and tongues. Every person is without excuse for not loving the Creator and serving God in truth; indeed, the whole created order testifies to Him. As Calvin observes: "[H]is essence is incomprehensible; hence, his divineness far escapes all human perception. But upon his individual works he has engraved unmistakable marks of his glory, so clear and so prominent that even unlettered and stupid folk cannot plead the excuse of ignorance" (cf. Ps. 104:2–4; Ps. 11:2). Wherever we look, there is not a nook or cranny of the universe that does not manifest "at least some sparks of his glory" (cf. Heb. 11:3). The fabric of the universe is like a mirror in which one can contemplate God (cf. Ps. 19:2; Rom. 1:19–20) (1.5.1).

Those schooled in the sciences and liberal arts—astronomy, medicine, and all natural science, etc.—penetrate even deeper into the secrets of divine wisdom, though the ignorant and uneducated have God's testimony of Himself ever before their eyes. Thus "men who have either quaffed or even tasted the liberal arts penetrate with their aid far more deeply into the secrets of the divine wisdom." The entire order of the universe, its mysteries and complexities, teaches us something about God. Hence, it is clear that "there is no one to whom the Lord does not abundantly show his wisdom" (1.5.2). Humans themselves are the loftiest proof of divine wisdom (1.5.3). We have within ourselves a veritable "workshop graced with God's unnumbered works and, at the same time, a storehouse overflowing with inestimable riches." Yet we rebelliously suppress the knowledge of God revealed in the creation. This is nothing other than "foul ungratefulness," for we should be moved to praise God but instead we are "puffed up and swollen with all the more pride." Calvin chides: "How detestable, I ask you, is this madness: that man, finding God in his body and soul a hundred times, on this very pretense of excellence denies that there is a God?" (1.5.4).

In addition, in this mad rebellion there are those who assert that man is nothing but a product of nature, with no immortal soul. There are also those who think that the creation actually is derived from itself, and therefore promote some kind of pantheism. God is either dismissed or confused with His creation (1.5.5). But God not only reveals His lordship over creation in all of His ordinary providential actions (1.5.6), He reveals His lordship in a "second kind of works, which are outside the ordinary course of nature…" (1.5.7). This is made clear from God's administration of human society, for "he so tempers his providence that, although kindly and beneficent toward all in numberless ways, he still by open and daily indications declares his clemency to the godly and his severity to the wicked and criminal" (1.5.7). There are no chance occurrences, no happenstances in the strict sense, no good luck; instead, God is the author of our lives and His heavenly providence provides for our needs and delivers us from troubles, even as His justice is administered against the wicked (1.5.8).

Although humans attempt to substitute nature for God, God remains the Lord of nature. It is futile to deny what actually is true. The creation declares God. God governs His creation, holding sovereign sway over all of life. For Calvin, this means that humans obtain a knowledge of God not through empty speculation into the divine essence, but by contemplating Him "in his works whereby he renders himself near and familiar to us, and in some manner communicates himself" (1.5.9).

This knowledge ought to awaken us to worship God and arouse us to the hope of the future life (1.5.10). Nonetheless, its proofs, due to our stupidity and dullness, are without profit.

> But although the Lord represents both himself and his everlasting Kingdom in the mirror of his works with very great clarity, such is our stupidity that we grow increasingly dull toward so manifest testimonies, and they flow away without profiting us. For with regard to the most beautiful structure and order of the universe, how many of us are there who, when we lift up our eyes to heaven or cast them about through the various regions of earth, recall our minds to a remembrance of the Creator, and do not rather, disregarding their Author, sit idly in contemplation of his works? In fact, with regard to those events which daily take place outside the ordinary course of nature, how many of us do not reckon that men are whirled and twisted about by blindly indiscriminate fortune, rather than governed by God's providence? (1.5.11).

Fallen people rebelliously fail to remember God, the Author of creation, when they gaze upon the stars or the beauty of the earth. They ignore God's providential care in the extra-ordinary events of life and ascribe them, instead, to coincidence, born of blind chance. This is a disease, as noted above, afflicting not only the slow-witted and unlearned, but those schooled and endowed with keen discernment (1.5.10–11).

Superstition and philosophical error choke this manifestation of God (1.5.12). But nature sufficiently testifies to God, even in our rebellion, that we feel the impulse to worship the God from whom we are estranged (cf. Acts 17:23). That, again, testifies to our guilt—all are under the verdict of guilt for suppressing the truth in unrighteousness. Few escape sharing in "the madness of the common herd" (1.5.13). Calvin concludes: "It is therefore in vain that so many burning lamps shine for us in the workmanship of the universe to show forth the glory of its Author. Although they bathe us wholly in their radiance, yet they can of themselves in no way lead us into the right path. Surely they strike some sparks, but before their fuller light shines forth these are smothered" (1.5.14).

We have no defense for our ignorance of God in light of the sure testimonies of God's creation and providence.

> ...although we lack the natural ability to mount up unto the pure and clear knowledge of God, all excuse is cut off because the fault of dullness is within us. And, indeed, we are not allowed thus to pretend ignorance without our conscience itself always convicting us of both baseness and ingratitude.... Therefore we are justly denied every excuse when we stray off as wanderers and vagrants even though everything points out the right way (1.5.15).

Observations

First, it is worth noting how Calvin's theology begins. It is rooted in creation, not redemption, and asks: how are we related to God as His creatures? Calvin refuses to talk about God in the abstract. We will not find, in Calvin, a philosophical discussion of God's being or essence. Calvin is always concerned to talk about God as He has revealed Himself to us, which casts his theology into a different light than the medieval scholastic tradition. Thomas Aquinas's theology begins with a discussion of what sacred doctrine is, i.e., what is theology? Is it necessary? Is it a science? How is it related to other sciences? Subsequent Reformed theology followed this scholastic or academic pattern of defining the nature of theology and arguing for its validity as a science, before embarking upon the task of theology itself. Whereas this is not an inappropriate aim, it was not Calvin's aim. His *Institutes*, even in its most developed redaction, seeks to be first of all a handbook to guide believers in the reading and understanding of Scripture, though it is also a textbook of doctrine. It is never, however, a doctrinal textbook that conceives of theology in the abstract; rather, Calvin writes for the life and well-being of the church. Theology serves the work of ministry and a life of piety. Indeed, the emphasis on piety as a life of reverence and humble service to God is always close at hand.

Second, in chapters one through five Calvin attempts to achieve two things. (1) Calvin wants to demonstrate that there is no way for humans to excuse themselves before God (we all stand guilty), for all have the knowledge of God written on their hearts—the seed of religion—and God's creation and providence irrefutably testify to Him. (2) In light of what he has shown under number one, Calvin wants to demonstrate that there is no way for humans to know God for their salvation apart from Scripture. Chapter six is entitled: "Scripture Is Needed as Guide and Teacher for Anyone Who Would Attain to God the Creator." This is an interesting feature of Calvin's work as well. Rather than beginning with a doctrine of Scripture in the abstract, he will introduce it in relation to its purpose—that is, the reasons for which it was given—namely, to make us wise unto salvation. Scripture alone is able to provide us the true knowledge of God, for the seed of religion and God's revelation of Himself in creation are themselves insufficient to lead corrupt humans to a true knowledge of God.

Questions for Reflection and Discussion

1. Look up Job 38:1ff, 42:1–6; Genesis 18:27; Judges 6:22–23, 13:22; Isaiah 6:1–5; Ezekiel 1:25–2:1. How do these passages confirm Calvin's argument about knowledge of God and of self? Discuss: Is "worm theology" unbiblical?

2. Is "piety," as Calvin defines it, the mark of modern Christianity? If you don't believe it is, what is the modern mark? Assuming you agree with Calvin's view of piety, do you struggle to find your complete happiness in God? Is the quality of your service and devotion to God rooted in this happiness?

3. Do you agree with Calvin that ostentatious worship is usually heartless? To whom was Calvin referring? Consider the worship emphases in North American Christianity today: Is there such a thing as great ostentation of emotion besides ostentation in ceremonies? Is this a welcome display? Explain.

4. Although Calvin does not specifically appeal to Romans 1 and 2 in his discussion, these chapters clearly serve as the framework for his argument. Look up Romans 1:18–2:18—especially verses 1:18–23; 1:28, 32; 2:1, 12. How do these verses confirm Calvin's teaching regarding human

knowledge of God and inexcusability? Why are all people without excuse? Would a modern atheist be convinced by Calvin's arguments?

5. How does Calvin refute the idea that all religions lead to God? Why would Calvin reject the view, "if one is sincere in his or her religion, that's all that matters"? In what way are all people religious?

6. Why are those who study the universe and the world—geologists, astronomers, physicists, biologists, etc.—better able to discover God's wisdom? Why are they even more inexcusable if they do not believe in and worship God?

7. In light of Calvin's discussion in chapters 1–5, is it possible to know God? How does Calvin's discussion help us understand unbelief and atheism today?

8. What are the implications of Calvin's views, presented in this chapter, for Christian apologetics? How should a defense of the Christian faith be conducted following Calvin's ideas?

The Necessity of Scripture

Chapters 6–9 of Book One

Chapter Six: Scripture is Needed as Guide and Teacher for Anyone Who Would Come to God the Creator

Orientation

WE HAVE NOTED that Calvin is concerned to establish two things in chapters one through five of Book One. On the one hand, all people are without excuse before God, for God has made Himself known to them. The fact that humans have suppressed and corrupted this knowledge does not negate its validity. All stand guilty. On the other hand, God cannot be known apart from Scripture. Because all people smother or pervert the general knowledge of God, another and superior help is needed to direct us to God our Creator. Scripture serves this purpose. Thus we come to a study of Scripture's nature and role, for Scripture alone places us in the arena where we can arrive at a true knowledge of God. In chapters six through nine Calvin focuses on why Scripture is necessary and credible, and how it guides us to the knowledge of God as our Creator and Redeemer.

Scripture—A Better Help

Calvin notes that humans need "another and better help" if they are to seek the true Creator of the universe and not succumb to some form of idolatry. The self-disclosure of God that comes to all people through the created order is not enough. God "added the light of his Word" by which we can know Him for our salvation (1.6.1). Scripture alone safeguards God's people from melting away from a pure knowledge of Him.

> Just as old or bleary-eyed men and those with weak vision, if you thrust before them a most beautiful volume, even if they recognize it to be

some sort of writing, yet can scarcely construe two words, but with the aid of spectacles will begin to read distinctly; so Scripture, gathering up the otherwise confused knowledge of God in our minds, having dispersed our dullness, clearly shows us the true God. This, therefore, is a special gift, where God, to instruct the church, not merely uses mute teachers but also opens his own most hallowed lips (1.6.1).

Twofold Knowledge of God Presented in Scripture
The knowledge of God that Scripture gives us is of a twofold nature: knowledge of Him as Creator (versus idols), and knowledge of Him as Redeemer. "First in order came that kind of knowledge by which one is permitted to grasp who that God is who founded and governs the universe. Then that other inner knowledge was added, which alone quickens dead souls, whereby God is known not only as the Founder of the universe and the sole Author and Ruler of all that is made, but also in the person of the Mediator as the Redeemer" (1.6.1). Calvin's chief concern, therefore, is to show us first how Scripture reveals God as our Creator over against idols, and then, in due order, he will show us God as our Redeemer. "God, the Artificer of the universe, is made manifest to us in Scripture, and…what we ought to think of him is set forth there, lest we seek some uncertain deity by devious paths" (1.6.1).

Such knowledge of God was first bestowed upon the Patriarchs—that is, upon Adam, Noah, Abraham, etc. The same oracles that God gave to the Patriarchs were recorded. In this way we received the law and the prophets (1.6.2). Scripture teaches us a twofold knowledge of God—God as our Creator and God as our Redeemer.

Therefore, however fitting it may be for man seriously to turn his eyes to contemplate God's works, since he has been placed in this most glorious theater to be a spectator of them, it is fitting that he prick up his ears to the Word, the better to profit. And it is therefore no wonder that those who were born in darkness become more and more hardened in their insensibility; for there are very few who, to contain themselves within bounds, apply themselves teachably to God's Word, but they rather exult in their own vanity. Now, in order that true religion may shine upon us, we ought to hold that it must take its beginning from heavenly doctrine and that no one can get even the slightest taste of right and sound doctrine unless he be a pupil of Scripture. Hence, there also emerges the beginning of true understanding when we reverently embrace what it pleases God there to witness of himself. But not only faith, perfect and in every way complete, but all right knowledge of God is born of obedience. And surely in this respect God has, by his singular providence, taken thought for mortals through all ages (1.6.2).

True religion, be it known, resides in heavenly doctrine, which we come to know through the reverent study of Scripture and obedience to it (1.6.2).

The Necessity of Scripture
This brings Calvin to discuss the necessity of Scripture, for if we are to know God in the fellowship of salvation, sacred Scripture is absolutely necessary. Indeed, God's revelation of Himself in creation is inadequate to bring us to communion with Him for our redemption.

Suppose we ponder how slippery is the fall of the human mind into forgetfulness of God, how great the tendency to every kind of error, how great the lust to fashion constantly new and artificial religions. Then we may perceive how necessary was such written proof of the heavenly doctrine, that it should neither perish through forgetfulness nor vanish through error nor be corrupted by the audacity of men. It is therefore clear that God has provided the assistance of the Word for the sake of all those to whom he has been pleased to give useful instruction because he foresaw that his likeness imprinted upon the most beautiful form of the universe would be insufficiently effective (1.6.3).

Thus, God's revelation in Scripture provides us with a knowledge of Him which we cannot obtain through creation—namely the testimony of God's mercy for our redemption. The scriptural Word is used by God to convert us, to give us wisdom, to enlighten us, and to lead us to worship Him (cf. Ps. 19; 18; also John 4:22). Without Scripture we stagger about in vanity and error (1.6.4).

Chapter Seven: Scripture Must Be Confirmed by the Witness of the Spirit. Thus May Its Authority Be Established as Certain; and It Is a Wicked Falsehood that Its Credibility Depends on the Judgment of the Church

Scripture's Authority and Authenticity from God, Not the Church
With chapter seven Calvin takes up the question of Scripture's authority. Calvin does not think it improper to reverence Scripture; and he is concerned

that we not doubt it. Scripture is the Word of God. Only the "deplorably insolent" question God's credibility. Rather than send daily oracles from heaven God chose to inscripturate His truth. The Bible, however, unless we are convinced that it is God's Word, will remain unopened or disregarded. The conviction that Scripture is God's Word is not born of ourselves. Scripture only obtains full authority among believers when they regard it as having sprung from heaven; only then do they read it as if they were hearing "the living words of God" (1.7.1).

This conviction requires the Spirit's testimony in our hearts. That testimony stands against the pernicious error that the authority of Scripture rests upon the determination of the church, which is nothing other than a mocking of the Holy Spirit. That error allows humans to sit in judgment upon Scripture. God is also put into subjection to human standards of judgment—as if we can declare His Word fit and worthy. In fact, Scripture is prior to the church. The church is founded upon Scripture. Furthermore, Scripture exhibits clear evidence of its own truth and needs no external witness, such as the church pretends to provide in order to confirm its authenticity (cf. 1.7.2). Although opponents try to cite Augustine in support of their view, they misconstrue his words (1.7.3).

The Inner Testimony of the Holy Spirit

For Calvin, God is not only the Author of Scripture, He is also the witness to its truth and authenticity. The witness of the Holy Spirit is stronger than all human-wrought proofs. "Thus, the highest proof of Scripture derives in general from the fact that God in person speaks in it" (1.7.4). This conviction comes to us through "the secret testimony of the Spirit." "They who strive to build up firm faith in Scripture through disputation are doing things backwards" (1.7.4). Even though Scripture skeptics can be refuted, such rebuttals do not lead to piety. "The testimony of the Spirit is more excellent than all reason. For as God alone is a fit witness of himself in his Word, so also the Word will not find acceptance in men's hearts before it is sealed by the inward testimony of the Spirit" (1.7.4). Scripture bears its own authentication.

> Let this point therefore stand: that those whom the Holy Spirit has inwardly taught truly rest upon Scripture, and that Scripture indeed is self-authenticated; hence, it is not right to subject it to proof and reasoning. And the certainty it deserves with us, it attains by the testimony of the Spirit. For even if it wins reverence for itself by its own

majesty, it seriously affects us only when it is sealed upon our hearts through the Spirit. Therefore, illumined by his power, we believe neither by our own nor by anyone else's judgment that Scripture is from God; but above human judgment we affirm with utter certainty (just as if we were gazing upon the majesty of God himself) that it has flowed to us from the very mouth of God by the ministry of men. We seek no proofs, no marks of genuineness upon which our judgment may lean; but we subject our judgment and wit to it as to a thing far beyond any guesswork! (1.7.5).

Calvin further explains that the inner testimony of the Spirit, by which the mysteries of God are comprehended, is granted to the elect alone, not to the multitude. True faith is sealed in our hearts also by the Holy Spirit (1.7.5).

Chapter Eight: So Far as Human Reason Goes, Sufficiently Firm Proofs Are at Hand to Establish the Credibility of Scripture

Proofs as Supplemental Aids
Calvin believes it is vain to fortify the authority of Scripture by arguments and proofs if the witness of the Spirit is lacking, "for unless this foundation is laid, its authority will always remain in doubt" (1.8.1). However, where the divine testimony is present, then such proofs become useful aids. Thus, "once we have embraced [Scripture] devoutly as its dignity deserves, and have recognized it to be above the common sort of things, those arguments—not strong enough before to engraft and fix the certainty of Scripture in our minds—become very useful aids" (1.8.1).

Calvin comments upon some of these "useful aids." He observes that Scripture exhibits a power all its own, which is different from that which marks human wisdom (cf. 1 Cor. 2:4–5). Scripture's power does not derive from the "realm of eloquence," at least not as such. Instead, Scripture more often bears the marks of a certain "rude simplicity." Yet truth, even if conveyed with rude simplicity, is its own prop and support (1.8.1). For "however much forward men try to gnaw at [Scripture], nevertheless it clearly is crammed with thoughts that could not be humanly conceived" (1.8.2). Moreover, says Calvin, "the very antiquity of Scripture has no slight weight" (1.8.3). Miracles, too, demonstrate that those who claimed to be God's messengers were His prophets (1.8.5). Moses' miracles were tested by severe proofs

(1.8.6). His prophecies were also subjected to severe scrutiny, being fulfilled many years later (1.8.7). This is true of all the prophets (1.8.8). Although the Scripture critics of Calvin's day sought to cast doubt upon the authenticity and reliability of the human authors of the Bible, Calvin counters by showing the inconsistency with which they apply their skepticism. They doubt whether Moses wrote Scripture but not whether Plato wrote his dialogues. In fact, "The law of Moses was wonderfully preserved by heavenly providence rather than by human effort." "But, to generalize concerning all sacred authors, it is absolutely certain that their writings passed down to posterity in but one way: from hand to hand. Some had heard their actual words; others learned that they had so spoken from hearers whose memories were still fresh" (1.8.9). Moreover, history itself testifies to the marvelous manner in which God has preserved His written Word (1.8.10).

But more than all of that, Scripture bears witness to its own authenticity. It is confirmed by miracles, by fulfilled prophecies, and by God's preservation of it; but the divine contents of Scripture also testify to its authority and authenticity (1.8.11). Especially when we come to the New Testament we see God at work in the lives of many of its (once skeptical or immoral) human authors. Calvin bids us to take note. These men, whom their fellows earlier regarded with contempt, suddenly began to speak most wonderfully about heavenly mysteries, which they could not do except they had been "instructed by the Spirit" (1.8.12).

Further, Calvin notes that the church throughout its history has clung to the Scriptures; and the blood of the martyrs testifies to the certitude they received from Scriptural doctrine (1.8.12–13). Having made that point, Calvin reiterates that such "proofs," for all they are worth, are not strong enough to provide "a firm faith." He concludes by saying:

> Therefore Scripture will ultimately suffice for a saving knowledge of God only when its certainty is founded upon the inward persuasion of the Holy Spirit. Indeed, these human testimonies which exist to confirm [faith] will not be vain if, as secondary aids to our feebleness, they follow that chief and highest testimony. But those who wish to prove to unbelievers that Scripture is the Word of God are acting foolishly, for only by faith can this be known (1.8.13).

Chapter Nine: Fanatics, Abandoning Scripture and Flying Over to Revelation, Cast Down All the Principles of Godliness

Orientation

With this chapter Calvin explores the relation between Word and Spirit or that bond between the Word given by the Spirit and the Spirit who binds Himself to the Word. This chapter is directed against the Libertines.

The Holy Spirit against Discarding Scripture

Calvin notes that certain "giddy men" exalt themselves as inspired by the Spirit, having freed themselves of "the dead and killing letter"—that is, Scripture. They are not merely gripped by error but carried away with frenzy. They despise the Scriptures, something the prophets and apostles did not do. "Hence we conclude that by a heinous sacrilege these rascals tear apart those things which the prophet joined together with an inviolable bond" (cf. Isa. 59:21) (1.9.1). "The Spirit, promised to us, has not the task of inventing new and unheard of revelations, or of forging a new kind of doctrine, to lead us away from the received doctrine of the gospel, but of sealing our minds with that very doctrine which is commended by the gospel" (1.9.1).

The Bond between Word and Spirit

For Calvin, Word and Spirit belong together. The Spirit speaks to us through the Word. It is important, then, that we zealously read and study the Bible. We must hearken to it with submissive hearts if we expect to benefit from the Spirit's work. However, since Satan disguises himself as an angel of light (2 Cor. 11:14), we cannot distinguish his work from the Spirit's work unless we make use of Scripture and look for the discerning mark of Scripture. For, again, Scripture is the Spirit's work (cf. 2 Tim. 3:16; 2 Pet. 1:21). As its Author, He cannot vary and differ from Himself. In fact, we discern the Spirit's very image in the Word. It is "the instrument by which the Lord dispenses the illumination of his Spirit to believers." There is no other Spirit than the One who dwelt and spoke in the apostles and prophets, whose oracles we have in the Scripture (1.9.2–3). "For by a kind of mutual bond the Lord has joined together the certainty of his Word and of his Spirit so that the perfect religion of his Word may abide in our minds when the Spirit, who causes us to contemplate God's face, shines; and that we in turn embrace the Spirit with no fear of being deceived when we recognize him in his own image, namely, in the Word" (1.9.3). The fanatics, however, swollen with pride, forfeit the Word and claim as divine revelation "whatever they may have conceived while snoring" (1.9.3).

Observations

It should be noted that Calvin does not think that humans can reach up to a saving knowledge of God through God's revelation of Himself in creation. Scripture is needed for that purpose. Although Scripture bears the marks of its divine authorship, and there are numerous other proofs for its authority, none of these are effectual in themselves to convince us that it is the Word of God. Only the internal testimony of the Holy Spirit persuades us of Scripture's divine origin and authority, for to regard Scripture on those terms requires faith. One must believe in God and be surrendered to Him, humbled and teachable, in order to have eyes to see what Scripture is—namely God's Word.

For this reason Scripture, the Word of the Spirit, communicates the gospel to us, whereby we are taught who God is and therefore who we are as His creatures. The Scripture never possesses a power in and of itself to move persons to faith. Yet the same Spirit who authored the Scripture, who is the best witness to the Scripture's authenticity, is the Spirit who authors faith in our hearts so that we receive Scripture as God's speech—indeed, a saving message concerning God as our Creator and Redeemer.

The Spirit also does not allow us to commune with Him independently of Scripture. Those who claim a liberation from the Bible, as though they are moved and touched by the Holy Spirit apart from Scripture, inauthenticate themselves, not Scripture. The bond between Word and Spirit is unbreakable, for the Spirit authors the Word, authors our faith in the Word, and authors our dependency upon the Word. He always speaks to the church through sacred Scripture.

Questions for Reflection and Discussion

1. Imagine the world without the Bible. How would your own religious experience change if you were without Scripture?

2. What does Calvin mean by likening Scripture to spectacles or glasses? What does Scripture bring into focus?

3. Do you agree with Calvin's analysis that without Scripture we stagger (note that word!) about in error? Give examples of how this is true if you do agree. Notice that Calvin combines the call to study Scripture with the call to obey Scripture. What are some New Testament examples of study without obedience? Why are both necessary?

4. What does Calvin mean in saying that the fall makes people forgetful of God? Give examples of this forgetfulness.

5. In light of Calvin's defense of Scripture as God's Word, if someone said to you: "Prove to me that the Bible is the Word of God," what would be your reply? The twentieth century will go down in church history as "the Battle for the Bible." Should that battle have been waged? Should it be waged now? Or is it enough to say that Scripture bears its own authentication, and let the critics spurn the Word of God?

6. How might Calvin have responded to the following comment: "Faith is the gift of God; but it does not in the least follow that the faith that God gives is an irrational faith, that is, a faith without grounds in right reason. It is beyond all question that only the prepared heart can fitly respond to the 'reasons'; but how can even a prepared heart respond, when there are no 'reasons' to draw out its action?" What is your response?

7. Why is the inner testimony of the Holy Spirit the foundation for even evaluating "the evidence" that Scripture is God's Word?

8. Who might qualify as fanatics today, that is, serve as examples or illustrations of Calvin's concern about fanatics overthrowing or grossly misusing Scripture as they testify to the Spirit's inward actions in their hearts? How should we respond to people who say, "The Lord spoke to me last night, and told me..."?

9. Does the testimony of the Holy Spirit apply to different parts of the Bible separately?

10. Is the appeal of certain mystics or fanatics to 2 Corinthians 3:6 to disprove the sufficiency of Scripture tenable?

≈ 4 ≈

The True God

Chapters 10–13 of Book One

Chapter Ten: Scripture, To Correct All Superstition, Has Set the True God Alone Over Against All the Gods of the Heathen

Orientation

WITH CHAPTER TEN, Calvin transitions from a discussion of the necessity of Scripture to its function, which is to reveal God as our Creator and Redeemer. As God's written Word, Scripture gives us a fuller and clearer revelation than God's revelation in creation. Specifically, Calvin explores *how* Scripture gives us knowledge of God. Although God is revealed to us quite clearly in the fashioning and governing of the universe, humans suppress this revelation. God gives Scripture as a remedy. As such, it "more intimately" and "more vividly" reveals the knowledge of God to us. From Scripture, Calvin briefly explores who God is and His chief attributes. Given this discussion, the eleventh chapter addresses the unlawfulness of making images of God. Then chapter twelve succinctly examines worshiping God versus idols and the false worship of God. Lastly, chapter thirteen brings us to the doctrine of the Trinity, which Calvin treats with care and at length.

Scripture on God as Creator

Calvin opens chapter ten with a summary statement: "We have taught that the knowledge of God, otherwise quite clearly set forth in the system of the universe and in all creatures, is nonetheless more intimately and also more vividly revealed in his Word" (1.10.1). What distinguishes God's inscripturated revelation of Himself as our Creator from His revelation in creation is its clarity and closeness. God draws near to us, using human speech, and shows Himself as our Creator.

Calvin knows that the doctrine of God is a huge topic, but his interest is merely to provide "a sort of index" to the biblical testimony concerning God (1.10.1). It is also not Calvin's interest in this chapter to consider God as our Redeemer, as the One who established a special covenant with Abraham for the salvation of sinners. Rather, at this point Calvin wants to explore Scripture as it pertains to the knowledge of God as our Creator and Provider. Even with this self-imposed limitation, we discover that both God's "fatherly goodness and his beneficently inclined will are repeatedly extolled; and examples of his severity are given, which show him to be the righteous avenger of evil deeds, especially where his forbearance toward the obstinate is of no effect" (1.10.1).

God's Chief Attributes

In looking for texts that provide "clearer descriptions" wherein God is suitably exhibited to us, Calvin turns to Exodus 34:6–7, where God says about Himself: "The LORD, the LORD, a merciful and gracious God, patient and of much compassion, and true, who keepest mercy for thousands, who takest away iniquity and transgressions...in whose presence the innocent will not be innocent, who visitest the iniquity of the fathers upon the children and the children's children." This passage concisely sets forth what we need to know about God. "Here let us observe," writes Calvin,

> that his eternity and his self-existence are announced by that wonderful name twice repeated. Thereupon his powers are mentioned, by which he is shown to us not as he is in himself, but as he is toward us: so that this recognition of him consists more in living experience than in vain and high-flown speculation. Now we hear the same powers enumerated there that we have noted as shining in heaven and earth: kindness, goodness, mercy, justice, judgment, and truth. For power and might are contained under the title *Elohim* (1.10.2).

Calvin also points readers to Psalm 145, which depicts "the sum" of God's powers, where indeed "nothing is set down there that cannot be beheld in his creatures." This passage elicits the following (though Calvin doesn't enunciate it): that God is king and unsearchable in His greatness; He is also majestic, the doer of wondrous works; mighty, gracious, full of compassion, slow to anger, of great mercy; He is likewise good, everlasting, providentially wise, caring, and just toward His creatures; He is righteous, holy, and a God who draws near to those who call on Him.

Another text Calvin cites is Jeremiah 9:24 ("Let him who glories, glory in this…that he knows that I am the Lord who exercises mercy, judgment, and justice in the earth").

> Certainly these three things are especially necessary for us to know: mercy, on which alone the salvation of us all rests; judgment, which is daily exercised against wrongdoers, and in even greater severity awaits them to their everlasting ruin; justice, whereby believers are preserved, and are most tenderly nourished. When these are understood, the prophecy witnesses that you have abundant reason to glory to God. Yet neither his truth, nor power, nor holiness, nor goodness is thus overlooked. For how could we have the requisite knowledge of his justice, mercy, and judgment unless that knowledge rested upon his unbending truth? And without understanding his power, how could we believe that he rules the earth in judgment and justice? But whence comes his mercy save from his goodness? If, finally, 'all his paths are mercy' [Ps. 25:10], judgment, justice [cf. Ps. 25:8–10], in these also is his holiness visible (1.10.2).

This knowledge of God, given to us in Scripture, invites us to fear God, to trust Him, and thus to worship Him with a pure life and genuine obedience as we depend on His goodness (1.10.2). As God manifests Himself in His work of creation and providential governance, so Scripture shows us God not as He is in Himself, but as He is toward us. Hence, the recognition of God "consists more in living experience than in vain and high-flown speculation" (1.10.2).

Calvin also points out that Scripture escorts us to "the true God." Scripture "distinctly excludes and rejects all the gods of the heathen, for religion was commonly adulterated throughout almost all ages" (1.10.3). The church fathers make this point as well. Indeed, if we do not worship the true God (cf. Hab. 2:20), we turn to idolatry (1.10.3).

Chapter Eleven: It is Unlawful to Attribute a Visible Form to God, and Generally Whoever Sets Up Idols Revolts Against the True God

Orientation

This chapter contains, in large measure, a polemic against the use of images as practiced by the Roman Catholic Church of Calvin's day. Calvin introduces the topic at this point by way of contrast with the true knowledge of God that Scripture renders.

Scripture's Rejection of Idols and Images

Whereas Scripture reveals God, images hide Him. Thus, Calvin rejects and wants nothing to do with "likenesses, pictures, and other signs by which the superstitious have thought [that God] will be near them" (1.11.1). Calvin cannot hide his contempt for bowing to dumb idols, while the true worship of God is ignored. His overriding concern is the neglect of piety. He refers his readers to Deuteronomy 4:15-20, where the Lord warns the Israelites to take heed to themselves, lest they corrupt themselves by making an idol or an image of some shape; even as they are also warned against bowing down and worshiping the moon and the stars—all the heavenly array—which are nothing more than things God has apportioned to all peoples. After citing numerous passages (e.g., Isa. 40:18-20; 41:7, 29; 45:9; 46:5-7), including Paul's words to the Athenians in Acts 17:29, Calvin writes, "From this it is clear that every statue man erects, or every image he paints to represent God, simply displeases God as something dishonorable to his majesty" (1.11.2).

To be sure, from time to time God has given "definite signs" of His majesty and presence; but, Calvin notes, "all the signs that [the Lord] ever gave forth aptly conformed to his plan of teaching and at the same time clearly told men of his incomprehensible essence" (1.11.3). Since God's essence is incomprehensible, it is folly to think that He can be depicted through images. Calvin offers an example:

> The mercy seat from which God manifested the presence of his power under the law was so constructed as to suggest that the best way to contemplate the divine is where minds are lifted above themselves with admiration. Indeed, the cherubim with wings outspread covered it; the veil shrouded it; the place itself deeply enough hidden concealed it [Ex. 25:17-21]. Hence it is perfectly clear that those who try to defend images of God and the saints with the example of those cherubim are raving madmen. What, indeed, I beg you, did those paltry little images mean? Solely that images are not suited to represent God's mysteries (1.11.3).

Scripture directly forbids the use of images and other visible representations to depict God (cf. Ps. 135:15; 115:4, 8; Isa. 44:12-17). "For surely there is nothing less fitting than to wish to reduce God, who is immeasurable and incomprehensible, to a five-foot measure!" (1.11.4). Such is a monstrous thing!

Although the defense set down for images is that they function as "the books of the uneducated," Jeremiah condemns this reasoning (cf. Jer. 10:8). In fact, contrary to the belief that images are the "books of the uneducated," Habakkuk teaches that "a molten image is a teacher of falsehood" (Hab. 2:18) (1.11.5). Even some of the doctors and theologians of the early church went astray on this matter (1.11.6). But more to the point, there would be no "uneducated" at all if the church had done its duty. "In the preaching of his Word and sacred mysteries [God] has bidden that a common doctrine be there set forth for all. But those whose eyes rove about in contemplating idols betray that their minds are not diligently intent upon this doctrine" (1.11.7).

Calvin asks: When the teachers of the church are mute, will they turn to voiceless idols to teach? People are left stupid and defrauded of the doctrine which is suited to bless them. The gospel in its proclamation presents Christ crucified clearly before our eyes (see Gal. 3:1). Calvin further asks: "What purpose did it serve for so many crosses—of wood, stone, silver, and gold—to be erected here and there in churches, if this fact had been duly and faithfully taught: that Christ died on the cross to bear our curse, in short, to reconcile us to God the Father? From this one fact they could have learned more than from a thousand crosses of wood or stone" (1.11.7).

The Rise and Misuse of Images
In an extended discourse, Calvin fills out the remainder of this chapter with a discussion of the origin and use of images, and how this increasingly devolved into the corruption of worship (1.11.8–16). We will not trace out this development, but we will note a few aspects of Calvin's discussion. As for those who contend that the idol (or the image) isn't being worshiped, Calvin argues that it makes no difference whether the idol or "God in the idol" is worshiped. It is idolatry because "divine honors are bestowed upon an idol," no matter the pretext or intention (1.11.9). The danger Calvin sees is that we "fasten God wherever we fashion him" (1.11.9). Moreover, when the church was strong and pure in doctrine it always rejected the use of images. Consider, too, that God has given us the images we need for the upbuilding of our faith in baptism and the Lord's Supper (1.11.13).

Calvin, however, does not wish to be misunderstood. He does not forbid the use of art altogether. Some get caught up in another form of superstition, he says, in thinking that absolutely no images are ever permissible in any circumstances. Calvin disagrees with this notion. Sculpture and painting are divine gifts. Therefore we are permitted "a pure and legitimate use of each, lest those things which the Lord has conferred upon us for his glory and our good be not only polluted by perverse misuse but also turned to our destruction" (1.11.12). But "only those things are to be sculptured or painted which the eyes are capable of seeing: let not God's majesty, which is far above the perception of the eyes, be debased through unseemly representations." Art gives us pleasure and has its place. Let us therefore resist the depravity to which some artists give themselves. In addition, let us not succumb to the folly of thinking that images, even when containing nothing evil, are suitable for teaching (1.11.12).

Calvin refutes the misuse of various biblical texts that some cite in an effort to lend God's authority to their idolatry (1.11.15). Finally, notes Calvin, the Eastern Orthodox Church is mistaken, just like Rome, in making subtle distinctions between worship and veneration. For example, Rome constantly promotes the distinction between *latria* (honor) and *dulia* (servitude), as if this delivers people from the idolatry of images. Neither God nor people are so easily hoodwinked (1.11.16).

Chapter Twelve: How God Is to Be Distinguished from Idols That Perfect Honor May Be Given to Him Alone

Orientation

This chapter serves as a sort of transfer station, taking us from the doctrine of God in general and the problem of idolatry (chapters ten and eleven) to the doctrine of the Trinity, which is treated at length in chapter thirteen. In this chapter, Calvin explores further the last point he made at the end of the previous chapter regarding *latria* and *dulia*. The knowledge of God as revealed in Scripture cuts off human speculation. Calvin continues to urge readers to follow the dictates of God's Word and to honor God according to those dictates.

God versus Idols

Calvin offers his own summary of what he has discussed to this point: "We said at the beginning that the knowledge of God does not rest in cold speculation, but carries with it the honoring of him. In passing, we also touched upon how he is to be rightly worshiped.... Now I only briefly repeat: as often as Scripture asserts that there is one God, it is not contending over the bare name, but also prescribing that nothing belonging to his divinity is to be transferred to another. From this it is also clear in what respect pure religion differs from superstition" (1.12.1). Calvin is zealous to convince us that we zealously distinguish God from idols. Nothing of God's divinity may be transferred to another. God alone is to be worshiped, and rightly worshiped. God's own law confirms this. This means that the worship of "saints" bears the same tendency to detract from God's glory as outright idolatry (1.12.1).

The Roman Catholic Church introduced the distinction between "honor" (*latria* or *cultus*) and "servitude" (*dulia* or *servitus*)—*latria* being reserved to God, *dulia* being offered to saints and angels. Calvin, however, wonders whether this isn't a distinction without a difference. Even if the distinction is apt, how does it help? Isn't enslavement to a human being of greater weight than rendering honor to God (1.12.2)? Calvin bids us to "drop fine distinctions and examine the thing itself" (1.12.3). Examining a number of scriptural passages, he observes that religious acts (like bowing, revering, and honoring) directed to anything other than God (even if God is the indirect target of these actions) cannot help but profane His honor. "Thus, if we wish to have one God, we should remember that we must not pluck away even a particle of his glory and that he must retain what is his own." For example, when Cornelius prostrated himself before Peter, "undoubtedly he did not intend to worship Peter in place of God, yet Peter earnestly forbade him to do it" (1.12.3).

We must follow God's Word, not our own speculations about the worship of God. "For by his law it pleases [God] to prescribe for men what is good and right, and thus to hold them to a sure standard that no one may take leave to contrive any sort of worship he pleases." As Calvin also states, "whenever any observances of piety are transferred to some one other than the sole God, sacrilege occurs" (1.12.3).

Observations

Chapters ten through twelve are connected by the common concern of the knowledge of God. If we would know God, we must know the true God over against idols. For God makes Himself known in His work of creation and providential governance; but also He makes Himself known in Scripture. Calvin reminds us that we must reject an icy speculation into God's nature as He is in Himself—which is to say, Calvin directs us away from philosophical subtleties. Instead, Calvin argues that the knowledge of God involves a proper worship of Him. In fact, we don't know God—God as He is toward us—until we do. The knowledge of God, then, has to do with the living experience of God, trusting and obeying Him, over against unproductive and pretentious speculations concerning Him, or worse, seeking to worship Him by images and idols or other superstitious rites.

For all that, however, we still do not have a true knowledge of God until we contemplate and trust Him as the Triune God, for the true God is Triune.

Chapter Thirteen: In Scripture, from the Creation Onward, We Are Taught One Essence of God, Which Contains Three Persons

Orientation

For Calvin, Scripture teaches us to know God as an "infinite and spiritual essence." In turn, we are called away from popular misconceptions of God, as well as deep subtleties of philosophy regarding the Deity. God's *infinity* warns us against any attempt to enclose Him within the confines of our own senses. That God has a *spiritual nature* tells us that we may not imagine Him according to what is earthly or carnal. Thus He accommodates Himself to our meager capacity. The use of anthropomorphisms in the Bible, where God, for example, is depicted as if He had a body, is emblematic of this accommodation. Calvin notes, "as nurses commonly do with infants, God is wont in a measure to 'lisp' in speaking to us.... To do this he must descend far beneath his loftiness" (1.13.1). This brings Calvin to discuss God's revelation of Himself as triune, that is, the doctrine of the Trinity.

Constructing the Doctrine of the Trinity

In many places and various ways Scripture distinguishes God from idols. One particularly noteworthy way in which God is so distinguished is His triune nature. That is, God manifests Himself as one God in three distinct persons. Not surprisingly, Calvin is careful to unfold this idea. Calvin first refers to Hebrews 1:3 ("who being the brightness of *his* glory, and the express image of his person"), where the apostle calls the Son of God "the express image of his person" or "the stamp of the Father's hypostasis." *Hypostasis* is the Greek term used here, translated "person" above. The Latin Vulgate uses the phrase *figura substantiae eius* (the exact representation of His substance).

Thus the Father and the Son have "subsistence" distinct (but not separate) from each other—that is, each possesses existence in a way which distinguishes the one from the other (1.13.2).

Calvin pauses to make clear that "the essence of God is simple and undivided, and he contains all in himself, without portion or derivation, but in integral perfection...." Here Calvin affirms God's fundamental unity (there is only one God) and simplicity, which means that God is not derived from other abstract perfections or composed of them, as if God were a collection of parts that come together to form Him. Thus the Father is distinct in His "proper nature" from the Son, but He "expresses himself wholly in the Son." Therefore the apostle says that the Father has made His *hypostasis* (His person) visible in His Son. Similarly, the Holy Spirit is "other than" the Father and the Son. This does not mean that the Father, Son, and Holy Spirit are distinct in essence; rather, they are distinct in "subsistence" or "person" or "hypostasis." "There are in God three hypostases" (1.13.2).

The Use of Technical Terms

Admittedly, this is technical language. Calvin knows that some object to using words to describe God not directly derived from Scripture, such as "Trinity" and "Person." Calvin replies that whether technical words are used or not, we cannot be shaken in our conviction that "three are spoken of, each of which is entirely God, yet that there is not more than one God" (1.13.3). Thus there is one essence or *ousia* in God but three persons, or *hypostases*, or subsistences, each distinct from the other (1.13.2). Although (as already noted) such technical terms are not strictly derived from the Bible, they aid us in understanding the scriptural teaching about God and therefore ought to be used. Moreover, such terms have helped the church unmask false teachers, such as Arius and Sabellius.

Arius acknowledged that Christ was God and the Son of God, while also maintaining that Christ was created and had a beginning, like other creatures. The church responded by asserting that Christ is "consubstantial" with the Father. The Greek word used to express this consubstantiality was the word *homoousios*, literally meaning "of the same substance" (as the Father). Arius was exposed in his error by this term, for he denied that the Son was God in the way the Father was God—of the same substance (the same divine essence) as the Father. One little word unmasked Arius (1.13.4).

The church also contended with Sabellius, who taught that the Father, the Son, and the Holy Spirit are nothing more than distinct names in God.

Thus Sabellius believed that the Father is not a distinct divine Person vis-à-vis the Son; rather, the Father is the Son; the Holy Spirit is the Father, etc., without rank, without distinction. In short, these distinct names merely refer to attributes of God, akin to calling God mighty, or just, or wise. Sabellius therefore denied that there are a trinity of Persons subsisting in the one God or subsisting in the unity of God. For Sabellius, the names Father, Son, and Holy Spirit refer to one person who is the one God, each name referring to one and the same person (1.13.4). The trinity of Persons exposed this writer in his error. Says Calvin, we must see, then, that technical terms were not rashly invented; and, similarly, we may not rashly discard them. On the contrary, technical language about the Trinity remains necessary so long as error obscures the truth about God and heresy is able to gain a foothold (1.13.4).

To be sure, the technical nature of these terms has had its drawbacks. Initially this language made it very difficult for the Eastern (Greek speaking) church and the Western (Latin speaking) church to understand one another. But ultimately understanding prevailed and the traitors to the biblical doctrine of the Trinity (like Arius and Sabellius) were unmasked and exposed in their mistaken views—the former being unmasked with the word "consubstantial," which testifies to a "unity of substance"; the latter being exposed when the church confessed against him that "in the one essence of God there is a trinity of persons," which bears witness to the truth that in God there are "three in one essence" (1.13.5).

Defining the Word "Person"

We see, then, that Calvin acknowledges that such terms have limits. He could wish their burial, "if only among all men this faith were agreed on: that Father and Son and Spirit are one God, yet the Son is not the Father, nor the Spirit the Son, but that they are differentiated by a peculiar quality" (1.13.5).

Calvin next takes a brief detour to define carefully the term "Person," which he calls a "subsistence in God's essence." Though each Person in the Trinity is related to the other Persons, each is also "distinguished by an incommunicable quality." Meanwhile the word "subsistence" must be distinguished from the word "essence" (1.13.6). Calvin elaborates on these ideas:

> For if the Word were simply God, and yet possessed no other characteristic mark, John would wrongly have said that the Word was always with God [John 1:1]. When immediately after he adds that the Word

was also God himself, he recalls us to the essence as a unity. But because he could not be with God without residing in the Father, hence emerges the idea of a subsistence, which, even though it has been joined with the essence by a common bond and cannot be separated from it, yet has a special mark whereby it is distinguished from it. Now, of the three subsistences I say that each one, while related to the others, is distinguished by a special quality. This "relation" is here distinctly expressed: because where simple and indefinite mention is made of God, this name pertains no less to the Son and the Spirit than to the Father. But as soon as the Father is compared with the Son, the character of each distinguishes the one from the other. Thirdly, whatever is proper to each individually, I maintain to be incommunicable because whatever is attributed to the Father as a distinguishing mark cannot agree with, or be transferred to, the Son (1.13.6).

The peculiar quality distinctive of each person of the Trinity is not a differentiation of essence but of economy. Calvin observes, with Tertullian, "that there is a kind of distribution or economy in God which has no effect on the unity of essence" (1.13.6). This is the distinction between what is called the ontological and economic Trinity.

The Divinity of the Son and of the Spirit

Calvin proceeds to make a scriptural case for the divinity of Christ and of the Holy Spirit. It is not our purpose to follow the full contours of that discussion except to observe that Calvin builds the case for the deity of Christ around various biblical texts. The Word (*Logos*), in Scripture, is not merely a transitory voice, but also a divine Person, through whom the Spirit has spoken by the prophets and apostles (1 Pet. 1:10–11). The Word has creative power (Gen. 1:1; Heb. 1:2–3). The Word is the personification of Wisdom, the essential Word of the Father, "presiding over the creation of things and all God's works" (Prov. 8:22; John 5:17; John 1:1–3). The Word, the Son of God, dwells with the Father from eternity, for God is the same forever and there is no change in His essence (cf. James 1:17; John 17:5).

In making the case for Christ's deity, Calvin looks to the Old and New Testaments (1.13.7–13; see Jer. 23:5–6; Hos. 12:5; Isa. 42:8; Zech. 2:3, 9; Mal. 3:1; also Isa. 8:14). But the New Testament especially demonstrates how "what had been foretold concerning the eternal God had already been revealed in Christ or was someday to be manifested in him" (1.13.11). For example, "when Isaiah prophesies that the Lord of Hosts is to be 'a stone of

stumbling and a rock of offense for the Judeans and Israelites' [Isa. 8:14 p.],
Paul declares this prophecy fulfilled in Christ [Rom. 9:32–33]. Therefore
he proclaims Christ to be Lord of Hosts" (1.13.11). Calvin cites numerous
examples of this sort of thing (Isa. 45:23 and Rom. 14:10–11; Ps. 68:18 and
Eph. 4:8; Isa. 6:1 and John 12:41; Ps. 101:26 and Heb. 1:10; Ps. 96:7 and
Heb. 1:6). Indeed, Christ is openly called God (Rom. 9:5), and He sits on
God's judgment throne (2 Cor. 5:10). He is God manifested in the flesh
(1 Tim. 3:16–17; Phil. 2:6–7). He is the true God and eternal life (1 John
5:20; cf. 1 Cor. 8:5–6; Acts 20:28; John 20:28) (1.13.11). Christ's divinity is
also proved from His works (cf. John 5:17–18; Heb. 1:3; Isa. 43:25; Matt.
9:4–6; John 2:25), from His miracles (Matt. 10:8; Acts 3:6; John 5:36;
10:37; 14:11; Acts 7:59; Col. 2:9; 1 Cor. 2:2), and from the biblical saluta-
tions (Rom. 1:7; 1 Cor. 1:3; 2 Cor. 1:2; Gal. 1:3, and the like) (1.13.7–13).

Calvin follows his case for Christ's divinity with a demonstration of the
divinity of the Spirit—the proof of which is evident from the Spirit's divine
activity and from direct biblical testimony (cf. 1.13.14–15). Calvin notes
that functions that belong to divinity are ascribed to the Holy Spirit, even
as they are ascribed to the Son (cf. 1 Cor. 2:10; 6:11; 12:4, 11). "If the Spirit
were not an entity subsisting in God, choice and will would by no means be
conceded to him." Thus we discover that the apostle "very clearly attributes
to the Spirit divine power, and shows that he resides hypostatically in God"
(1.13.14). Appealing to an array of texts, Calvin shows that the Holy Spirit
is a divine Person, and when Ananias lied to the Holy Spirit he lied to God
(Acts 5:3–4). Blasphemy against the Spirit is the unpardonable sin (Matt.
12:31; Mark 3:29; Luke 12:10; also see various other texts that Calvin takes
up to varying degrees in arguing for the deity of the Spirit, such as 1 Cor.
3:16–17; 6:19; 2 Cor. 6:16, 19; Isa. 6:9; Acts 28:25–26; Isa. 63:10; Gen. 1:2;
Ps. 33:6; Isa. 11:4).

The Distinction between and Unity of the Persons

Having shown that there are three who are divine, that is, about whom we
may rightly say, "He is God," Calvin advances his discussion of the Trinity
by explaining the distinction and unity of the three Persons. Here Calvin
expounds on the Oneness and Threeness of God as triune. First, there is only
one God. We confess only one faith, one baptism; and Christ commissions
the church to baptize in the one name of God the Father, the Son, and the
Holy Spirit. Yet Father, Son, and Spirit are not mere titles, but Persons dis-

tinct from the other. They are not, however, divided or separated from one another (1.13.16–17).

If division among the Persons existed, if they were separated from one another, we would have to say that there are three Gods. That is entirely contrary to Scripture. God is one; there is only one God. Yet the Persons of the Trinity are distinct from one another; and the Bible makes clear that we must distinguish each from the other. Scripture allows us to distinguish the Persons of the Trinity as follows:

> …to the Father is attributed the beginning of activity, and the fountain and wellspring of all things; to the Son, wisdom, counsel, and the ordered disposition of all things; but to the Spirit is assigned the power and efficacy of that activity. Indeed, although the eternity of the Father is also the eternity of the Son and the Spirit, since God could never exist apart from his wisdom and power, and we must not seek in eternity a *before* or an *after*, nevertheless the observance of an order is not meaningless or superfluous, when the Father is thought of as first, then from him the Son, and finally from both the Spirit. For the mind of each human being is naturally inclined to contemplate God first, then the wisdom coming forth from him, and lastly the power whereby he executes the decrees of his plan. For this reason, the Son is said to come forth from the Father alone; the Spirit, from the Father and the Son at the same time (1.13.18).

Here Calvin clearly sides with the Western church in affirming the *filioque*, a phrase that the Latin church added to the Nicene Creed, namely that the Spirit proceeds from the Father *and the Son* (*filioque*).

Calvin's comments above do not compromise God's "utterly simple unity." On the contrary, for "in each hypostasis the whole divine nature is understood, with this qualification—that to each belongs his own peculiar quality" (1.13.19). Calvin urges us to soberness and to profess our faith in one God. Under that name we understand "a single, simple essence, in which we comprehend three persons, or hypostases." Meanwhile, "because the peculiar qualities in the persons carry an order within them, e.g., in the Father is the beginning and the source…, the name *God* is peculiarly applied to the Father." Likewise, "unity of essence is retained, and a reasoned order is kept, which yet takes nothing away from the deity of the Son and the Spirit" (1.13.20).

Calvin is very aware of the anti-trinitarian heresies that have plagued the church in former times and his own times. As he writes: "Moreover, Satan, in order to tear our faith from its very roots, has always been instigating great battles, partly concerning the divine essence of the Son and the Spirit, partly concerning the distinction of the persons. He has during nearly all ages stirred up ungodly spirits to harry orthodox teachers over this matter and today also is trying to kindle a new fire from the old embers. For these reasons, it is important here to resist the perverse ravings of certain persons" (1.13.21). In particular Calvin defends the doctrine against the deceptions of Servetus and Valentine Gentile (cf. 1.13.22–29).

Christ's personhood as human and divine is, in particular, at stake in the debate on the Trinity. As our Mediator the nature and meaning of salvation is drawn up into this matter. Calvin urges his readers to "impose a limit upon their curiosity, and not seek out for themselves more eagerly than is proper troublesome and perplexed disputations" (1.13.29). As he says in another place: "Let us then willingly leave to God the knowledge of himself" (1.13.21).

Observations

With his discussion of the doctrine of the Trinity Calvin has shown us the most important aspect of who God is and His relation to us as our Creator. In the chapters that now follow on creation and providence, Calvin will further unpack what it means to know God as He is toward us. Book One is about the knowledge of God our Creator. Calvin will therefore expound upon God's works of creation and providence, which show us why we owe all that we are and have to God, and why we can find solace in the rough-and-tumble of life, in the face of its uncertainties and sorrows, for the true God governs all things according to His wise plan.

Questions for Reflection and Discussion

1. Why does a knowledge of God consist more in living experience than in vain and high-flown speculation? What does Calvin mean? What is the knowledge of "living experience"?

2. What does God's aseity or self-existence mean? Why is this important to affirm about God? *Self sufficient*

3. List all the attributes of God that Calvin mentions in this chapter.

4. Calvin mentions attributes of God that can be "beheld in his creatures." What are these attributes? What attributes of God cannot be beheld in His creatures? *anger love mercy self sustane immutability*

5. How would you respond to a person who says about a stained glass picture of a gentle-looking Jesus, "It teaches me that God is a loving God"? How would Calvin respond? Moreover, would Calvin disapprove of passion plays or Sunday school materials with pictures of Jesus?

6. Is the modern church sensitive to questions about idolatry, or jealous that not one particle of God's glory be stolen from Him? Explain how this is or isn't the case.

7. What are some common trinitarian heresies? Do you recall the false teachings of Arius and Sabellius concerning the Trinity? What about the Jehovah's Witnesses, the Mormons, and other sects that fly a flag under the name of Christ?

8. Are you helped by the technical terms used by theologians (including Calvin) to explain the doctrine of the Trinity? If not, what would help you? Analogies?

9. What are the key features, following Calvin, that build the biblical case for the Son's divinity and for the Spirit's divinity?

10. What is the meaning of the term "subsistence"?

11. What does the term "hypostasis" mean? How does this word differ from the way we commonly use our word "person" in English—i.e., how do we define "person" in English and how does the word "hypostasis" differ from our definition?

12. What are the implications of knowing God as triune for your life as a believer and in communion with other believers?

13. How ought knowing God as triune influence our prayer life and corporate worship?

14. In the Trinity there is consubstantiality—each Person has and is the same divine essence—but in God there are also three distinct subsistences—"ways of existing" which are the three Persons of the Trinity. Thus each Person exists in a certain distinct manner from the others and, in turn, this brings forth a distinct "work" unique to each Person. This reveals, for example, a functional subordination of the Son to the Father, and of the Spirit to the Father and the Son. In this light, how does seeing a functional difference among the Persons (while being one God) help us live a Christian life with unity but functional differences or as one body with many gifts?

15. What is the practical significance of the doctrine of the Trinity—or better, to know God as triune?

❦ 5 ❦

The Creation of All Things

Chapters 14–15 of Book One

Chapter Fourteen: Even in the Creation of the Universe and of All Things, Scripture by Unmistakable Marks Distinguishes the True God from False Gods

Orientation

WITH THIS CHAPTER, Calvin launches on an exposition of the doctrine of creation—that is, he expounds on the activity of the triune God as Creator. Creation is, for Calvin, part of God's revelation of Himself. In this way, the faith of the church finds comfort in contemplating the Lord as our Creator; and the account of creation as recorded in the Bible teaches us to "seek no other God but him who was put forth by Moses as the Maker and Founder of the universe" (1.14.1). Creation takes us back to "the primal source of the human race and of all things," namely God. Moreover, creation testifies to God's eternity, for creation is part of the finitude of time, which stands in marked contrast to God's eternity. "When a certain shameless fellow mockingly asked a pious old man what God had done before the creation of the world, the latter aptly countered that he had been building hell for the curious" (1.14.1). We must resist "wicked and hurtful speculations" and reverently accept "God's secret purposes" (1.14.1).

God's Goodness Revealed in Creation

Calvin notes that God revealed His work of creation in order that we might properly conceive of Him, not wander into speculations like unbelievers and pagans. The creation story refutes the mythic accounts of Egyptian fables (1.14.1). Without this revelation of God concerning the origin of all things, we will never distinctly discern who God is or who we are as His creatures (1.14.1).

The account of creation presented in Scripture also manifests God's eternity and the order with which God fashioned the world (1.14.1–2). God's work of creation was not accomplished in a single moment or by one definitive act, but in six days. This process is not "foreign to God's power," but He uses it for our benefit. By means of this order or arrangement—God distributing His work into six days—Calvin bids us "to contemplate God's fatherly love toward mankind, in that he did not create Adam until he had lavished upon the universe all manner of good things." On the contrary, creation is ordered for man's habitation and well-being. This is all evidence of God's "wonderful goodness toward us" (1.14.2).

Creation of the Spirit-world

God created the visible world, but also the things invisible. This brings Calvin to an exposition of the creation of angelic beings. He is concerned that we view angels as God's *creatures*. Angelic creatures possess neither "eternity" nor "self-existence," which are attributes belonging to God alone. That is an important point to make since some have posited the notion that good and evil are simultaneously and eternally existent things. On the contrary, says Calvin, all depravity and malice, including that of the devil, "do not spring from nature" but are derived "from the corruption of nature" (1.14.3).

We must, says Calvin, resist all speculation concerning the order, rank, form, and number of angels. As with all matters pertaining to doctrine we must follow the rule "to seek out and meditate upon those things which make for edification." Piety or godliness should be our aim, for it is the theologian's task not to tickle ears but "to strengthen consciences by teaching things true, sure, and profitable" (1.14.4). Thus concerning angels Calvin wishes to circumscribe and limit his discussion according to Scripture.

By way of definition, "angels are celestial spirits whose ministry and service God uses to carry out all things he has decreed [e.g., Ps. 103:20–21]" (1.14.5). They are God's "intermediary messengers," being referred to in Scripture as "hosts," "principalities," "powers," and "dominions." They are sometimes called "thrones" and "gods" (1.14.5). In all these descriptions and terms we are comforted in being taught that angels are "dispensers and administrators of God's beneficence toward us" who "keep vigil for our safety, take upon themselves our defense, direct our ways, and take care that some harm may not befall us" (1.14.6). We note, however, that Calvin is not confident of the biblical validity of what some call "guardian angels," that is, an angel personally assigned to an individual believer (1.14.7). Although Acts 12:15 lends some credibility to this notion, Calvin believes it is more appropriate to understand the care of each of us as being the labor of not "one angel only" but all the angels, who "with one consent watch over our salvation" (1.14.7).

We must remember that divine glory does not belong to the angels and therefore they are not to be worshiped. Our gaze must not be diverted from the Lord and directed to them—rather, the reverse, the ministry of angels testifies to the nearness of God to us (cf. 1.14.8–12).

It is difficult to talk about "ranks" of angels other than to affirm that Michael is called "the great prince" in Daniel 12:1 and "the archangel" in Jude 9. As to the number of angels, we know that they constitute "a great multitude" (Ps. 34:7) and consist of "many myriads" (Dan. 7:9) (1.14.8). More importantly, we should remember that they are spirit-beings, having real existence. They are not mere phantoms or products of our minds. As real existent creatures they "are 'ministering spirits' [Heb. 1:14], whose service God uses for the protection of his own, and through whom he both dispenses his benefits among men and also carries out his remaining works" (1.14.9).

God's glory must not be diverted to them, for we may worship God alone (cf. Rev. 19:10; 22:8–9). Scripture also plainly teaches the superiority of Christ to the angels (cf. Col. 1:16, 20; Heb. 1:4–6, 13–14) (1.14.10).

Because God is mindful of our weakness in the face of life's numerous hazards and the enmity we face as His children in this life, He uses angels "to comfort our weakness." The Lord is indeed our protector. "But when we see ourselves beset by so many perils, so many harmful things, so many kinds of enemies—such is our softness and frailty—we would sometimes be filled with trepidation or yield to despair if the Lord did not make us realize the presence of his grace according to our capacity." In this light, God informs us of "innumerable guardians whom he has bidden to look after our safety; that so long as we are hedged about by their defense and keeping, whatever perils may threaten, we have been placed beyond all chance of evil." This is all an expression of God's "immeasurable kindness and gentleness." It is a serious mistake to disregard this teaching of Scripture, for we can take a lesson from Elisha's servant who needed his eyes opened in order to see the angelic hosts protecting him and the prophet (2 Kings 6:17). We can take courage from a knowledge of God's care for us through angels (1.14.11). We are therefore urged to trust God more and to place our hope in Him, while we are likewise urged not to conceive of using angels as our mediators to commune with God or to offer them our praise alongside of God (1.14.12).

Fallen Angels

Calvin next discusses fallen angels or demons, acknowledging that Scripture has little to say about them. The Bible teaches us that though they were created as good servants of God, by "degeneration they ruined themselves, and became the instruments of ruin for others." Peter and Jude profit us by their plain teaching on this subject. "God did not spare those angels who sinned [2 Peter 2:4] and kept not their original nature, but left their abode [Jude 6]." Likewise, Paul, "in speaking of the 'elect angels' [1 Tim. 5:21], is no doubt tacitly contrasting them with the reprobate angels" (1.14.16). The Bible bids us to be on guard, for, writes Calvin, "All that Scripture teaches concerning devils aims at arousing us to take precaution against their stratagems and contrivances, and also to make us equip ourselves with those weapons which are strong and powerful enough to vanquish these most powerful foes" (1.14.13). We are in a war with a great army of evil. As believers we must wage an unceasing struggle against the devil (cf. 1.14.13–16). Inasmuch as Satan is our enemy, seeking to devour us as a raging lion, we do well to be cautious and vigilant. Scripture calls us to resist him and to take up the implements for this battle (cf. 1 Pet. 5:9; Eph. 6:13ff.), even as we plead God's help to "supply us with counsel and strength, courage and armor" (1.14.13).

The number of demons is not minuscule. Satan is the prince of this dark empire (1.14.14). He is not only our enemy, he is God's adversary too. Christ called him a murderer and liar from the beginning (cf. John 8:44). Therefore we must venture an "irreconcilable war" with the devil, for he constantly sets snares to overthrow the kingdom of Christ. He is, following his fall, by nature "depraved, evil, and malicious." In fact, Scripture depicts him as "the author, leader, and architect of all malice and iniquity" (1.14.15). Scripture speaks rather slenderly about the origin of evil in the angelic world, but by way of a summary conclusion Calvin offers these comments about the nature of demons: "they were when first created angels of God, but by degeneration they ruined themselves, and became the instruments of ruin for others." Thus the Bible speaks of angels who sinned (2 Pet. 2:4), who left their abode, forsaking their original nature (Jude 6), and clearly were not faithful to God as "elect angels," but proved themselves to be otherwise (1.14.16).

Calvin is careful to delimit Satan's power, lest we overestimate it. Calvin reminds us that Satan "can do nothing unless God wills and assents to it" (1.14.17). The story of Job is most instructive in this regard. Satan is also used as God's instrument, as we see in the incidents involving Ahab and Saul (cf. 1 Kings 22:20–22; 1 Sam. 16:14; 18:10). "Satan is clearly under God's power, and is so ruled by his bidding as to be compelled to render him service." To clarify this point Calvin adds these comments about the devil as God's vessel: "From himself and his own wickedness...arises his passionate and deliberate opposition to God.... But because with the bridle of his power God holds him bound and restrained, he carries out only those things which have been divinely permitted to him; and so he obeys his Creator, whether he will or not, because he is compelled to yield him service wherever God impels him" (1.14.17). Although Satan acts out of his own passionately evil motives and desires, willy-nilly he fulfills God's purpose.

In addition, Satan does not reign over believers, though he with his demons may "exercise believers in combat, ambush them, invade their peace, beset them in combat, and also often weary them, rout them, terrify them, and sometimes wound them; yet they never vanquish or crush them" (1.14.18). The wicked are not so protected. Believers are consoled in knowing that Satan's defeat, along with the defeat of all the wicked, is certain. Christ, the seed of the woman, and those who are that seed in the way of faith, will crush Satan's head (cf. Gen. 3:15; Rom. 16:20). To be sure, believers "fall under violent blows, but afterward they are raised up; they are wounded, but not fatally; in short, they so toil throughout life that at the last they obtain the victory." In Christ the Head, however, the victory has never been in doubt and in fact has "always fully existed" (1.14.18).

In this connection Calvin explains what it means that Christ has brought forth His kingdom into this world.

> To the extent that Christ's Kingdom is upbuilt, Satan with his power falls; as the Lord himself says, "I saw Satan fall like lightning from heaven" [Luke 10:18]. For, by this answer he confirms what the apostles had related concerning the power of their preaching. Likewise: "When a prince occupies his own palace, all his possessions are undisturbed. But when one stronger than he overcomes him, he is cast out," etc. [Luke 11:21–22 p.]. And Christ, by dying, conquered Satan, he had "the power of death" [Heb. 2:14], and triumphed over all his forces, to the end that they might not harm the church. Otherwise, at every moment [these forces] would do away with it a hundred times over. For,

such is our weakness and such is the power of his fury, how could we stand even in the slightest against his manifold and continuous attacks, unless we relied upon the victory of our leader? Therefore God does not allow Satan to rule over the souls of believers, but gives over only the impious and unbelievers, whom he deigns not to regard as members of his own flock, to be governed by him (1.14.18).

Satan's rule is unchallenged only in the realm of unbelief (cf. Luke 11:21; 2 Cor. 4:4; Eph. 2:2; John 8:44; 1 John 3:8–10). Given the gravity of the battle believers find themselves waging and the hostile sway of Satan in the world—a world without faith in God—it is foolhardy to suppose demons do not exist or that they are figments of our imaginations or "evil emotions ...which come upon us from our flesh" (1.14.19).

Creation as God's Beautiful Theater
Having discussed the spirit world, Calvin returns to the material world and urges us to godly meditation upon the greatness and beauty of creation. For the creation is "the first evidence in the order of nature" that calls us to faith in God. Calvin likens creation to a "most beautiful theater" and we should take "pious delight" in it. From Scripture's record of "the history of the creation" we see how God created the universe *ex nihilo*, that is, out of nothing, by His Word and Spirit. Thereafter,

> he brought forth living beings and inanimate things of every kind, that in a wonderful series he distinguished an innumerable variety of things, that he endowed each kind with its own nature, assigned functions, appointed places, and stations; and that, although all were subject to corruption, he nevertheless provided for the preservation of each species until the Last Day. We...likewise learn that he nourishes some in secret ways, and, as it were, from time to time instills new vigor into them; on others he has conferred the power of propagating, lest by their death the entire species perish; that he has so wonderfully adorned heaven and earth with as unlimited abundance, variety, and beauty of all things as could possibly be, quite like a spacious and splendid house, provided and filled with the most exquisite and at the same time most abundant furnishings. Finally, we...learn that in forming man and in adorning him with such goodly beauty, and with such great and numerous gifts, he put him forth as the most excellent example of his works (1.14.20).

Beyond these brief comments Calvin is not interested in offering an elaborate exposition of the six days of creation, though readers could consult his commentaries and sermons for such an exposition.

God and His Creator Call Us to Gratitude

Calvin's concern is that we grasp the practical implications of the doctrine of creation. In the first five sections of chapter five (Book I) Calvin has already shown how the knowledge of God shines forth in the fashioning of the universe and the continuing government of it. Here Calvin bids us to be gratefully thoughtful and remember "those conspicuous powers which God shows forth in his creatures...." He regards this as a "universal rule." We must see that God has created all creatures and blessed them with a unique place and function and sustains them in the same (1.14.21). Besides this, we must see "that God has destined all things for our good and salvation but at the same time to feel his power and grace in ourselves and in the great benefits he has conferred upon us, and so bestir ourselves to trust, invoke, praise, and love him" (1.14.22). The very ordering of creation, unfolding in six days, demonstrates how God first prepared all that was needful and blessed for His human creatures before He fashioned man with His own hands. God also made all things on earth subject to us, which further illustrates His liberality towards us. Thus to call God "the Creator of heaven and earth" is to recognize that we are His children, under His care, for He has received us "into his faithful protection to nourish and educate." We must therefore look for all good things from Him alone and trust Him completely to care for us and grant us what we need for our salvation. We must also "petition him for whatever we desire" and with gratitude acknowledge every good that comes into our lives. Indeed, "let us study to love and serve him with all our heart" (1.14.22).

Chapter Fifteen: Discussion of Human Nature as Created, or the Faculties of the Soul, of the Image of God, of Free Will, and of the Original Integrity of Man's Nature

Orientation

Following his discussion of the doctrine of creation, with a focus on angels and their fall, Calvin next turns to discuss the creation of man. As God's creation, man represents "the noblest and most remarkable" of His creative works, testifying to His "justice, wisdom, and goodness." At this juncture we are brought back to what Calvin observed at the outset of the *Institutes*, namely that true wisdom is twofold, consisting of a knowledge of God and of ourselves. If we are to rightly know God we must also have a proper knowledge of ourselves. Such knowledge requires that we first understand how we were originally constituted or the state of integrity in which God first fashioned us before Adam's fall, when we were free from the evil and guilt that now clings to us and characterizes human nature. If we fail to do this we are liable to blame God for human misery, as if our tainted nature and sad condition comes from Him. In our sinful condition we always look for excuses and seek to shift the blame for our depravity to another. On the contrary, we must see that in the beginning God created man good and in His own image (1.15.1).

Man Created as Body and Soul
God fashioned man from the earth, which reminds us of our humble origins and how creaturely we are, being formed out of dust (see Gen. 2:7; 18:27). In fact, God made us for Himself, that we could glorify Him. He also, according to His "great liberality," gave man "an immortal spirit." A human being thus consists of a soul and a body. Elaborating on this dual aspect of human nature Calvin says, "Now I understand by the term 'soul' an immortal yet created essence, which is [our] nobler part. Sometimes it is called 'spirit'" (1.15.2). Generally speaking, the words soul and spirit are synonyms (see Eccl. 12:7; Luke 23:46; Acts 7:59). As for the body, it is the receptacle of the soul. Calvin is not even adverse to referring to it as the "prison house" of the soul, which reflects some residual Platonism in his thinking.

In calling the soul "immortal" Calvin is not denying that it is created—that it has a beginning—but he is asserting that we are creatures that cannot suffer annihilation. The soul is not subject to death or mortality. The soul is an "essence" distinct from the body, meaning it is a thing other than the body. It is its own unique thing. To understand what Calvin means by the soul it is necessary to consider its faculties, which consists of understanding or intellect and will. Calvin will discuss this in more detail below. Here it suffices to say that through our intelligence we conceive of God, though He is invisible, and we "grasp things that are right, just, and honorable, which are hidden from the bodily senses" (1.15.2). Scripture confirms the soul's immortality as well (see Job 4:19; 2 Cor. 7:1; 1 Pet. 2:25; 1:9; 2:11; Heb. 13:17; 12:9; Luke 16:22, 23; 2 Cor. 5:6, 8; Acts 23:8). Consider, too, Matthew 10:28 and Luke 12:5 where Christ tells us to fear

Him who not only can kill the body but also "can send the soul into the Gehenna of fire" (1.15.2).

Man Created in God's Image

Adam, the first man, was created in God's image. Calvin explains that there is no difference between "image" and "likeness," except that the term "likeness" helps to explain the term "image." For Calvin, that Adam was made in the image of God means that he was endowed with certain benefits or qualities: (a) right intelligence, (b) affections kept within bounds of reason, (c) senses tempered in right order, (d) understanding to refer all gifts to his Maker (1.15.3). This is not to deny that man's physical or outer appearance reflects something of God's glory; indeed, "there was no part of man, not even the body itself, in which some sparks did not glow"; nevertheless, the image of God resides properly "in the mind and heart, or the soul and its powers" (1.15.3).

In order to come to a full definition of the image of God we must turn to the New Testament. Here we find a richer and fuller understanding of what it means to be image-bearers of God, for "Christ is the most perfect image of God." To be restored to the image of God is to be restored with "true piety, righteousness, purity, and intelligence." This is rooted in our renewal in Christ. Restoration and renewal, however, bespeak the loss of the divine image in Adam and his descendants. Calvin is careful to explain that "God's image was not totally annihilated and destroyed" in fallen man, but "it was so corrupted that whatever remains is frightful deformity" (1.15.4). The Apostle Paul shows us that our renewed image is "in Christ" and consists of true knowledge, righteousness, and holiness [see Eph. 4:24; Col. 3:10; 2 Cor. 3:18]. In summing up his position Calvin states that

> God's image is the perfect excellence of human nature which shone in Adam before his defection, but was subsequently so vitiated and almost blotted out that nothing remains after the ruin except what is confused, mutilated, and disease-ridden. Therefore in some part it now is manifest in the elect, in so far as they have been reborn in the Spirit; but it will attain its full splendor in heaven (1.15.4).

Calvin rejects the notion that the divine image resides in man's dominion mandate. He also rejects the notion that the soul emanates from God, as the Manicheans and Servetus foolishly taught. Likewise he rejects the idea of the wayward Lutheran theologian, Osiander, who taught that the divine image in man consists of the transfusion of divine righteousness into him. The renewal of the image in man is not a matter of participating in the divine substance but in being transformed by the Holy Spirit (see 2 Cor. 3:18) (1.15.5).

The Faculties of the Soul

As for the human soul, Calvin maintains that its powers or faculties are best described as consisting of two things: understanding and will. People are led by their understanding, whereas their will chooses and follows what the understanding pronounces good. Hence, in being human we have been endowed with the faculty of understanding in order to distinguish good from evil, right from wrong, what we should do and what we should avoid. We have been endowed with the faculty of will in order to make decisions; it is the seat of free choice (1.15.7–8).

However, Calvin also argues that it is important not to "confuse two very diverse states of man"—unfallen and fallen, something Augustine distinguished by referring to man's ability to sin before the fall and his inability not to sin after the fall. In his unfallen state, man "excelled in these pre-eminent endowments"—that is, before the fall, man was sufficiently guided by reason, understanding, prudence, and judgment not only "for the direction of his earthly life" but also to rise up "even to God and eternal bliss" (1.15.8). Choice was added, as well, in order to direct the appetites and regulate all the organic motions, and in this way make the will completely surrendered to the government of reason. Thus in this upright state, before the fall, man possessed "free will," and if he had exercised that freedom rightly—"if he so willed"—he had the power "to attain eternal life" (1.15.8). Calvin elaborates on this idea:

> Therefore Adam could have stood if he wished, seeing that he fell solely by his own will. But it was because his will was capable of being bent to one side or the other, and was not given the constancy to persevere, that he fell so easily. Yet his choice of good and evil was free, and not that alone, but the highest rectitude was in his mind and will, and all the organic parts were rightly composed to obedience, until in destroying himself he corrupted his own blessings (1.15.8).

Calvin shall take up the loss of free will at length in connection with man's fall (see 2.2–5). Here his aim is directed elsewhere, namely that we perceive clearly that man, as originally created, was free from the corruption and depravity that now defines his nature as fallen in Adam. In Adam, all his descendants have an hereditary taint that rests upon their entire nature. The faculties of the soul—the understanding and the will—have been compromised. Note, at the first creation man's powers were upright, his mind was sound and stood firm, and his will was "free to choose the good"; now, given the fall, his understanding is confused and his will is in bondage to sin.

Lest someone object that God should have created Adam less prone to sin or in a more secure position, so that Adam's will was less liable to weakness, Calvin bids us to "sobriety" as the way of wisdom. It is not for us to know why God ordained Adam's fall and did not sustain him in his integrity. This lies hidden in the divine plan. Calvin will say this, however: "Man...received the ability [to persevere in his unfallen state] provided he exercised the will; but he did not have the will to use his ability, for this exercising of the will would have been followed by perseverance." In other words, had Adam withstood the temptation of the serpent, he (with his posterity) would have been made secure in his integrity and righteousness and no longer subject to temptation and sin. But he did not do this and therefore he, with his descendants, is without excuse. He brought about his own ruin. God did not impose any necessity on him except to endow him with a mutable will or what Calvin calls "a mediocre and even transitory will." God did this to occasion His own glory (1.15.8).

Observations

Calvin's theological anthropology or doctrine of humanity must not be divorced from his wider theological enterprise. Calvin's doctrine of redemption only makes sense in light of the original good creation, including humans created good in the image of God. Calvin therefore is concerned that we not confuse man's original state of true righteousness and holiness with the present condition of depravity, corruption, and guilt. Calvin grounds God's creative operations in the divine plan—a plan that has Christ at its center and God's glory in the salvation of His people as its outcome. Calvin will next take up God's governance and preservation of creation in the doctrine of divine providence, which then becomes the driving engine of all that God does in the world and all that transpires in history for the coming of Christ and, finally, the consummation of all things.

Questions for Reflection and Discussion

1. Calvin says that the creation is like a beautiful theater reflecting God's glory. In what ways is this so? How does it apply even after the fall?

2. What is the alternative to the doctrine of creation? Why is this doctrine so important for the Christian faith?

3. What extremes should be avoided regarding the relation between God and the world?

4. Even in Calvin's day there were those who advocated a kind of "naturalism." What is naturalism and what is the scriptural rebuke of it?

5. Do you agree with Calvin's use of the term "prison house" to refer to the body? What are the implications for our daily earthly labors if we view the body as a prison house? How is the flesh (though not our body as such) our enemy according to the Bible (cf. Rom. 7:23; Gal. 5:17)?

6. Do we—as Reformed believers—need our eyes opened like Elisha's servant to perceive the reality of angels and their ministry among us? How can we cultivate a proper sense of their presence and task for our blessedness, while avoiding a useless speculation and preoccupation with them?

7. What is the image of God according to Calvin? To what degree is it lost with Adam's fall? How is it being restored in Christ?

8. Give examples of how human understanding and will—faculties of the soul—are tainted with sin's corruption but not entirely lost. What is Calvin's definition of "will" and why does he want to rid the church of the term "free will"?

∽ 6 ∽

Divine Providence

Chapters 16–18 of Book One

Chapter Sixteen: God by His Power Nourishes and Maintains the World Created by Him, and Rules Its Several Parts by His Providence

Orientation

WE HAVE SEEN that Calvin wants to distinguish the God of Scripture from false gods and to accentuate the fact that we know the true God only from Scripture. Calvin argues that God is set apart from idolatrous notions of deity by two "special marks": (1) God is infinite spiritual essence; and (2) God is one essence in three persons. The Triune God is the Creator. But more, He is the sustainer and governor of the creation. Thus Calvin is prompted next to take up the difficult subject of God's providence.

God Active in Providence

God's providence stands in opposition to any notion of God as cold and aloof—that is, the notion that God is unavailable to us or uninvolved in the world He has made. Calvin directly opposes the idea of "a momentary Creator" (1.16.1). On the contrary, "we see the presence of divine power shining as much in the continuing state of the universe as in its inception." This is a point often forgotten. What is more, without a correct doctrine of God's providence our confession that God is the Creator of the universe becomes empty talk. Even "carnal sense" realizes that all things are sustained by "an energy divinely bestowed" (1.16.1). Faith reaches more deeply into this matter. If God is the Creator, then "he is also everlasting Governor and Preserver...." God does not so much direct the whole machine of the world, with its several parts, by a universal motion; rather, by a particular providence "he sustains, nourishes, and cares for, everything he has made, even to the least sparrow" (cf. Matt. 10:29; and also Ps. 33:6; 32:6, 13–14; 33:13) (1.16.1). We see that providence entails God's own active sustaining, nurturing, and governing care over His creation. It is comprehensive and detailed—everything is under God's providential rule—all things and all creatures. Indeed, in God all creatures live, move, and have their being (Acts 17:28). All creatures look to God to give them their food in due season (Ps. 104:27–30). Providence is an extension of creation since the Maker cares for the work of His hands (1.16.1).

Providence against Chance
Calvin is also concerned that we see how providence warns us away from all notions of fortune or chance or other superstitions, like astrology or the fate of cards, etc. Although it opposes any notion of fate or chance, most people accept one of these as an integral part of reality. This depraved opinion, observes Calvin, beclouds if not buries providence. Instead, we need to understand that our lives, even with their burdens and disappointments, are directed by God's providence (1.16.2). Calvin offers an explanation:

> Suppose a man falls among thieves, or wild beasts; is shipwrecked at sea by a sudden gale; is killed by a falling house or tree. Suppose another man wandering through the desert finds help in his straits; having been tossed by the waves, reaches harbor; miraculously escapes death by a finger's breadth. Carnal reason ascribes all such happenings, whether prosperous or adverse, to fortune. But anyone who has been taught by Christ's lips that all the hairs on his head are numbered [Matt. 10:30] will look farther afield for a cause, and will consider that all events are governed by God's secret plan. And concerning inanimate objects we ought to hold that, although each one has by nature been endowed with its own property, yet it does not exercise its own power except in so far as it is directed by God's ever-present hand. These are, thus, nothing but instruments to which God continually imparts as much effectiveness as he wills, and according to his own purpose bends and turns them to either one action or another (1.16.2).

The changing of the seasons is according to providence. Providence reminds us that God is not idle and empty and unconscious; rather, He is watchful, effective, active, attentive, and engaged in ceaseless activity. "Nothing takes place without his deliberation." Thus, "in times of adversity believers comfort themselves with the solace that they suffer nothing except by God's ordinance and command, for they are under his hand." By His omnipotence, God has power ample enough to supply for our good and to keep us in His protection. Calvin urges us to forsake the infidelity of transferring to objects power or purpose that belongs to God alone. Calvin also tells us to "ever remember that there is no erratic power, or action, or motion in creatures, but that they are governed by God's secret plan in such a way that nothing happens except what is knowingly and willingly decreed by him" (1.16.3).

Erroneous Conceptions of Providence

Calvin elaborates on the nature of God's providence by distinguishing between general and special providence. Calvin begins by rejecting some errors. As the Lord of all creation, God, so to speak, stands at "the helm" of the universe and regulates all events. Providence therefore is not mere foreknowledge, as some erroneously affirm. Rather, providence is a divine act or activity; it is God acting. Neither is providence to be thought of as a general kind of oversight which does not "specifically direct the action of individual creatures" (1.16.4). This error embraces a certain conception of the free choice that acts contingently and independently of God's rule, which makes human affairs unfold independently of "God's determination" (1.16.4). Calvin likewise rejects the error of the Epicureans who conceive of God as slothful or inert. For Calvin, any conception of God's providence that renders some things under His care while other things float independently of His rule and governance is "patent madness" (1.16.4). Calvin disputes as well a certain conception of a general or universal providence which states that while God does not direct everything according to His wisdom and purpose, He does exercise "some kind of blind and ambiguous motion." This means that while God does not have "control" of the world, the world nonetheless requires God's power in order to exist and function. This is true so far as it goes, says Calvin, but it does not go far enough. On the contrary, "God so attends to the regulation of individual events, and they all so proceed from his set plan, that nothing takes place by chance" (1.16.4). But Calvin is careful not to reject a general or universal providence as such, for there is an "order of nature" that God rules and this order exists, "moved by a secret impulse of nature," according to the exercise of God's "especial care over each of his works." In God we live, move, and have our being (Acts 17:28). All things are sustained by the mighty command of Christ (Heb. 1:3). Here Calvin affirms a doctrine of "concurrence," wherein God is universally active in all things, such that they are sustained and derive their energy to do anything at all (1.16.4–5).

It is therefore mistaken to think that God only directs ordinary affairs or merely guides the common arrangement, cycle, or order of nature. It is likewise mistaken to think that God exercises His providence merely in granting to heaven and earth "an ordinary power" which supplies for the needs of His creatures. Such notions leave room neither for "God's fatherly favor" nor for "his judgments." Scripture clearly testifies that when crops flourish or fail because of favorable or unfavorable weather patterns we must not neglect to see both "God's fatherly favor" on the one hand or "his certain and special vengeance" on the other. "It is certain that not one drop of rain falls without God's sure command" (1.16.5). Here we see that Calvin is concerned to affirm God's special providence.

God's Providential Care of Human Beings
Calvin expands on this point by showing how God's providence relates particularly to the human race. There is no person who can direct his or her own way (cf. Jer. 10:23). Likewise, "it is an absurd folly that miserable men take it upon themselves to act without God, when they cannot even speak except as he wills!" (1.16.6; cf. Prov. 16:1, 9).

All people are under God's direction. Therefore, nothing is fortuitous or without divine determination—even a person who is killed from a falling branch. Both the branch falling and that the person is killed is according to God's governance (cf. Exod. 21:13). The Lord, not chance, determines the outcome of cast lots. Similarly, one person is rich and another is poor; God assigns each condition by His "secret plan." This reality bids us to patience and undermines various erroneous notions—such as the notion that success lies within our power, or the notion that our toil achieves our blessing, or the notion that all things are in the hands of fortune (1.16.6).

Divine providence enables us to see that nothing occurs in the world that is not directed by God. Wind and wave are ever expressive of "God's express command." We see this throughout God's dealings with Israel, with Jonah and Jacob, and in our own daily needs for His care (see Ps. 103:3–4; 104:3–4; 106:25; 107:25, 29; Jonah 1:4; Amos 4:9; Gen. 30:2; Ps. 136:25; 34:15). We must see that God's "general providence not only flourishes among creatures so as to continue the order of nature," but it is also following "his wonderful plan adapted to a definite and proper end" (1.16.7).

God's Providence Not to Be Confused with Fate

Many, however, dislike the idea of God's comprehensive providential governance of all things, branding it a doctrine of "fate" as taught by the Stoics. Calvin disagrees. He is careful to separate divine providence from fate and emphatically rejects the fatalism of the Stoic philosophers. Fatalism teaches that nature contains a necessity consisting of a perpetual complex and "intimately related series of causes," such that blind chance or fortune, not God, rules human affairs. This is contrary to God's providence (1.16.8).

In defending divine providence, Calvin doesn't believe we need to give up using terms like "haply, perchance, mayhap, perhaps, fortuitously," for we know everything comes under divine providence. Likewise when we speak of "chance occurrence" we refer only to things "ruled by a secret order," the reason or cause of which we cannot discern. We must follow Augustine who taught "that nothing is more absurd than that anything should happen without God's ordaining it, for that would mean it would happen without any cause" (1.16.8). Indeed, "if every success is God's blessing, and calamity and adversity his curse, no place now remains in human affairs for fortune or chance" (1.16.8). Providence, then, is nothing else than the execution of God's eternal decree. As the ruler and governor of all things, according to His wisdom, God has ordained from all eternity "what he was going to do, and now by his might carries out what he has decreed." This means that "not only heaven and earth and the inanimate creatures, but also the plans and intentions of men are so governed by his providence that they are borne by it straight to their appointed end" (1.16.8).

Calvin admits that, for us humans, events can *appear* fortuitous, that is, can appear to be by chance or random, "since the order, reason, end, and necessity of those things which happen for the most part lie hidden in God's purpose, and are not apprehended by human opinion...." Yet Scripture is clear in teaching us that even those things which seem to come to us by chance "take place by God's will" (1.16.9).

Chapter Seventeen: How We May Apply This Doctrine to Our Greatest Benefit

God's Purpose for Us in Providence

Calvin is concerned that we see the practical implications of divine providence. He explains that "God always has the best reason for his plan: either to instruct his own people in patience, or to correct their wicked affections and tame their lust, or to subjugate them to self-denial, or to arouse them from sluggishness; again, to bring low the proud, to shatter the cunning of the impious and to overthrow their devices" (1.17.1).

For those who cavil at this doctrine Calvin replies that their fight is with Scripture. "Since God assumes to himself the right (unknown to us) to rule the universe, let our law of soberness and moderation be to assent to his supreme authority, that his will may be for us the sole rule of righteousness, and the truly just cause of all things" (1.17.2). Providence itself calls us not to cross-examine God's ways but, in reverence and fear, to humbly submit ourselves to God's secret plans, for God's judgments are a deep abyss (Ps. 36:6; also see Rom. 11:33–34; Isa. 40:13–14). Moses reminds us that the secret things belong to the Lord (cf. Deut. 29:29). The Book of Job is exhibit front and center as an illustration of this truth. Job had to learn, as we must learn, to submit to God's supreme authority, for His will is our sole rule of righteousness. Submitting ourselves to divine providence, being prepared to do God's will completely, shows forth the wonderful blessing of this doctrine (1.17.2).

Distortion of the Doctrine of Providence

Not surprisingly, however, God's providence is a doctrine that can be twisted and abused. Profane persons will argue that all human attempts to be prudent are a waste of time; prayers are reckoned superfluous; or they maintain that devising of plans or planning ahead, making provision for the future, stands against divine providence. Similarly, all that transpires, even those things carried out from wicked motives, are ascribed immediately to God's providence. If an assassin murders an upstanding citizen, then they claim that the killer did God's will. If a woman commits adultery against her husband, they say that God's plan has been carried out. If a thief robs your home, he is (it is said) a minister of God's providence, for he has done what was ordained of the Lord. Should parents fail to take their sick child to the physician for medicine to heal him, they claim that that omission was appointed from eternity and therefore the parents could not resist God's plan. Such persons call all crimes virtues, since all misdeeds are subject to God's ordinance (1.17.3).

In saying that God governs all things, Calvin does not mean to relieve people of responsibility for their wickedness. As Proverbs 16:9 says, "Man's heart plans his way, but the Lord will direct his steps." Practically speaking, providence does not compete with human action. Our duty is clear: we are to plan ahead and make use of means.

> This means that we are not at all hindered by God's eternal decrees either from looking ahead for ourselves or from putting all our affairs in order, but always in submission to his will. The reason is obvious. For he who has set the limits to our life has at the same time entrusted to us its care; he has provided means and helps to preserve it; he has also made us able to foresee dangers; that they may not overwhelm us unaware, he has offered precautions and remedies. Now it is very clear what our duty is: thus, if the Lord has committed to us the protection of our life, our duty is to protect it; if he offers helps, to use them; if he forewarns of dangers, not to plunge headlong; if he makes remedies available, not to neglect them.... These fools do not consider what is under their very eyes, that the Lord has inspired in men the arts of taking counsel and caution, by which to comply with his providence in the preservation of life itself (1.17.4).

We are not God, and it is folly to fail to use the means He provides for us (this too is His providence) in order to secure our future in spite of our limited understanding.

Calvin reminds us that God does not always meet us in "naked form." He often clothes His care in the form of other instruments and means. Moreover, God's providence does not exonerate our wickedness. Here we see that Calvin understands Scripture to allow a distinction between God's "will of decree" and God's "will of command." Some raise an objection in this regard: "If God governs all things, then how can he blame the thief for his thievery, or the murderer for his killing, or the adulterer for her infidelity?" In other words, "If all such men are serving God's will, why shall they be punished?" (1.17.5). But, replies Calvin, they are not serving God's will as revealed in His Word. To be sure, they do not act *outside* of God's providence but they do act *contrary* to God's command. The evil is within them, not God! They are motivated by desires in opposition to God's revealed, moral law, and do not render service to God or do His bidding. For God calls us to do what He commands and we may not violate His commands with impunity. But the objection is raised: "Unless He willed it, we would not do it." Calvin replies,

> I agree. But do we do evil things to the end that we may serve him? Yet he by no means commands us to do them; rather we rush headlong, without thinking what he requires, but so raging in our unbridled lust

that we deliberately strive against him. And in this way we serve his just ordinance by doing evil, for so great and boundless is his wisdom that he knows right well how to use evil instruments to do good.

Calvin offers an illustration:

Whence ... comes the stench of a corpse, which is both putrefied and laid open by the heat of the sun? All men see that it is stirred up by the sun's rays; yet no one for this reason says that the rays stink. Thus, since the matter and guilt of evil repose in a wicked man, what reason is there to think that God contracts any defilement, if he uses his service for his own purpose? Away, therefore, with this doglike impudence, which can indeed bark at God's justice afar off but cannot touch it (1.17.5; also see 1.18.1–4, where Calvin treats this topic more in depth, including the twofold aspects of the one divine will).

Making Use of the Doctrine of God's Providence

Believers do well to meditate upon God's providence, for we are consoled to know that our lives, that life itself and the happenings that surround us, are completely in God's hands. God is the principal cause of all things, but this does not negate secondary causes in their proper place. Even when evil men act against us, we do not lose sight of God's hand, for He watches over the welfare of believers by His providence (cf. Isa. 49:15; 1 Pet. 5:7; Ps. 91:12). We are of greater value to God than sparrows, small creatures that He likewise nurtures (Matt. 10:31). Further, our meditation should not be ungrateful when we contemplate God's rich provisions in our lives, in the favorable unfolding of events and circumstances. Likewise, we should be patient in adversity and wean ourselves from a life of worry as we ponder God's fatherly care over us in the way of His providence. Indeed we learn that all blessing comes from the Lord alone (1.17.6–7).

Providence teaches us to look for God's care in times of adversity and hardship. A powerful example is manifest in the life of Job. After he faces adversity, God ushers forth prosperity. We behold it in Christ's words that the Father watches over the sparrows and provides His children even closer care. God's providence offers us patience in adversity, as is evident in the story of Joseph and his brothers' cruel treachery against him. When sorrow strikes, we find comfort in knowing the Lord willed it—discovering peace in the knowledge that "he wills nothing but what is just and expedient" (1.17.8). Practically and concretely this means that "when we are unjustly wounded by men, let us overlook their wickedness (which would but worsen our pain and sharpen our minds to revenge), remember to mount up to God, and learn to believe for certain that whatever our enemy has wickedly committed against us was permitted and sent by God's just dispensation" (1.17.8).

Conversely, when we enjoy good health and this life's many benefits, all the praise and reverence belongs to God, who is the principal author of such blessings, though persons can be secondary ministers or agents through whom God works His benevolence to us. God's providence does not neglect means but establishes them. Neither does providence make secondary causes superfluous. Rather, secondary causes are usually the very channels through which God works to accomplish His purposes, which is nothing else than the execution of His decree (1.17.9). Thus those with a godly frame of mind can be consoled.

> Innumerable are the evils that beset human life; innumerable, too, the deaths that threaten it. We need not go beyond ourselves: since our body is the receptacle of a thousand diseases—in fact holds within itself and fosters the causes of diseases—a man cannot go about un-burdened by many forms of his own destruction, and without drawing out a life enveloped, as it were, with death. For what else would you call it, when he neither freezes nor sweats without danger? Now, wherever you turn, all things around you not only are hardly to be trusted but almost openly menace, and seem to threaten immediate death. Embark upon a ship, you are one step away from death. Mount a horse, if one foot slips, your life is imperiled. Go through the city street, you are subject to as many dangers as there are tiles on the roofs. If there is a weapon in your hand or a friend's, harm awaits. All the fierce animals you see are armed for your destruction. But if you try to shut yourself up in a walled garden, seemingly delightful, there a serpent sometimes lies hidden. Your house, continually in danger of fire, threatens in the daytime to impoverish you, at night even to collapse upon you. Your field, since it is exposed to hail, frost, drought, and other calamities, threatens you with barrenness, and hence, famine. I pass over poison-ings, ambushes, robberies, open violence, which in part besiege us at home, in part dog us abroad. Amid these tribulations must not man be most miserable, since, but half alive in life, he weakly draws his anxious and languid breath, as if he had a sword perpetually hanging over his neck? (1.17.10).

Even if such events rarely touch us, they lurk around the corner, so to speak. We cannot conclude that they won't touch us. The godly person finds his or her solace in the knowledge that the "Heavenly Father so holds all things in his power, so rules by his authority and will, so governs by his wisdom, that nothing can befall except he determine it." We dwell under "God's safekeeping." Even the angels are assigned a caring role for us. Nothing can harm us except in so far as God judges it wise and good for our sakes. Truly, the Lord is our helper (Ps. 118:6; 117:6). The world does not aimlessly tumble and turn, for God orders all things and works to promote our welfare. God restrains evil like a horse bridled. Nothing happens without His permission, just as He also fetters the devil and his crew. May all such thoughts comfort our hearts and strengthen us in times of difficulty or uncertainty (1.17.11). For providence teaches us that God is in control, and, knowing that, our fear and anxiety can give way to comfort and assurance. Furthermore, providence teaches us that the devil and his demons are fettered to God's service. Ignorance of providence is "the ultimate of all miseries"; but within a knowledge of it resides "the highest blessedness" (1.17.11).

Chapter Eighteen: God So Uses the Works of the Ungodly, and So Bends Their Minds to Carry Out His Judgments, That He Remains Pure From Every Stain

Orientation
In this chapter, Calvin extends his argument from the previous chapter. The title sufficiently reflects its contents. Calvin builds his argument around such passages as Job 1:21; Acts 4:28; 2:23; 3:18; 2 Sam. 16:22; 12:12, and the like. This chapter also treats some objections to Calvin's view of divine providence.

Willing and Permitting—A False Distinction
Calvin is aware that his vision of God's providence, where the Lord is active in all events and things, leaves many people puzzled and burdened. The puzzlement takes on two issues: (1) how God escapes contracting "some defilement" from the transgressions of sinful creatures; and (2) how God is free of "all blame" when He is providentially active in all events and human endeavors. Some seek a solution to these issues by distinguishing between "doing" and "permitting." The idea is that God only permits but does not will

the wicked acts of wicked people. Calvin does not believe that this offers any kind of solution to the supposed problem. Humans can do nothing "except by God's secret command," so that even their deliberations are under God's eternal decree and according to His "secret direction." Scripture presents us with a multitude of texts that bear this out (cf. Ps. 115:3) (1.18.1).

In particular, the story of Job illustrates this. Satan cannot undertake anything against Job "unless God so wills" it. Job acknowledges this himself. After suffering terrible disasters in succession, he says that the Lord gives and the Lord takes away (Job 1:21). It is the Lord who has done these things to him. To be sure, Satan acts with his evil intentions, as do the Sabaeans. But Job knows he was "stripped of all his property" by God. "Therefore, whatever men or Satan himself may instigate, God nevertheless holds the key, so that he turns their efforts to carry out his judgments" (1.18.1). Bare permission is a figment of our imaginations, says Calvin (cf. 1 Kings 22:20, 22). God doesn't merely permit that which He wills to accomplish; rather, He wills and decrees what is to take place (1.18.1).

Similarly, Christ's trial and crucifixion are conducted by impious and evil men, but all of this is according to God's plan (Acts 4:28). "So Peter …preached that 'by the definite plan and foreknowledge of God, Christ had been given over' to be killed [Acts 2:23, cf. Vg.]" (1.18.1). Calvin offers various examples: Absalom (2 Sam. 12:12; 16:22;), the Chaldeans (Jer. 1:15; 7:14; 50:25), Nebuchadnezzar (Jer. 25:9, 27:6), the Assyrians (Isa. 10:5), David (2 Sam. 16:10), and others. "Yet from these it is more than evident that they babble and talk absurdly who, in place of God's providence, substitute bare permission—as if God sat in a watchtower awaiting chance events, and his judgments thus depended upon human will" (1.18.1).

God is sovereign over the human heart (Prov. 21:1). God works "inwardly in men's minds" (Ezek. 7:26). God also "blinds men's minds" (Isa. 29:14; cf. Rom. 1:28) and hardens hearts (Exod. 9:12). None of this language allows us to speak of a "bare permission." Indeed, notes Calvin, "it is often by means of Satan's intervention that God acts in the wicked, but in such a way that Satan performs his part by God's impulsion and advances as far as he is allowed" (1.18.2). Summing up, Calvin writes the following: "since God's will is said to be the cause of all things, I have made his providence the determinative principle for all human plans and works, not only in order to display its force in the elect, who are ruled by the Holy Spirit, but also to compel the reprobate to obedience" (1.18.2).

Answering Objections

This brings Calvin to examine a key objection to his stated view, namely, that his understanding of God's providence means that there are "two contrary wills" in God. For if nothing happens apart from God's will, i.e., in willing things according to His own "secret plan" (His decree), then God wills what He has "openly forbidden by his law." Calvin replies to this criticism of his view by observing that Scripture allows us to speak of God willing wicked things—even our sinful actions. Again, Christ's crucifixion is the prize example, for Christ was crucified according to God's will. And this does not mean that God's will is "at war with itself," nor does God's will change, nor does God pretend not to will what He wills. God's will is "one and simple in him," though it appears to be diverse to us. But more, says Calvin, our mental capacities aren't capable of digging into God's ways and wisdom (1.18.3).

The key for solving this objection is to recognize that God has His own righteous motive for evil acts, while the immediate human agent of the evil has wicked motives driving him or her to act. "For through the bad wills of evil men God fulfills what he righteously wills," as Augustine says. Humans act against God's will in the sense that they have unrighteous motives and violate God's moral law. God, however, performs His will upon them according to His righteousness. As Augustine further states: "in a wonderful and ineffable manner nothing is done without God's will, not even that which is against his will. For it would not be done if he did not permit it; yet he does not unwillingly permit it, but willingly; nor would he, being good, allow evil to be done, unless being also almighty he could make good even out of evil" (1.18.3).

But is this just? That is the second objection raised against Calvin's doctrine of providence. More specifically, if God wills all things that come to pass, then humans are not culpable for their sinful actions and they are "undeservedly damned" for carrying out God's decreed will regarding them. Calvin replies that this objection wrongly confuses God's "decree" with God's "precept": "innumerable examples clearly show how utterly different these two are." Absalom commits adultery with his father's wives, violating God's precept—His moral law—but he fulfilled God's decree "to punish David's adultery with this shameful act." We should therefore hold tight to this truth: "while God accomplishes through the wicked what he has decreed by his secret judgment, [sinful persons] are not excusable, as if they had obeyed his precept which out of their own lust they deliberately break" (1.18.4).

If we still chafe under divine providence, then Calvin bids us to humility. "For our wisdom ought to be nothing else than to embrace with humble teachableness, and at least without finding fault, whatever is taught in Sacred Scripture. Those who too insolently scoff, even though it is clear enough that they are prating against God, are not worthy of a longer refutation" (1.18.4).

Observations

With this chapter Calvin brings to a conclusion his treatment of the knowledge of God as our Creator. The sum of all wisdom, we must not forget, is the twofold knowledge of God and of ourselves. In the next Book of the *Institutes* Calvin will explore the knowledge of God as our Redeemer. Here, too, we will learn something more about God and about ourselves. If we have already learned that we are God's creatures, fashioned in His image, next we will discover that we are fallen image-bearers of God, depraved and corrupted, in bondage to sin, and under God's just judgment and curse, and therefore desperate for rescue. God as our Redeemer answers this need— more especially Christ as our Redeemer.

Questions for Reflection and Discussion

1. Look up Job 1:6, 12; 2:1, 6; 1 Kings 22:20–22; 1 Samuel 16:14; 18:10; Psalm 78:49; 2 Thessalonians 2:9, 11. How do these verses defend Calvin's remark that God wills and assents to Satan's work? How does a knowledge of this give believers the assurance of victory?

2. The story of Joseph is a powerful testimony of God's providence (see Gen. 37–47). What is predicted in the story? How is this fulfilled? What bearing does this doctrine have on so-called games of chance, e.g., the lottery?

3. How would you respond to someone who tells you, "I don't buckle my seatbelts—if God wants me to die, then I will die; it is all according to His providence"?

4. Many people dislike the idea of all things being governed and controlled by God, since it seems to undermine human freedom. How do you respond to this worry? What does it mean that God works through secondary causes?

5. Why is God's providence a blessed doctrine to contemplate in connection with prayer?

6. Reflect on your own life, with its ups and downs, joys and heartbreaks: How does a knowledge of God's sovereign control comfort you in the face of adversity or tragedy? What if God was not in control?

7. Farmers in particular are affected by the weather; how does a knowledge of God's providence lend comfort in a year of flooding or drought?

8. Why are we so prone to arrogance when things go our way—good health, good looks, good children, financial success, talents, gifts, etc.? Even if we acknowledge God as the source of blessing and that we are under His providence, we can harbor pride in our hearts. How do we combat this? How might God wean us from such arrogance?

9. Open Theism, a modern view of God, argues that the future is open and uncertain because it has yet to take place. Not even God knows the future in its details (though He can bring the future to the outcome He wants because of His wisdom). Nonetheless, God is neither omniscient nor omnipotent—all-knowing and all-powerful—and so the future is not yet planned. How would Calvin respond to this view and why would he insist it is unbiblical and absurd?

Institutes of the Christian Religion

Book Two

The Knowledge of God the Redeemer in Christ,
First Disclosed to the Fathers Under the Law,
and Then to Us in the Gospel

The Fall and Human Corruption

City of God

Chapters 1–5 of Book Two

Chapter One: By the Fall and Revolt of Adam the Whole Human Race Was Delivered to the Curse, and Degenerated from Its Original Condition; the Doctrine of Original Sin

Orientation

WITH BOOK TWO of the *Institutes* Calvin sets out to expound the knowledge of God as our Redeemer. In knowing God as Redeemer we come to know ourselves as sinners who need redemption. As Calvin stated in the first chapter of Book One, true and sound wisdom consists of the knowledge of God and of ourselves, and the two parts of this knowledge are joined with many bonds. Book Two begins with the story of treachery—man's rebellion against God and its wretched aftermath. We learn of accursedness and death, of toil and suffering, of estrangement and depravity, and of the origin of human misery. The defilement that flows from the fall leaves humans both unable and unwilling to save themselves. In exploring the depths of human depravity, as well as the frown of God's wrath that abides on all people apart from Christ, Calvin will show us our desperate need for salvation. He will also show us God's warm gaze of mercy, of a promised Seed to heal and bless us, of Christ our Redeemer.

The opening chapters of Book Two treat the fall and corruption of human beings. Specifically, chapter one deals with Adam's fall, the spread of sin to the human race, and the doctrine of original sin. Chapter two concerns the loss of free will, which is part of original sin. Given this loss, chapter three explores the nature and extent of human depravity. Chapter four considers how God works in humans—even bending their wills—without being blameworthy for their sins. Finally, in chapter five Calvin answers arguments that oppose his doctrine of the enslaved will.

True Knowledge of Self Destroys Self-Assurance

Human beings love to inflate themselves, to look at themselves and boast of their dignity and fineness. Calvin presents a biblical portrait of human beings *as fallen*, empty, unseemly, and degenerate. Calvin presents this picture of fallen humans against the deceptions of ancient philosophers and renaissance humanists who believed self-knowledge resulted in a vision of human worth and excellence. Without knowledge of God we misjudge ourselves, says Calvin, for proper self-knowledge does not "puff up" or offer "empty assurance." Rather,

> knowledge of ourselves lies first in considering what we were given at creation and how generously God continues his favor toward us, in order to know how great our natural excellence would be if only it had remained unblemished; yet at the same time to bear in mind that there is in us nothing of our own, but that we hold on sufferance whatever God has bestowed upon us. Hence we are ever dependent on Him. Secondly, to call to mind our miserable condition after Adam's fall; the awareness of which, when all our boasting and self-assurance are laid low, should truly humble us and overwhelm us with shame (2.1.1).

Unless we see "the sorry spectacle of our foulness," we won't comprehend the loss of our original integrity, which in turn leads us to abhor ourselves and come to true humility. This displeasure with ourselves also kindles in us "a new zeal to seek God, in whom each of us may recover those good things which we have utterly and completely lost" (2.1.1). Again Calvin writes: "Here, then, is what God's truth requires us to seek in examining ourselves: it requires the kind of knowledge that will strip us of all confidence in our own ability, deprive us of all occasion for boasting, and lead us to submission" (2.1.2). We are inclined to self-admiration and delusion. "For, since blind self-love is innate in all mortals, they are most freely persuaded that nothing inheres in themselves that deserves to be considered hateful" (2.1.2). Humans love the "alluring talk that tickles the pride that itches in his very marrow." Such self-congratulation "delights in its own sweetness," driving us to ruin and blocking the way to true self-knowledge; instead, we are "plunged into the worst ignorance" (2.1.2).

To be sure, many fallen people, with no knowledge of God, seek to improve or reform themselves, to promote virtues and renounce vices in themselves. But when God's moral nature is the standard by which we measure ourselves, then we are more sober in our self-assessment and find no reason to lift our hearts to self-confidence. In fact, we discover many reasons to become dejected and flounder in the path we should take (2.2.3).

God as our moral compass not only reminds us of our sin, He reminds us of "our original nobility," which serves to show us the righteousness and goodness that should be our zeal to pursue. We were created for immortality, not mortality. We have fallen from our created virtue and the end of our creation. We have lost these things. This is why we are sick and miserable. We groan, for we have slipped far from our original rectitude (2.1.3).

Calvin, therefore, asserts that the knowledge man needs about himself issues forth into two imperatives:

> First, he should consider for what purpose he was created and endowed with no mean gifts. By this knowledge he should arouse himself to meditation upon divine worship and the future life. Secondly, he should weigh his own abilities—or rather, lack of abilities. When he perceives this lack, he should lie prostrate in extreme confusion, so to speak, reduced to nought. The first consideration tends to make him recognize the nature of his duty; the second, the extent of his ability to carry it out (2.1.3).

Calvin will examine both of these in due order. Only, this point is fundamental: under divine scrutiny we find nothing about which to boast. The standard of divine judgment deprives us of self-assurance and self-confidence. When we contemplate the glorious state from which we have fallen and the corruption that spoils us, including the gifts we have lost, we discover our profound inability to remedy our fault or even seek divine help on our own (2.1.3).

Adam's Fall and Its Consequences
• *Estrangement, Curse, and Death.* Next Calvin carefully looks at the narrative in Genesis 3, which records for us the temptation and fall of Adam in paradise. Adam's fall from his original state was "no light sin"; rather, it was "a detestable crime" (2.1.4). Adam—man—deserted God's Word and authority when he ignored God's command regarding the tree of the knowledge of good and evil. That Adam was denied this tree, says Calvin, was in order "to test his obedience and prove that he was willingly under God's command."

Indeed, the name of the tree pointed to the nature of God's precept, for Adam needed to learn to be "content with his lot" and take heed to himself lest he become "puffed up with wicked lust." "But the promise by which he was bidden to hope for eternal life so long as he ate from the tree of life, and, conversely, the terrible threat of death once he tasted of the tree of the knowledge of good and evil, served to prove and exercise his faith" (2.1.4).

Adam didn't heed God's Word; neither did Eve. Instead, Adam heeded another word (see Rom. 5:19). He "revolted from God's authority" and embraced falsehood. Once God's Word was disregarded and Adam treated God with irreverence, unfaithfulness manifested itself. In fact, says Calvin, not just pride, "Unfaithfulness...was the root of the Fall" (2.1.4). Then coupled with pride and ambition, along with ingratitude, Adam spurned his good situation and committed "a monstrous wickedness!" He showed contempt for the truth, disbelieved God's Word, spurned God's great bounty; and being swayed by Satan's lies he ambitiously and proudly sought a higher state than bestowed to him by his Creator. Apostasy is Adam's sin, "a foul and detestable offense" (2.1.4). Adam vilely reproached God in listening to Satan. Rather than heeding the Word of his Maker, after whose image he was formed, he gave ear to the devil. Adam's sin, then, was both *infidelity*, for he failed to trust God, and *rebellion*, since he refused to look for his contentment and happiness in the Lord alone (2.1.4).

• *The Spread of Adam's Sin to His Posterity.* Moreover, we learn from Scripture that Adam's sin brings with it estrangement from his Creator and "the death of his soul." In addition, Adam's fall brought ruin not only upon himself but upon his entire progeny. His fall was the forfeiture of humankind's original endowments and ushered all human beings into misery and death. That is, Adam's sin has spread to all his offspring; all die (Rom. 5:12ff.). "Therefore, after the heavenly image was obliterated in him, he was not the only one to suffer this punishment—that in place of wisdom, virtue, holiness, truth, and justice, with which adornments he had been clad, there came forth the most filthy plagues, blindness, impotence, impurity, vanity, and injustice—but he also entangled and immersed his offspring in the same miseries" (2.1.5). This inherited corruption is *original sin*, that is, "the depravation of a nature previously good and pure" (2.1.5). Calvin is aware that people chafe under the idea that all are guilty through the guilt of one man. He is also aware that Pelagius proposed a solution to this matter which proved to be nothing else than a "profane fiction." For Pelagius claimed that Adam's sin only harmed himself and did not affect his descendants, and that the apostle's words in Romans 5, which speaks of the transmission of Adam's sin to all his offspring, is a matter of "imitation" not "propagation." Calvin, however, sides with Augustine who contended against Pelagius's views. We "are corrupted not by derived wickedness"; rather, "we bear inborn defect from our mother's womb" (2.1.5). We are perverse from our very conception (Ps. 51:5). "Therefore, all of us, who have descended from impure seed, are born infected with the contagion of sin" (2.1.5).

Calvin offers further arguments against the notion that the depravation of our original nature has come to us through imitation, as Pelagius erroneously asserted. Calvin returns to Romans 5. The apostle Paul makes clear that the poisoning of our nature is through an inherited corruption (2.1.6). Our pollution goes back to our original "progenitor," to be sure, but even more, Adam is "the root of human nature." Thus, writes Calvin, "in his corruption mankind deserved to be vitiated." This is why the apostle compares Adam with Christ in Romans 5. If Adam's sin spread by mere imitation, then Christ's righteousness likewise is transmitted to us merely as an example set before us to emulate. Calvin denounces this notion as "sacrilege!" No, we lost righteousness and life in Adam; and in Christ the same "are ours by communication." "Here, then, is the relationship between the two: Adam, implicating us in his ruin, destroyed us with himself; but Christ restores us to salvation by his grace" (2.1.6).

Calvin also refers to 1 Corinthians 15:22. All of us died in Adam; we are infected with the disease of sin and we are all condemned. Not one of us is "untouched by the guilt of iniquity" (2.1.7). Christ's righteousness must be communicated to us to cure this malady (cf. Rom. 8:10). To die in Adam, then, means that "Adam, by sinning, not only took upon himself misfortune and ruin but also plunged our nature into like destruction. This was not due to the guilt of himself alone, which would not pertain to us at all, but was because he infected all his posterity with that corruption into which he had fallen" (2.1.6). We are all *by nature* children of wrath because we are already "cursed in the womb" (Eph. 2:3). Here "nature" refers to human nature as violated, spoiled, and sullied with sin and pollution. Adam's corruption spread to all his offspring. As Christ says, "whatever is born of flesh is flesh" (John 3:6) (2.1.6).

• *Original Sin.* From here Calvin briefly comments on the controversy regarding the origin of the soul in each person, that is, whether it is derived from one's parents or in some other way. The question has significance since the contagion of human sin and corruption principally resides in the soul. Calvin rejects the notion that our souls are propagated to us from our parents. He offers these remarks, which he regards as sufficient on this matter: "the Lord entrusted to Adam those gifts which he willed to be conferred upon human nature. Hence Adam, when he lost the gifts received, lost them not only for himself but for us all" (2.1.7). Clearly Adam acts for the human race and not for himself alone. We may liken our relationship to Adam as that of rotten branches which sprout from a rotten root.

> For thus were the children corrupted in the parent, so that they brought disease upon their children's children. That is, the beginning of corruption in Adam was such that it was conveyed in a perpetual stream from the ancestors into their descendants. For the contagion does not take its origin from the substance of the flesh or soul, but because it had been so ordained by God that the first man should at one and the same time have and lose, both for himself and for his descendants, the gifts that God had bestowed upon him (2.1.7).

Believers and unbelievers alike beget "guilty children," for each are begotten from a "corrupted nature." Guilt is "of nature" (2.1.7).

From his discussion of sin's transmission Calvin turns to a fuller discussion of sin's effects upon or consequences to human nature, i.e., original sin. He offers this formal definition: "Original sin…seems to be a hereditary depravity and corruption of our nature, diffused into all parts of the soul, which first makes us liable to God's wrath, then also brings forth in us those works which Scripture calls 'works of the flesh' [Gal. 5:19–21]" (2.1.8).

Calvin proceeds to unpack this definition.

> First, we are so vitiated and perverted in every part of our nature that by this great corruption we stand justly condemned and convicted before God, to whom nothing is acceptable but righteousness, innocence, and purity. And this is not liability for another's transgression. For, since it is said that we became subject to God's judgment through Adam's sin, we are to understand it not as if we, guiltless and undeserving, bore the guilt of his offense but in the sense that, since we through his transgression have become entangled in the curse, he is said to have made us guilty. Yet not only has punishment fallen upon us from Adam, but a

contagion imparted by him resides in us, which justly deserves punishment (2.1.8).

We are all defiled and stained with original sin from our mothers'
wombs. Even infants are subject to condemnation, for they carry fault
within themselves. "For, even though the fruits of their iniquity have not yet
come forth, they have the seed enclosed within them. Indeed, their whole
nature is a seed of sin; hence it can be only hateful and abhorrent to God"
(2.1.8). In short, since humans are corrupted in every part of their nature,
they are justly condemned. We are not reckoned guilty because of the guilt
of another; rather, we are guilty with our own guilt, inheriting our corruption from Adam. We are infected and dirty, given to every kind of evil. This
concludes Calvin's comments on the first thing.

Now Calvin moves to the second thing that emerges from his definition of original sin, namely, "that this perversity never ceases in us, but
continually bears new fruits—the works of the flesh that we have already
described—just as a burning furnace gives forth flame and sparks, or water
ceaselessly bubbles up from a spring." Fallen humans are like a fountain ever
spouting sinful habits, actions, deeds, thoughts, desires, and feelings. This
corruption isn't merely the deprivation of the good but the propagation of
evil. "Our nature is not only destitute and empty of good, but so fertile and
fruitful of every evil that it cannot be idle." It is aptly termed "concupiscence," which refers in this context to evil desire as the source and cause of
continual sinning. All of our nature, whatever is in man, every part, is "defiled and crammed with this concupiscence," says Calvin. "The whole man is
of himself nothing but concupiscence" (2.1.8).

Original sin, then, is that depravity of our nature that seeps into all
parts of the soul, including our understanding, our will, and even our flesh.
It strikes to the depth of our hearts, so that pride resides there. Paul depicts
this in detail for us in Romans 3. We need the complete transforming and
renewing work of the Holy Spirit, "the full reformation of all the parts,"
because sin's pollution reaches to all parts. We must put on a new nature
(2.1.8–9). As Calvin observes, "the whole man is overwhelmed—as by a
deluge—from head to foot, so that no part is immune from sin and all that
proceeds from him is to be imputed to sin" (2.1.9).

Having defined and expounded upon original sin—or man's per-
vasive depravity of nature—Calvin moves to chastise those who would
dare write God's name upon their faults," as if our depravity of nature is

from God or that God is at fault since we are now naturally sinful. No, says Calvin. "Our destruction…comes from the guilt of our flesh, not from God, inasmuch as we have perished solely because we have degenerated from our original condition" (2.1.9). We must ignore, even loathe, the overly curious objection that God should have intervened to prevent Adam's fall. Such things belong to God's secret predestination. Rather than accuse God of blame for our fall and depravity, we must incriminate ourselves. "Obviously, man's ruin is to be ascribed to man alone; for he, having acquired righteousness by God's kindness, has by his own folly sunk into vanity" (2.1.10).

Calvin also feels obliged to explain more overtly what he means by our "natural" condition, for after Adam's fall "natural" refers to our fallenness— i.e., the nature with which we are now born—because of Adam's sin. Our fallenness, however, is not natural in the sense of being part of the original creation. Rather, that constitutes a terrible falling away from nature, a loss of our original endowments (2.1.11).

Observations

It should be noted that Calvin's discussion of Adam's fall, the spread of sin to his posterity, and original sin are fundamental anthropological issues which will shape his doctrine of salvation. It is interesting that in discussing Adam's fall, Calvin (like Augustine) sets forth a rudimentary doctrine of the covenant of works. He does not use that language, of course, but the ingredients that would compose that doctrine in later Reformed thinking are present, namely (1) the testing of God's image-bearer to live by God's authority in the way of faith; (2) a paradisal eschatology, i.e., the promise of eternal life; (3) symbolical trees, whose names bespeak the promise of life or the threat of death; and (4) Adam functioning as a public person, i.e., acting on behalf of the whole human race, so that the outcome for him is the outcome for all his posterity—meaning that he did not sin only to his own loss but harmed all his descendants by his one act of sin.

We must further note that Calvin's treatment of the spread of sin is ambiguous in its definition and categorization, but bears some of the marks of the doctrine of mediate imputation. However, it is probably better to say that, for Calvin, original sin is a hereditary evil and we do well to leave unexplained in any precise sense how original sin is transmitted from one person to another. Calvin is clear, however, in affirming that Adam acted not merely for himself but for all his posterity. All are fallen in him and have lost every good gift.

Chapter Two: Man Has Now Been Deprived of Freedom of Choice and Bound Over to Miserable Servitude

Orientation

With chapter two Calvin comes to the question of the extent of sin's corruption upon our faculty of volition or willing. Has the corruption of sin so impaired our freedom of choice that we are properly said to be under the servitude of sin? That is, is human will free or in bondage? Do we possess the power of free choice or have we forfeited this ability?

Human Freedom and the Enslavement of the Will

Before answering these sorts of questions, Calvin first urges us to reckon with the perils that plague the words "freedom of choice." There are two perils, as Augustine observes, which we must consider if we are to avoid error.

> (1) When man is denied all uprightness, he immediately takes occasion for complacency from that fact; and, because he is said to have no ability to pursue righteousness on his own, he holds all such pursuit to be of no consequence, as if it did not pertain to him at all. (2) Nothing, however slight, can be credited to man without depriving God of his honor, and without man himself falling into ruin through brazen confidence (2.2.1).

The first error to be avoided is complacency, the second false boasting. Addressing the first fault, Calvin says that although we are empty of good and deprived of freedom, we should aspire for both. In seeing our own poverty, let us not acquiesce to passivity; rather, let us be "aroused from inactivity" (2.2.1). Then in addressing the second fault, Calvin reminds us that man, even in his state of integrity, with all his blessed endowments intact, was not "permitted to boast about himself." Even less, now that we are fallen and cast into "extreme disgrace," may we venture to credit ourselves for any achievement. Instead, we must recognize God's beneficence to us, confess our own poverty, and give all glory to God. In fact, "we flatter our strength unduly when we compare it even to a reed stick!" For Calvin, these points are fundamental for true religion and profit us in no small degree (2.2.1).

Turning to the question at hand, Calvin surveys the history of the doctrine of free will, beginning with the ancient philosophers, then the church fathers, and then the sophisticated discussion of this topic in the Middle Ages (see 2.2.2–9). The philosophers, for their part, argued that reason "is a sufficient guide for right conduct." Meanwhile, the will is subject to reason, and since it is free, "it cannot be hindered from following reason as its leader in all things" (2.2.3). Many of the church fathers followed this lead (2.2.4). Calvin disputes this view, and finds himself most in agreement with Augustine, who did not hesitate to call the will "unfree" (2.2.1, 8).

In evaluating human freedom, Calvin notes that "in the schools three kinds of freedom are distinguished: first from necessity, second from sin, and third from misery" (2.2.5). The first of these, freedom from necessity, by which Calvin means freedom from the necessity of compulsion, is basic and inherently attached to human nature. All humans *as humans* are free from this sort of necessity, for it is impossible to be a moral agent and under a necessity of compulsion. However, Calvin is not averse to asserting that, as fallen, we are under the necessity of sin. Although Calvin doesn't use this terminology, we can call it a conditioned necessity or a necessity of consequences, for all are now subject to the necessity of an evil disposition. Thus Calvin affirms that we have lost or forfeited the other types of freedom, namely freedom from sin and freedom from misery (2.2.5; cf. 2.3.5).

Calvin says if we follow him in the recognition of these sorts of distinctions, "it will be indisputable that free will is not sufficient to enable man to do good works, unless he be helped by grace, indeed by special grace, which only the elect receive through regeneration" (2.2.6). Returning to his discussion regarding freedom from compulsion, Calvin again asserts that even fallen humans have this sort of freedom of decision. This doesn't mean that man "has a free choice equally of good and evil"; rather, it only means that "he acts wickedly by will, not by compulsion" (2.2.7). But, says Calvin, to label this sort of freedom with the noble title "free will" when we are such willing slaves to sin and under the necessity of a fallen nature is not apt or helpful. "Indeed, I abhor contentions about words.... But I have scrupulously resolved to avoid those words which signify something absurd, especially where pernicious error is involved." Coming to the real problem, Calvin explains why he refuses to speak of free will: "But how few men are there, I ask, who when they hear free will attributed to man do not immediately conceive him to be master of both his own mind and will, able of his own power to turn himself toward either good or evil?" The term leads to "ruinous self-assurance" (2.2.7). After examining Augustine on this matter, Calvin will concede this much: "If anyone...can use this word without understanding it in a bad sense, I shall not trouble him on this account." Then he immediately adds: "But I hold that because it cannot be retained without great peril, it will, on the contrary, be a great boon for the church if it be abolished" (2.2.8). Calvin urges us to follow Augustine who said that believers should glory in nothing inasmuch as nothing is theirs. We are destitute. Every good gift is from God. We must "forsake confidence in our own virtue" and acknowledge that all our strength "rests in God alone" (2.2.9).

According to Calvin, the very idea of a free (that is, unhindered or untainted) will puffs us up. If we are truly to advance in a keen knowledge of ourselves, we must be "cast down" and "overwhelmed" by the recognition of our "calamity, poverty, nakedness, and disgrace." When we admit this about ourselves we are truly advancing far in self-knowledge (2.2.10). Our danger is not to underestimate our achievements or gifts but to overestimate them. We must learn that what we have lost and now lack God alone can recoup for us (2.2.10).

With Augustine, Calvin asserts that "humility" is the heart of the Christian faith (2.2.11). The fall has stripped humans of all "supernatural gifts," such as, faith, love of God, charity toward our neighbor, and zeal for holiness and righteousness. As for their "natural gifts" of reason and will, though the fall did not obliterate them, they were corrupted. Humans thus retain enough of their innate faculties to be distinguished from brute beasts, but their will, while it does not perish, is now "so bound to wicked desires that it cannot strive after the right" (2.2.12). Calvin extends his treatment of both reason (or understanding) and will.

Humans Corrupted in the Faculty of Intellect
• *Regarding Earthly Life.* The power of understanding (the faculty of the intellect) is not without any effect or value pertaining to things below or this present life, but its power regarding things above, or the life to come, is much more precarious and frail. Calvin offers this distinction:

> ...there is one kind of understanding of earthly things; another of heavenly. I call "earthly things" those which do not pertain to God or his Kingdom, to true justice, or to the blessedness of the future life; but which have their significance and relationship with regard to the present life and are, in a sense, confined within its bounds. I call "heavenly life" the pure knowledge of God, the nature of true righteousness, and the mysteries of the Heavenly Kingdom. The first class includes government, household management, all mechanical skills, and the liberal arts. In the second are the knowledge of God and of his will, and the rule by which we conform our lives to it (2.2.13).

By natural instinct man fosters and preserves human society. Natural law accounts for the universality of practice in establishing laws for the ordering of communal life and "a certain civic fair dealing and order." These seeds have been "implanted in all men." Although persons violate such laws and chafe under the rule of others, this reality does "not nullify the original conception of equity." Calvin continues: "For, while men dispute among themselves about individual sections of the law, they agree on the general conception of equity. In this respect the frailty of the human mind is surely proved: even when it seems to follow the way, it limps and staggers. Yet the fact remains that some seed of political order has been implanted in all men. And this is ample proof that in the arrangement of this life no man is without the light of reason" (2.2.13).

This applies to the the arts and sciences as well. Whether speaking of the liberal arts or manual skills, there is "a universal apprehension of reason and understanding by nature implanted in men." In witnessing the sorry spectacle of those who might be referred to as "imbeciles," that is, those who suffer severe mental and physical challenges, we are reminded of the endowments of reason and skill that remain with us. These are "natural gifts," being granted to the believer and unbeliever alike (2.2.14). Indeed, many persons with no saving knowledge of God are not for that reason without any knowledge at all—that is, there is still an "admirable light of truth shining in them" to teach and show us God's excellent gifts. Calvin offers these important words on this topic:

> If we regard the Spirit of God as the sole fountain of truth, we shall neither reject the truth itself, nor despise it wherever it shall appear, unless we wish to dishonor the Spirit of God. For by holding the gifts of the Spirit in slight esteem, we contemn and reproach the Spirit himself. What then? Shall we deny that the truth shone upon the ancient jurists who established civic order and discipline with such great equity? Shall we say that the philosophers were blind in their fine observation and artful description of nature? Shall we say that those men were devoid of understanding who conceived the art of disputation and taught us to speak reasonably? Shall we say that they are insane who developed medicine, devoting their labor to our benefit? What shall we say of all the mathematical sciences? Shall we consider them the ravings of madmen? No, we cannot read the writings of the ancients on these subjects without great admiration. We marvel at them because we are compelled to recognize how preeminent they are. But shall we count

anything praiseworthy or noble without recognizing at the same time that it comes from God? Let us be ashamed of such ingratitude.... Those men whom Scripture [1 Cor. 2:14] calls "natural men" were, indeed, sharp and penetrating in their investigation of inferior things. Let us, accordingly, learn by their example how many gifts the Lord left to human nature even after it was despoiled of its true good (2.2.15).

Calvin sums up his discussion of fallen and unsanctified man's power of understanding pertaining to earthly things in this way:

We see among all mankind that reason is proper to our nature; it distinguishes us from brute beasts, just as they by possessing feeling differ from inanimate things. Now, because some are born fools or stupid, that defect does not obscure the general grace of God. Rather, we are warned by that spectacle that we ought to ascribe what is left in us to God's kindness.... Some men excel in keenness; others are superior in judgment; still others have a readier wit to learn this or that art. In this variety God commends his grace to us, lest anyone should claim as his own what flowed from the sheer bounty of God (2.2.17).

• *Regarding Heavenly Life.* Turning now to fallen and unsanctified man's power of understanding pertaining to heavenly life or the things that constitute the life to come and the way of redemption, i.e., the kingdom of God, Calvin asserts that it involves three things: "(1) knowing God; (2) knowing his fatherly favor in our behalf, in which our salvation consists; (3) knowing how to frame our life according to the rule of his law" (2.2.18). Humanity, fallen in sin, is blind, ignorant, and altogether lost regarding these things. In fact, the "greatest geniuses" are "blinder than moles" when it comes to spiritual insight into God's fatherly favor and the way of salvation in Jesus Christ. Humanity resides in darkness (John 1:4–5), does not comprehend God, and is without "any ability of spiritual understanding." We must be reborn of God (John 1:13), which means: "Flesh is not capable of such lofty wisdom as to conceive God and what is God's, unless it be illumined by the Spirit of God" (2.2.19). In fact, inasmuch as we obtain any knowledge of God, it is His own work (John 3:27 and 1 Cor. 2:14). We need divine illumination, for "nothing is accomplished by preaching him if the Spirit, our inner teacher, does not show our minds the way" (2.2.20). Our minds must be "made new by the illumination of the Holy Spirit" (see 1 Cor. 1:13ff.; 2:9ff.; Eph. 1:17ff.) (2.2.20–21). Neither does fallen humanity know how to conduct itself rightly in a way pleasing and honoring to God. For we corrupt even the light of nature (Rom. 2:14–15). "There is nothing more common than for a man to be sufficiently instructed in a right standard of conduct by natural law (of which the apostle is here speaking)." Indeed, conscience stands in place of the written law of Moses, and man befouled by sin stands condemned on that basis. "The purpose of natural law, therefore, is to render man inexcusable." Calvin offers this definition of natural law as it functions in Romans 2: "natural law is that apprehension of the conscience which distinguishes sufficiently between just and unjust, and which deprives men of the excuse of ignorance, while it proves them guilty by their own testimony" (2.2.22). In human depravity and ignorance, every person is capable of excusing his or her own sin, forgetting the general moral principle which is otherwise affirmed (2.2.23).

Calvin next expounds this theme in connection with the moral law or the Ten Commandments—"the pattern of perfect righteousness." He remarks that fallen humanity is completely blind, indeed, wholly incapable of meeting the standards of the First Table of the law, such as trusting in God, praising Him, calling on His name, keeping the Sabbath. As for the Second Table of the law, though fallen humans have some grasp of it inasmuch as it relates to the preservation of civil society, they fall short here as well (2.2.24). In this way we begin to see how desperately we need the Holy Spirit to guide our way and illumine our hearts and minds. We are evil in our heart's imaginings (Gen. 6:5), our reasoning subject to vanity (Ps. 119:34), and we need God's direction at every moment (2.2.25).

Humans Corrupted in the Faculty of the Will

Calvin next addresses the power of volition or the faculty of the will. As fallen, our power of volition, the determiner of choice, is now subject to bondage. Like an animal, man "follows the inclination of his nature, without reason, without deliberation." What is needed is that he "discern good by right reason; that knowing it he choose it; that having chosen it he follow it." But in fact our reason is not right but disordered. "To sum up," writes Calvin, "much as man desires to follow what is good, still he does not follow it" (2.2.26). Calvin also reminds us that the person described in Romans 7 refers to one regenerated, to "the Christian struggle." This, then, is not a description of fallen humanity in darkness. We are all slaves to sin in that darkness, "under the yoke of sin," which also includes our will unless the Spirit works His grace in us (2.2.27).

Observations

Calvin acknowledges that sinners act willingly and not by compulsion. He, however, dislikes labeling such willful action "free will" since this locution is easily misunderstood and leads to persons thinking they are equally as capable of performing good as doing evil. The term is simply problematic due to its ambiguity and openness to misinterpretation; consequently, Calvin opts to abandon the term. For Calvin, fallen humans can still discern good and evil because of the light of nature. But even this light is turned into darkness when fallen persons, ceasing to ponder the common things for the ordering of life, turn their minds to seek after God or heavenly things or the way of redemption. Both in the faculties of intellect and volition humans are incapable of finding God. Humans, however, remain choice-makers, i.e., they still possess the faculty of volition, but it is in bondage to sin and humans are without freedom to act righteously unless God provides the way.

Chapter Three: Only Damnable Things Come Forth from Man's Corrupt Nature

The Whole of Human Nature Sinful

Having discussed the bondage of human will in a non-regenerate state, Calvin looks deeper into the corruption of original sin or what is sometimes labeled "total depravity." He demonstrates that Scripture depicts the whole man as subject to corruption and bondage. The Bible calls man in such a state flesh (John 3:6); such persons are at enmity with God (Rom. 8:6–7), need rebirth (John 3:3), and they are darkened in understanding and blind of heart (Eph. 4:17–20). Says Calvin, "We, indeed, infer from these words that the grace of Christ is the sole remedy to free us from that blindness and from the evils consequent upon it" (2.3.1). Romans 3 also catalogues the nature and scope of human corruption (2.3.2).

Human Depravity and God's Restraining Grace

Although in the previous chapter Calvin treated to some degree the question of gifts, talents, and intellectual virtues in those who do not belong to Christ and possess nothing of the Spirit's saving influence, now he confronts this issue more directly. More specifically, in assessing man's fallen nature as wholly corrupted, Calvin believes we need to qualify that assessment as it pertains to certain capacities of some human beings. Calvin notes that in every age there are individuals, guided by the law of nature, who have sought after virtue throughout their lives. In spite of their moral failings, in the very pursuit of a more virtuous life, they evidence an honesty which bespeaks "some purity in their nature" (2.3.3). Calvin will explain how much these "virtues" lack any merit or standing with God; nonetheless, he does want to acknowledge an observable fact of life. Examples of this sort ought to give us caution in how we speak of man's depravity, for some persons, prompted by the law of nature, conduct themselves "most honorably throughout life." "But," says Calvin, in witnessing such a fact, "here it ought to occur to us that amid this corruption of nature there is some place for God's grace; not such grace as to cleanse it, but to restrain it inwardly" (2.3.3). Indeed, because of the magnitude of human perversion, we need the restraining grace of God lest in wickedness fallen persons give full vent to their lusts, which would make life unlivable. Calvin expands on this point:

> If every soul is subject to such abominations as the apostle boldly declares [in Rom. 3:10–18], we surely see what would happen if the Lord were to permit human lust to wander according to its own inclination. No mad beast would rage as unrestrainedly; no river, however swift and violent, burst so madly into flood. In his elect the Lord cures these diseases in a way that we shall soon explain. Others he merely restrains by throwing a bridle over them that they may not break loose, inasmuch as he foresees their control to be expedient to preserve all that is. Hence some are restrained by shame from breaking out into many kinds of foulness, others by the fear of the law—even though they do not, for the most part, hide their impurity. Still others, because they consider an honest manner of life profitable, in some measure aspire to it. Others rise above the common lot, in order by their excellence to keep the rest obedient to them. Thus God by his providence bridles perversity of nature, that it may not break forth into action; but he does not purge it within (2.3.3).

We see that Calvin recognizes the various and distinct motives that move persons to restrain their sinful nature. We see, too, that this restraining grace of God is exercised through His providence. It is outward or external in its application to individuals, not inward or internal. There is no renewal of heart or mind. In this way we see what we might term natural virtues in unregenerate persons. Calvin refers to such virtues as "special graces of God, which he bestows variously and in a certain measure upon men otherwise wicked" (2.3.4). "Special graces" here means non-saving gifts of God given in an unequal and diverse manner to befouled human beings who deserve His wrath.

Humans under the Necessity of Sin, Not the Necessity of Compulsion

In making this point, Calvin does not want us to think that human will is somehow not in bondage to sin. It is in terrible and complete bondage. That does not mean, however, that humans are deprived of the faculty of will itself; no, they are deprived of "soundness of will" (2.3.5). Fallen humans are under the bondage of sin which renders them unable to desire the good, seek the good, or dispose themselves toward the good apart from God's intervention. When persons actually want righteousness in a righteous manner, this must be "ascribed entirely to God's grace." "Therefore simply to will is of man; to will ill, of a corrupt nature; to will well, of grace" (2.3.5).

Calvin knows that to speak of persons willing ill of necessity often gets a cold reception. Yet he bids us to remember the difference between necessity and compulsion. Just as God acts according to His holy and good nature, so that He cannot not be good (which means He is free but under the necessity of His nature), so fallen humans must act according to their depraved natures (that is, they are under the necessity of their sinful natures), and therefore they cannot will righteousness from themselves. This sort of necessity is congruent or compatible with human responsibility, for humans do will what they want in accord with what their sinful hearts desire. That is their bondage to sin and describes what it means to be under the necessity of sin.

> The chief point of this distinction, then, must be that man, as he was corrupted by the Fall, sinned willingly, not unwillingly or by compulsion; by the most eager inclination of his heart, not by forced compulsion; by the prompting of his own lust, not by compulsion from without. Yet so depraved is his nature that he can be moved or impelled only to evil. But if this is true, then it is clearly expressed that man is surely subject to the necessity of sinning (2.3.5).

In short, depraved human beings are under the necessity of sin but they are not compelled to act or will sinfully from a force outside themselves or apart from their own willing. Humans sin of necessity but no less do they sin voluntarily. They are not under the necessity of compulsion.

Human Depravity of Will Requires Divine Remedy
In that light, given the necessity of sin, redemption must be a divine gift. Humans cannot achieve it themselves. It is God who begins the good work in us (cf. Phil. 1:6). He is the author of rebirth. He arouses in us a love, desire, and zeal for righteousness. And He finishes this good work, preserving and ushering us into glory. Calvin refers to Ezekiel 36:26–27; Philippians 2:13; 1 Corinthians 12:6; Ephesians 2:10 (cf. 2.3.6). Grace is not a cooperative effort, for grace precedes every good work. The Lord Himself heals our evil will, and this may not and must not be attributed to man (2.3.7). "Only in the elect does one find a will inclined to good" (2.3.8). This seeking and willing righteousness is from God, by His initiative, His persistence, and His victory in us (2.3.9). It is the Spirit who "directs, bends, governs our heart and reigns in it as in his own possession" (2.3.10). Hence even good works and perseverance in faith are God's gifts (2.3.11). We are so dependent upon divine grace, we may not assign any virtue or good performance to ourselves except God's grace precede us, accompany us, and keep us (2.3.12). As Augustine says, by God's grace acting in us choice and will in the heart are formed within us, "so that whatever good works then follow are the fruit and effect of grace…" (2.3.13). We are completely dependent upon God's grace if we are to will according to His holy will. Again using Augustine's words, "the human will does not obtain grace by freedom, but obtains freedom by grace…" (2.3.14).

Chapter Four: How God Works in Men's Hearts

Orientation
The title of this chapter might give the impression that Calvin is now going to discuss how God works in our hearts in order to bring them to faith and repentance. That, however, is not his focus at this point. In fact, he will address that topic in the first chapter of Book Three. Calvin's focus here has to do with why God isn't culpable for human sinning. More precisely, Calvin considers the manner in which God uses sinful instruments to fulfill His purposes in human beings while He remains free of their crimes. Satan's influence upon sinful man is also discussed in this connection.

God's Providential Rule in Satan and the Reprobate
Calvin's view of human depravity is that "man is so held captive by the yoke

of sin that he can of his own nature neither aspire to good through resolve nor struggle after it through effort" (2.4.1). Meanwhile, God can operate in the affairs and hearts of men without becoming entangled in human culpability. Calvin notes Augustine's example of the horse under the command of its rider—the rider can be either God or the devil. When Satan is the rider we are not to think that human will is like an unwilling slave compelled to take orders from a master. Rather, "the will, captivated by Satan's wiles, of necessity obediently submits to all his leading." Such persons the Lord surrenders to the devil's work. Thus Satan works his purpose in the reprobate but not without their will (2.4.1).

Calvin elaborates on this theme. He explains that God, Satan, and an individual can each be active in the same event, each with a diversity of purpose—for example, the attack of the Chaldeans on Job's servants (Job 1:17). Consequently, while God's intent may be the legitimate testing of Job's faith, Satan and the Chaldeans work with evil intent and, thereby, are blameworthy. As Calvin states, "The distinction in purpose and manner causes God's righteousness to shine forth blameless there, while the wickedness of Satan and of man betrays itself" (2.4.2).

That the Lord works blessing in human hearts is of grace. But the Lord need not be gracious; He can judge and punish the wicked in their wickedness. The hardening of Pharaoh serves as an example. "When [God's] Spirit is taken away, our hearts harden into stones"; or "when his guidance ceases, [our hearts] are wrenched into crookedness. Thus it is properly said that [God] blinds, hardens, and bends those whom he has deprived of the power of seeing, obeying, and rightly following" (2.4.3). Part of God's wrath against the wicked is to blind them to His truth (2.4.4). Calvin quotes Augustine to fortify his point: "The fact that men sin is their own doing; that they by sinning do this or that comes from the power of God, who divides the darkness as he pleases" (2.4.4).

Satan is under God's providential direction as well, for God uses Satan to act upon the reprobate in ways that serve the divine purpose. Here Calvin appeals to 1 Samuel 16:14; 18:10; 19:9, where an evil spirit (under God's will and power) acts as "God's instrument" (2.4.5).

God's Providence and Human Willing

But what about matters that are not right or wrong, good or evil? How does God act in us in such things? In answering this question, Calvin insists that it is "of God's special grace" when humans act in ways that are advantageous for themselves or their wills incline in that direction. God's providence doesn't merely extend to external events but also in giving humans the will to choose in a way that conforms and serves the outcome He desires (cf. Ps. 106:46; 2 Sam. 17:14; 1 Kings 12:10, 14; Deut. 28:65) (2.4.6).

God exercises His providence to achieve His purpose, which includes, then, bending human will in external matters. This is only to say that God's will reigns over human decision and our acts of volition. "Whether you will or not, daily experience compels you to realize that your mind is guided by God's prompting rather than by your own freedom to choose." Calvin further explains this: "In the simplest matters judgment and understanding often fail you, while in things easy to do the courage droops." Also the reverse is seen: "In the obscurest matters, ready counsel is immediately offered; in great and critical matters there is courage to master every difficulty" (2.4.7).

Calvin explains that free will does not have to do with the ability to effect outcomes but with the ability to choose freely, i.e., according to our desires, which in fact accords with our nature. Thus the debate about free will has to do with whether a person has both freedom in (1) "choice of judgment" and (2) "inclination of will." Calvin affirms that we are free to be choice-makers, but we are not free to incline our wills as we please, for the will is guided by the desires of our natures, which are sinful. But those who urge free will insist on humans possessing freedom in each way (2.4.8).

Chapter Five: Refutation of the Objections Commonly Put Forward in Defense of Free Will

Orientation
Calvin is aware that a number of objections are put forward against his denial of free will. In this chapter he first presents these objections, and then he sets forth a number of passages which are said to support the freedom of the will. In each case, Calvin offers refutations of these counter proposals.

Answering Arguments in Favor of Free Will
In order to defend free will, opponents of Calvin's view present various objections against the enslavement of the will. The first argument opposing the will's enslavement asserts that if sin is a matter of necessity, then sin ceases to be sin; and if sin is voluntary, then it can be avoided. In opposition Calvin argues that "he who sins of necessity sins no less voluntarily" (2.5.1). The

second argument opposing the denial of free will is that unless both virtues and vices come from the free choice of the will, reward and punishment lose their meaning. Calvin replies that sin takes its source from us. What is more, since we sin from our own voluntary desires, it does not matter that we sin from "servile judgment." Therefore God is just in punishing us. As for rewards, they depend on God's grace and kindness. Human merit has nothing to do with it. In rewards, God crowns His own gifts, as Augustine says. A key text to which Calvin appeals is 1 Corinthians 4:7 ("For who maketh thee to differ *from another?* and what hast thou that thou didst not receive? now if thou didst receive *it,* why dost thou glory, as if thou hadst not received *it?*"). This text deprives free will of everything and leaves no room for merits. "But nevertheless, inexhaustible and manifold as God's beneficence and liberality are, he rewards, as if they were our own virtues, those graces which he bestows upon us, because he makes them ours" (2.5.2).

The third argument against the bondage of the will is that without the ability to choose good and evil, humans must be either wholly bad or wholly good. But, says Calvin in reply, the apostle's words in Romans 3 cannot be gainsaid. All persons are depraved, sunk in wickedness, and remain that way unless God intervenes to rescue us by His mercy. That some choose the good is by God's healing hand; others He passes by and allows to rot in their own waywardness (2.5.3). The fourth argument against the doctrine of the will's bondage states that all exhortation and admonition are meaningless unless we have the power to obey. Calvin responds by pointing to various biblical texts that make clear that we are dependent upon God if we are to obey His exhortations (cf. John 15:5; Rom. 9:16; Isa. 5:24; 24:5; Deut. 10:16; Jer. 4:4; 31:33; Ezek. 11:19). This dependency, however, does not undermine exhortation. Calvin offers this as his principal answer to the stated objection: "God works in his elect in two ways: within, through his Spirit; without, through his Word. By his Spirit, illuminating their minds and forming their hearts to the love and cultivation of righteousness, he makes them a new creation. By his Word, he arouses them to desire, to seek after, and to attain the same renewal. In both he reveals the working of his hand according to the mode of dispensation" (2.5.5). Naturally, with respect to the reprobate, exhortation serves a different purpose, most expressly to stir their conscience and at the Last Judgment to leave them without excuse (2.5.5).

We discover that each one of the arguments presented by those who oppose the notion of the bondage of the will rests on the Pelagian notion that "(in)ability limits obligation" or, conversely, "obligation requires ability."

Misappropriating Texts Which Allegedly Teach Free Will

Next Calvin turns to consider various passages which allegedly teach the freedom of the will (2.5.6–19). We need not trace out Calvin's detailed presentation of this material inasmuch as the above mentioned assumption—namely, that "ought implies can"—is operative in how the proponents of free will understand divine commands, promises, and rebukes. Calvin argues, on the contrary, that divine imperatives do not assume the power or ability to comply with them, that God can have a variety of motives and reasons for issuing imperatives, rebukes, and promises, and that the biblical testimony is ample and clear that insofar as we will what is right, such is by the prompting of the Holy Spirit. The Spirit is free to use external means for His inward operations. In short, the notion that (in)ability limits obligation or that obligations require ability is untenable. Calvin concludes his discussion of human depravity with these words:

> Therefore let us hold this as an undoubted truth which no siege engines can shake: the mind of man has been so completely estranged from God's righteousness that it conceives, desires, and undertakes, only that which is impious, perverted, foul, impure, and infamous. The heart is so steeped in the poison of sin, that it can breathe out nothing but a loathsome stench. But if some men occasionally make a show of good, their minds nevertheless ever remain enveloped in hypocrisy and deceitful craft, and their hearts bound by inner perversity (2.5.19).

Questions for Reflection and Discussion

1. How is "low self-esteem" different from Calvin's idea of true knowledge of self?

2. Given Calvin's discussion of hereditary depravity, is original sin itself enough to make us "children of wrath" and subject to "God's condemnation"? Why is the answer to this question so important?

3. Is Calvin's view of human nature too pessimistic? Defend your answer biblically! How does Calvin's view differ from much modern psychology and the self-esteem movement? What is your assessment of the need for self-esteem?

4. How ought Calvin's doctrine of "general grace" shape our view of art, science, technology, music, etc.?

5. Look up Ephesians 4:17ff. and Romans 3:9–20. What are the abominations to which sinners are subject? Why do only "damnable" things come forth from corrupt human nature, according to Calvin?

6. Read Ezekiel 36:26–27, Philippians 2:13, 1 Corinthians 12:6, and Ephesians 2:10. Do you believe Calvin has made his case, namely, that even the good works believers do and their perseverance in faith are God's gifts? Explain.

7. Why, according to Calvin, is it fair of God to harden hearts?

8. Explain how the notion that "ability limits obligation" permits sin to carry excuse in its own bosom.

9. Why does Calvin wish to abandon the idea of "free will"?

Canon of Dort
3–4

The Way of Redemption in Christ

Chapter Six: Fallen Man Ought to Seek Redemption in Christ

Orientation

IN THE FIRST five chapters of Book Two Calvin presents us with the doctrine of human depravity. We have seen that original sin leaves the human race fallen and corrupted, morally and spiritually incapable of seeking after God. With chapter six, Calvin begins to expound the answer to our predicament, pointing us to Christ who is our only hope for redemption. Christ alone, bestowed to us from the Father as a gift, rescues us from the fall. Indeed, just as Adam was the progenitor, even the root, of the human race, so Christ is the head of the new humanity. Or as Calvin stated back in chapter one: "Here, then, is the relationship between the two: Adam, implicating us in his ruin, destroyed us with himself; but Christ restores us to salvation by his grace" (2.1.6).

Calvin now embarks upon an exposition of God's unfolding plan for human redemption. In chapters six through eight he expounds upon the old covenant and the role of the law—especially the moral law or the Ten Commandments—as part of God's work of salvation, all of which teaches us to know God as our Redeemer. Chapter six, which we now examine, is introductory to this discussion.

The Need for the Mediator

Calvin argues that since the human race has fallen into death, it cannot rescue itself from that predicament. It is necessary that God salvage His fallen creation. Indeed, appearing as our Redeemer in the person of His only-begotten Son, God secures the way of salvation. In addition, the knowledge of God the Creator becomes useless to us unless faith in Him as our Redeemer is imparted to us. Through faith we come to know God as our Father in Christ. However, without the light of faith, without knowledge of Christ as our Mediator, we behold only God's curse in the creation. Consequently, as we contemplate the universe we cannot "infer that [God] is Father." Rather, conscience justly accuses us. Given our sin, conscience reveals to us that God has just cause to disown us and to regard us no longer as His sons and daughters. We in turn respond with "dullness" and "ingratitude," "for our minds, as they have been blinded, do not perceive what is true. And as all our senses have become perverted, we wickedly defraud God of his glory" (2.6.1). Thus if anybody is to come to faith, it must be God's work. Indeed, it is God's work. He uses the folly of preaching as the outward means for that purpose (see 1 Cor. 1:21). We find, then, that the way of salvation is presented to us in Christ alone. All humanity is estranged from God and lies under curse. Meanwhile, in seeking redemption or peace on its own terms, the human heart invents its own gods. All pagan religions have emerged in this way; and that is also why they are false. No worship pleases God except worship that looks to Christ (see Eph. 2:12), for only those engrafted into Him "have the place and rank of children" (2.6.1).

The way of salvation in Christ applied to the people of the old covenant as well as the people of the new covenant (2.6.2). Even the old covenant people hoped for and looked to Christ as the Mediator. God's pledge of mercy always, even in the Old Testament and under the Law of Moses, rested on Christ, the Redeemer (2.6.3). Calvin is emphatic in affirming and maintaining this point: "Apart from Christ the saving knowledge of God does not stand. From the beginning of the world he had consequently been set before all the elect that they should look unto him and put their trust in him" (2.6.4).

Chapter Seven: The Law was Given, Not to Restrain the Folk of the Old Covenant under Itself, But to Foster Hope of Salvation in Christ Until His Coming

Orientation
Calvin now examines the law, for by the law God shows fallen humans their desperate need for redemption. God's covenantal dealings with estranged

sinners find a particular focus in His law, since the law plays a unique role in driving sinners to Christ.

The Law of God

In treating God's law, Calvin explains that in the Old Testament God provided witnesses to remind His chosen people of the One to come. He did this to urge them to look for that coming, to await Him, "to hold their minds in readiness until his coming; even to kindle desire for him, and to strengthen their expectation..." (2.7.1). Calvin also explains what he means by the law. "I understand by the word 'law' not only the Ten Commandments, which set forth a godly and righteous rule of living, but the form of religion handed down by God through Moses." This law did not cancel the gracious covenant that God had established with Abraham. On the contrary, Moses frequently reminds Israel "of that freely given covenant made with their fathers of which they were the heirs." In fact, through the ceremonies of the Mosaic law God renews this covenant. They are typological or figurative in pointing ahead to the sacrifice to come. Calvin argues that the moral and ceremonial laws point us to Christ. The whole cultus of the law, seen as shadows and figures corresponding to the truth, points us to God's mercy in Christ. For "God did not command sacrifices in order to busy his worshipers with earthly exercises. Rather, he did so that he might lift their minds higher" (2.7.1).

In that light, Calvin also wants us to see that the Mosaic law contains the gospel promise of Christ to come. In both the Levitical priesthood and in the royal figure of David the Old Testament presents us with "a double mirror" that shows us Christ. The law and the prophets repeatedly testify that the ceremonial laws of sacrifice, for example, look ahead to "a single sacrifice" (cf. Isa. 53:5; Dan. 9:26–27; Ps. 110:4; and Heb. 5:6; 7:21). The Ten Commandments—God's moral law written down for us—teach righteousness in vain "until Christ confers it by free imputation and by the Spirit of regeneration" (cf. Rom. 10:4) (2.7.2). This is what it means that Christ is "the fulfillment or end of the law." The law shows us our faults and condemns us (cf. Gal. 3:19). Only when we are humbled by the law are we prepared to look for divine aid and seek Christ (2.7.2).

The law was never given to provide a way of salvation apart from Christ, as if the law could lead us to righteousness. The law arouses guilt in us so that we look outside ourselves for pardon. Seeing ourselves guilty before God's tribunal humbles us so that we are ready to seek His pardon. Since the law teaches perfect righteousness, we can only obtain righteousness before God if we observe the law perfectly. The law, however, displays its "feebleness" in that it cannot actually make us righteous or even obedient. Hence, the law shows us our curse and failure; its threatening judgments loom over us, announcing certain damnation. But it cannot save us. "Because observance of the law is found in none of us, we are excluded from the promises of life, and fall back into the mere curse" (2.7.3).

Thus in condemning us, the law leaves us despondent and despairing (cf. Gal. 3:10). Even the conditional—"do this and live"—promises contained in the law of Moses (conditions we can never meet) were not given in order to mock us, says Calvin. Rather, when we discover our inability to fulfill such conditions and that such conditional promises are "fruitless and ineffectual for us," we also discover that God must intervene on our behalf, from His free goodness, and "receive us without looking at our works." In faith, then, we embrace His goodness presented to us in the gospel, the promises that "do not lack effectiveness even with the condition attached" (2.7.4). The law, indeed, contains promise, that is, the gospel. This gospel promise is also revealed in the law—the law here referring to the entirety of the Old Testament, not merely the Ten Commandments. God supplies what we don't have and performs what we cannot do. He meets the condition that we cannot fulfill. This is our justification, which Calvin says he will treat in its due place. We discover, then—even more, the Lord shows us—the necessity of God's free grace, for we cannot fulfill the law. Scripture often bears witness to this reality (Eccl. 7:21; Ps. 143:2; Gal. 5:17; 3:10; Deut. 27:26). The way of self-righteousness is truly impossible. "Let us be quite agreed, then, that the law cannot be fulfilled in this life of the flesh, if we observe the weakness of our own nature…" (cf. Rom. 8:3) (2.7.5).

The Three Uses of the Law

Calvin believes this discussion comes to greater clarity when we examine the moral law which functions in a threefold way, i.e., it has three uses.

• *The First Use of the Law.* The first use of the law is that it functions as a mirror showing us God's righteousness and our sin. This, in turn, leads us to implore divine help. As Calvin writes:

> While the [moral law] shows God's righteousness, that is, the righteousness alone acceptable to God, it warns, informs, convicts, and lastly

condemns, every man of his own unrighteousness. For man, blinded and drunk with self-love, must be compelled to know and to confess his own feebleness and impurity. If man is not clearly convinced of his own vanity, he is puffed up with insane confidence in his own mental powers, and can never be induced to recognize their slenderness as long as he measures them by a measure of his own choice. But as soon as he begins to compare his powers with the difficulty of the law, he has something to diminish his bravado. For, however remarkable an opinion of his powers he formerly held, he soon feels that they are panting under so heavy a weight as to stagger and totter, and finally even to fall down and faint away. Thus man, schooled in the law, sloughs off the arrogance that previously blinded him (2.7.6).

"The law is like a mirror," writes Calvin. We see our weakness and wickedness by means of it, and also the resultant curse (2.7.7). Through the law comes knowledge of sin (Rom. 3:20; 5:20; 4:15). All people stand condemned before God's law. Nobody escapes. While the wicked are terrified, God's chosen ones come to realize their empty-handedness before God (Rom. 3:19; 11:32). Consequently, they seek God's mercy most earnestly, "dismissing the stupid opinion of their own strength." We stand before God "naked and empty-handed." In this condition we flee to God's mercy, "repose entirely in it, hide deep within it, and seize upon it alone for righteousness and merit." "In the precepts of the law," writes Calvin, "God is but the rewarder of perfect righteousness, which all of us lack, and conversely, the severe judge of evil deeds. But in Christ his face shines, full of grace and gentleness, even upon us poor and unworthy sinners" (2.7.8).

This is why the law in its accusing function drives us to seek God's grace in Christ. Even the reprobate discover that their consciences are "buffeted" by the waves of God's verdict of condemnation and impending judgment so that they know in themselves that they are deserving of divine justice (2.7.9).

• *The Second Use of the Law.* The second use of the law is its restraining effect upon evildoers and unbelievers. The law threatens punishment. The fear of punishment serves "to restrain certain men who are untouched by any care for what is just and right unless compelled by hearing the dire threats in the law." Thus some people are restrained from sin and evil-doing, "not because their inner mind is stirred or affected, but because, being bridled, so to speak, they keep their hands from outward activity, and hold inside the depravity that otherwise they would wantonly have indulged. Consequently, they are neither better nor more righteous before God" (2.7.10).

Calvin argues that "this constrained and forced righteousness is necessary for the public community of men, for whose tranquility the Lord herein provided when he took care that everything be not tumultuously confounded" (2.7.10). This fear of punishment is even to the benefit of God's children before they have come to faith. Thus the law serves as a deterrent both for those who are confident of their own self-righteousness, for it brings them to humility, and for those who abandon themselves to their lusts, since it restrains them with fear of retribution (2.7.11).

• *The Third Use of the Law.* The third use of the law is to admonish believers and urge them on in well doing or obedience. Calvin considers this use the "proper purpose" of the law. It "finds its place among believers in whose hearts the Spirit of God already lives and reigns. For even though they have the law written and engraved upon their hearts by the finger of God [Jer. 31:33; Heb. 10:16], that is, have been so moved and quickened through the directing of the Spirit that they long to obey God, they still profit by the law in two ways": (1) the law helps them to learn more thoroughly each day the Lord's will; and (2) the law exhorts them to obedience, strengthening them in it, and pulling them back from the slippery path of transgression. "The law," writes Calvin, "is to the flesh like a whip to an idle and balky ass, to arouse it to work. Even for a spiritual man not yet free of the weight of the flesh the law remains a constant sting that will not let him stand still" (2.7.12).

In this connection, Calvin contends against antinomianism, which teaches that the law no longer has any role or function in the Christian life. Calvin's plea to us is forthright: "Banish this wicked thought from our minds!" The law provides us the perfect pattern of righteousness (cf. Deut. 32:46–47). Calvin also points to the words of David in Psalm 1:2 ("But his delight *is* in the law of the LORD; and in his law doth he meditate day and night"), which are "just as applicable to every age, even to the end of the world" (2.7.13). To be sure, the law sets forth a high standard of righteousness that can frighten us, for we cannot meet its strict demands. Yet in its third function, the law does not come to us as "a rigorous enforcement officer who is not satisfied unless the requirements are met." No, here the law shows us the goal after which we strive, even as it presents us with the course of the race we are to run (2.7.13).

The Abrogation of the Law

We see, then, that the law has a threefold function. At the same time, Calvin is careful to explain in what manner the believer has been liberated from the law.

> The law has power to exhort believers. This is not a power to bind their consciences with a curse, but one to shake off their sluggishness, by repeatedly urging them, and to pinch them awake to their imperfection. Therefore, many persons, wishing to express such liberation from that curse, say that for believers the law—I am still speaking of the moral law—has been abrogated. Not that the law no longer enjoins believers to do what is right, but only that it is not for them what it formerly was: it may no longer condemn and destroy their consciences by frightening and confounding them (2.7.14).

We must not forget that when the apostle says, "All Scripture is inspired by God" (2 Tim. 3:16ff.), he is referring to the Old Testament Scripture. Note well that the Old Testament Scripture is profitable for teaching, for reproof, for correction, and for training New Testament believers in every good work. The law no longer condemns believers, for Christ was made a curse for them, releasing them from the law's requirements. Nevertheless, being released from the law's demands does not mean believers cease to venerate and obey the law (2.7.15).

Likewise, the ceremonial laws "have been abrogated not in effect but only in use. Christ by his coming has terminated them, but has not deprived them of anything of their sanctity; rather, he has approved and honored it" (2.7.16). What is more, the law's verdict of continual and repeated condemnation—its written bond—is blotted out. Calvin interprets Colossians 2:14 in light of Hebrews 9:15. He writes:

> We hold that ceremonies, considered in themselves, are very appropriately called 'written bonds against' the salvation of men. For they were, so to speak, binding legal documents, which attested men's obligation. When the false apostles wanted to bind the Christian church again to observe them, Paul with good reason, more profoundly restating their ultimate purpose, warned the Colossians into what danger they would slip back if they allowed themselves to be subjugated to the ceremonial law in this way [Col. 2:16ff.]. For at the same time they were deprived of the benefit of Christ, since, when once he had carried out the eternal atonement, he abolished those daily observances, which were able only to attest sins but could do nothing to blot them out (2.7.17).

Chapter Eight: Explanation of the Moral Law (The Ten Commandments)

Orientation

Given the importance of the moral law for the Christian life—in each of its three functions—Calvin introduces the Ten Commandments and offers a brief exposition of each commandment. A clear explanation of God's moral law will only serve to reinforce and illustrate the points Calvin has earlier made, namely that the law is still in force today and that the Jews already in the Old Testament were taught the standard of godliness and their inability to meet that standard, so that being in dread of God's judgment they were "drawn inevitably though unwillingly to the Mediator" (2.8.1). At this juncture, Calvin offers his own summary of his chief point:

> …that, empty of all opinion of our own virtue, and shorn of all assurance of our own righteousness—in fact, broken and crushed by the awareness of our own utter poverty—we may learn genuine humility and self-abasement. Both of these the Lord accomplishes in his law. First, claiming for himself the lawful power to command, he calls us to reverence his divinity, and specifies wherein such reverence lies and consists. Secondly, having published the rule of his righteousness, he reproves us both for our impotence and for our unrighteousness. For our nature, wicked and deformed, is always opposing his uprightness; and our capacity, weak and feeble to do good, lies far from his perfection (2.8.1).

The Ten Commandments and Natural Law

Calvin is ready to proceed. He begins by showing the connection between the law of nature and the moral law set forth in the Ten Commandments. The "inward law" or the natural law which is "written, even engraved, upon the hearts of all, in a sense asserts the very same things that are to be learned from the two Tables." Conscience testifies to and expresses this law as "an inner witness and monitor of what we owe God." It testifies as well to what is good and evil and points the accusing finger at us for failure to do our duty. Only, natural law cannot lead us to worship God in an acceptable manner. Moreover, fallen humans are so conceited and "blinded by self-love" that they cannot look into themselves to discover why they should be moved to humility before God. "Accordingly," Calvin observes, "(because it is necessary both for our dullness and for our arrogance), the Lord has provided us with a written law to give us a clearer witness of what was too obscure in the natural law, shake off our listlessness, and strike more vigorously our mind and memory" (2.8.1).

The Unyielding and Righteous Claims of the Law

The law expresses God's righteousness. What God declares in the law is holy, right, and good, for God can only demand of us these things. The law expresses His will, which is righteousness and opposed to sin and wickedness. As such, the law calls us to love God with reverence, love, and fear, giving Him the glory that is His due. It also calls us away from our own will to conform to His. The law likewise bids us to worship God in the way of holiness, purity, and all that is good (2.8.2).

From this standpoint, then, the law bids us to examine ourselves. In doing so we discover the first function of the law, for in comparing ourselves with God's righteous standards, we learn that our lives are far removed from His holy will. We are guilty. We also learn that we are unable to heal ourselves. We cannot keep the law. We are powerless to fulfill its demands or keep ourselves from its prohibitions. Finally we learn to seek "God's mercy alone" for help, for the law judges us and threatens us with death. God's grace is our "only haven of safety." The end result: we are moved, despairing in ourselves, to look for divine aid (2.8.3).

Indeed, the threats and promises of the law serve the purpose to "imbue our hearts with love of righteousness and with hatred of wickedness…" (2.8.4). It is not enough to fear divine judgment through the law's testimony. We need to be shown the beauty of righteousness. This is why God, as a loving Father, to attract us by means of rewards, calls us to seek after Him in love. Obedience brings blessing. However, the converse also applies—that is, disobedience meets with punishment. As Calvin writes, speaking of obedience: "And to urge us in every way, [God] promises both blessings in the present life and everlasting blessedness to those who obediently keep his commandments." Similarly, he writes regarding disobedience: "[God] threatens the transgressors no less with present calamities than with the punishment of eternal death" (cf. Lev. 18:5; Ezek. 18:4). Eternal life constitutes the principal reward, eternal perdition the principal threat. Of course, reward is a matter of grace. Calvin says that God "yields his own right when he offers a reward for our obedience, which we do not render voluntarily or as something not due" (2.8.4).

Obedience is not a trifle, for obedience is following the rule of perfect righteousness. This disallows all contrived schemes to acquire righteousness before God apart from His Word (cf. Deut. 12:28, 32). "The best remedy to cure that fault will be to fix this thought firmly in mind: the law has been divinely handed down to us to teach us perfect righteousness; there no other righteousness is taught than that which conforms to the requirements of God's will; in vain therefore do we attempt new forms of works to win the favor of God, whose lawful worship consists in obedience alone; rather, any zeal for good works that wanders outside God's law is an intolerable profanation of divine and true righteousness" (2.8.5).

Three Observations for Rightly Understanding the Law
Before proceeding to an exposition of the Ten Commandments, Calvin wants to point out three things about the moral law which help us to discern what each commandment is burdened to do and how it functions.

Calvin's first observation about the law is that the law is spiritual. "Let us agree that through the law man's life is molded not only to outward honesty but to inward and spiritual righteousness" (2.8.6). The law teaches us about "the Lawgiver," for it shows us His character and perfections. A merely human lawgiver is concerned only with outward conformity to the stated rule, not the inward purity of heart. God, however, is "a spiritual lawgiver" who aims both at the outward conformity of our actions to His rule and no less the disposition and submission of our soul to His truth. Human laws aim at the prevention of wrongdoing. God's law is given for our hearts and souls, that we may be constrained from within ourselves. Against this purpose, though, the human heart is content to congratulate itself when it has achieved this outward conformity. For example, "common folk" hear the law say: "'You shall not kill; you shall not commit adultery; you shall not steal.' They do not unsheathe a sword for slaughter; they do not join their bodies to prostitutes; they do not lay hands on another's goods. So far so good. But wholeheartedly they breathe out slaughter, burn with lust, look with jaundiced eye upon the goods of all others and devour them with covetousness. They are lacking in the chief point of the law" (2.8.6). Calvin thus reminds us that the law makes an absolute claim on us.

In making this point further Calvin takes us to Christ's teaching against the Pharisees. No one interpreted the law better than our Lord. The Pharisees, on the other hand, had infected the people with "a perverse opinion," so that mere outward observance to the law was counted as obedience. Jesus' instruction in Matthew 5 undermines and exposes this whole defiled scheme (2.8.7).

Calvin's second observation about the law is that each commandment has a wider scope of meaning and application than its narrowly stated stipulation. Calvin observes that each of the divine commandments function through "synecdoche"—that is, in the commandments a general rule is laid down, and from the general rule every sort of particular prohibition is included as well. For example, the commandment not to kill extends to the prohibition not to vent your anger toward your neighbor. The negative prohibition of a commandment applies in a positive way, too, for each commandment contains a positive mandate. "Thou shalt not kill," as a positive mandate means: "Don't sit idly by when your neighbor's life is threatened. Take measures to protect your neighbor." Each commandment expands to a wider and more general application. In Calvin's words: "the commandments and prohibitions always contain more than is expressed in words" (2.8.8). To properly interpret the law we must go "beyond the words." Calvin presents this as "the best rule": "if attention be directed to the reason of the commandment; that is, in each commandment to ponder why it was given to us" (2.8.8). Calvin's aim here is that we see how each commandment has a definite *intent* or *purpose*, which then reveals the core *content* or the *substance* of the specified commandment. In the First Commandment we are called to have no other gods except the One who is God. The purpose of the commandment is that we worship God and no other. The substance of that precept is "true piety"—which is to say, that our lives are directed to the One who is our Creator and Lord, and that God "abominates impiety" (2.8.8). From this observation we must also see that there are two sides to every commandment: (1) something enjoined, with its opposite prohibited; and (2) something prohibited, with its opposite enjoined (2.8.8).

> Thus in each commandment we must investigate what it is concerned with; then we must seek out its purpose, until we find what the Lawgiver testifies there to be pleasing or displeasing to himself. Finally, from this same thing we must derive an argument on the other side, in this manner: if this pleases God, the opposite displeases him; if this displeases, the opposite pleases him; if he commands this, he forbids the opposite; if he forbids this, he enjoins the opposite (2.8.8).

We see, then, that we are called to faithful right doing, not mere restraint from wrong doing (2.8.9). Calvin notes that God issues these "half commandments"—which by synecdoche press over into every part of our lives—in order to expose our penchant to make excuses for ourselves. Thus

God prohibits murder—the most heinous element in that sort of transgression—to make us shudder, with the aim that our minds should detest every sort of sin that lies underneath murder or the whole mass of vices that give birth to murder. This includes anger and hatred (2.8.10).

Calvin's third observation about the law is that the Ten Commandments are to be divided into two Tables. The first Table contains the commandments regarding the duties we owe God; the second Table presents the commandments concerning the duties we owe our neighbors. Worship of God is the foundation of righteousness. Only then are we in a position to act righteously toward one another. Hence the law is summed up by loving God and our neighbor (2.8.11). In speaking of the two Tables of the law, Calvin argues that the commandments should be divided so that the first four compose the first Table and the next six comprise the second Table (2.8.12).

The Ten Commandments Expounded

Calvin now turns to an exposition of the Ten Commandments. We present only a bare sketch of his more extended commentary, beginning with the Preface to the commandments, that is, the words "I am the Lord, thy God...." The Preface to the law reminds us that we may not hold the law in contempt; rather, we must remember that the law is from God, and God's authority is affixed to the law, even as He reveals Himself as the One who promises mercy and who has in the past demonstrated that mercy in the blessings of their deliverance from bondage. This forms the context to the law God calls His people to keep and to observe and do (2.8.13–15).

The First Commandment: God alone is to be preeminent among His people. Thus God alone is to be worshiped. We owe God adoration, trust, invocation, and thanksgiving. We must ever be on our guard against superstition (2.8.16).

The Second Commandment: Here we are shown what kind of God we worship and how He should be honored. God calls us to true spiritual worship. This commandment forbids trying to depict God by some material representation, as it forbids the worship of any images. Violation of this commandment brings curse upon us. God is like a husband to us; He will not have His marriage bed defiled by our apostasy (2.8.17–21).

The Third Commandment: God's will for us in this commandment is that we hallow the majesty of His name. We may not treat His name carelessly or contemptuously. In dealing with this commandment, Calvin gives a detailed discussion about "oaths" (2.8.22–27).

The Fourth Commandment: Here we are exhorted to recognize the futility of our evil works and inclinations, and therefore we should meditate on God's kingdom in the ways He has established. It involves "spiritual" rest, which includes a specific day for assembly to worship and a day of rest for servants, etc. Only at rest are we receptive to God's working in us; thus our labors must cease (2.8.28–34).

The Fifth Commandment: God establishes rank and degrees of preeminence among humans which should be honored. We are thus called to respect those placed over us by God and treat them with honor, obedience, and gratefulness, not detracting from their dignity by contempt or ungratefulness. It is monstrous if one does not honor his parents. We must render to them, along with all other authorities placed over us, due reverence, obedience, and gratitude, unless they incite us to disobey God (2.8.35–38).

The Sixth Commandment: We are called to concern ourselves with one another's safety. Harm to our neighbor is forbidden. The prohibition involves our neighbor's physical and spiritual well being. This commandment exposes anger, hatred, and all evil intention to bring harm on others as forms of murder (2.8.39–40).

The Seventh Commandment: Because God loves modesty and purity, all uncleanness must be far from His people. Thus we are called not to defile ourselves with any filth or lustful intemperance of the flesh. Chastity is virtuous, and marriage is given as the only acceptable arena in which to exercise our sexuality. This commandment bids us to modesty and forbids fornication, as well as seduction by alluring dress, conduct, gestures, or speech. In this context Calvin also deals with questions surrounding celibacy (cf. 2.8.41–44).

The Eighth Commandment: Since injustice is abominable to God, He bids us to render to every person his or her due. We should not pant after another person's possessions. Instead, we should help him keep his goods, as it is God who gives to each what he has. Theft comes in many forms: by violence, fraud, legal craft, by flattering pretense of gift. We should protect our neighbor's property. And more, we should give generously to the needy out of our abundance (2.8.45–46).

The Ninth Commandment: God abhors lies. We must, therefore, practice truth toward each other. We are called to protect our neighbor's good name and reputation, as we are forbidden to harm anyone with slander or evil speaking. Sadly, humans enjoy talking scandalously about others. Evil speech that defames is condemned by God, as is the *listening* to it (2.8.47–48).

The Tenth Commandment: With this commandment God wills us to be disposed to love; therefore, we must banish all desires contrary to love. This means all covetous thoughts are forbidden. In this way we see that not only is the inclination to evil forbidden, but even the prompting thereto. Covetous hearts are diseased, standing in the way of love (2.8.49–50).

The Summary of the Law

Calvin sums up his exposition of the Moral Law by stating: "Now it will not be difficult to decide the purpose of the whole law: the fulfillment of righteousness to form human life to the archetype of divine purity" (2.8.51). We see God's own character outlined for us in the law. The law is not an elementary textbook about righteousness; it is better viewed as the perfect guide to all the duties of piety and love. It isn't merely presented in order to lead us in our "apprenticeship"; rather, it guides us to our true goal, which is good works, since we cannot desire a greater perfection than what is presented to us in God's law (2.8.51).

Moreover, its perfection is seen in that even its mandates pertaining to our neighbor serve to summarize the whole law for us, for love is the essence of the law (2.8.52–53). The law directs our self-love to others, which is to be expressed most beautifully toward those who are our brothers and sisters in Christ (2.8.54). Indeed, the law is only kept by loving God and our neighbor, forsaking self. An evil life is easily seen in self-interest and self-centered striving (2.8.54). However, love for our neighbors does not only pertain to those who live in our physical vicinity but to all persons without exception—even our enemies (2.8.55–57). We are called to self-sacrifice, loving our neighbor, seeking the welfare of even the remotest stranger (2.8.55).

The False Distinction between Venial and Mortal Sins

The last matter Calvin briefly addresses pertains to the distinction that has been made between venial and mortal sins. Venial sin refers to transgressions of the law whereby in committing the sin the transgressor has "desire without deliberate assent, which does not long remain in the heart" (2.8.58). This is set in contrast to mortal sin which involves full knowledge and deliberate consent. The idea is that mortal sin is a grave violation of God's law, and since it has one's heart and mind assenting to it, it destroys love in our heart and turns us away from God. Venial sin, however, is more a matter of weakness, in which one's heart is still directed to God; and though it wounds our love for God, love still resides in our heart. Thus it is a less grave sin.

Calvin rejects this distinction as it stands, since all sins are a violation of the law and derive from hearts divided or directed away from God. Sin is sin, and every sin merits "the death penalty." Every little transgression is setting aside God's authority. As the apostle says, "The wages of sin is death" (Rom. 6:23). "Let the children of God hold that all sin is mortal. For it is rebellion against the will of God, which of necessity provokes God's wrath, and it is a violation of the law, upon which God's judgment is pronounced without exception" (2.8.59).

Questions for Reflection and Discussion

1. How is a denial of "Christ as the only way of salvation" a denial of the entire covenant of grace in the Old and New Testaments?

2. What is God's law? What are the three *types* of law? What are the three *uses* of the law that Calvin mentions? Give examples of each "use" of the law. For example, how does law restrain sin today?

3. How can we use the law in the "third way" without slipping back into the first use? Is it possible to avoid the "first use" of the law even when it serves as a "guide to gratitude"? What are the dangers and obstacles? (See Heidelberg Catechism, Q/A 115.)

4. Is antinomianism still with us today? If so, what are some examples?

5. What is Calvin's conception of natural law? What are the limitations of natural law?

6. Calvin presents the law of God and the Ten Commandments as he embarks upon teaching us the way of redemption in Christ. How does the law function to bring us to salvation?

7. What are Calvin's three general observations about the law and how do they help us apply the law to our lives today?

8. What is the distinction between mortal and venial sins? Why is this distinction not helpful?

Christ the Redeemer—Promise and Fulfillment

Chapters 9–11 of Book Two

Chapter Nine: Christ, Although He Was Known to the Jews Under the Law, Was at Length Clearly Revealed Only in the Gospel

Orientation

HAVING SHOWN US the depth of human depravity in the opening chapters of Book Two, Calvin next introduces us to the promise of redemption through Jesus Christ. Already in the Old Testament we are shown the nature of God's mercy, for God announces the promise of salvation through the seed of the woman; and God has given us His law in order to make known and preserve the standard of holiness that sin obscures and ignores. The law of God, however, especially the Ten Commandments, convinces us of our need for redemption by showing us our guilt before God. In this way the moral law serves the gospel, which is the message concerning Jesus Christ and God's free mercy to us through Him.

Now Calvin demonstrates how Christ was revealed under the law but is now clearly and fully revealed in the gospel. Christ, our Redeemer, was promised to us in the Old Testament in the way of shadows, ceremonies, and symbols, but the promise has reached fulfillment in the New Testament with the incarnation of the Son of God and the work He undertook for our redemption.

Law and Gospel

Already in the Old Testament, says Calvin, God gave His people the promise of Christ to come. He did this by means of expiations and sacrifices, showing that He is their Father and they are His chosen people. As Malachi declares, "The sun of righteousness shall rise" (Mal. 4:2). "By these words he teaches that while the law serves to hold the godly in expectation of Christ's coming, at His advent they should hope for far more light." Indeed, the treasure about which the ancient prophets bore witness is now our possession. They (the people of the Old Testament revelation) saw from afar; we (the people of the New Testament revelation) have been brought near. The law—here referring to the Old Testament—declares Christ, but the gospel—meaning the New Testament—imparts to us "the clear manifestation of the mystery of Christ" (2.9.1). In speaking of law and gospel, we need to understand that Calvin (and Scripture) uses the word "gospel" also in a more specific sense, so that "gospel" is also revealed in the law or in the Old Testament. For "the word 'gospel,' taken in the broad sense, includes those testimonies of [God's] mercy and fatherly favor which God gave to the patriarchs of old." Then Calvin immediately adds, "In a higher sense... the word refers...to the proclamation of the grace manifested in Christ" (2.9.2). In this sense the gospel (Christ revealed in the New Testament) is the fulfillment of what God promised in the Old Testament, for the truth of His promises are realized in the person and work of Christ (2.9.3).

Calvin, unlike Luther, does not as such oppose law and gospel to one another. He is careful to show how "law" and "gospel" can have different nuances of meaning.

> We refute those who always erroneously compare the law with the gospel by contrasting the merit of works with the free imputation of righteousness. This is indeed a contrast not at all to be rejected. For Paul often means by the term 'law' the rule of righteous living by which God requires of us what is his own, giving us no hope of life unless we completely obey him, and adding on the other hand a curse if we deviate even in the slightest degree....
>
> But the gospel did not so supplant the entire law as to bring forward a different way of salvation. Rather, it confirmed and satisfied whatever the law had promised, and gave substance to the shadows.... Where the whole law is concerned, the gospel differs from it only in clarity of manifestation (2.9.4).

The importance of Calvin's remark here is not to be underestimated. The law can refer to the entirety of Old Testament revelation; in that sense the gospel is revealed in the law. Sometimes the law can, instead, refer to God's perfect standard of righteousness, which demands from us perfection if we would enjoy fellowship with God. Then the law stands entirely opposed to the gospel, for the gospel tells us that Christ has met the demands of the law; Christ is our perfection, who suffers the sanction of the law in our place, who fulfills righteousness on our behalf or in our stead.

John the Baptist—the Prophet Standing between Law and Gospel
Calvin observes that John the Baptist "stood between the law and the gospel, holding an intermediate office related to both." The sum of the gospel is declared by John when he calls Christ the lamb of God who takes away the sins of the world (John 1:29). John the Baptist here is a messenger of the gospel, preparing the way of salvation that is wrought by God's Son, manifest in the flesh (2.9.5).

Chapter Ten: The Similarity of the Old and New Testaments

Orientation
This chapter unfolds for us Calvin's understanding of God's covenant. The way in which God enters into fellowship with human beings is through a covenant. In fact, "all men adopted by God into the company of his people since the beginning of the world were covenanted to him by the same law and by the bond of the same doctrine as obtains among us"—that is, among us who have the fuller revelation of Jesus Christ in the New Testament.

The Unity of the Covenant of Grace
This brings Calvin to consider the similarities that exist between the Old and New Testaments. In other words, there is a continuity between the one and the other. The patriarchs of old "participated in the same inheritance and hoped for a common salvation with us by the grace of the same Mediator" (2.10.1). This is not to deny that differences also exist between the testaments—something Calvin will explore in the next chapter—but first Calvin wishes to show us the similarities between the covenant God made with the Israelites in the Old Testament, before Christ came in the flesh, and what God has made known to us after Christ's incarnation.

Calvin points out the continuity as follows: "The covenant made with all the patriarchs is so much like ours in substance and reality that the two are actually one and the same." Then he writes, "Yet they differ in the mode of dispensation" (2.10.2). The key words or phrases here are "substance" and "reality," and also "mode of dispensation." A fundamental unity exists between the two testaments—for they are the same in substance and reality. Substance here means that basic stuff that makes something uniquely what it is, and without which it wouldn't be what it is. Concretely, this means that the grace of God and the way of salvation through Jesus Christ—promised to come in the Old Testament and having come in the New Testament—is one and the same in both testaments. More specifically Calvin observes that in the Old Testament the goal of the covenant for the patriarchs was not "carnal prosperity and happiness" but the adoption into "the hope of immortality" and "assurance of this adoption." In other words, the goal of the covenant in the Old Testament is the same as that which is depicted in the New Testament. Besides this, "the covenant by which they were bound to the Lord was supported, not by their own merits, but solely by the mercy of the God who called them." Stated differently, this means that the way of salvation by God's grace alone, by the One He provides, is the same in both testaments. There isn't one way of salvation in the Old Testament, say, by works, and another way of salvation in the New Testament: by grace through Christ. In addition, more explicitly, Calvin states that the patriarchs "had and knew Christ as Mediator, through whom they were joined to God and were to share in his promises" (2.10.2).

Old Testament Saints Looked for Eternal Blessedness

In this context Calvin is particularly concerned to emphasize his first point, namely that the people of the Old Testament were not seeking merely material blessing and felicity in earthly obtainments. Rather, "the Old Testament was particularly concerned with the future life" (2.10.3). Thus "the Old Testament was established upon the free mercy of God, and was confirmed by Christ's intercession." It "always had its end in Christ and in eternal life" (2.10.4). Calvin points out that the warnings of the covenant that applied in the Old Testament also apply in the New Testament (cf. 1 Cor. 10:1–6, 11) (2.10.5). Even the manna that rained from heaven was not merely provided in order to fill the stomachs of the Israelites. The manna, if received in faith, testified to the eternal and heavenly life God promises to give us (2.10.6).

The people of the Old Testament looked for the fulfillment of the covenant promises in the life to come. They entered into God's immortal kingdom and eternal life (2.10.7). To possess God's pledge that He would be their God and they would be His people was life and salvation. This didn't refer to earthly happiness—as if God pledges to be a God of their bodies alone and not their souls; rather, it referred to eternal blessedness. For "souls, unless they be joined to God through righteousness, remain estranged from him in death" (2.10.8). God is the God to a thousand generations, such that His goodness overflows to the posterity of His own. Indeed, He is not the God of the dead but of the living (cf. Matt. 22:23–32) (2.10.9).

Calvin demonstrates how the patriarchs (Adam, Abel, Noah, Abraham, Isaac, and Jacob) did not seek deliverance from sin's misery and the curse in merely material or earthly prosperity. No, each sought after heavenly and eternal life as promised in God's covenant through the seed of the woman (2.10.10–13). They "set before themselves the blessedness of the future life" (2.10.14). Calvin also provides examples of this in the life of David, Job, Ezekiel, and others (2.10.15–22).

Calvin closes out this chapter with two observations about the Old Testament fathers: first, they "had Christ as pledge of their covenant"; and, second, they "put in him all trust of future blessedness." Thus Calvin resolutely declares this principle as unassailable: "the Old Testament or Covenant that the Lord had made with the Israelites had not been limited to earthly things, but contained a promise of spiritual and eternal life" (2.10.23).

Chapter Eleven: The Difference Between the Two Testaments

Orientation
From what Calvin has said about the similarity and continuity between the two testaments it might appear that he is neglecting some obvious dissimilarities that exist between them, or that he is not reckoning with how the law and the gospel—each defined in a certain way—might legitimately be said to differ from one another. It certainly is not the case that Calvin places the Old and New Testaments on the same level of clarity. Calvin's chief concern is to demonstrate both the continuity and discontinuity between the testaments. In doing so, he shows how they relate to each other.

The Chief Differences between the Two Testaments
For Calvin, the essential unity of the testaments must be accented and maintained, but this still leaves room for differences between them. Calvin mentions five chief differences. Each of these differences has to do with "the manner of dispensation rather than the substance" of the covenant as manifest in the two testaments.

The first difference consists of this: "the Lord of old willed that his people direct and elevate their minds to the heavenly heritage; yet, to nourish them better in this hope, he displayed it for them to see and, so to speak, taste, under earthly benefits. But now that the gospel has more plainly and clearly revealed the grace of the future life, the Lord leads our minds to meditate upon it directly, laying aside the lower mode of training that he used with the Israelites." What is crucial to grasp in this connection is that the earthly blessings promised to the Israelites were never intended to be ends in themselves. What is more, to the degree that earthly ends were in view, they were, subsequent to the revelation of Christ, transformed into typological portraits of the heavenly inheritance. "We contend," writes Calvin, "…that, in the earthly possession they enjoyed, they looked, as in a mirror, upon the future inheritance they believed to have been prepared for them in heaven" (2.11.1; also see 2:11.2–3).

The second difference between the testaments resides in figures. Whereas the Old Testament used images and shadows in anticipation of that reality, which is Christ the Lord, the New Testament reveals that the reality has come, that the very substance of truth is present (2.11.4). Therefore, in the Old Testament we find the covenant wrapped in shadowy images, communicated through indirect encounters, and enacted by means of ineffectual ceremonial observances. In the New Testament, however, we find the covenant renewed, confirmed, and consecrated in and through the blood of Christ. As Calvin writes, the Old Covenant "became new and eternal only after it was consecrated and established by the blood of Christ" (2.11.4). The law contained the shadow of the blessings to come—as such, it contained the gospel. It thereby introduced the better hope to be manifested in the gospel (Heb. 7:19).

To be sure, if the substance of the promises is under consideration, the covenant under Moses (i.e., the covenant of the law) stands in sharp contrast to the covenant of the gospel. For the covenant of grace—that eternal and never-perishing gospel covenant—finds its fulfillment in Christ; He is its confirmation and ratification. Even in the covenant under Moses, through its ceremonies and sacrifices, we find the solemn symbols of that confirmation. Precisely in this respect, these may be abrogated "to give place to Christ, the Sponsor and Mediator of a better covenant" (cf. Heb. 7:22). This is the substance of the covenant that never changes, while the ceremonies and sacrifices are displaced by Christ. "The Testament of God attained its truth when sealed by his [Christ's] blood." This is how it "becomes new and eternal" (2.11.5).

The third difference is seen in the words of Jeremiah who speaks of a *new* covenant to come (Jer. 31:31–34). This leads the apostle Paul "to make a comparison between the law and the gospel, calling the former literal, the latter spiritual doctrine; the former he speaks of as carved on tablets of stone, the latter as written upon men's hearts; the former is the preaching of death, the latter of life; the former of condemnation, the latter of righteousness; the former to be made void, the latter to abide" [2 Cor. 3:3–11] (2.11.7). It is important not to misconstrue the nature of this contrast. Calvin carefully explains it inasmuch as the apostle Paul is making a very particular point:

> ... both Jeremiah and Paul, because they are contrasting the Old and New Testaments, consider nothing in the law except what properly belongs to it. For example: the law contains here and there promises of mercy, but because they have been borrowed from elsewhere, they are not counted part of the law, when only the nature of the law is under discussion. They ascribe to it only this function: to enjoin what is right, to forbid what is wicked; to promise a reward to the keepers of righteousness, and threaten transgressors with punishment; but at the same time not to change or correct the depravity of heart that by nature inheres in all men (2.11.7).

Thus the law is of the letter, functioning without the Spirit, whereas the gospel is spiritual since the Lord engraves "it spiritually upon men's hearts" (2 Cor. 3:6a). The law brings death, for without perfect obedience to it, it pronounces the curse of death upon its violators. The gospel, by contrast, is the instrument of life, for it frees us from the curse of the law through the One who underwent the law's curse for us (cf. 2 Cor. 3:6b). The law is the ministry of condemnation, but the gospel is the ministry of righteousness inasmuch as "it reveals God's mercy, through which we are justified" (2 Cor. 3:9). Finally, the law in its ceremonial features pointed ahead, typologically, to what had not yet become a reality; thus it had to give way and be pushed aside. The gospel, however, "because it reveals the very substance, stands fast forever" (2 Cor. 3:10–11) (2.11.8). We see, then, that the Old Testament anticipates and foreshadows the coming of the Spirit but it could not bring it about. The New Testament, however, brings forth the reality and power of the Spirit. The law—minus the gospel—calls us to obedience, issues demands and prohibitions, and even points to the good news of the gospel, but *as law* it cannot produce or accomplish any change in the human heart. The gospel, by contrast, is potent precisely where the law is impotent, for it can produce or accomplish such change, for the gospel fulfills the law.

"The fourth difference arises out of the third. Scripture calls the Old Testament one of 'bondage' because it produces fear in men's minds; but the New Testament, one of 'freedom' because it lifts them to trust and assurance" (2.11.9). Thus the Old Testament afflicted consciences and made them tremble, but the New Testament brought joy, casting off the yoke of bondage and bringing emancipation. Calvin references Galatians 4:22–31 where the apostle

> ... allegorically interprets Abraham's two sons in this way: Hagar, the bondwoman, is the type of Mt. Sinai where the Israelites received the law; Sarah, the free woman, is the figure of the heavenly Jerusalem whence flows the gospel. Hagar's offspring were born in bondage, never to arrive at the inheritance; Sarah's, free and entitled to it. In like manner, we are subjected to bondage through the law, but are restored to freedom through the gospel alone.... To sum up: the Old Testament struck consciences with fear and trembling, but by the benefit of the New they are released into joy. The Old held consciences bound by the yoke of bondage; the New, by its spirit of liberality, emancipates them into freedom (2.11.9).

The fifth difference on which Calvin elaborates "lies in the fact that until the advent of Christ, the Lord set apart one nation within which to confide the covenant of grace" (2.11.11). This means that He manifested His grace and bestowed His mercies to a single people. "'But,' notes Calvin, 'when the fullness of time came' [Gal. 4:4] which was appointed for the restoration of all things, [Christ] was revealed as the reconciler of God and men; 'the wall' that for so long had confined God's mercy within the boundaries of Israel 'was broken down' [Eph. 2:14]. 'Peace was announced to those who were far off, and to those who were near' [Eph. 2:17] that together they might be reconciled to God and welded into one people [Eph. 2:16]. Therefore there is now no difference between Jew and Greek [Gal. 3:28]."

We see that whereas the Old Testament revelation was confined to the Jewish nation, the New Testament revelation has become universal in its scope. In short, the calling and welcoming of the Gentiles into the sphere of God's saving mercy distinguishes the New from the Old Testament (2.11.12).

Observations

In his treatment of the continuity and discontinuity between the Testaments, Calvin argues most robustly for the continuity that exists between them. This is not to shortchange the five differences that mark the two Testaments and upon which Calvin expounds, but it is proper to note that they do not differ as to substance—and the substance of a thing is most fundamental and important. God's will is one and immutable—the plan of salvation contained in the two Testaments is therefore singular and unchanging. Christ forms the content of grace in both Testaments. The entire Levitical priesthood and ceremony is pointing finally to the one Lamb of God, to the one Sacrifice for sin, to the one Mediator between God and humans. The covenant is singular and so are the signs and seals of that covenant, namely the sacraments, which though the elements and rites change from one Testament to another, the grace they declare and the promise of forgiveness they portray are the same.

The two Testaments are, therefore, identical in their content or substance, which is God's grace in Christ—the seed of the woman. There is no difference at this root and fundamental level. If there were, two different ways of salvation would be posited—one pertaining to believers in the Old Testament and another pertaining to believers in the New Testament. This is not the case. Calvin maintains a radical unity and continuity between the Testaments. The Old Testament is cluttered with ceremonial encumbrances that have served their purpose now that the reality to which they pointed has arrived. Now the covenant, established in the Old Testament, is fulfilled or brought to its fullness in the New Testament. Rightly understood, the Old Testament in its content is one and the same with the New Testament.

Questions for Reflection and Discussion

1. Following Calvin, what is law? What are different ways in which law can be understood?

2. What is gospel, according to Calvin? How can gospel be present in the law (i.e., the law defined in a particular way)?

3. How is Calvin's understanding of Law/Gospel different from modern fundamentalism or dispensationalism?

4. What are the similarities and the differences between the Old and New Testaments? Why is it important to recognize each of these?

5. Why is it so important to understand and appreciate both the continuity and the discontinuity between the Testaments? How is the Christian life affected by both the continuity and the discontinuity between the testaments?

6. What is the unity of the covenant of God between the two testaments? Explain the importance of that unity.

7. What is meant by the contrast between the "letter" and the "spirit"? How does this relate to law and gospel in a very particular sense?

8. What does it mean that Christ is the fulfillment of the law and that the gospel is Christ?

❦ 10 ❧

The Person of Christ

Chapter Twelve: Christ Had to Become Man in Order to Fulfill the Office of Mediator

Orientation

CALVIN REMINDS US of the sort of remedy requisite to save those who have sinned against God's supreme majesty. We need a Mediator who is very God and very man. This is not an absolute necessity, but flows from God's eternal decree upon which human salvation depends. God knows the best means to reconcile us with Himself inasmuch as our sins have wholly alienated us from His fellowship. Thus we need a Mediator of a very peculiar sort. Calvin takes up this topic in chapter twelve wherein he first shows us why we need a Mediator who is very God and very man; then Calvin answers various objectors and the mistaken views they espouse.

The Necessity of the God-Man

Calvin states that it is "of the greatest importance for us that he who was to be our Mediator be both true God and true man" (2.12.1). The depth of human depravity requires this cure. "Since our iniquities, like a cloud cast between us and [God], had completely estranged us from the Kingdom of Heaven (cf. Isa. 59:2), no man, unless he belonged to God, could serve as the intermediary to restore peace." A mere human being cannot reach up to God; what is more, we are all fallen in Adam. Truly, says Calvin, the situation would have been beyond solution "had the very majesty of God not descended to us, since it was not in our power to ascend to him" (2.12.1). "Hence," Calvin continues, "it was necessary for the Son of God to become for us 'Immanuel, that is, God with us' [Isa. 7:14; Matt. 1:23], and in such a way that his divinity and our human nature might by mutual connection grow together." Even without sin man stands in need of a mediator to reach God, writes Calvin—so all the more now that we are sinners, "befouled with many spots" and under His curse. Jesus Christ, Son of God, Son of man, is the Mediator that God has provided for our redemption (cf. 1 Tim. 2:5; Heb. 4:15; Eph. 5:29-31) (2.12.2).

Calvin expands on this theme. The task of this Mediator was most uncommon—Christ's task for our sakes—namely, to bring the estranged back into God's favor, to make "of the children of men, children of God; of the heirs of Gehenna, heirs of the Heavenly Kingdom" (2.12.2). God's natural Son, i.e., His only-begotten Son, "Ungrudgingly…took our nature upon himself to impart to us what was his, and to become both the Son of God and the Son of man in common with us" (2.12.2) Thus, says Calvin,

> …it was also imperative that he who was to become our Redeemer be true God and true man. It was his task to swallow up death. Who but the Life could do this? It was his task to conquer sin. Who but very Righteousness could do this? It was his task to rout the powers of world and air. Who but a power higher than world and air could do this? Now where does life or righteousness, or lordship and authority of heaven lie but with God alone? Therefore our most merciful God, when he willed that we be redeemed, made himself our Redeemer in the person of his only begotten Son [cf. Rom. 5:8] (2.12.2).

"The second requirement of our reconciliation with God," Calvin observes,

> was this: that man, who by his disobedience had become lost, should by way of remedy counter it with obedience, satisfy God's judgment, and pay the penalties for sin. Accordingly, our Lord came forth as true man and took the person and the name of Adam in order to take Adam's place in obeying the Father, to present our flesh as the price of satisfaction to God's righteous judgment, and, in the same flesh, to pay the penalty that we had deserved. In short, since neither as God alone could he feel death, nor as man alone could he overcome it, he coupled human nature with divine that to atone for sin he might submit the weakness of the one to death; and that, wrestling with death by the power of the other nature, he might win victory for us (2.12.3).

In addition, this Mediator is born from the line of God's covenantal promise, of the seed of Abraham and of David, the One promised in the

Old Testament and now bringing that promise to fulfillment in His Person and work. He is the Anointed One, the promised Messiah; and more importantly, as God's Anointed He takes on our nature, so that "clothed with our flesh he vanquished death and sin together that the victory and triumph might be ours" (2.12.3).

Reply to Objections and Errors
Calvin rejects all speculations that Christ would have "come-in-the-flesh" regardless of human sin. Here he refutes various notions of Andreas Osiander (1498–1552), an unorthodox Lutheran theologian who opposed among other things Luther's doctrine of Christ's imputed righteousness (2.12.4–7; also see 3.11.5–12).

It is worth noting that Calvin rejects the idea that Christ would have become man even if man had remained unfallen so that redemption was unnecessary. Christ was ever and only promised to us in the way of blood and sacrifice, and that for the expiation of our sins. It is foolish to speculate that His office would not require His death for our sakes. It is not biblically permissible to pursue such questions (2.12.4–5).

Chapter Thirteen: Christ Assumed the True Substance of Human Flesh

Orientation
This chapter mostly consists of a refutation of heresies. Specifically, Calvin contends against those who deny that Christ took on real human flesh. The positive teaching presented here is of a fundamental nature—that is, that Christ possesses a true human nature, and though He is fully human, He is also sinless. This chapter sets the stage for the more extended and technical chapter that follows which treats the Person of Christ comprehended in two natures.

Refutation of Heresies
The interest of Calvin's discussion at this point is not the divinity or the divine nature of Christ, for he treated this topic when he expounded upon the doctrine of the Trinity. Calvin thus considers the humanity or true human nature of Christ against ancient heresies. Already during the New Testament era, false teachers taught that Christ did not take on a genuine human

nature. In subsequent church history, certain Manicheans and Marcionites likewise taught that Christ's body was mere appearance, a mere phantom (2.13.1–2). Calvin rejects such views as nonsense inasmuch as they represent a gross distortion of various biblical texts, e.g., Philippians 2:5–8; 1 Corinthians 15:47.

The genealogies of the Gospels of Matthew and Luke make clear that Christ sprang from the line of David, and further back from the line of Adam (2.13.3). But coming from Adam's line does not mean Christ inherited the corruption of Adam's sin (cf. Rom. 5:12, 18). Rather, He "is true man, but without fault and corruption." The first Adam was of the earth, an earthly and natural man. The second Adam, Christ, was of heaven, heavenly and without sin (1 Cor. 15:47). Christ, then, is true and righteous man— free from inherited pollution—"because he was sanctified by the Spirit," and so took on our flesh, "pure and undefiled." "Whenever Scripture calls our attention to the purity of Christ, it is to be understood of his true human nature, for it would have been superfluous to say that God is pure" (2.13.4). Christ, then, is true man, yet sinless; and as true man, He is also true God.

Yet another erroneous view to which Calvin responds states that "if the Word of God became flesh, then he was confined within the narrow prison of an earthly body." Calvin rejoins by calling this view "mere impotence!" "For," he continues, "even if the Word in his immeasurable essence united with the nature of man into one person, we do not imagine that he was confined therein." Consider this: "the Son of God descended from heaven in such a way that, without leaving heaven, he willed to be borne in the virgin's womb, to go about the earth, and to hang upon the cross; yet he continuously filled the world even as he had done from the beginning!" (2.13.4).

Observations

This last point is what became known as the *extra-Calvinisticum,* a Lutheran sneer word against Calvin and the Reformed. Calvin insists that the incarnation means that though the Second Person of the Trinity was fully united to a human nature, He was never fully contained within that human nature. Hence the Word became flesh, but wasn't confined to the flesh. Christ's divinity could not be bound by His humanity, so the Son of God existed beyond *(extra)* the human nature.

Chapter Fourteen: How the Two Natures of the Mediator Make One Person

Orientation

Calvin now takes up what we might regard as the intricacies of the doctrine of Christ's Person, specifically how the Person of the Son of God exists in two natures, divine and human. Calvin shows high regard for the church's labors to define and understand this important doctrine. He has already demonstrated the necessity of the incarnation—the Son of God taking on human nature. Calvin has also already presented the case for Christ's divinity when he dealt with the doctrine of the Trinity. In the previous chapter Calvin defended Christ's genuine humanity against various errors. Now Calvin turns to explain how these two natures co-exist and relate to one another in the one Person of the Son. After presenting the orthodox understanding of the two natures, he then treats several Christological errors that must be refuted.

The Human and Divine Natures of Christ

If the doctrine of the Trinity presents us with the puzzle of oneness/threeness, the doctrine of Christ's two natures gives us the problem of oneness/twoness—one divine Person, but two natures, one divine, one human. Calvin begins chapter fourteen with John 1:14, "The Word became flesh," which shows us that our Mediator, the Son of God, has become also the Son of man. This does not take place through a confused commingling of the two natures together, a stirring together of the divine and the human. Rather, the divine and human natures remain distinct and altogether intact. The Son of God becomes the Son of man, but "not by confusion of substance"; rather, "by unity of person." That is, says Calvin, "we affirm [Christ's] divinity so joined and united with his humanity that each retains its distinctive nature unimpaired, and yet these two natures constitute one Christ" (2.14.1). This is the heart of the doctrine that Calvin proceeds to expound.

Calvin appeals to an analogy in order to help us grasp this doctrine, namely our own constitution as humans in which we consist of two substances, body and soul. Neither is mingled with the other, each remains distinct, yet a human being has both body and soul in the unity of personhood. Two diverse natures, each distinct and fundamental, make up one Person. "Thus, also, the Scriptures speak of Christ: they sometimes attribute to him what must be referred solely to his humanity, sometimes what belongs uniquely to his divinity; and sometimes what embraces both natures but fits neither alone" (2.14.1). The church fathers sought to capture this "union of the two natures," so earnestly depicted for us in Scripture, by speaking of "the communicating of properties" (*communication idiomatum*) (2.14.1). This refers to the way that the properties of the divine and human natures of Christ are communicated or interchanged in the unity of His Person—which means, for Calvin, the interchange takes place in the Person of Christ. This is not an interchange between the natures themselves, for this would produce a commingling and confusion of the natures.

Calvin cites many texts that refer either exclusively to Christ's divinity (cf. John 8:58; Col. 1:15, 17; John 17:5), or conversely, exclusively to His humanity (cf. Isa. 42:1; Luke 2:52; John 8:50; Mark 13:32; John 14:10; John 6:38). Either way, the "communicating of characteristics or properties" consists in the unity of Christ's Person, for He is true God and true man (2.14.2).

There are as well texts that "comprehend both natures at once, very many of which are to be found in John's Gospel..." (2.16.3). In such texts Christ's deity and humanity are together in view. In the union of His Person, He forgives sins (John 1:29), raises the dead, bestows righteousness, holiness, and salvation; and judges the living and the dead (John 5:21–23). So too as the God-man, He is the light of the world, the good shepherd, the only door, and the true vine (cf. John 9:5; 8:12; 10:9, 11; 15:1). Calvin expands on this theme:

> In the same sense we ought also to understand what we read in Paul: after the judgment "Christ will deliver the Kingdom to his God and Father" [1 Cor. 15:24]. Surely the Kingdom of the Son of God had no beginning and will have no end. But even as he lay concealed under the lowness of flesh and "emptied himself, taking the form of a servant" [Phil. 2:7], laying aside the splendor of majesty, he showed himself obedient to his Father. Having completed his subjection, "he was at last crowned with glory and honor" [Heb. 2:9], and exalted to the highest lordship that before him "every knee should bow" [Phil. 2:10]. So then will he yield to the Father his name and crown of glory, and whatever he has received from the Father, that "God may be all in all" [1 Cor. 15:28]. For what purpose were power and lordship given to Christ, unless by his hand the Father might govern us? In this sense, also, Christ is said to be seated at the right hand of the Father [cf. Mk. 16:19; Rom. 8:34]. Yet this is but for a time, until we enjoy

the direct vision of the Godhead.... But when as partakers in heavenly glory we shall see God as he is, Christ, having then discharged the office of Mediator, will cease to be the ambassador of his Father, and will be satisfied with that glory which he enjoyed before the creation of the world (2.14.3).

Even the name "Lord" belongs to Christ in the unity of His Person (2.14.3).

Christological Heresies

In this light Calvin turns to refute the errors of Nestorius, Eutyches, and Servetus (see 2.14.4–8). Briefly (perhaps too briefly) we sum up Calvin's discussion. Nestorius pulled the natures of Christ apart, destroying the unity of His Person, in effect giving us a "two personed" Christ or a "double Christ!" This means that the Person who became flesh, God's Son, is divine; the (other) Person, Jesus of Nazareth, is human. By dividing the two natures in this way, rather than distinguishing them, Nestorius ended up with forfeiting the union of Christ's two natures in His one Person as the Son of God. Calvin asserts that we must maintain that the two natures are united but not mingled in Christ's Person (2.14.4).

Eutyches fell into a different error. He commingled or mixed together the two natures of Christ, thereby destroying the distinctiveness of each nature, particularly compromising Christ's humanity. Eutyches aimed to keep the unity of Christ's Person; but he so merged the natures together that he compromised the integrity of each nature—so that Christ's humanity gets swallowed up into His divinity. This mixing of the two natures of Christ produced a muddle that misses Christological orthodoxy. Says Calvin, we must neither commingle nor pull apart Christ's two natures (2.14.4). Meanwhile, Servetus, that "deadly monster," advanced the wild notion that the incarnation, Christ becoming flesh, means His flesh was turned into God, i.e., Christ's "flesh was of the same substance with God, and...the Word was made man by the conversion of flesh into God." In this way Servetus obliterates Christ's true humanity (2.14.5).

Thus Calvin defends the church's understanding of the one Person and two natures of Christ against these errors, affirming the "hypostatic union," i.e., the union of the two natures in the one Person, the Son of God (see 2.14.5–8).

Observations

Calvin's stated Christological views line up with standard Chalcedonian Christology. He affirms the hypostatic union, and argues the standard Chalcedonian formula: the two natures of Christ exist in the unity of Christ's Person without mixture, without change, and without confusion. For Calvin, the importance of the Person of Christ is grounded in the work of salvation, for unless the Son of God takes on the human nature that sinned, as a pure and righteous man, He cannot be our Mediator or God's Lamb of sacrifice. But unless He is God, He cannot bear the penalty of our sin without Himself being consumed. The power of His divinity enables Him to undergo and come through the divine judgment against our sins.

Questions for Reflection and Discussion

1. Why does the Mediator have to be fully human and fully divine in order to achieve salvation? Why do theologies of salvation that fail to depend upon Christ as the God-man destroy the work of salvation itself? How does Calvin argue this point?

2. What is the tendency today—to compromise Christ's humanity? His divinity? Or mix them together? Give examples if you can.

3. What is the "hypostatic union"?

4. Who was Nestorius and what was his Christological error?

5. Who was Eutyches and what was his Christological error?

6. Who was Apollinarius and what was his Christological error?

7. What are the Christological errors of Jehovah's Witnesses and Mormons?

8. What does modernism, classic theological liberalism, teach regarding the Person of Christ? Is it orthodox?

⊸ 11 ⊷

The Work of Christ

Chapters 15–17 of Book Two

Chapter Fifteen: To Know the Purpose for Which Christ Was Sent by the Father, and What He Conferred upon Us, We Must Look above All at Three Things in Him: the Prophetic Office, Kingship, and Priesthood

Orientation

HAVING EXPOSITED AT length upon the Person of Christ, Calvin now turns his attention to the work of Christ. The remainder of Book Two takes up this theme. The current chapter explores the threefold office of Christ; the next expounds upon the articles of faith concerning Christ as expressed in the Apostles' Creed, that is, Christ's mighty acts of redemption; and the last chapter of Book Two takes up the meritorious nature of Christ's sacrificial work of atonement.

The Threefold Office of Christ

Christ discharges His Mediatorial office in the unity of His Person. This was the burden of the previous chapter concerning the incarnation and Christ's two natures. With chapter fifteen, Calvin explores the nature of the Mediatorial office. Some take Christ's name upon their lips yet they divest Him of His dignity and office and consequently worship a fantasy. "Therefore," writes Calvin, "in order that faith may find a firm basis for salvation in Christ, and thus rest in him, this principle must be laid down: the office enjoined upon Christ by the Father consists of three parts. For he was given to be prophet, king, and priest" (2.15.1). Indeed, the Son of God, who is the Son of man, is the Messiah, God's Anointed One, which bespeaks His office. He comes into the world with a task and a commission. "The title 'Christ' pertains to these three offices: for we know that under the law prophets as well as priests and kings were anointed with holy oil. Hence the illustrious name of 'Messiah' was also bestowed upon the promised Mediator" (2.15.2).

• *Christ as Prophet.* Christ was anointed by the Holy Spirit to be the prophet of the Father's mercy and grace—an anointing that extends to the church and its preaching of the gospel. Jesus, the Messiah, takes the words of Isa. 61:1–2 upon Himself. The Voice rumbled from heaven, both at the transfiguration and at Jesus' baptism, declaring that He is God's Beloved (Matt. 17:5; 3:17); and as such He is God's Anointed, anointed with the Holy Spirit. Christ, however, is no ordinary teacher. We must see that He is anointed as prophet "not only for himself that he might carry out the office of teaching, but for his whole body"—that is, so that "the power of the Spirit might be present in the continuing preaching of the gospel." This means that Jesus Christ is God's definitive prophet, for "the perfect doctrine he has brought has made an end to all prophecies" (2.15.2). As Calvin notes, "outside of Christ there is nothing worth knowing, and all who by faith perceive what he is like have grasped the whole immensity of heavenly benefits" (2.15.2).

• *Christ as King.* Coming to Christ's kingship, Calvin first emphasizes that it is spiritual in nature, which means it is eternal and cannot be vanquished. As King, Christ's reign "pertains to the whole body of the church," but it also pertains "to each individual member" (2.15.3). First, He preserves His church in the face of all adversaries and tribulations, for the church is founded on Christ's "eternal throne." Whenever we hear the biblical testimony concerning Christ's eternal power, we should remember that "the perpetuity of the church is secure in this protection." In fulfilling His royal office, Christ "assures the godly of the everlasting preservation of the church, and encourages them to hope, whenever it happens to be oppressed" (2.15.3). The devil can never destroy the church. Second, as His kingship applies to each one of us, we can hope for "blessed immortality," that is, "the better life," when we shall receive the "full fruit" of God's grace in the age to come (2.15.3).

Calvin is jealous to accent the spiritual character of Christ's kingship. The hardships and trials we face under Christ's cross are enough to remind us that we seek sanctuary beyond the wretchedness of this earthly life. "For this reason we ought to know that the happiness promised us in Christ does not consist in outward advantages—such as leading a joyous and peaceful life, having rich possessions, being safe from all harm, and abounding with delights such as the flesh commonly longs after. No, our happiness belongs to the heavenly life!" (2.15.4). Christ gives us what we need for the eternal salvation of our souls and to stand firm and undefeated against the assaults of every spiritual foe. "From this we infer that he rules—inwardly and outwardly—more for our own sake than his." This is why He bestows the gifts of the Spirit, and the Spirit Himself, to us (cf. Rom. 14:17). The kingdom of God is within us (Luke 17:20–21). Thus, Christ never leaves His own destitute; rather, He brings them to glory (2.15.4).

Christ's anointing was not with oil or aromatic perfumes; He was anointed with the Holy Spirit—Christ means "Anointed One" (cf. John 1:32; Luke 3:22). "Christ's Kingdom lies in the Spirit, not in earthly pleasures or pomp." As citizens of His kingdom we must forsake the kingdom of this world. In our King we "stand unconquered," surrounded by His "spiritual riches." Consequently, we are called Christians. We abide in the strength of our King. As our King He is our pastor; but as King He also holds a "rod of iron" to break the nations (cf. Ps. 2:9; Rev. 2:27; 12:5). Truly, toward the ungodly Christ is the Ruler who shall dash them to pieces like pottery [Ps. 2:9] (2.15.5).

• *Christ as Priest.* "As a pure and stainless Mediator [Christ] is by his holiness to reconcile us to God." But without Him, sinners are unclean, estranged, and at enmity with God. More, "…God's righteous curse bars our access to him, and God in his capacity as judge is angry toward us. Hence, an expiation must intervene in order that Christ as priest may obtain God's favor for us and appease his wrath. Thus Christ to perform this office had to come forward with a sacrifice" (2.15.6). That sacrifice is Christ Himself, for we are freed from our guilt and delivered from the penalty of our sins in the sacrifice of His death alone. He is our access to God; He is our everlasting Intercessor (cf. Heb. 9:22; 5:6; 7:15).

Believers find solace in knowing that Christ, their Intercessor, pleads their cause on the basis of His sacrifice. Even more, He enlists them as "his companions in this great office [Rev. 1:6]." We, too, are priests in Him, offering ourselves as sacrifices of service to the Lord; and, through Him we enter the heavenly sanctuary with our sacrificial prayers (2.15.6).

Chapter Sixteen: How Christ Has Fulfilled the Function of Redeemer to Acquire Salvation for Us. Here, also, His Death and Resurrection Are Discussed, as well as His Ascent into Heaven

Orientation

Calvin now considers the mighty acts of Christ for our redemption as expressed in the articles of the Apostles' Creed—thus His suffering under Pontius Pilate, crucifixion, death, burial, descent into hell, resurrection, ascension, reign at God's right hand, and return to judge the living and the dead.

Divine Wrath and Divine Love

Calvin begins chapter sixteen with these words, "What we have said so far concerning Christ must be referred to this one objective: condemned, dead, and lost in ourselves, we should seek righteousness, liberation, life, and salvation in him, as we are taught by that well-known saying of Peter: 'There is no other name under heaven given to men in which we must be saved' [Acts 4:12]" (2.16.1). In explaining the significance of the title "Christ" in the previous chapter, Calvin now discusses the meaning of the name "Jesus" (Savior), for Christ is what His name signifies. "Accordingly," writes Calvin, "the moment we turn away even slightly from him, our salvation, which rests firmly in him, gradually vanishes away" (2.16.1).

Christ is divinely sent to be our Savior, for God's wrath must be appeased. We abide under God's wrath and righteous vengeance. We are estranged from Him, deserving of His fury, under the curse of eternal death, enslaved to Satan, and destined to eternal punishment, except Christ intercede as our Advocate. Indeed, the good message of the gospel is that Christ has interceded for us in just this way, taking on Himself God's righteous judgment, washing us by His blood of all our sins, thereby expiating our sins and making satisfaction to God's justice for us. This is our peace. To sum up, "since our hearts cannot, in God's mercy, either seize upon life ardently enough or accept it with the gratefulness we owe, unless our minds are first struck and overwhelmed by fear of God's wrath and by dread of eternal death, we are taught by Scripture to perceive that apart from Christ, God is, so to speak, hostile to us, and his hand is armed for our destruction; [and we are taught] to embrace his benevolence and fatherly love in Christ alone" (2.16.2).

Beyond question, God cannot abide our unrighteousness; yet His love precedes our reconciliation in Christ. We deserve God's hatred, but God does not abandon the work of His hands. As Calvin states:

> However much we have brought death upon ourselves, yet [God] has created us unto life. Thus he is moved by pure and freely given love of us to receive us into grace.... Therefore, to take away all cause for enmity and to reconcile us utterly to himself, he wipes out all evil in us by the expiation set forth in the death of Christ; that we, who were previously unclean and impure, may show ourselves righteous and holy in his sight (2.16.3).

This work of Christ derives from God's love (1 John 4:19). Hence God is at enmity with us while, simultaneously, He is favorable and loving toward us. In His love God sends Christ to suffer His wrath on our behalf; and so we fix our eyes on Christ alone. Lest we think that God only begins to love us after redemption is accomplished, Calvin quotes the words of Augustine, demonstrating that God's love for us is grounded in eternity:

> The fact that we were reconciled through Christ's death must not be understood as if his Son reconciled us to him that he might now begin to love those whom he had hated. Rather, we have already been reconciled to him who loves us, with whom we were enemies on account of sin..." [cf. Rom. 5:8]. Therefore, he loved us even when we practiced enmity toward him and committed wickedness. Thus in a marvelous and divine way he loved us even when he hated us (2.16.4).

• *Christ Suffered under Pontius Pilate.* Christ does not only redeem us by His death, but also by His life of obedience. He fulfilled all righteousness; and His obedience was an obedience even unto death. Calvin further explains that Christ abolished sin, reconciled us to God, and acquired righteousness for us "by the whole course of his obedience" (2.16.5). That is what it means that He was subject to the law (Gal. 4:4–5). "Thus in his very baptism, also, he asserted that he fulfilled a part of righteousness in obediently carrying out his Father's commandment [Matt. 3:15]." Calvin is clear on this pont: "from the time when [Christ] took on the form of a servant, he began to pay the price of liberation in order to redeem us" (2.16.5). This isn't to disparage or even shortchange the centrality and focus of His saving work in His death, but none of His obedience is excluded from the work of salvation (see Phil. 2:7–8). Even Christ's death involves His obedience to lay down His life (2.16.5).

However, His death deserves special notice, for death is the curse of sin and that death-sentence threatens us at God's judgment seat. "Accordingly, Scripture first relates Christ's condemnation before Pontius Pilate, governor of Judea, to teach us that the penalty to which we were subject had been imposed upon this righteous man" (2.16.5). For Calvin, that Christ "suffered under Pontius Pilate" means He was condemned by Pilate. The peculiar form of Christ's death, based on a trial and judicial sentence, was necessary to transfer to Himself the condemnation determined for us. The sinless One had to die for the sinner. Hence, our guilt was transferred to Christ.

> To take away our condemnation, it was not enough for him to suffer any kind of death: to make satisfaction for our redemption a form of death had to be chosen in which he might free us both by transferring our condemnation to himself and by taking our guilt upon himself. If he had been murdered by thieves or slain in an insurrection by a raging mob, in such a death there would have been no evidence of satisfaction. But when he was arraigned before the judgment seat as a criminal, accused and pressed by testimony, and condemned by the mouth of the judge to die—we know by these proofs that he took the role of a guilty man and evildoer.... [Indeed] 'He was reckoned among the transgressors' [Mark 15:28,... cf. Isa. 53:12]. Why so? Surely that he might die in the place of the sinner, not of the righteous or innocent man. For he suffered death not because of innocence but because of sin (2.16.5).

Thus, when Pilate acquitted Christ and found no fault in Him, though that governor nevertheless condemned Him, we need to see "the person of a sinner and evildoer represented in Christ." The "shining innocence" of Christ also makes it clear that He "was burdened with another's sin rather than his own." Therefore,

> This is our acquittal: the guilt that held us liable for punishment has been transferred to the head of the Son of God [Isa. 53:12]. We must, above all, remember this substitution, lest we tremble and remain anxious throughout life—as if God's righteous vengeance, which the Son of God has taken upon himself, still hung over us (2.16.5).

The transfer of our guilt onto Christ is something Calvin wants us to remember every day of our lives, for it frees us from fear and anxiety (2.16.5).

• *Christ Crucified.* In Christ being "crucified," we are shown that His death was under divine accursedness, for the cross—hanging on the tree—

signified accursedness (Gal, 3:13–14; 1 Pet. 2:14; Deut. 21:23). Christ shed His blood as a sacrifice for us, to cleanse us, and to satisfy God's justice (2.16.6). He died so that we would not be swallowed by death (cf. Heb. 2:14–15). His crucifixion and death are an expiatory sacrifice for sin, for the curse of our sin was transferred to Christ's flesh. Although this curse was upon Him, He was not crushed by it. Rather, He crushed, broke, and scattered the whole force of that curse (cf. Col. 2:14–15). His shed blood is not only an appeasement of wrath, but a laver that washes us pure (cf. Eph. 5:26; Titus 3:5; Rev. 1:5) (2.16.6).

• *Christ Dead and Buried.* As for Christ's death and burial, again, Calvin accents its substitutionary character. He died and was buried *for us* (Heb. 2:9). "By dying, he assured that we would not die, or—which is the same thing—redeemed us to life by his own death" (2.16.7). Christ dies to conquer death, to crush the head of the one who had the power of death, the devil, and to deliver us from fear of death (1 Pet. 3:22; Heb. 2:14–15). This is the first great benefit of Christ's death and burial; the second is our own death, i.e., the mortification of our old self so that we can live new life in Him (cf. Rom. 6:4–5; Gal. 2:19; 6:14; Col. 3:3). "Therefore, in Christ's death and burial a twofold blessing is set forth for us to enjoy: liberation from the death to which we had been bound, and mortification of our flesh" (2.16.7).

• *Christ Descended into Hell.* Calvin next offers an explanation of the meaning of the phrase "descended into hell." In short this expression refers to the spiritual torment Christ endured for us. He underwent the severity of God's vengeance and wrath (cf. Isa. 53:5; Ps. 22:1; Matt. 27:46) (2.16.11). Others interpret this article of the Creed very differently. Calvin considers these views and offers rebuttals of them. For Calvin, Christ's descent into hell signifies the hellish penalty He suffered on the cross (2.16.10). Calvin reminds us of the words Christ uttered from the cross, "My God, my God, why hast thou forsaken me?" (Ps. 22:1; Matt. 27:46). These words teach us that Christ "bore the weight of divine serverity, since he was 'stricken and afflicted' [cf. Isa. 53:5] by God's hand, and experienced all the signs of a wrathful and avenging God" (2.16.11). (Calvin offers an extended defense of this view in the next section; see the whole of 2.16.12.)

• *Christ Rose Again from the Dead.* It is in Christ's resurrection, however, inseparable from His death, where the victory of our faith over death lies.

Although Christ's cross and Christ's resurrection produce different effects, they must not be separated. Through His death we have "the complete fulfillment of salvation," says Calvin; nevertheless, through His resurrection we are born to a living hope (1 Pet. 1:3). Scripture shows us that through Christ's death, sin and death are wiped out; through His resurrection, righteousness is restored and life raised up; and so through resurrection, the saving and healing power of Christ's death is manifested in us. Indeed, Christ was raised for our justification (Rom. 4:25) (2.16.13).

We must resist the artificial separation of Christ's death and resurrection. Calvin bids us to understand that when Scripture mentions Christ's death alone, "we are to understand at the same time what belongs to his resurrection" and vice-versa. Synecdoche, i.e., a part for the whole or a whole for the part, applies to such words. Believers share not only in Christ's death but also in His resurrection. Being engrafted into Him, we seek to walk in newness of life (Rom. 6:4; Col. 3:3, 5). Furthermore, Christ's resurrection from the dead guarantees our own resurrection; His victory over death certifies and secures our own bodily resurrection, and the attendant victory over sin's curse (1 Cor. 15:12–26) (2.16.13).

• *Christ Ascended into Heaven.* Christ also ascended into heaven, where He now reigns. He has laid aside His "mean and lowly state of mortal life and the shame of the cross," and now with His resurrection and ascension has begun "to show forth his glory and power more fully" (2.16.14). Even more, Christ "truly inaugurated his Kingdom only at his ascension into heaven," says Calvin (see Eph. 4:10). Although He is no longer with us in His flesh, He abides with us by His Spirit (see John 16:7, 14; 14:18–19; Matt. 28:20) (2.16.14).

• *Christ Seated at the Right Hand of the Father.* That Christ was received into glory and sits at the Father's right hand declares that He is "invested with lordship over heaven and earth" and possesses the kingdom committed to Him, awaiting Judgment Day (see Eph. 1:20–21; Phil. 2:9; 1 Cor. 15:27; Eph. 1:22). Here we see the purpose of Christ's session or "sitting": "that both heavenly and earthly creatures may look with admiration upon his majesty, be ruled by his hand, obey his nod, and submit to his power." But some wonder what it means that Stephen, when he was being martyred, saw Christ standing (Acts 7:55). This should cause us no concern. As Calvin explains, Christ's sitting at the Father's right hand "means nothing else than to preside at the heavenly judgment seat" (2.16.15).

The benefits of Christ's ascension and reign are, says Calvin, threefold:

> First [our faith] understands that the Lord by his ascent to heaven opened the way into the Heavenly Kingdom, which had been closed through Adam…. Secondly, as faith recognizes, it is to our great benefit that Christ resides with the Father. For, having entered a sanctuary not made with hands, he appears before the Father's face as our constant advocate and intercessor. Thus he turns the Father's eyes to his own righteousness to avert his gaze from our sins…. Thirdly, faith comprehends his might, in which reposes our strength, power, wealth, and glorying against hell. "When he ascended into heaven he led captivity captive" [Eph. 4:8], and despoiling his enemies, he enriched his own people, and daily lavishes spiritual riches upon them (2.16.16).

• *Christ Will Return as Judge.* Finally, coming to the last article of the Creed concerning Christ's mighty acts of redemption, we arrive at the words, "he will come to judge the living and the dead." Truly, Christ shall return, visibly, in the flesh, and in His glory—i.e., "with the glow of immortality, with the boundless power of divinity, [and] with a guard of angels" (cf. Acts 1:11; Matt. 24:30). He ushers in Judgment Day—all shall come before Him, both "the living and the dead." No one shall escape His verdict (cf. Matt. 25:31–33; 1 Thess. 4:16–17) (2.16.17).

But connected with that, says Calvin, we must perceive "a wonderful consolation," namely—

> …that we perceive judgment to be in the hands of him who has already destined us to share with him the honor of judging [cf. Matt. 19:28]! Far indeed is he from mounting his judgment seat to condemn us! How could our most merciful Ruler destroy his people? How could the Head scatter his own members? How could our Advocate condemn his clients? For if the apostle dares exclaim that with Christ interceding for us there is no one who can come forth to condemn us [Rom. 8:34, 33], it is much more true, then, that Christ as Intercessor will not condemn those whom he has received into his charge and protection (2.16.18).

What wonderful assurance! Our Redeemer is our Judge—our Judge is our Redeemer!

Thus in all these phrases of the Apostles' Creed, which sum up in so few words the main points of our salvation, we see that the whole of our redemption rests in Christ. No part of it has another source: our salvation is in His name; our gifts, in His anointing; our strength, in His dominion; our purity, in His conception; our gentleness, in His birth; our redemption, in His passion; our acquittal, in His condemnation; our remission from curse, in His cross; our satisfaction, in His sacrifice; our purification, in His blood; our reconciliation, in His descent into hell; our mortification of the flesh, in His tomb; our newness of life, in His resurrection; our immortality, in the same; our inheritance of the heavenly kingdom, in His entrance into heaven; our protection, security, abundant supply of all blessings, in His kingdom; our untroubled expectation of judgment, in His power given Him to judge (2.16.19).

Observation

In expositing the articles of the Apostles' Creed pertaining to Christ, Calvin has grounded redemption in the historical labors of Christ in the flesh. The theology of the cross is founded on the work of Christ in the flesh. In fact, Calvin shall next consider the theological significance of the person and work of Christ for the blessing of forgiveness and pardon. We do well to see this unbreakable connection. The person and work of Christ bring about a theological reality and truth pertaining to the believing sinner's status before God, namely the changed status of estrangement from God to reconciliation and peace, from guilt to innocence, from being under wrath to being under God's favor, from dirty to clean, from being "not my people," to being "my people."

Chapter Seventeen: Christ Rightly and Properly Said to Have Merited God's Grace and Salvation for Us

Orientation

Now Calvin takes up the question of merit, a term that has liabilities and is open to misunderstanding. In fact, Calvin responds to "certain perversely subtle men" who wish to abandon all talk of merit in relation to salvation or to Christ's work of salvation for us. How can merit and mercy stand together? If we are saved by divine mercy, then there is no room for merit; if we are saved by merit, then mercy is excluded. Calvin addresses this issue and answers this perverse subtlety.

The Unity of Mercy and Merit

For Calvin, the denial of merit, i.e., claiming divine mercy absent merit, trivializies Christ's sacrifice and turns Him into "a mere instrument or minister" of salvation. This is a mistake. Scripture does not treat Him as a mere instrument; rather, Scripture portrays Him as "the Author" of redemption, as "the Prince of life" (cf. Acts 3:15). To be sure, says Calvin, man as man cannot merit before God. Even the human nature of Christ cannot merit before God. "For no worthiness will be found in man to deserve God's favor" (2.17.1). It is therefore quite wrong to regard Christ as merely an instrument for redemption.

Christ, as very God and very man, as our Head, is "the very foundation of grace," as Augustine says. In treating the question of Christ's meriting for us, notes Calvin, we must see that it is grounded in "God's ordinance," which is "the first cause." "For God solely of his own good pleasure appointed him Mediator to obtain salvation for us." This exposes the absurdity of playing merit against God's mercy. There is no conflict between one thing subordinate to another. "For this reason nothing hinders us from asserting that men are freely justified by God's mercy alone, and at the same time that Christ's merit, subordinate to God's mercy, also intervenes on our behalf." Salvation is born of divine mercy. In love God appoints His Son to be our Mediator, who comes to take on our flesh and our sin; and God has determined to accept Christ's work of redemption for us. "Both God's free favor and Christ's obedience, each in its degree, are fitly opposed to our works." Again, Christ could not merit anything for us unless God appointed Him to that task and determined to accept His sacrifice as appeasement of wrath—and this according to God's good pleasure. In summary, "inasmuch as Christ's merit depends upon God's grace alone, which has ordained this manner of salvation for us, it is just as properly opposed to all human righteousness as God's grace is" (2.17.1).

God's love is the highest cause and origin of our redemption (John 3:16). Faith in Christ is the second and proximate cause. "For if we attain righteousness by a faith that reposes in him, we ought to seek the matter of our salvation in him" (2.17.2). Many biblical passages bear this out—e.g., in the words of 1 John 4:10, "Herein is love, not that we loved God, but that he loved us, and sent his Son *to be* the propitiation for our sins." Propitiation means to appease wrath; and that idea is important for us to grasp. "For, in some ineffable [indescribable] way, God loved us and yet was angry toward us at the same time, until he became reconciled to us in Christ" (see 1 John 2:2; Col. 1:19–20; 2 Cor. 5:19, 21; Eph. 2:3, 15–16) (2.17.2). Christ is, in this sense, a means to an end, for He gives to us "something of what he has acquired" (2.17.2).

The Merits of Christ

We may therefore legitimately speak of Christ's merits and of His meriting salvation for us. As Calvin states:

> By his obedience...Christ truly acquired and merited grace for us with his Father. Many passages of Scripture surely and firmly attest this. I take it to be a commonplace that if Christ made satisfaction for our sins, if he paid the penalty owed by us, if he appeased God by his obedience—in short, if as a righteous man he suffered for unrighteous men—then he acquired salvation for us by his righteousness, which is tantamount to deserving it. But, as Paul says, "We were reconciled, and received reconciliation through his death [Rom. 5:10–11 p.]. But reconciliation has no place except where an offense precedes it. The meaning therefore is: God, to whom we were hateful because of sin, was appeased by the death of his Son to become favorable toward us (2.17.3).

The merits of Christ are nothing else than the work of Christ, particularly the shedding of His blood by which we are cleansed (Heb. 9:22, 26). His death is an expiation of our sins (1 John 1:7; Matt. 26:28; Luke 22:30). He pays redemption's price, for He takes away our sins (John 1:29). Calvin points to an abundance of texts, especially from Hebrews, which directly show that salvation is not by divine fiat, a mere declaration of pardon. Grace sends a Mediator, and He is the way of pardon through genuine sacrifice—indeed, the power of Christ's sacrifice is in "expiating, appeasing, and making satisfaction." Christ became a curse for us (see Gal. 3:13). Commenting on this text, Calvin writes, "It was superfluous, even absurd, for Christ to be burdened with a curse, unless it was to acquire righteousness for others by paying what they owed" (2.17.4). When Peter says, "He...bore our sins...on the tree," he means that "the burden of condemnation, from which we were freed, was laid upon Christ" (2.17.4; cf. Eph. 5:2).

Calvin further explains that Christ endured our death penalty (Rom.

3:24–25). We have been ransomed through His blood (1 Pet. 1:18–19). He paid the price and satisfied divine justice (1 Cor. 6:20; 1 Tim. 2:5–6). We are redeemed by His blood, which is "the forgiveness of sins" (Col. 1:14). Christ's shed blood corresponds to satisfaction for our sakes (Col. 2:14). Galatians 2:21 ("for if righteousness *come* by the law, then Christ is dead in vain") shows us, says Calvin, that "we must seek from Christ what the law would give if anyone could fulfill it; or, what is the same thing, that we obtain through Christ's grace what God promised in the law for our works" (cf. Lev. 18:5) (2.17.5). Indeed, Christ took the burden of the law's requirements upon Himself (both positively and negatively, both fulfilling its just demands and suffering its penalties for our sakes) in order to reconcile us to God. It is as if we had kept the law (cf. Acts 13:39; Gal. 4:4–5). Christ subjects Himself to the law "to acquire righteousness for us" by "undertaking to pay what we could not pay" (2.17.5). This is why we may speak of the imputation of righteousness (Rom. 4). "For the righteousness found in Christ alone is reckoned as ours" (2.17.5).

The outcome of Christ's work *for us* is that satisfaction has been made for *our sins*, the requirements of the law have been honored *for our* redemption, and the Father is favorable toward us, and this is *our* reconciliation. Salvation is thus bestowed by God's love, and achieved through Christ's merit.

Christ Needed No Merits for Himself

Calvin concludes this chapter by responding briefly to a question raised by certain medieval theologians, that is, whether Christ merited anything for Himself. Calvin regards this query as a "stupid curiosity," but he is not in doubt regarding the biblical and theological answer to it. "What need was there for God's only Son to come down in order to acquire something new for himself?" (2.17.6). Christ came not to merit anything for Himself, but to merit salvation for us. We are the enemies of God that need redemption and pardon; He is God's beloved Son who is sent to us according to God's love (cf. Rom. 5:10; John 3:16; Rom. 8:32, 35, 37). Christ is obedient for our sakes, and sanctifies Himself for our sakes (John 17:19). "For he who gave away the fruit of his holiness to others testifies that he acquired nothing for himself." In short, Christ forgot Himself in pursuing our salvation (2.17.6).

Questions for Reflection and Discussion

1. The word "Messiah" is a title, not a name. What does this title mean and signify? Why is it important to see Christ's work as a divine commission?

2. How can we be comforted in knowing that God loves us even while we were "children of wrath"? Look at Romans 5:6–11.

3. Why don't more Christians live with the kind of assurance Calvin speaks of in connection with Christ's work *for us*? What can be done to strengthen assurance in the life of believers?

4. Christ is our Prophet, Priest, and King—explain how this threefold office of Christ comprehends all that Christ does. For example, Jesus calls Himself the Good Shepherd. How is Jesus the Good Shepherd as Prophet, Priest, and King?

5. Calvin speaks of two benefits that come to us from Christs' resurrection. What are they and how can we make use of each in our Christian life?

6. Calvin mentions three benefits that result from Christ's ascension and session. Name them. Which of them do we most often forget and why?

7. How can we face Judgment Day with biblical assurance? In other words, how can we know our assurance is proper, and not mere presumption?

8. Calvin tells us that Christ's kingdom does not consist of the blessings and benefits of this life which are fading and precarious. In that light, how should we assess the health-and-wealth gospel propagated today, often by those who are dispensationalists? What is wrong-headed in that message?

9. Many moderns are offended and scandalized by the doctrine of penal substitution, that is, that Christ suffered the wrath of God on the cross.

Respond to the charge that this doctrine gives us a God of violence, a Father who may be likened to a child-beater, making His Son suffer.

10. What is the ransom theory of the atonement? What is the example theory of the atonement? What are the serious errors and "moments of truth" in each theory?

11. What do each of the following words mean: atonement, propitiation, expiation, redemption, and reconciliation? Cumulatively, what do these words teach us about Christ's work to save us?

Institutes of the Christian Religion

Book Three

The Way in Which We Receive the Grace of Christ:
What Benefits Come to Us from It, and What Effects Follow

≈ 12 ≈

The Holy Spirit—Our Bond to Christ:
Faith and Repentance

Chapters 1–5 of Book Three

Chapter One: The Things Spoken Concerning Christ Profit Us by the Secret Working of the Spirit

Orientation

WITH BOOK THREE of the *Institutes* Calvin wants us to comprehend how the blessings which the Father committed to His Son come to reach us, seeing that the Son did not receive them for His own use. Rather, the Son bestows these blessings to poor and needy sinners like ourselves. This is the burden of Book Three. We must not, however, create a division where there is only a distinction. It is not that Christ's Person and work are left behind, for part of the title of the third Book is, "The Way in which We Receive the Grace of Christ." We are still treating the knowledge of God as our Redeemer, with His work now fastened to the Holy Spirit whose operations bring us into union with Christ.

With Book Three, then, Calvin explores the believer's appropriation of Christ's work through the Holy Spirit. It is here that Christ's work and the Holy Spirit's secret operation come together. An overview of the chapters under consideration here shows that Calvin begins, in chapter one, by providing an introduction to the work of the Holy Spirit. Next Calvin gives an extended exposition of faith in chapter two. Chapter three considers the flip side of faith, which is repentance. Chapters four and five are disputative or argumentative in nature, treating the medieval scholastic doctrine of penance and auricular confession, as well as indulgences and purgatory.

The Holy Spirit's Work

The principal issue to be considered is how believers can seize upon Christ's saving work in order to benefit by it. "We must understand," states Calvin,

> that as long as Christ remains outside of us, and we are separated from him, all that he has suffered and done for the salvation of the human race remains useless and of no value for us. Therefore, to share with us what he has received from the Father, he had to become ours and to dwell within us. For this reason, he is called "our Head" [Eph. 4:15], and "the first-born among many brethren" [Rom. 8:29]. We also, in turn, are said to be "engrafted into him" [Rom. 11:17], and to "put on Christ" [Gal. 3:27]; for, as I have said, all that he possesses is nothing to us until we grow into one body with him (3.1.1).

Since it is beyond doubt that not all embrace Christ by faith and commune with Him, we need to understand how we can become part of Christ. Therefore we need to examine "the secret energy of the Spirit, by which we come to enjoy Christ and all his benefits" (3.1.1). For "the Holy Spirit is the bond by which Christ effectually unites us to himself" (3.1.1). Notice, Christ isn't passive in this work! *He* unites us to Himself in the Spirit.

The Spirit who indwells believers first indwelt Christ. The Holy Spirit is called the "Spirit of sanctification" (2 Thess. 2:13; 1 Pet. 1:2; Rom. 1:4). He is "the root and seed of heavenly life in us." He is the "Spirit of the Father," the "Spirit of the Son," and is called the "Spirit of Christ" (Rom. 8:9). He is the "life-giving Spirit" (1 Cor. 15:45). The Spirit is coupled with the Father and the Son in holy benediction and the work of our salvation (cf. 2 Cor. 13:14; Rom. 5:5) (3.1.2). He is given titles that reflect His work. He is the "Spirit of adoption" (Rom. 8:15; Gal. 4:6), the "guarantee and seal" of our inheritance (2 Cor. 1:22), and He is "life" (Rom. 8:10). Our Lord calls Him "fire" (Luke 3:16) and the "spring" from which issues all heavenly riches to us (John 4:14).

The practical impact of this is important to see. For "until our minds become intent upon the Spirit, Christ, so to speak, lies idle because we coldly contemplate him as outside ourselves—indeed, far from us" (3.1.3). Calvin explains that we remain coldly aloof from Christ until He becomes our Head. Only through "union with Christ" do the benefits of Christ apply to us, by which we are assured that His saving work is not unprofitable. This union makes us flesh of His flesh and bone of His bone (Eph. 5:30). We become one with Him. This doesn't mean that we are deified or absorbed into

Christ, as if our humanity is mingled with His divinity. No! But we are truly part of Him, and this union with Christ is the way we are bonded or connected and receive all that Christ has accomplished for His people (3.1.3).

This union is not apart from faith or the Holy Spirit, for the Spirit alone is the bond that secures this marriage between Christ and His members (3.1.3), and faith is the Spirit's principal work (3.1.4). Paul depicts the Spirit as "the inner-teacher" so that the promise of the gospel "penetrates into our minds, a promise that would otherwise only strike the air or beat upon our ears." The Holy Spirit is the "source" of our faith; He is also the source of our assurance that we belong to Christ (2 Thess. 2:13; 1 John 3:24; 4:13). It is the Spirit's office to teach us inwardly and call to mind what Christ had taught verbally (John 14:17). We are baptized in the Spirit, the One who illumines our hearts and minds, draws us to faith, and brings us to rebirth and renewal (cf. Luke 3:16; 2 Cor. 3:6; John 6:44; 12:32; 17:6; 2 Cor. 5:17). The Holy Spirit also consecrates us to be God's temples (cf. 1 Cor. 3:16ff.; 2 Cor. 6:16; Eph. 2:21).

Chapter Two: Faith: Its Definition Set Forth, and Its Properties Explained

The chief work of the Holy Spirit is to bond us to Christ through faith, drawing us to Him and giving us ears to hear and eyes to see, renewing our wills, and changing our hearts. It is very important therefore that we understand what we mean by "faith."

At the beginning of this chapter Calvin provides a summary of our sin and ruin, which the law exposes, and of the depravity that clings to us, leaving us unable to rescue ourselves, and of the only remedy in Christ our Redeemer. Then Calvin offers the reminder that we need "firm faith" which embraces Christ and rests in His mercy. For that, however, we need the Holy Spirit to arouse us and draw us to seek Him (3.2.1).

Faith Defined

Before providing us with a definition of faith, Calvin wants to clear away some misconceptions that we have inherited from the Schoolmen (i.e., the medieval scholastic theologians), especially the notion of "implicit faith"—a doctrine that bids believers to place their faith in the church and its prescribed teaching even when they don't grasp or understand for themselves what is to be believed; or worse, a faith which remains ignorant of Christ but trusts in the judgment of the church. "Faith," writes Calvin, "rests not on ignorance, but on knowledge. And this is, indeed, knowledge not only of God but of the divine will" (3.2.2). We obtain salvation "when we know that God is our merciful Father, because of reconciliation effected through Christ [2 Cor. 5:18–19], and that Christ has been given to us as righteousness, sanctification, and life" (3.2.2). Thus we need "explicit recognition of the divine goodness upon which our righteousness rests" (3.2.2). Ignorance tempered by humility and reverence for the church ought not to be termed "faith." This breeds superstition (3.2.3).

While Calvin freely admits that faith always is clouded with error and doubt, in that sense an "implicit faith" does exist; nevertheless, such an implicit faith must possess the seeds of *true* faith to be *saving faith* (3.2.4). The "preparation" for faith may likewise be called implicit faith, which exhibits an openness and teachableness for the truth of the gospel and the things of God. This is very different from "sheer ignorance," says Calvin (3.2.5).

True faith isn't ignorance but "the true knowledge of Christ," that is, "if we receive him as he is offered by the Father: namely, clothed with his gospel" (3.2.6). For Calvin, faith is dependent upon God's Word. We know Christ, the object of faith, as He is "clothed with his gospel" (3.2.6). In the Word alone are we shown God's kindness and love in his gracious promises (3.2.6). Faith, then, is "a knowledge of God's will toward us, perceived from his Word" (3.2.6). Faith must keep to the Word and to Christ as presented in the Word. The Word supports and sustains faith. "Therefore, take away the Word and no faith will then remain." "The Word itself," says Calvin, "however it is imparted to us, is like a mirror in which faith may contemplate God." Faith not only affirms that God exists, it also embraces a knowledge of His will for us (3.2.6).

Hence, a partial definition of faith is that it is "a knowledge of God's will toward us, perceived from his Word" (3.2.6). What is missing is that God is favorable toward us, that is, the content of the gospel must fill up faith. To believe in Christ for salvation, we must be "attracted to seek him." "Accordingly, we need the promise of grace, which can testify to us that the Father is merciful; since we can approach him in no other way, and upon grace alone the heart of man can rest" (3.2.7). God in His love and mercy attracts us to Himself. The gospel must form the content of faith, otherwise we would not seek God for help (cf. Ps. 89:14, 24; 92:2; 98:3; 100:5; 108:4; 115:1; 36:5; 40:10f.; 117:2). God gives abundant witness that He is "well disposed toward us." "But...the sole pledge of his love is Christ, without whom the signs of hatred and wrath are everywhere evident" (3.2.7). Our hearts, then, rest in God's goodness.

What, then, is the nature of true faith? Calvin defines it as "a firm and certain knowledge of God's benevolence toward us, founded upon the truth of the freely given promise in Christ, both revealed to our minds and sealed upon our hearts through the Holy Spirit" (3.2.7).

Before Calvin explores this definition in more depth (see 3.2.14–15) he wants to remove another "worthless" scholastic distinction, namely the one drawn between "formed" and "unformed" faith. Unformed faith is mere assent to the truth of the gospel without the works of love. Formed faith is assent combined with works of love. In other words, faith is "formed" when piety is added to assent. For Calvin, unformed faith is not faith at all. Although certain medieval theologians conjured up this idea, giving the word faith to an assenting act of the mind void of a life of virtue, love, or fear of God, Calvin maintains that this is pure invention. Faith cannot be conceived apart from love, although the virtue of love is in no way meritorious for salvation. As he says, "faith can in no wise be separated from devout disposition" (3.2.8). While faith certainly involves an assenting act, says Calvin, this is "more of the heart than of the brain, and more of the disposition than of the understanding" (3.2.8). Calvin gathers an arsenal of arguments to further refute this notion, using principally 1 Corinthians 13:2 (see 3.2.9–11).

Calvin also considers the manner in which some of the reprobate seem to have faith. To be sure, only the elect are the recipients of true faith, yet "the reprobate are sometimes affected by almost the same feeling as the elect, so that even in their own judgment they do not in any way differ from the elect." The Spirit sometimes works in their lives—Calvin calls it a "lower working"—that shows some of the traits or shadows of faith but comes short of the reality (3.2.11). That faith can be copied or mimicked explains why there is such a thing as false versus true faith (3.2.12). In addition, Scripture shows us that the word "faith" can be used in a variety of senses (3.2.13).

Exploring the Definition of Faith

Now Calvin returns to his definition of faith earlier presented (see 3.2.7), treating its individual parts. He starts with knowledge. What is meant when we define faith as "knowledge"? Calvin does not mean to suggest that faith is mere comprehension of things we perceived through our senses. Neither is it a question of rational proof. The knowledge of faith is certainly "far more lofty than all understanding." It is often linked to "recognition," for we know we are God's children (cf. Eph. 1:17; 4:13; Col. 1:9; 3:10; 1 Tim. 2:4) (3.2.14). The knowledge-aspect of faith is more a persuasion; it "consists in assurance rather than in comprehension" (3.2.14).

Faith also consists of certainty. Faith is knowledge but also "sure and firm" knowledge—i.e., a "solid constancy of persuasion." "For, as faith is not content with a doubtful and changeable opinion, so is it not content with an obscure and confused conception; but requires full and fixed certainty, such as men are wont to have from things experienced and proved" (3.2.15). Calvin acknowledges that some doubt God's mercy toward them and struggle with the comforting promise of the gospel. They endure "miserable anxiety." In their mind, grace is confined to a narrow circle, available for all but themselves. This sentiment comes well short of that feeling of "full assurance that in the Scriptures is always attributed to faith." Confidence, then, is born of assurance. Confidence begets boldness. "This boldness arises only out of a sure confidence in divine benevolence and salvation" (3.2.15).

The Certainty of Faith

Calvin enlarges on the above discussion. Since he defines faith as knowledge or, more precisely, as a "certain" knowledge, the reality of faith as manifested in our lives is born of certainty. Calvin's passion on this point is noteworthy: "Here, indeed, is the chief hinge on which faith turns: that we do not regard the promises of mercy that God offers as true only outside ourselves, but not at all in us; rather that we make them ours by inwardly embracing them. Hence, at last is born that confidence which Paul elsewhere calls 'peace' [Rom. 5:1]" (3.2.16). Calvin amplifies his comments on this score: "Now it is an assurance that renders the conscience calm and peaceful before God's judgment. Without it the conscience must be harried by disturbed alarm, and almost torn to pieces; unless perhaps, forgetting God and self, it for the moment sleeps. And truly for the moment, for it does not long enjoy that miserable forgetfulness without the memory of divine judgment repeatedly coming back and very violently rending it" (3.2.16). This brings Calvin to conclude that for a person to be a true believer, he must be "convinced by a firm conviction that God is a kindly and well-disposed Father toward him," and that God promises all things "on the basis of his generosity." The true believer clasps "an undoubted expectation of salvation." Calvin further states that "no one hopes well in the Lord except him who confidently glories in the inheritance of the Heavenly Kingdom. No man is a believer, I say, except him who, leaning upon the assurance of his salvation, confidently triumphs over the devil and death…" (3.2.16). For Calvin, believers only grasp God's goodness by gathering it from "the fruit of great assurance."

Now, the certainty of faith is not to suggest that believers do not face temptation. Calvin is fully aware of this struggle. God's children are plagued with inescapable afflictions to their faith.

> Surely, while we teach that faith ought to be certain and assured, we cannot imagine any certainty that is not tinged with doubt, or any assurance that is not assailed by some anxiety. On the other hand, we say that believers are in perpetual conflict with their own unbelief. Far, indeed, are we from putting their consciences in any peaceful repose, undisturbed by any tumult at all. Yet, once again, we deny that, in whatever way they are afflicted, they fall away and depart from the certain assurance received from God's mercy (3.2.17).

No doubt, every believer knows this faith struggle. As Calvin explains: "the godly heart feels in itself a division because it is partly imbued with sweetness from its recognition of the divine goodness, partly grieves in bitterness from an awareness of its calamity; partly rests upon the promise of the gospel, partly trembles at the evidence of its own iniquity; partly rejoices at the expectation of life, partly shudders at death." All of this is reflective of faith's "imperfection." Life ever presents us with obstacles and hindrances, so that "it never goes so well with us that we are wholly cured of the disease of unbelief and entirely filled and possessed by faith." This explains, too, the constant assault we are under. Unbelief, attached to our fleshly nature, "rises up to attack the faith that has been inwardly conceived" (3.2.18).

Does this mean, then, that the certainty of faith is destroyed? Calvin replies, "Not at all. For even if we are distracted by various thoughts, we are not on that account completely divorced from faith. Nor if we are troubled on all sides by the agitation of unbelief, are we for that reason immersed in its abyss." To suffer assault is not to suffer loss of faith, but it is to know struggle. The conflict, however, always ends this way: "that faith ultimately triumphs over those difficulties which besiege and seem to imperil it" (3.2.18).

Faith that is weak and immature, and even ignorant in part, is nonetheless genuine faith (3.2.19). Consider 1 Corinthians 13:9, 12: "we know in part and prophesy in part"; and we "see in a mirror dimly." Though faith is weak, even a small drop of faith is real faith and adequate, though mixed with "doubt," "trepidation," and "the wrappings of ignorance" (3.2.20). But

the Word of God serves as a shield for faith (cf. Eph. 6:16). The promises
of God's Word reassure and fortify our faith. Even when faith is sorely as-
saulted by unbelief, "its light is never so extinguished or snuffed out that it
does not at least lurk as it were beneath the ashes" (3.2.21). Faith is strengthened, too, in seeing the severity of God's judgment upon the wicked. Even
the Gentiles are taught to learn from God's rejection of the Jews (3.2.22).
Faith looks only and completely to Christ.

> For we await salvation from him not because he appears to us afar
> off, but because he makes us, engrafted into his body, participants not
> only in all his benefits but also in himself.... [H]is righteousness over-
> whelms your sins; his salvation wipes out your condemnation; with his
> worthiness he intercedes that your unworthiness may not come before
> God's sight. Surely this is so: We ought not to separate Christ from
> ourselves or ourselves from him. Rather we ought to hold fast bravely
> with both hands to the fellowship by which he has bound himself to
> us (3.2.24).

The Basis of Faith

Calvin reminds us repeatedly that "faith properly begins with [God's] promise [in the gospel], rests in it, and ends in it. For in God faith seeks life: a
life that is not found in commandments or declarations of penalties, but
in the promise of mercy, and only in a freely given promise" (3.2.29). This
is an important point lest we are tempted to begin in faith but then derail,
so to speak, and end in works, to start with promise and end in law. "For in
God faith seeks life: a life that is not found in commandments or declarations of penalties, but in the promise of mercy, and only in a freely given
promise." Calvin adds, "For a conditional promise that sends us back to our
own works does not promise life unless we discern its presence in ourselves."
This is a recipe for doubt and despair. "Therefore, if we would not have faith
tremble and waver, we must buttress it with the promise of salvation, which
is willingly and freely offered to us by the Lord in consideration of our misery rather than our deserts" (3.2.29). The promises of the gospel are given
in Christ and fulfilled through Christ. Calvin makes this point even more
pointedly: "If someone believes that God both justly commands all that he
commands and truly threatens, shall he therefore be called a believer? By
no means!" Why? Because "there can be no firm condition for faith unless
it rests upon God's mercy" (3.2.30). Thus faith needs divine mercy, which is

offered us in Christ in the gospel. Faith, then, also needs the Word as much as fruit needs the living root of the tree (cf. 3.2.31–32).

The Holy Spirit's Work in Bringing Us to Faith

The Word, however, is ineffectual without the Spirit's labor. "Our mind has such an inclination to vanity that it can never cleave fast to the truth of God; and it has such a dullness that it is always blind to the light of God's truth." For this reason, the Word is impotent and can achieve nothing "without the illumination of the Holy Spirit." In this way we see that "faith is much higher than human understanding." In other words, it is not "enough for the mind to be illumined by the Spirit of God." We need illumination wedded to the Spirit's power in strengthening our hearts. Both illumination and this strengthening belong to the Spirit. "In both ways, therefore, faith is a singular gift of God, both in that the mind of man is purged so as to be able to taste the truth of God and in that his heart is established therein. For the Spirit is not only the initiator of faith, but increases it by degrees, until by it he leads us to the Kingdom of Heaven" (3.2.33). Among the biblical texts to which Calvin appeals are Matthew 16:17; 1 Corinthians 2:14, 16; John 6:44–45; Luke 24:45; 2 Thessalonians 1:11; 1 Corinthians 2:4–5; Ephesians 1:13–14; and 2 Corinthians 1:21–22 (cf. 3.2.34–40).

Faith, Hope, and Love

Calvin also considers the relationship between faith, hope, and love. Faith moves us to love God even while we fear Him (3.2.41). Faith also moves us to hope, that is, to expect from God what He has promised. Hope flows from a living faith and without it faith is empty (cf. 3.2.41–43).

Chapter Three: Our Regeneration by Faith: Repentance

Repentance as the Fruit of Faith

Having discussed faith in detail, Calvin now turns his attention to the most prominent fruit of faith—repentance and holiness of life. The believer, being united to Christ, seeks divine mercy. Faith produces that inevitable effect. As Calvin states: "With good reason, the sum of the gospel is held to consist in repentance and forgiveness of sins [Luke 24:47; Acts 5:31]" (3.3.1). Repentance follows faith and is born of faith. Indeed, repentance (and all that goes with it in the way of sanctification) is impossible without faith. Calvin explains that when we rightly understand the topic of repentance we will be better prepared to understand "how man is justified by faith alone," i.e., by God's "simple pardon." Our justification is not by repentance or by holiness of life (3.3.1).

Repentance is grounded in the gospel. Persons turn to God in repentance because they know they belong to God. "But no one is truly persuaded that he belongs to God unless he has first recognized God's grace" (3.3.2). Besides this, we must believe that "God is propitious" to us. We will not turn to God for help unless we are confident that He is mercifully disposed toward us in Christ. For God's grace precedes even repentance (the Anabaptists and Jesuits try to turn this around) (3.3.2).

Repentance itself is said to consist of two parts: mortification and vivification. Mortification is aptly enough defined "as sorrow of soul and dread conceived from the recognition of sin and the awareness of divine judgment," consisting of a hatred for and an abhorrence of sin and displeasure with oneself, confessing one's sins in humility of heart. That is, it is contrition. Vivification refers to "the desire to live in a holy and devoted manner, a desire arising from rebirth; as if it were said that man dies to himself that he may begin to live to God" (3.3.3).

Repentance as Regeneration

Calvin, for his part, thinks it is best not to confuse faith with repentance, for they are two distinct, though related, things. Repentance refers to our whole conversion of life, and so includes the pursuit of holiness. Calvin therefore defines repentance as "the true turning of our life to God, a turning that arises from a pure and earnest fear of him; and it consists in the mortification of our flesh and of the old man, and in the vivification of the Spirit" (3.3.5). Calvin amplifies this definition, explaining that we need to examine it under three main heads. He writes, "First, when we call it a 'turning of life to God,' we require a transformation, not only in outward works, but in the soul itself. Only when it puts off its old nature does it bring forth the fruits of works in harmony with its renewal" (3.3.6).

The second main head of repentance, says Calvin, derives from a sincere fear of God.

> For, before the mind of the sinner inclines to repentance, it must be aroused by thinking upon divine judgment. When this thought is deeply and thoroughly fixed in mind—that God will someday mount

his judgment seat to demand a reckoning of all words and deeds—it will not permit the miserable man to rest nor to breathe freely even for a moment without stirring him continually to reflect upon another mode of life whereby he may be able to stand firm in that judgment (3.3.7).

We see, then, that an awareness of being under God's judgment precedes repentance. There must be a sense of need. Scripture confirms this since it "often mentions judgment when it urges to repentance" (cf. Jer. 4:4; Acts 17:30–31) (3.3.7).

The third main head of repentance has to do with its two parts, namely, mortification of the flesh and vivification of the spirit. The prophets express this twofold idea vividly and with simplicity when they say, "Cease to do evil, and do good" (Ps. 36:8, 3, 27; also see Isa. 1:16–17). We are often exhorted to put off the old man and to put on the new man, to renounce the world, the flesh, and the devil's way, and to be renewed in the spirit of our mind (Eph. 4:22–23). "Indeed, the very word 'mortification' warns us how difficult it is to forget our previous nature. For from 'mortification' we infer that we are not conformed to the fear of God and do not learn the rudiments of piety, unless we are violently slain by the sword of the Spirit and brought to nought" (3.3.8).

Both mortification and vivification happen to us through our participation in Christ. We share in Christ's death and resurrection. Repentance then is nothing other than regeneration, which means we are dying to the old life and coming to life in the new. We are being restored to the image of God which had been almost obliterated in us through Adam's fall (cf. Rom. 6:6; 2 Cor. 3:18; Eph. 4:23; Col. 3:10). We are being fully restored through Christ. "Indeed," says Calvin, "this restoration does not take place in one moment or one day or one year; but through continual and sometimes even slow advances God wipes out in his elect the corruptions of the flesh, cleanses them of guilt, consecrates them to himself as temples, renewing all their minds to true purity that they may practice repentance throughout their lives and know that this warfare will end only at death" (3.3.9). Thus Calvin conceives of repentance as regeneration, understood in the comprehensive sense of spiritual renewal and restoration.

The Walk of Repentance

What this means for believers is that though liberation has come, perfection has not. We are not yet done with our battle with sin. In Calvin's words, "there remains in a regenerate man a smoldering cinder of evil, from which desires continually leap forth to allure and spur him to commit sin" (3.3.10). This does not mean that sin has dominion in the life of believers; but it does mean sin yet dwells within them. Sin no longer reigns, but it is still present; vestiges remain which humble us by reminding us of our own weakness (3.3.11). Calvin shows that Augustine taught this as well. Calvin also challenges the antinomian and perfectionistic notions of the Anabaptists (cf. 3.3.12–14).

From 2 Corinthians 7:11 Calvin observes seven aspects ("causes, effects, or parts") of repentance, which are *earnestness or carefulness*, born of sorrow for sin; *excuse*, which expresses desire for purification and pardon; *indignation*, wherein sinners moan inwardly and fault themselves; *fear*, which is trembling at the thought of what our sin deserves; *longing*, which shows the desire to reform our ways; *zeal*, which is linked to longing except now we are spurred on with ardor; and *avenging*, where we condemn ourselves" (3.3.15). Repentance is not something primarily external, but internal, although there are occasions when the public display of repentance is necessary (2.3.16–19).

Repentance and forgiveness of sins are interrelated; not that repentance constitutes the basis for forgiveness or is the cause of salvation. That belongs to the obedience and sacrifice of Christ. At the same time, no one embraces Christ in faith without repentance. "For no one ever hates sin unless he has previously been seized with a love of righteousness" (3.3.20).

Repentance and the Unpardonable Sin

God's mercy is inseparably bound with faith and repentance, for each is His gift (3.3.21). Repentance, like faith, is altogether a gift of God (Acts 11:18; 2 Cor. 7:10). The call to salvation is one thing, but "the efficacy of this depends upon the Spirit of regeneration" (cf. Eph. 2:10). Repentance doesn't save us, but in saving us God brings us to repentance. Truly, all who repent shall be saved (3.3.21).

However, not all sins are pardonable, which brings Calvin to discuss the unpardonable sin—that is, the sin for which there is no repentance or pardon. He describes it as the sin against the Holy Spirit, which consists of persons' willful intention and resistance to God's truth, even though the brightness of God's truth so touches them that they cannot remain ignorant (see Matt. 12:31ff.). "Such resistance alone," says Calvin, "constitutes this sin." Persons "whose consciences, though convinced that what they repudiate and impugn is the Word of God, yet cease not to impugn it—these are said to blaspheme against the Spirit, since they strive against the illumination that is the work of the Holy Spirit" (3.3.22). The unpardonable sin, then, describes an inability to return to the light of the knowledge of Christ for those who have willfully rejected it. They cannot be forgiven, for they cannot repent. They are stricken by God's just judgment, being rendered eternally and perpetually blind (cf. 3.3.22–24).

Chapter Four: How Far from the Purity of the Gospel is All that the Sophists in Their Schools Prate about Repentance; Discussion of Confession and Satisfaction

The Scholastic Doctrine of Penance

With this chapter, Calvin wages a polemic against the scholastic (i.e., the school or academic) theology that had gained the day in the Western church during the medieval period, and was being defended by Roman Catholic contemporaries of Calvin. Calvin calls them "Sophists" because he regards their deceptively subtle reasoning as a kind of sophistry. More specifically, Calvin argues against the sophistry of their doctrine of penance.

Calvin maintains that Rome has not only misused the writings of the church fathers in an attempt to gird up its erroneous doctrine, but misused Scripture as well. First, the Scholastics (the late medieval doctors of the church), in defining repentance, doggedly focus upon "outward exercises," making it into "a discipline and austerity that serves partly to tame the flesh, partly to chastise and punish faults." Meanwhile, they remain woefully silent about "the inward renewal of the mind, which bears with it true correction of life." Second, they wrongly divide repentance into three parts: contrition of heart, confession of mouth, and satisfaction of works. They maintain that each of these is necessary for true or perfect repentance to be manifest (3.4.1).

What is of principal importance here is the forgiveness of sins, for the three parts of repentance delineated above become, for Rome, "necessary to attain forgiveness of sins." This brings believers to a torment of conscience, where they have no peace with God, no assurance of salvation, and finally become so vexed and tormented they hate God and flee from Him (3.4.2).

Forgiveness is not obtained from the weight and depth of our contrition; rather, we must look to the Lord's mercy alone. So is the believer to have no sorrow for sin? Calvin offers this explanation: "It makes a great difference whether you teach forgiveness of sins as deserved by just and full contrition, which the sinner can never perform; or whether you enjoin him to hunger and thirst after God's mercy to show him—through the recognition of his misery, his vacillation, his weariness, and his captivity—where he ought to seek refreshment, rest, and freedom; in fine, to teach him in his humility to give glory to God" (3.4.3).

Furthermore, believers do not need to make confession to priests in order to achieve repentance. For scriptural confession is to be a mutual confession among the members of the church, even as we are to pray for one another (cf. James 5:16), not the prerogative of priests alone. Besides, Rome wrongly makes this compulsory (see 3.4.4–6).

Criticisms of Rome's Practices

Calvin presents the biblical case for private and public confession and challenges the Roman Catholic use of the confessional, also refuting their claim that the confessional is a proper use of the keys of the kingdom (see 3.4.7–23). He summarizes his view as follows: "Now when that thing which God wished to be free is prescribed as necessary to obtain pardon, I call it an utterly intolerable sacrilege, because there is no function more proper to God than the forgiveness of sins, wherein our salvation rests" (3.4.24). In short, the Roman Catholic doctrine of repentance imposes a tyrannical law upon believers, wounds their conscience, wrests forgiveness out of God's hands, casts miserable souls into despair, or if persons are not concerned about their sins, "soothes them with empty blandishments and renders them more sluggish" (3.4.24).

Christ's Satisfaction and Peace of Conscience

As for the third aspect of contrition according to Roman doctrine, i.e., the making of satisfaction, Calvin gathers arguments against this notion as well. Rome teaches that "it is not enough for the penitent to abstain from past evils, and change his behavior for the better, unless he makes satisfaction to God for those things which he has committed." Satisfaction can take the form of "tears, fasting, offering, and works of charity," which pay a debt to God and redeem us from punishment for our transgressions. Writes Calvin, "Over against such lies I put freely given remission of sins; nothing is more clearly set forth in Scripture [Isa. 52:3; Rom. 3:24–25; 5:8; Col. 2:13–14; 2 Tim. 1:9; Titus 3:5]" (3.4.24). Forgiveness is "a gift of sheer liberality." This is because Christ has made full satisfaction for our sins. The Roman doctrine displaces Christ's work of atonement, robs Him of the honor that is His due, and undermines the peace of conscience that belongs to believers who look to Christ for pardon (3.4.25–27).

More Roman Catholic Practices Evaluated

Strictly speaking, Rome does not claim that guilt is remitted by our making satisfaction, for God alone remits our guilt; rather, only penalty or punishment that remains needs to be satisfied. Calvin insists that such a distinction is wholly unbiblical and appeals to numerous scriptural texts to prove his point (see 3.4.29). In turn, this leads Calvin to point again to Christ's work of atonement for us. Calvin asks, "What…would Christ have bestowed upon us if the penalty for our sins were still required?" Indeed, the punishment due our sins, because of our guilt—note, punishment due because we are guilty—is what Christ takes upon Himself; He is punished. And although Roman Catholic writers try to escape this obvious point by distinguishing between temporal and eternal punishments—so that, they claim, Christ bore and removed from us the eternal punishments of God, while we must bear our own temporal punishments—Calvin will have none of it (3.4.29–30). No, God does not punish us; instead He imposes the loving chastisements of a father upon us, for He is our Heavenly Father. "In the judgment of chastisement he is not so harsh as to be angry, nor does he take vengeance so as to blast with destruction. Consequently, it is not, properly speaking, punishment or vengeance, but correction and admonition" (3.4.31). Calvin elaborates on the distinction between fatherly chastisement and divine vengeance in sections that follow (see 3.4.32–37).

Chapter Five: The Supplements That They Add to Satisfactions, Namely, Indulgences and Purgatory

The Question of Indulgences

Exploring this topic further, Calvin takes up two of the most pernicious errors in the Roman Catholic doctrine of penance, that is, the making of satisfaction in the form of indulgences and purgatory. It is not our interest to examine these matters at length. We do well, however, to note what is the Roman doctrine of indulgences and purgatory, and some of Calvin's arguments against each.

Indulgences refer to the remittance of temporal punishments for our sins—and more specifically, the temporal punishment that is absolved refers to the time the soul must spend in purgatory, prior to going on to heaven, to satisfy for sins committed in this life. Indulgences, then, are directly tied to the doctrine of purgatory. Eventually, by the time of the Protestant Reformation, indulgences had developed into the practice of offering money as an act of penance, and the merit in them came from the treasury of Christ's merits and the merits of the saints. This was the origin of "the sale" of indulgences. Meanwhile, purgatory refers to an intermediate state of purification between death and heaven; its purpose is the satisfaction of temporal penalties for sins committed, with the aim that, once satisfaction is made, the soul can enter into eternal communion with God. Purgatory, then, is part of the process of sanctification. Purgatory is not an escape from any sort of eternal punishment; neither is it any kind of opportunity for conversion not achieved in one's temporal life. Rather, it is an interval between the believer's final purification and perfection and his or her former life of sin (see 3.5.1–2).

Calvin vehemently opposes these two doctrines, as they were paired together and had become so integral to the Roman Catholic doctrine of penance. "Now very many persons see the base tricks, thefts, and greediness with which the indulgence traffickers have heretofore mocked and beguiled us, and yet they do not see the very fountain of the impiety itself" (3.5.2). Calvin regards them as "a profanation of the blood of Christ, a Satanic mockery," in fact lead "Christian people away from God's grace, away from the life that is in Christ, and turn them aside from the true way of salvation." This is because indulgences look to the blood of saints and their works, rather than Christ alone, for the cleansing of sins (3.5.2–5).

The Question of Purgatory

As for purgatory, Calvin regards it as "a deadly fiction of Satan, which nullifies the cross of Christ," and along with this offense, it "inflicts unbearable contempt upon God's mercy, and overturns and destroys our faith" (3.5.6). Calvin offers a more fulsome explanation of its faults: "[I]f it is perfectly clear from our preceding discourse that the blood of Christ is the sole satisfaction for the sins of believers, the sole expiation, the sole purgation, what remains but to say that purgatory is simply a dreadful blasphemy against Christ?" (3.5.6). Most importantly, it shows itself to be contrary to Scripture and leads to superstition (see 3.5.7–9). "Now, since the entire law and gospel do not furnish so much as a single syllable of leave to pray for the dead, it is to profane the invocation of God to attempt more than he has bidden us" (3.5.10).

Questions for Reflection and Discussion

1. Look up 2 Corinthians 5:17; Romans 8:1; Ephesians 1:1; Colossians 1:2; also 1 Thessalonians 2:14; Galatians 2:4; Romans 12:5. How is life *in Christ* different from *outside* of Christ? (Also see Rom. 8:8.)

2. Why is an *explicit* recognition of Christ and His work necessary for salvation versus a mere implicit or vague recognition of Him? Moreover, why must faith manifest itself in "the fear of the Lord" in order to be called faith?

3. Calvin addresses the problem of assurance of salvation. What is his analysis of doubting faith and what solutions does he propose?

4. How does David's life confirm Calvin's point? Look up Psalm 42:5, 11; 43:5; and 116:7. Why is assurance so essential to faith?

5. Calvin maintains that people will not turn to God in repentance unless they are persuaded that He will receive them in mercy. Explain Calvin's remark that faith must begin with God's promise in the gospel, rest in it, and end with it. Why is this so important?

6. If faith is a gift from God, does that negate "the call to faith"? Why or why not?

7. (a) How does repentance as transformation challenge the common notion that one can have Jesus as Savior without surrendering to Him as Lord?

   (b) How does a lack of "earnest fear" affect the health of the church today?

   (c) Why is it important to see "knowledge of sin" as a perpetual part of the Christian life?

8. May a believer declare without qualification, "I'm not a sinner, I'm a saint"? Defend your answer.

9. What might be instances or examples of the unpardonable sin today?

The Christian Life

Chapters 6–10 of Book Three

Chapter Six: The Life of the Christian Man; and First, by What Arguments Scripture Urges Us to It

Orientation

WITH THESE CHAPTERS we come to some of the most treasured portions of Calvin's *Institutes*. Calvin moves from the question of regeneration—that is, a renewed life marked by faith and repentance—to the question of regenerated living. As he had stated earlier, "The object of regeneration . . . is to manifest in the life of believers a harmony and agreement between God's righteousness and their obedience, and thus to confirm the adoption that they have received as sons [Gal. 4:5; cf. 2 Peter 1:10]" (3.6.1). Calvin therefore turns to a discussion of the Christian life, since the whole of Christian living is comprehended in a life of faith and repentance.

Calvin covers this topic over five chapters. Chapter six sets out some basic ideas which frame what he will explore in the ensuing chapters. This is followed in chapter seven with an analysis of self-denial, which constitutes the sum of the Christian life. Chapter eight treats cross-bearing as an aspect of self-denial. Meditation on the future life is explored in chapter nine. Lastly, chapter ten expounds on how we should use this life—and its helps—in living the Christian life.

Motives of the Christian Life

To live the Christian life one needs to keep two aspects in mind: (1) that our hearts are filled with a love of righteousness; and (2) that we are guided by a rule for righteousness, for Scripture bids us to heed the call to holiness. The call to holiness isn't optional; it constitutes our first motivation to walk in conformity to our salvation (cf. 1 Pet. 1:15–16). In fact, holiness is the bond of our union with God. We have been delivered out of "the wickedness and pollution of the world" in which we once wallowed with the purpose that we might dwell in the New Jerusalem. How unfitting that God's sanctuary should be turned into a barn "crammed with filth" (3.6.2).

We should understand that Christ serves as our supreme example. "Scripture shows that God the Father, as he has reconciled us to himself in his Christ [cf. 2 Cor. 5:18], has in him stamped for us the likeness [cf. Heb. 1:3] to which he would have us conform" (3.6.3). We are called to conform to His pattern; our life is to express His. As members of Christ's body, as adopted children of God, dare we disfigure it? Let us, therefore, wholeheartedly "aspire heavenward" and strive to keep ourselves "pure and uncorrupted until the Day of the Lord" (3.6.3).

Nominal Christian Living Not to
Be Confused with Imperfect Christian Living
Calvin reprimands those who would make the Christian life merely a matter of the tongue. We are urged to put off the old man and to put on Christ. A pretended knowledge of Christ insults God, for the Christian life "is not apprehended by the understanding and memory alone, as other disciplines are, but it is received only when it possesses the whole soul, and finds a seat and resting place in the inmost affection of the heart" (3.6.4). The Christian life is expressed in "daily living."

Though we cannot insist upon or find perfection in our moral walk, we should aim for it. Perfection is the goal, though progress is slow. As Calvin states:

> No one in this earthly prison of the body has sufficient strength to press on with due eagerness, and weakness so weighs down the greater number that, with wavering and limping and even creeping along the ground, they move at a feeble rate. Let each one of us, then, proceed according to the measure of his puny capacity and set out upon the journey we have begun. No one shall set out so inauspiciously as not daily to make some headway, though it be slight. Therefore, let us not cease so to act that we may make some unceasing progress in the way of the Lord. And let us not despair at the slightness of our success; for even though attainment may not correspond to desire, when today outstrips yesterday the effort is not lost. Only let us look toward our mark with sincere simplicity and aspire to our goal; not fondly flatter-

ing ourselves, nor excusing our own evil deeds, but with continuous effort striving toward this end: that we may surpass ourselves in goodness until we attain to goodness itself. It is this, indeed, which through the whole course of life we seek and follow. But we shall attain it only when we have cast off the weakness of the body, and are received into full fellowship with him (3.6.5).

Chapter Seven: The Sum of the Christian Life: The Denial of Ourselves

The Meaning and Necessity of Self-Denial

Calvin explains that we are called to offer ourselves to God as living sacrifices of thanksgiving (Rom. 12:1–2). We are to be people consecrated and dedicated to God inasmuch as we are not our own but the Lord's (1 Cor. 6:19). This has consequences upon which Calvin comments:

> We are not our own: let not our reason nor our will, therefore, sway our plans and deeds. We are not our own: let us therefore not set it as our goal to seek what is expedient for us according to the flesh. We are not our own: in so far as we can, let us therefore forget ourselves and all that is ours.
>
> Conversely, we are God's: let us therefore live for him and die for him. We are God's: let his wisdom and will therefore rule all our actions. We are God's: let all the parts of our life accordingly strive toward him as our only lawful goal (3.7.1).

Along this path, step one is that we must expend ourselves in the Lord's service. For Calvin, the word "service" comprises both obedience to the divine Word and, over against carnal sensibilities, a mind surrendered to "the bidding of God's Spirit." Reason submits to the Holy Spirit; then, our lives become Christ's life in us (Gal. 2:20) (3.7.1).

Step two is that we pursue not the things limited to the temporal life but the things "which are of the Lord's will and will serve to advance his glory." We must become "almost forgetful of ourselves" and "leave off self-concern." Then we will have the ability to "devote our zeal to God and his commandments." This is what the denial of self comprises, and to which Christ calls us. For Calvin, self-interest is a "pestilence" leading to our destruction. We must deny ourselves as Christ enjoins, for self-denial "leaves no place at all first either to pride, or arrogance, or ostentation; then either to avarice, or desire, or lasciviousness, or effeminacy, or to other evils that our self-love spawns [cf. Matt. 16:24; 2 Tim. 3:2–5]." Yet, "on the other hand," notes Calvin, "wherever denial of ourselves does not reign, there either the foulest vices rage without shame or if there is any semblance of virtue, it is vitiated by depraved lusting after glory" (3.7.2).

Titus 2:11–14 sculpts an image of self-denial for us ("For the grace of God that bringeth salvation hath appeared to all men. Teaching us that, denying ungodliness and worldly lusts, we should live soberly, righteously, and godly, in this present world; looking for that blessed hope, and the glorious appearing of the great God and our Saviour Jesus Christ; who gave himself for us, that he might redeem us from all iniquity, and purify unto himself a peculiar people, zealous of good works"). Here the apostle removes two obstacles that stand in the way of holiness: ungodliness and worldly lusts. He also presents three parts to the life of holiness: *soberness*, which calls us to chastity, temperance, and frugality; *righteousness*, which comprehends all the demands of equity so that all are given what is properly their due; and *godliness*, which bids us to separate from the world's multiple transgressions. This is not a vain pursuit (1 Thess. 3:5). Christ shall return and scatter "all the allurements that becloud us and prevent us from aspiring as we ought to heavenly glory." We must journey "as pilgrims in this world that our celestial heritage may not perish or pass away" (3.7.3).

Self-Denial Exercised toward Our Neighbor

The denial of self directs itself partly to our fellow man, and partly, chiefly, to God. Scripture bids us to esteem others above ourselves (Phil. 2:3), and to do well to them (Rom. 12:10). Many similar commands are urged upon us. Yet, we are incapable of heeding these exhortations

> unless our mind be previously emptied of its natural feeling. For, such is the blindness with which we all rush into self-love that each one of us seems to himself to have just cause to be proud of himself and to despise all others in comparison. If God has conferred upon us anything of which we need not repent, relying upon it we immediately lift up our minds, and are not only puffed up but almost burst with pride. The very vices that infest us we take pains to hide from others, while we flatter ourselves with the pretense that they are slight and insignificant, and even sometimes embrace them as virtues. If others manifest the same endowments we admire in ourselves, or even superior ones, we spitefully belittle and revile these gifts in order to avoid yielding

place to such persons. If there are any faults in others, not content with
noting them with severe and sharp reproach, we hatefully exaggerate
them. Hence arises such insolence that each one of us, as if exempt
from the common lot, wishes to tower above the rest, and loftily and
savagely abuses every mortal man, or at least looks down upon him as
an inferior (3.7.4).

We must examine ourselves, for our faults call us to humility against the
tendency of our hearts which try to convince us of our "own pre-eminence."
We attain true gentleness by only one path: "a heart imbued with lowliness
and with reverence for others" (3.7.4).

The denial of ourselves calls us to seek our neighbor's benefit. We are
repeatedly exhorted to labor for the edification of the community of faith, as
well-functioning parts of a healthy body (cf. 1 Pet. 4:10; 1 Cor. 12:12ff.). But
how difficult this is to do! Says Calvin, "Unless you give up all thought of self
and, so to speak, get out of yourself, you will accomplish nothing here. For
how can you perform those works which Paul teaches to be the works of love,
unless you renounce yourself, and give yourself wholly to others?" (3.7.5).

We must also remember the image of God in others, "to which we owe
all honor and love." Self-denial is the way of love (1 Cor. 13). We may not
refuse to lend assistance to those in need, even though they be contempt-
ible and worthless or an enemy (Matt. 6:14; 18:35). We are called "to love
those who hate us, to repay their evil deeds with benefits, to return blessings
for reproaches" (Matt. 5:44). We must look upon God's image in unlovable
persons, for the beauty of that image, "with its beauty and dignity allures us
to love and embrace them" (3.7.6).

Calvin tells us that the way of self-denial carries with it the grace of
mercy and generosity toward others. Believers, in dying to self, are to be
kind in their disposition and actions. This shows itself in the intentions of
the heart, with genuine pity felt for those who suffer ill fortune, followed
by deeds of assistance. Nothing other than "duties of love" accomplish this
mortification (3.7.7). We should see ourselves as debtors to our neighbors
and thus manifest a kindness toward them which gives to the limit of re-
sources (3.7.7).

Self-Denial Exercised toward God
Self-denial is also directed toward God, and this is its foremost aspect. We
must, says Calvin, resign ourselves and our possessions to the Lord's will
(3.7.8). How prone we are, driven by mad lust and boundless desire "to covet

wealth and honors, to strive for authority, to heap up riches, to gather together all those follies which seem to make for magnificence and pomp." To resist this we must instead desire the Lord to prosper and care for us, to see these worldly cravings as nothing—even legitimate blessings are as nothing without the Lord's blessing upon them. Not the least particle of happiness is ours unless the Lord gives His blessing and turns away misfortune (3.7.8). This means that we will not greedily

> strive after riches and honors—whether relying upon our own dexterity of wit or our own diligence, or depending upon the favor of men, or having confidence in vainly imagined fortune—but for us always to look to the Lord so that by his guidance we may be led to whatever lot he has provided for us.... He who rests solely upon the blessing of God...will neither strive with evil arts after those things which men customarily madly seek after, which he realizes will not profit him, nor will he, if things go well, give credit to himself or even to his diligence, or industry, or fortune. Rather, he will give God the credit as its Author (3.7.9).

Self-denial also helps us bear adversity. When we are resigned to and governed by God's will we accept life's trials without complaint or ill will (3.7.10). And how necessary this is, given the many things that touch our lives unexpectedly. As Calvin writes:

> Various diseases repeatedly trouble us: now plague rages; now we are cruelly beset by the calamities of war; now ice and hail, consuming the year's expectation, lead to barrenness, which reduces us to poverty; wife, parents, children, neighbors, are snatched away by death; our house is burned by fire. It is on account of these occurrences that men curse their life, loathe the day of their birth, abominate heaven and the light of day, rail against God, and as they are eloquent in blasphemy, accuse him of injustice and cruelty. But in these matters the believer must also look to God's kindness and truly fatherly indulgence.... Whatever happens, because he will know it ordained of God, he will undergo it with a peaceful and grateful mind so as not obstinately to resist the command of him into whose power he once for all surrendered himself and his every possession (3.7.10).

The rule of piety is unmistakable: God's hand alone bestows or withholds gifts and trials, all according to His justice (3.7.10).

Chapter Eight: **Bearing the Cross, A Part of Self-Denial**

Christ's Cross and Ours

Self-denial is not duly understood until we contemplate Christ's call for every believer to bear his or her own cross (Matt. 16:24). "For whomever the Lord has adopted and deemed worthy of his fellowship ought to prepare themselves for a hard, toilsome, and unquiet life, crammed with very many and various kinds of evil. It is the Heavenly Father's will thus to exercise them so as to put his own children to a definite test" (3.8.1). Christ Himself endured such a test. We mustn't think ourselves exempted. We are called to commune with His sufferings, wherein we are also blessed (3.8.1).

The Purposes of Cross-bearing

God has specific reasons for us constantly to bear the cross. First, we congratulate ourselves for our achievements, which shows our inclination to the flesh. God therefore unmasks our feebleness, along with our haughty hearts and stupid confidence in ourselves. In fact, we are frail and feeble. God afflicts us to prove it to us. Disgrace, poverty, bereavement, disease, calamities—these things expose us in our weakness and pride. Hypocrisy must learn humility. Believers must "betake themselves to God's grace" (3.8.2). Bearing a perpetual cross in this life teaches us humility. It also teaches us, maintains Calvin, not to esteem our virtue above its due. Moreover, being humbled we learn to call on God's power, "which alone makes us stand fast under the weight of afflictions." In this way we are brought to a deeper knowledge of our Lord. We should remember the words of Romans 5:3–4 ("Tribulation worketh patience; and patience, experience; and experience, hope.") As Calvin passionately writes: "And it is of no slight importance for you to be cleansed of your blind love of self that you may be made more nearly aware of your incapacity; to feel your own incapacity that you may learn to distrust yourself; to distrust yourself that you may transfer your trust to God; to rest with a trustful heart in God that, relying upon his help, you may persevere unconquered to the end; to take your stand in his grace that you may comprehend the truth in his promises; to have unquestioned certainty of his promises that your hope may thereby be strengthened" (3.8.3).

Bearing the cross also teaches us patience and obedience (3.8.4). Peter reminds us that our faith is proved by trials (1 Pet. 1:7). By this means God brings to light "the graces he has conferred upon the saints...." We learn to obey God, for we are taught to seek His will rather than chase our own. We don't learn to follow God by acting according to our whims (3.8.4).

Cross-bearing is a kind of medicine for God's people. We ever want to discard "God's yoke." When we experience abundance we grow wild and untamed like horses too long in the pasture. Fat and flabby with God's beneficence toward us, we kick against our own Master. Hence, the Lord, knowing what is expedient for us, puts us under "the remedy of the cross." God tries us with one kind of cross or another—they may come in many different forms. Whether the discipline is gentle or more extreme, God aims at our health and "he leaves no one free and untouched, because he knows that all, to a man, are diseased" (3.8.5).

Cross-bearing also functions as a form of God's fatherly discipline or chastisement to correct us from our sins. In facing affliction, we should remember our past wrongdoing and misdeeds. We should recall that we are deserving of God's chastisement. It is for our good. God uses hardships to "correct past transgressions so that he may keep us in lawful obedience to himself.... For [our Father] afflicts us not to ruin or destroy us but, rather, to free us from the condemnation of the world" (3.8.6). Even when we suffer for righteousness' sake we find God's comfort (3.8.7). Poverty, exile, contempt, prison, disgrace, even death—each of these can befall us without a loss of God's love and favor toward us. We must learn what it is to suffer for Christ's sake and to be counted worthy to suffer for Him (Matt. 5:19; John 15:18–20; Acts 5:41).

We have God's promises to uphold us in our sufferings. We can be slandered but God knows the truth. We can lose our homes but God makes us secure in His family. We can be vexed and despised, but God loves us in Christ. We can be disgraced and held in derision, but God gives us a fuller place in His kingdom. We can be delivered to death, but God takes us into the eternity of the blessed life. Every believer must be ready to suffer for Christ's sake. This is bearing the cross of Christ, too (cf. 1 Pet. 4:12ff.) (3.8.7–8). Such cross-bearing is a kind of death.

> If there were no harshness in poverty, no torment in diseases, no sting in disgrace, no dread in death—what fortitude or moderation would there be in bearing them with indifference? But since each of these, with an inborn bitterness, by its very nature bites the hearts of us all, the fortitude of the believing man is brought to light, if—tried by the feeling of such bitterness—however grievously he is troubled with it, yet valiantly resisting, he surmount it. Here his forbearance reveals itself: if

sharply pricked he is still restrained by the fear of God from breaking into any intemperate act. Here his cheerfulness shines if, wounded by sorrow and grief, he rests in the spiritual consolation of God (3.8.8).

Christian Cross-bearing, Suffering, and Patience

Unlike the Stoics who seek to turn themselves into cold rocks, we have the example of Christ who mourned for His own and expressed sorrow and compassion for others. Jesus wept (John 11:35). We are counted blessed if we mourn (Matt. 5:4) (3.8.9). We suffer but we do not despair. In being Christ's disciple, God knows what we must endure in order to be shaped after the image of His Son.

> Thus it will come to pass that, by whatever kind of cross we may be troubled, even in the greatest tribulations of mind, we shall firmly keep our patience. For the adversities themselves will have their own bitterness to gnaw at us; thus afflicted by disease, we shall both groan and be uneasy and pant after health; thus pressed by poverty, we shall be pricked by the arrows of care and sorrow; thus we shall be smitten by the pain of disgrace, contempt, injustice; thus at the funerals of our dear ones we shall weep the tears that are owed to our nature. But the conclusion will always be: the Lord so willed, therefore let us follow his will. Indeed, amid the very pricks of pain, amid groaning and tears, this thought must intervene: to incline our heart to bear cheerfully those things which have so moved it (3.8.10).

We patiently endure suffering to learn of God's righteousness and equity, and to pursue our own salvation. God's providence directs our lives. God's will brings us our situations and circumstances. And God does everything according to His "well-ordered justice." In fact, we bear the cross, knowing that "our innumerable and daily offenses deserve to be chastised more severely and with heavier rods than the afflictions he lays upon us out of his kindness" (3.8.11). We are therefore called to patience. We can be comforted in this patience as well. We know that "in the very act of afflicting us with the cross [God] is providing for our salvation." Thus we don't merely endure affliction, we do so with thankful and quiet spirits. We consent to God's providence as "for our own good." Then "the bitterness of the cross" can be "tempered with spiritual joy" (3.8.11).

Chapter Nine: Meditation on the Future Life

The Sufferings of the Present Life

With chapter nine Calvin shows us that the cross we bear has duration for this life alone. Beyond is the future life which believers should contemplate, for surely God uses the afflictions and tribulations we endure in order to wean us from excessive love of the present life. As Calvin states: "Whatever kind of tribulation presses upon us, we must ever look to this end: to accustom ourselves to contempt for the present life and to be aroused thereby to meditate upon the future life" (3.9.1). By the miseries of this life, that is, the miseries that perpetually afflict us, God shows us the vanity of the present life. Therefore, in order that believers might not delude themselves with a false sense of security in this world, or try to find peace in it, God

> permits them often to be troubled and plagued either with wars or tumults, or robberies, or other injuries. That they may not pant with too great eagerness after fleeting and transient riches, or repose in those which they possess, he sometimes by exile, sometimes by barrenness of the earth, sometimes by fire, sometimes by other means, reduces them to poverty, or at least confines them to a moderate station. That they may not too complacently take delight in the goods of marriage, he either causes them to be troubled by the depravity of their wives or humbles them by evil offspring, or afflicts them with bereavement (3.9.1).

Thus, "we conclude that in this life we are to seek and hope for nothing but struggle; when we think of our crown, we are to raise our eyes to heaven. For this we must believe: that the mind is never seriously aroused to desire and ponder the life to come unless it be previously imbued with contempt for the present life" (3.9.1).

Calvin believes there is no middle ground with respect to this question. "Either the world must become worthless to us or hold us bound by intemperate love of it" (3.9.2). This life is transient, like smoke or shadow (Ps. 102:3, 11). How easily, though, we take the things of this life "as if we were establishing immortality for ourselves on earth." When we face a grave we are usually brought to a more sober mind, but this vanishes quickly. God must constantly shake us "out of our sluggishness" so that we may strive for our heavenly life and hold this world, with its sins, in disdain (3.9.2).

Desiring the Life to Come

This isn't to say that we are without gratitude for life and the blessings of this life, which, after all, afford us a foretaste of the blessings of heavenly glory (3.9.3). But presently the earth is for us a place of exile. If the life to come is a deliverance from bondage, then what is this life but a grave and this body but a prison? We are not to hate this earthly life "except in so far as it holds us subject to sin" (3.9.4). "Let the aim of believers in judging mortal life, then, be that while they understand it to be of itself nothing but misery, they may with greater eagerness and dispatch betake themselves wholly to meditate upon that eternal life to come" (3.9.4).

Thus we are called to long for the Lord's coming, and not merely long, but groan and sigh for it "as the happiest thing of all." Likewise, believers who have made progress in the school of Christ "joyfully await the day of death and final resurrection" (3.9.5). The Lord promises to wipe every tear from our eyes (Rev. 7:17). And when God's children are troubled by wicked persons and bear their evil insult, suffer at the hand of their thievery, or are afflicted with other wickedness "they will without difficulty bear up under such evils also," for "they have ... lifted their heads above everything earthly" (3.9.6). Further, when we see the unbelievers and ungodly persons prosper, enjoying peace, living in luxury, brimming with delight, we await the day of reckoning that God has promised. God will receive the faithful into His presence and bliss. The evildoer will meet divine justice and be "cast into utter disgrace" (Rev. 7:17; 21:3–4, 8; Isa. 66:24; Matt. 25:41; Mark 9:43, 46; 2 Thess. 1:6–7). Truly, this is the consolation of believers: "To conclude in a word: if believers' eyes are turned to the power of the resurrection, in their hearts the cross of Christ will at last triumph over the devil, flesh, sin, and wicked men" (3.9.6).

Chapter Ten: How We Must Use the Present Life and Its Helps

The Right Use of the Present Life

The call for meditation upon the future life does not mean that Calvin rejects the creation. His piety is not "other worldly" as such, for Calvin directs us to enjoy the good things of this life as God's gifts to us. However, we do need instruction in "the right use of earthly benefits." To live the Christian life and order it well we need to know how "to use those helps necessary for living," whether "for necessity" or "for delight" (3.10.1). We may not forget that God's people are on a pilgrimage in this world as they journey to the heavenly kingdom (Heb. 11:8–10; 1 Pet. 2:11). The principle which Calvin lays forth seeks to escape both asceticism and intemperance. These are the two errors we must avoid—the first "too severe," the second given to "unbridled excess." Asceticism puts consciences in chains. Its advocates live by depending on the necessary things. "To them necessity means to abstain from all things that they could do without; thus, according to them, it would scarcely be permitted to add any food at all to plain bread and water." Intemperance or licentiousness leaves the conscience without limits or regulation. Its devotees give way to unchecked indulgence, ignoring scriptural rules and guidelines altogether (3.10.1).

Calvin argues that we are to use the Lord's gifts by directing them to the end and use for which He created them.

> Now if we ponder to what end God created food, we shall find that he meant not only to provide for necessity but also for delight and good cheer. Thus the purpose of clothing, apart from necessity was comeliness and decency. In grasses, trees, and fruits, apart from their various uses, there is beauty of appearance and pleasantness of odor.... Has the Lord clothed the flowers with the great beauty that greets our eyes, the sweetness of smell that is wafted upon our nostrils, and yet will it be unlawful for our eyes to be affected by that beauty, or our sense of smell by the sweetness of that odor? What? Did he not so distinguish colors as to make some more lovely than others? What? Did he not endow gold and silver, ivory and marble, with a loveliness that renders them more precious than other metals or stones? Did he not, in short, render many things attractive to us, apart from their necessary use? (3.10.2).

Moderation and Generosity

Mere utility is not a correct use of God's gifts. Calvin, however, is also aware how easily we succumb to the lusts of the flesh: gorging ourselves at banquets, falling into conceit with our apparel. Some people are so allured by material things that they have no sense or appetite for spiritual matters. Ingratitude marks this path. We must heed the apostle's warning to resist the abuse of creation's good gifts, and especially to make no provision for the flesh, to satiate its wicked desires (Rom. 13:14). "If we yield too much to these, they boil up without measure or control" (3.10.3).

If we are spiritually minded in the proper way, we will learn a certain contempt for the present life and treasure the heavenly immortality to come. "For from this two rules follow: those who use this world should be so affected as if they did not use it; those who marry, as if they did not marry; those who buy, as if they did not buy, just as Paul enjoins [1 Cor. 7:29–31]. The other rule is that they should know how to bear poverty peaceably and patiently, as well as to bear abundance moderately" (3.10.4). Calvin urges us to see how these two rules deliver us from two different sets of sins. On the one hand if we heed the first rule, we destroy "the intemperance of gluttony"—the excessiveness in all things: dining, buildings, and clothing; ambition, pride, arrogance, and overfastidiousness. We also destroy all the daily cares of life that keep us from contemplating our heavenly life or prevent the nurture of our souls (3.10.4). Calvin offers this tenet to guide us: "to indulge oneself as little as possible; but, on the contrary, with unflagging effort of mind to insist upon cutting off all show of superfluous wealth, not to mention licentiousness, and diligently to guard against turning helps into hindrances" (3.10.4).

On the other hand if we heed the second rule, to exercise patience in poverty and bear abundance moderately, we "will make considerable progress in the Lord's school." Persons who begrudge their poverty will boast in their prosperity. "This is my point: he who is ashamed of mean clothing will boast of costly clothing; he who, not content with a slender meal, is troubled by the desire for a more elegant one, will also intemperately abuse those elegances if they fall to his lot." If we grumble at meagerness, we will also become arrogant in having abundance. We must learn contentment (Phil. 4:12). Let us beware of excess, pride, ostentation, and vanity, which "befog the mind." Instead, let us embrace abstinence, sobriety, frugality, and moderation. Moreover, we must be good stewards of the gifts God has bestowed upon us (3.10.5).

Finally, so Calvin instructs, every believer must be faithful to his calling. "Each individual has his own kind of living assigned to him by the Lord as a sort of sentry post so that he may not heedlessly wander about throughout life." Thus every person has his station and task. He ought not to grumble, since God has placed him there.

> It will be no slight relief from cares, labors, troubles, and other burdens for a man to know that God is his guide in all these things. The magistrate will discharge his functions more willingly; the head of the household will confine himself to his duty; each man will bear and swallow the discomforts, vexations, weariness, and anxieties in his way of life, when he has been persuaded that the burden was laid upon him by God. From this will arise also a singular consolation: that no task

will be so sordid and base, provided you obey your calling in it, that it will not shine and be reckoned very precious in God's sight (3.10.6).

Questions for Reflection and Discussion

1. Does Calvin's depiction of the Christian struggle ring true to you? Why or why not? Is modern Christianity in North America in harmony with the melody of the Christian life that Calvin plays? Explain.

2. What is the "natural feeling" of the mind to which Calvin refers? How would the practice of self-denial heal human relationships?

3. What does self-denial exercised toward our neighbor impact social welfare programs, catastrophic relief assistance, benevolence giving in church, etc.?

4. Apply Calvin's remarks about "evil arts" to the "profit motive." What do his remarks have to say about lotteries and other modern schemes to get rich?

5. How does self-denial help us cope with the painful side of life? How did Calvin suffer?

6. What would Calvin think of the modern practice to promote oneself? How does this fit with the vision of the Christian life that Calvin depicts?

7. How can we come to see that even in our afflictions God is gracious? What would happen if God treated us as our sins deserve?

8. Karl Marx said that religion was "the opium of the people." What did he mean by that phrase and what would he have thought of Calvin's remarks about meditation on the future life? What is the answer to Marx and to people of his ilk?

9. What is asceticism and what is intemperance? How are they harmful?

10. How does Calvin's idea of "calling" shape our view of the Christian life? Is it all just witnessing and winning souls? How is Calvin's view different from the conception of the Christian life in Roman Catholicism and in Fundamentalism?

11. What most impresses you about Calvin's doctrine of the Christian life? How can the modern church put his vision into practice?

≈ 14 ≈

Justification by Faith Alone

Chapters 11–14 of Book Three

Chapter Eleven: Justification by Faith: First the Definition of the Word and of the Matter

Orientation

As CALVIN EMBARKS upon his treatment of justification by faith alone, he arrives at the second aspect of that "double grace" believers receive in being united to Christ. Earlier Calvin had explained that the sum of the gospel consists of repentance and forgiveness of sins—that is, in newness of life and free reconciliation. Christ confers both of these graces upon us through faith. Moreover, these blessings are never separated from one another, for holiness of life and the free imputation of Christ's righteousness are parts of the single tapestry of His work of salvation. He bestows both benefits to believers united to Him.

Calvin treats justification in detail, covering nine chapters in the *Institutes*. An overview of his discussion will serve us well. Chapter eleven presents the doctrine of justification. As foils for his presentation of the doctrine, Calvin presents the views of the aberrant theologian Andreas Osiander and his doctrine of an infused righteousness; Calvin also presents and refutes the medieval scholastic doctrine, which wrongly blends or combines sanctification and justification. Chapter twelve demonstrates the serious nature of the justification of sinners who stand before God's tribunal. The thirteenth chapter looks at various features of the doctrine of justification, especially how it consoles believers and gives them peace of conscience. Chapter fourteen examines the practicality of the doctrine as it is worked out in the Christian life. Here Calvin argues that good works or works of faith are inevitable but form no part of justification itself. Chapter fifteen rebuts the doctrine of human merit that has long infected this doctrine. Chapters sixteen and seventeen follow in that strand, taking up the place of works in relation to justification by faith alone. Chapter eighteen treats rewards and the false notion that rewards attest works-righteousness. Finally, the nineteenth chapter takes up Christian freedom, which Calvin calls an appendage and the power of justification.

The Other Aspect of the "Double Grace"

The question of the believer's justification before God was one of the key controversies of the Protestant Reformation. Before Calvin engages this topic, he reviews what we have learned so far concerning our redemption. "Christ was given to us by God's generosity, to be grasped and possessed by us in faith. By partaking of him, we principally receive a double grace: namely, that being reconciled to God through Christ's blamelessness, we may have in heaven instead of a Judge a gracious Father; and secondly, that sanctified by Christ's spirit we may cultivate blamelessness and purity of life" (3.11.1).

Calvin conceives of regeneration, as noted earlier, not in the narrow sense of a momentary spiritual awakening but in the broad sense of an ongoing life of faith and repentance. This is one aspect of the double grace he cites, mentioned second in the quotation above but treated first in his order of teaching. In choosing this order we must not think that Calvin regards justification as chronologically later than or subsequent to regeneration. Calvin does not think that some sort of "causal relation" exists between them. Neither does he wish to make one the final aim of the other. Both blessings are granted to us immediately in union with Christ.

So why take this order of exposition? Why expound the Christian life *before* the doctrine of justification? Calvin explains: "It was more to the point to understand first how little devoid of good works is the faith, through which alone we obtain free righteousness by the mercy of God; and what is the nature of the good works of the saints, with which part of this question is concerned" (3.11.1). In other words, by first showing us that justifying faith is not destitute of good works, properly understood, he can refute the charge that the Reformers were subverting a Christian walk of godliness and well-doing. He could also show that the works believers produce cannot in any way mount up to the righteous standard of God's holiness and contribute to the believers' acceptance before God.

Calvin views justification of principal importance for Christian doctrine and life. He calls it "the main hinge on which religion turns," and then elaborates: "For unless you first of all grasp what your relationship to God is, and the nature of his judgment concerning you, you have neither a foundation on which to establish your salvation nor one on which to build piety toward God" (3.11.1).

Justification Defined and Explained
Calvin offers the following definition of justification: "He is said to be justified in God's sight who is both reckoned righteous in God's judgment and has been accepted on account of his righteousness. Indeed, as iniquity is abominable to God, so no sinner can find favor in his eyes in so far as he is a sinner and so long as he is reckoned as such. Accordingly, wherever there is sin, there also the wrath and vengeance of God show themselves. Now he is justified who is reckoned in the condition not of a sinner, but of a righteous man; and for that reason, he stands firm before God's judgment seat while all sinners fall" (3.11.2). Calvin clearly accents two aspects of justification: (1) being reckoned righteous before God; and on that basis (2) being accepted by God. "Therefore, we explain justification simply as the acceptance with which God receives us into his favor as righteous men. And we say that it consists in the remission of sins and the imputation of Christ's righteousness" (3.11.2). Again, two important aspects emerge: (1) the forgiveness of sins; and (2) the imputation of (or the being reckoned righteous with) Christ's righteousness. Our own works have no part to play in this. Faith alone "grasps the righteousness of Christ." The person who is clothed in Christ's righteousness appears before God's scrutiny not as a sinner but as one who is righteous (3.11.2).

Turning to Scripture, Calvin explains that "to justify" means nothing else than "to acquit of guilt him who was accused, as if his innocence were confirmed." Romans 8:33–34 demonstrates that justification involves an absolution, for it is God who justifies; and no one can condemn those whom He defends with Christ's intercession. "Therefore," writes Calvin, "since God justifies us by the intercession of Christ, he absolves us not by the confirmation of our own innocence but by the imputation of righteousness, so that we who are not righteous in ourselves may be reckoned as such in Christ" (3.11.3). As an example, Calvin looks at Acts 13:38–39 ("Be it known unto you therefore, men *and* brethren, that through this man is preached unto you the forgiveness of sins; and by him all that believe are justified from all things, from which ye could not be justified by the law of Moses"). This passage shows us that justification is an explanation or interpretation of what it means to have the forgiveness of sins. It is absolution, received by faith, apart from the performance of our obedience to the law (3.11.3).

Justification is denoted also by the word "acceptance." That this is the case is made plain in Ephesians 1:5–6. The grace of election and adoption are coupled with our acceptance in the beloved, in Christ. God justifies us freely (Rom. 3:24). Acceptance bespeaks welcome and fellowship. This is the opposite of estrangement and enmity. In Christ the believer is welcomed into God's fellowship and favor. Moreover, justification may be denoted as the "imputation of righteousness" and as "reconciliation to God," for that imputation renders us acceptable in His sight (Rom. 4:6–7). Even better is 2 Corinthians 5:18–21, for God in Christ does not count our sins against us. The apostle adds the explanation that the One who had no sin was made sin for our sakes. All of this produces reconciliation between God and the sinner, and this acceptance is our justification (cf. Rom. 5:19) (3.11.4).

Refutation of Infused Righteousness

Calvin has set forth the doctrine of justification by faith alone in a synoptic form. In order to expound and expand upon it, he sets it next to aberrant views. Specifically, he first sets justification by faith alone against the view of Osiander, who introduced the "strange monster of 'essential' righteousness" (3.11.5).

Osiander taught that we are righteous not merely by Christ's obedience and sacrificial death, but we are "substantially righteous in God by the infusion both of his essence and of his quality" (3.11.5). Thus we are *made* righteous with the essence of God. For Osiander, "to justify" means, finally, "to be made righteous, and [therefore] righteousness is not a free imputation but the holiness and uprightness that the essence of God, dwelling in us, inspires." As for Christ's redemptive work for us, Osiander "sharply states that Christ is himself our righteousness, not in so far as he, by expiating sins as Priest, appeased the Father on our behalf, but as he is eternal God and life" (3.11.6). This means that we are saved not through pardon or justification but through regeneration or sanctification. In other words, for Osiander, justification has become sanctification. He blends and confuses these ideas. Calvin argues that we may not tear Christ asunder, and so we must keep both aspects intact as distinct and necessary but not as one and the same (3.11.6).

Turning to the faith that justifies, Calvin wants to clear away some confusion in this regard. Osiander does not want faith to be viewed as having the power of justifying. Calvin agrees. Faith receives Christ. It doesn't perform a work or possess a power of itself. "For if faith justified of itself or through some intrinsic power, so to speak, as it is always weak and imperfect it would effect this only in part; thus the righteousness that conferred a fragment of salvation upon us would be defective" (3.11.7). Calvin, of course, completely rejects that conception of justifying faith. He writes, properly speaking, "we say... God alone justifies; then we transfer this same function to Christ because he was given to us for righteousness." So what is faith? "We compare faith to a kind of vessel; for unless we come empty and with the mouth of our soul open to seek Christ's grace, we are not capable of receiving Christ." Faith receives Christ, but Christ justifies. Faith is merely an instrument; Christ is "the Author and Minister of this great benefit"—that is, "the material cause," which means His righteousness is the content and stuff of our pardon and acceptance before God (3.11.7).

Osiander's view of justification really makes Christ's humanity, with the cross and resurrection, unnecessary. Since Christ infuses us with His divine nature, making us righteous, His humanity is expendable. Says Calvin, Osiander leads us away "from the priesthood of Christ and the person of the Mediator to his outward deity" (3.11.8).

Calvin, however, shows that justification comes by way of Christ's mediatorial work, according to His divine and human nature. He offers this explanation: "For even though Christ if he had not been true God could not cleanse our souls by his blood, nor appease his Father by his sacrifice, nor absolve us from guilt, nor, in sum, fulfill the office of priest, because the power of the flesh is unequal to so great a burden, yet it is certain that he carried out all these acts according to his human nature. For if we ask how we have been justified, Paul answers, 'By Christ's obedience' [Rom. 5:19 p.]." The righteousness of God by which we are justified is not an infusion of the divine essence into us. Instead, it is the righteousness by which God approves of us—Christ's righteousness according to His obedience—so that we stand acquitted and innocent before His judgment seat. To be sure, Christ, as He is God and man, justifies sinners. His righteousness, imputed to us for our justification, is wrought in His mediatorial office, which is His obedience to the law and sacrificial death for us (3.11.9).

Calvin maintains that Christ remains outside of us until the Head is joined to His members. The "mystical union" between Christ and His people has the "highest degree of importance." In Christ being made ours, we become sharers in all His benefits. This is why we must "put on Christ" and be "engrafted into his body." None of this, however, devolves into Osiander's error, where there is "a gross mingling of Christ and believers." We participate in the righteousness of Christ because God reckons His righteousness to us, received through faith, and in union with the Beloved (cf. 2 Pet. 1:4; 2 Cor. 5:21; 1 John 3:2) (3.11.10).

Another dimension of Osiander's doctrine that vexes Calvin is its practical outcome. Calvin is convinced that Osiander's view "enfeebles" our assurance of salvation. Osiander scorns the doctrine of a legal declaration of righteousness—i.e., imputation. He maintains that justification refers to the sinner actually becoming righteous with intrinsic righteousness, not mere pardon or acquittal.

Calvin counters this view. If the believer is intrinsically righteous—not just pardoned, forgiven, declared righteous, but actually holy—then what of the sins that linger in us and infect us? What is this newness of life, of which Osiander boasts, that walks in old ways? The biblical doctrine of justification teaches that believers receive acquittal. 2 Corinthians 5:19 explicitly teaches that believers are declared or reckoned righteous by imputation, not infusion; justification is by Christ's extrinsic work of expiation, not by their own intrinsic holiness (3.11.11). Because sin always remains in those justified, they are taught to rest in Christ's work throughout their lives. Infused righteousness either leads to presumption (I'm holy no matter how I live) or doubt (since I'm not holy Christ isn't really in me) (cf. 3.11.11). We must not forget that justification and sanctification, though distinct, are not separated.

In answer to Osiander's objection that we insult God in saying he justifies "those who actually remain wicked," Calvin notes that since "traces of sin always remain in the righteous, their justification must be very different from reformation into newness of life [cf. Rom. 6:4]," that is, sanctification (3.11.11). Thus, for Osiander to be correct, all traces of sin must be extinguished. If the righteous are intrinsically righteous before God's tribunal and not merely forensically or extrinsically so, why do the justified still sin? "No portion of righteousness," writes Calvin, "sets our consciences at peace until it has been determined that we are pleasing to God, because we are entirely righteous before him." Justification is perverted when doubt is injected into our minds, so that the assurance of salvation is shaken and we no longer freely and confidently call upon God. "For faith totters if it pays attention to works, since no one, even of the most holy, will find there anything on which to rely" (3.11.11). Upon his own uprightness as a believer Paul passed this verdict: "Wretched man that I am!" (Rom. 7:24). But justification brings consolation, for no one can bring a charge of accusation against those whom God justifies (Rom. 8:33ff.). We are righteous not because we possess righteousness in our own person; on the contrary, we are righteous through the obedience of the One God provided for our pardon and reconciliation (Rom. 5:19) (3.11.11–12).

Refutation of Confused Righteousness

Calvin next turns his attention to the medieval scholastic doctrine of justification, wherein sanctification and justification are melded into each other or confused with one another. For Rome, justification includes sanctification, for good works—in the way of regeneration or sanctification—are given an effectual place for our justification before God.

Calvin writes, "A great deal of mankind imagine that righteousness is composed of faith and works" (3.11.13). The contrast he presents is between "faith righteousness" and "works righteousness." If one stands, the other must fall. He begins with Philippians 3:8–9, where the apostle counts all "as dross" in order that he may gain Christ and be found in Him, "not having a righteousness of [his] own, based on law but one that is through faith" (3.11.13). This sets before us a clear "comparison of opposites," showing that a person, to obtain Christ, must forsake his or her own righteousness. The Jews failed at just this point; they appealed to their own righteousness rather than turn to God's mercy in Christ (Rom. 10:3). As Calvin affirms, faith, not works, excludes all boasting, for faith makes us look away from ourselves to Christ (Rom. 3:27). Abraham was justified not by works but by faith (Rom. 4:2). Moreover, reward given for works is a matter of debt—work performed and debt owed (Rom. 4:4). But righteousness in the way of faith is by grace. Therefore our justification "does not arise from the merit of works. Farewell, then, to the dream of those who think up a righteousness flowing together out of faith and works" (3.11.13).

Calvin proceeds to answer the claim that the works that count for justification are divine gifts wrought in us. They are the fruit of regeneration, not *our own* works. This still misses the contrast between the law and the gospel, says Calvin. All works are excluded for our justification, even if they are born of God's regenerating Spirit (Gal. 3:11–12). The law requires that all righteous demands be fulfilled. But the righteousness that is by faith calls us to believe in the One who has fulfilled all righteousness on our behalf in

His death and resurrection (Rom. 10:5, 9). "Not even spiritual works come into account when the power of justifying is ascribed to faith" (3.11.14). Calvin reminds us that believers are accounted righteous wholly "outside themselves" (cf. 3.11.14). This stands in direct contrast to finding justification as a doer of the law, for the works necessary to achieve justification before God through the law must meet the law's strict standard. Our works, however, according to that standard, avail us nothing. We are destitute such works (3.11.15).

The Roman doctrine points us not to the imputation of Christ's righteousness for our justification; rather, it assures us that the Spirit is helping us in the pursuit of holiness. This is sanctification, not justification (3.11.15).

> But Scripture, when it speaks of faith righteousness, leads us to something far different: namely, to turn aside from the contemplation of our own works and look solely upon God's mercy and Christ's perfection. Indeed, it presents this order of justification: to begin with, God deigns to embrace the sinner with his pure and freely given goodness, finding nothing in him except his miserable condition to prompt Him to mercy, since he sees man utterly void and bare of good works; and so he seeks in himself the reason to benefit man. Then God touches the sinner with a sense of his goodness in order that he, despairing of his own works, may ground the whole of his salvation in God's mercy. This is the experience of faith through which the sinner comes into possession of his salvation when from the teaching of the gospel he acknowledges that he has been reconciled to God: that with Christ's righteousness interceding and forgiveness of sins accomplished he is justified. And although regenerated by the Spirit of God, he ponders the everlasting righteousness laid up for him not in the good works to which he inclines but in the sole righteousness of Christ (3.11.16).

Calvin returns to the nature of faith in God's work of justifying us, for Rome misperceives what role faith occupies in this act. As we saw in his comments toward Osiander, faith has, for Calvin, merely an instrumental function in justification. That is, "Faith is said to justify because it receives and embraces the righteousness offered through the gospel. Moreover, because righteousness is said to be offered through the gospel, all consideration of works is excluded" (3.11.17). Commenting on Romans 10, Calvin writes: "For in comparing the law and the gospel in the letter to the Romans [Paul] says: 'the righteousness that is of the law' is such that 'the man who practices these things will live by them' [Rom. 10:5]. But the 'righteousness that is of faith' [Rom. 10:6] announces salvation 'if you believe in your heart and confess with your mouth that Jesus is Lord and that the Father raised him from the dead' [Rom. 10:9 p.]." Then Calvin asks, "Do you see how he makes this the distinction between law and gospel: that the former attributes righteousness to works, the latter bestows free righteousness apart from the help of works?" (3.11.17).

Faith righteousness is "freed of all conditions of the law." It is a matter of promise (Gal. 3:18). Of course, the law had promises too, but they were of a conditional nature: "Do this and live." The promises of the gospel, however, "are free and dependent solely upon God's mercy" (3.11.17).

Another important passage is Galatians 3:11–12 ("But that no man is justified by the law in the sight of God, *it is* evident: for, the just shall live by faith. And the law is not of faith"). Righteousness or justification is not by the law but by faith. The law is not of faith. The law is of performance and obedience and meeting its strict perfection. "The law…is different from faith." Why? "Because works are required for law righteousness." But our works don't apply for faith righteousness. To be justified by faith is to be justified without the merit of works—indeed, our works are without merit in any case. Faith receives what our works could not achieve—that is, the righteousness that the gospel bestows, the righteousness of Christ. This is where the gospel distinguishes itself from the law. The law—being law—demands righteous works. The gospel lodges this righteousness in God's merciful provision. Faith receives what God gives (3.11.18). And nothing accompanies faith in this work. This is why it is by faith *alone*. Any addition to faith, be it our half-righteous or tainted good works, denies the righteousness of the gospel (Rom. 1:17; cf. Gal. 3:10). We are freely justified, apart from the law (Rom. 3:21, 24, 28). The law judges and condemns us; it brings us under the sentence of God's wrath (Rom. 4:15). The gospel pardons and forgives; it brings us under the sentence of God's mercy in Christ. All boasting is therefore excluded (Rom. 3:27; Gal. 3:21ff.) (3.11.19).

Calvin also counters those who try to insert love into faith in order to re-insert works into justification. Since faith works through love, and genuine faith produces works of repentance, righteousness is then claimed for faith. Yes, says Calvin, "no other faith justifies 'but faith working through love' [Gal. 5:6]. But faith does not take its power to justify from that working of love. Indeed, it justifies in no other way but in that it leads us into fellowship with the righteousness of Christ" (3.11.20).

The righteousness of faith is the forgiveness of sins. Faith doesn't bring any works of righteousness to Christ. As Calvin explains, Christ receives us into union with Himself and we are justified. This is because God cannot receive us as forgiven nor join us to Himself in fellowship unless He changes us into righteous persons. This righteousness is the forgiveness of our sins. Justification is the turning away of God's wrath inasmuch as we are pardoned (3.11.21). This is free acceptance because of Christ's righteousness (3.11.22). More explicitly, we are justified in God's sight "by the intercession of Christ's righteousness" (3.11.23). Our righteousness is in Christ, not ourselves. By faith we turn away from ourselves and our works and we turn to Him. All riches and blessings are found in Him (Rom. 8:1–4). We are no longer under the sentence of condemnation because we are under the sentence of acquittal and forgiveness, justified through one man's obedience (Rom. 5:19). "To declare that by him alone we are accounted righteous, what else is this but to lodge our righteousness in Christ's obedience, because the obedience of Christ is reckoned to us as if it were our own?" (3.11.23). Using an illustration from Ambrose, Calvin says that our justification in Christ may be likened to our hiding "under the precious purity of our first-born brother, Christ, so that we may be attested righteous in God's sight" (3.11.23).

Chapter Twelve: We Must Lift Up Our Minds to God's Judgment Seat That We May Be Firmly Convinced of His Free Justification

Justification before God's Perfection
With this chapter Calvin shifts the discussion of justification to the believer's appropriation of the doctrine, or how the believer ought to benefit from a knowledge of God's grace given to us as free acceptance in Christ. This is necessary because the law ever reminds us that no one, apart from Christ, is righteous in God's sight. Without an appreciation of this simple truth, justification by faith is of "precious little value." Calvin chastises human vanity:

> In the shady cloisters of the schools anyone can easily and readily prattle about the value of works in justifying men. But when we come before the presence of God we put away such amusements! For there we deal with a serious matter, and do not engage in frivolous word battles. To this question, I insist, we must apply our mind if we would profitably inquire concerning true righteousness: How shall we reply to the

Heavenly Judge when he calls us to account? Let us envisage for ourselves that Judge, not as our minds naturally imagine Him, but as He is depicted for us in Scripture: by whose brightness the stars are darkened; by whose strength the mountains are melted; by whose wrath the earth is shaken; whose wisdom catches the wise in their craftiness; beside whose purity all things are defiled; whose righteousness not even the angels can bear; who makes not the guilty man innocent; whose vengeance when once kindled penetrates to the depths of hell. Let us behold him, I say, sitting in judgment to examine the deeds of men: Who will stand confident before his throne? (3.12.1).

Indeed, "unless every man admit his guilt before the Heavenly Judge, and concerned about his own acquittal, willingly cast himself down and confess his nothingness," the whole discussion about justification is not only useless, but also foolish and weak (3.12.1).

Calvin is in fact offering a practical observation about justification. Many persons do not regard the doctrine as cool water for parched souls but as unnecessary information that may be ignored. For Calvin, if persons do not rise up to a contemplation of God in His majestic holiness (instead consoling themselves with a comparison of others), they will have no sense of their desperate need for rescue or for divine mercy. Only when we look away from our fellows, with their sins, and look to God in His righteousness do we come to the right assessment of ourselves and discover in the gospel the answer to the malicious and melancholic malady of our sin. How easy to justify ourselves before human beings; how impossible to do so before God (3.12.2). Calvin volunteers Augustine and Bernard of Clairvaux as respected theologians who eloquently make this point (3.11.3).

Conscience Condemns Our Works

From another angle, Calvin makes the same point. Only when we see ourselves as under God's frown, with His just penalty against us because of our guilt and corruption, will our consciences grow worried and seek refuge. Just as the stars lose their brilliance in the light of day before the sun, so we cease to think ourselves innocent in the light of God's purity (3.11.4). Human vanity, self-flattery, and the practice of comparing ourselves with others soothe the conscience and console us in our haughtiness. God, however, sets the standard that unmasks the filth and defilement of our supposed works of righteousness. Then we also cease to admire and flatter ourselves. Self-love blinds us to our true need. God sees into the heart and detects every impurity (cf. Job 25:6; 15:16; 14:4; 9:20; Isa. 53:6). When we examine ourselves according to Scripture, says Calvin, we are cast down "into complete consternation." This consternation, however, is the very thing needed to prepare us "to receive Christ's grace." For God gives His grace to the humble (1 Pet. 5:5; James 4:6) (3.11.5). It is noteworthy, as Calvin has asserted earlier, we need to see our sin and God's judgment, but we also need to see that God is favorable and loving toward us.

The psalmist reminds us of this very truth. Calvin bids us to heed the words of Psalm 18:27 and Psalm 17:28, which instruct us about the proud and about the humble. Concerning these passages Calvin writes:

> first consider that the gateway to salvation does not lie open unless we have laid aside all pride and taken upon ourselves perfect humility; secondly, that this humility is not some seemly behavior whereby you yield a hair of your right to the Lord, as those who do not act haughtily or insult others are called humble in the sight of men, although they rely upon some consciousness of excellence. Rather, this humility is an unfeigned submission of our heart, stricken down in earnest with an awareness of its own misery and want. For so it is everywhere described by the Word of God (3.12.6).

God comes to the lowly and contrite (Isa. 66:2). The humbled publican goes away justified (Luke 18:13) (3.12.7). Conversely, arrogance and complacency are both a pestilence. Sinners arrogantly regard themselves as righteous and commendable to God. Alternatively, sinners complacently become "drunk with the sweetness of their vices" and don't give God's judgment a moment's thought. We will never trust Christ until we are contrite and distrust ourselves (cf. 3.12.8).

Chapter Thirteen: Two Things to Be Noted in Free Justification

Justification Glorifies God

Calvin, as we have seen, is concerned that believers neither rob God of His honor nor rob themselves of peace and consolation. These concerns are the burden of chapter thirteen. Hence his words, "Here, indeed, we are especially to note two things: namely, that the Lord's glory should stand undiminished and, so to speak, in good repair, and that our consciences in the presence of his judgment should have peaceful rest and serene tranquility" (3.13.1).

When we claim honor for ourselves, we inevitably cheat God of the honor belonging to Him. That is to say, to the degree we claim for ourselves "even a crumb of righteousness," to just that degree we pluck and take away "the glory of God's righteousness" (3.13.2).

Justification Brings Tranquility to Our Consciences
Meanwhile, any righteousness we claim as our own cannot give us peace of conscience. Is there anyone who has not sunken into infinite filth? Indeed, our conscience calls us to account. Our works cry out for condemnation. Instead of peace our conscience is plagued with torment (3.13.3). Besides, if we look to ourselves we are not looking to the promises of God for our salvation. God's promises are truly embraced when we receive them with the assurance of conscience. This assurance can only come by finding ourselves in Christ, the King of peace (Isa. 9:6; Eph. 2:14). "In short, we must seek peace for ourselves solely in the anguish of Christ our Redeemer" (3.13.4).

Thus Calvin solicits believers to rest in God's promises. Indeed, can rest ever be found in either faith or regeneration? No! These are always imperfect. Hence we are driven to the sole remedy, which is "that believers should be convinced that their only ground of hope for the inheritance of a Heavenly Kingdom lies in the fact that, being engrafted in the body of Christ, they are freely accounted righteous. For, regarding justification, faith is something merely passive, bringing nothing of ours to the recovering of God's favor but receiving from Christ that which we lack" (3.13.5).

Chapter Fourteen: The Beginning of Justification and Its Continual Progress

Four Classes of Persons
To bring more clarity to his discussion of this doctrine, Calvin notes that there are four classes of people with regard to justification: (1) those who are in rank unbelief, without Christ's righteousness; (2) those who are initiated into the church by means of the sacraments, yet because they lead such impure lives they deny God through their actions, even though they vainly confess Him with their lips—these possess Christ in name only; (3) those who are false brothers, hiding their hypocrisy and wicked heart from others; and (4) those who are regenerated by the Holy Spirit and are truly

concerned to live holy lives (3.14.1). Only the fourth class of people escapes divine punishment.

• *Unbelievers.* Calvin acknowledges the "notable endowments" and virtues that believers discern in those "outside Christ." These come from God's hand; He bestows them as gifts (3.14.2). Yet, says Calvin, we must understand that such virtues fall well short of the height of God's glory and purity. Consequently, the beneficiaries of these gifts deserve punishment because, by the pollution of their hearts, they defile even these wonderful endowments from the Lord (cf. 3.14.2–3). In addition, since unbelievers do not serve God with the gifts He bestows unto them, their virtuosity is a sham. The good they perform isn't intended "to serve God" and consequently must, "by its perverse intention," be reckoned "sin" (3.14.3). Moreover, "those who have no part in Christ, whatever they may be, whatever they may do or undertake, yet hasten all their lives to destruction and to the judgment of eternal death" (3.14.4). Calvin is emphatic: "God finds nothing in man to arouse him to do good to him but that he comes first to man in his free generosity" (3.14.5). Our works are excluded. Calvin observes that words like Titus 3:4–5 ("But after that the kindness and love of God our Saviour toward man appeared, not by works of righteousness which we have done, but according to his mercy he saved us") deprive humans of even "the slightest particle" of righteousness. "If the righteousness of works brings anything to justify us, we are falsely said to be justified by grace" (3.14.5). Since we need the cleansing of Christ's blood (1 Pet. 1:2), let us not deceive ourselves into thinking that we are anything less than miserable sinners apart from Christ. Indeed, faith in Christ is itself the beginning of our journey from death to life (3.14.6).

• *Nominal Christians and Hypocrites.* Calvin groups together the second and third type of persons in relation to justification—that is, name-only Christians and hypocrites (3.14.7). Like outright unbelievers, nominal Christians and false brothers are under condemnation. Since they are unregenerated, they are subject to God's wrath. Lacking faith, they lack Christ. In short, they are unreconciled to God. Their so-called "good works" are nothing of the sort. Their "religious performances" are mere hypocrisies. The works of such people are so far from the righteousness God requires that they can only be reckoned sins (cf. Isa. 1:13–16; Prov. 15:8). No difference that matters exists between the first three classes of people pertaining to justification before God (3.14.7–8).

• *The Regenerated.* As for the fourth class of people, those "in Christ," Calvin says this about them:

> We confess that while through the intercession of Christ's righteousness God reconciles us to himself, and by free remission of sins accounts us righteous, his beneficence is at the same time joined with such a mercy that through his Holy Spirit he dwells in us and by his power the lusts of our flesh are each day more and more mortified; we are indeed sanctified, that is, consecrated to the Lord in true purity of life, with our hearts formed to obedience to the law. The end is that our especial will may be to serve his will and by every means to advance his glory alone (3.14.9).

Throughout our lives, even while led by the Spirit, enough failure besets our striving after godliness to keep us humble and dependent upon Christ alone. Even more, "we have not a single work going forth from the saints that if it be judged in itself deserves not shame as its just reward" (3.14.9). Whoever fails at one point of the law, fails in the whole law (James 2:10). The law perpetually condemns us without justification (3.14.10). This is why "there never existed any work of a godly man which, if examined by God's stern judgment, would not deserve condemnation"—even if such a work existed, the doer of such a work is still contaminated with other sins which wholly corrupt him (3.14.11). If works play a part, then our boasting plays a part, the very thing the apostle denies (Eph. 2:8–9) (3.14.11).

Rome's Objections to Faith Justification
The remainder of this chapter deals with Roman Catholic teachings on justification. We will not cover the various facets of this discussion, except to pause at some pertinent highpoints. Calvin combats the Roman doctrine of "works of supererogation" (3.14.12–17). Works of supererogation refer to the believer's performance of works beyond what God requires, such that the believer acquires merit through them. For Calvin, this is pure fantasy. Luke 17:10 makes clear that we owe all to God and in giving all to Him we have merely done our duty as unprofitable servants. Besides, as earlier observed, our works are tainted in any case. Without the righteousness of

Christ to cover them, we cannot be acceptable in God's sight; neither can our works (3.11.13–16).

Calvin makes an appeal to the philosophical distinction of fourfold causality—which might better be termed four ways of explaining something, namely the efficient cause, the material cause, the formal (or instrumental) cause, and the final cause. He does this to clarify the parts of justification, which in turn shows that no part or parcel of it consists of our works.

> For Scripture everywhere proclaims that the efficient cause of our obtaining eternal life is the mercy of the Heavenly Father and his freely given love toward us. Surely the material cause is Christ, with his obedience, through which he acquired righteousness for us. What shall we say is the formal or instrumental cause but faith? And John includes these three in one sentence when he says: "God so loved the world that he gave his only-begotten Son that everyone who believes in him may not perish but have eternal life" [John 3:16]. As for the final cause, the apostle testifies that it consists both in the proof of divine justice and in the praise of God's goodness... (3.14.17).

Romans 3:23–26 exhibits these four explanations of our justification as well.

Calvin does not deny that our good works can serve to fortify faith. Good works strengthen faith but make no contribution whatsoever to our salvation. We may even say that good works are a sign of "divine benevolence" (3.14.18). Works can function to undergird and strengthen our faith, for they are exhibits of God's kindness toward us. They are fruits of regeneration and signify the indwelling of the Holy Spirit (3.14.19). Indeed, works that are "good" are a gift from God. As such they become, for believers, signs confirming their election. Thus, good works in themselves are not antithetical to free justification (3.14.20). Yet they can never constitute the foundation or ground of our justification. Our free acceptance, which alone consoles and assures us, is founded on Christ's righteousness and none other (3.14.21).

Observations

In the order of teaching, Calvin has treated the doctrine of sanctification and the Christian life prior to an exposition of justification. Calvin explains that he did this for a twofold reason: (1) to show that justification by faith alone does not produce a Christian walk destitute of good works; (2) to show the

nature of those good works. By expounding sanctification prior to justification, Calvin can refute the charge that was perpetually made against free
justification, namely, that this doctrine leads to a life absent of good works
and the practice of godliness. In order to demonstrate that the Reformed,
with the doctrine of justification by faith alone, have neither forfeited good
works nor failed to urge believers to seek to do good, Calvin first examined,
at some length, the Christian life, which is a life of faith and repentance. He
also sketched for us the chief characteristics of Christian piety.

So, Calvin presents sanctification before justification, in part, to meet a
polemical concern about good works as part of the Christian life. But Calvin
adds a second explanation for this order of presentation, and it has to do
with the weighty theological point pertaining to our justification, namely,
with this order of presentation he can show us "what is the nature of the
good works of the saints." The nature of those works must be noted, for in
fact we discover why we may put no confidence in our well-doing and why
good works have no part to play in the believer's justification. Our good
works—even our best works—are bankrupt and polluted in themselves.
Consequently, with this understanding, we can be more assured that our
justification is absent any merit of our own. This is a key point in Calvin's discussion of justification. The theological and pedagogical purpose is primary:
believers, standing before God, with their best sanctified foot put forward,
so to speak, must see how empty-handed they are and thus reach for the gift
of salvation in Christ and His righteousness alone. Only then do believers
discover that even their "good works" of faith—produced in them by the
Holy Spirit—fail to meet the standard of God's perfect righteousness.

Questions for Reflection and Discussion

1. What do phrases like "reckoned righteous" and "imputation of Christ's
   righteousness" mean? Do we do enough with the "acceptance" dimension of justification?

2. What is the difference between "Christ in the believer" versus "the be-
   liever in Christ"? Look up Galatians 3:8; Luke 16:15; Ephesians 1:5–6;
   Romans 3:26–28, 4:4–7, 5:19, 8:33, 10:5–6; 2 Corinthians 5:18–21.
   These are some of the texts Calvin comments upon. Why is the doctrine

of "essential righteousness" (*a la* Osiander) so dangerous? (Note: It is promoted today by the "Exchanged Life" teaching.)

3. Does the modern church today think of God as wrathful, needing to be appeased?

4. Is the church or the world interested in the question of justification? Does modern crusade evangelism preach "God" the way Calvin does? Should it?

5. Why is it false to say that justification by faith alone leads to cockiness, presumption, or smugness?

6. Have you ever thought of your works as "justified"? How does this help bring assurance to doubting believers?

7. Many modern Christians are bored with the doctrine of justification by faith alone. In former times, people sacrificed their lives for it. What accounts for this boredom, i.e., what are the factors, social and theological, that lie behind this apathy for the heart of the gospel?

∝ 15 ∾

Justification, Good Works,
and Christian Liberty

Chapters 15–19 of Book Three

Chapter Fifteen: Boasting About the Merits of Works Destroys
Our Praise of God for Having Bestowed Righteousness,
As Well As Our Assurance of Salvation

Orientation

• CALVIN PRESENTED HIS doctrine of justification by faith alone in the previous chapter. Now he offers a further defense of the doctrine in the face of various criticisms and objections. He also examines an assortment of ancillary questions and issues that seem to threaten or undermine free justification. In particular, Calvin addresses various questions about the role of works in the Christian life. He closes out his discussion of justification by demonstrating how this doctrine generates a Christian life marked by freedom rather than bondage, for justification's power delivers us from the yoke of the law.

Human Merit and Justification

Calvin begins with a short review. Our righteousness depends wholly upon God's grace in Christ by faith—that is, righteousness "is confined solely to God's mercy, solely to communion with Christ, and therefore solely to faith." If our righteousness depended in any way, to any degree, on our works, it must "entirely collapse" in God's sight (3.15.1).

With this summary of his doctrine of justification by faith alone in place, Calvin next takes up the question of merit—a term that needs to be carefully understood lest we fall into error. Calvin could wish that this boastful word was altogether banished from our theological vocabularies. The ancient writers, however, did use the word in a non-offensive way, so we likewise do well to define it in a way that does justice to scriptural teaching (3.15.2).

"Scripture shows what all our works deserve when it states that they cannot bear God's gaze because they are full of uncleanness." Thus even if we should perfectly do all that the law requires of us, we must admit that we are at best unprofitable servants, having only fulfilled our duty (Luke 17:10). We certainly haven't merited anything before God. Yet the Bible teaches us that God rewards good works. Calvin explains that "whatever is praiseworthy in works is God's grace; there is not a drop that we ought by rights to ascribe to ourselves." Once we see this point, we will cease to inflate ourselves with any confident notions of our merit. Even the idea of our own merit will disappear. This being clear, we must remember, insofar as He rewards our works, He is rewarding His own righteousness in them. In this way, "good works...are pleasing to God and are not unfruitful for their doers." That good works are rewarded at all, however, is not due to any merit in them or because God regards them as deserving His blessing. It is only "because God's kindness has of itself set this value on them" (3.15.3). It is divine generosity, not human merit that accounts for this.

Calvin returns to a theme he has already touched on, namely, that all our works are tainted with sin. "Now it is the teaching of Scripture that our good works are always spattered with much uncleanness, by which God is rightly offended and is angry against us" (3.15.4). So how can our works receive a reward? This comes from the fact that God considers "our works according to his tenderness, not his supreme right," and so He "accepts them as if they were perfectly pure; and for that reason, although unmerited, they are rewarded with infinite benefits, both of the present life and also of the life to come" (3.15.4).

Christ's Merit—the Foundation of Our Justification

Jesus Christ and His righteousness stand at the foundation of this blessed reckoning of our works—that is, the reward granted to our (tainted) good works is grounded in the righteousness of Christ. As Calvin asks:

> What sort of foundation have we in Christ? Was he the beginning of our salvation in order that its fulfillment might follow from ourselves? Did he only open the way by which we might proceed under our own power? Certainly not. But, as Paul had set forth..., Christ, when we acknowledge him, is given us to be our righteousness [1 Cor. 1:30]. He alone is well founded in Christ who has perfect righteousness himself:

since the apostle does not say that He was sent to help us attain righteousness but himself to be our righteousness [1 Cor. 1:30].... In brief, because all his things are ours and we have all things in him, in us there is nothing. Upon this foundation, I say, we must be built if we would grow into a holy temple to the Lord [cf. Eph. 2:21] (3.15.5).

Before returning to the theme of Christ as the foundation of reward, Calvin sets Rome's doctrine in contrast to what he has articulated above. He finds it lacking (see 3.15.6–7).

Union with Christ is the key to Calvin's discussion. When persons are engrafted into Christ through faith, they become God's children, heirs of heaven, partakers in righteousness, possessors of life, and receive "all the merits of Christ." Union with Christ doesn't bestow to them the opportunity to obtain merits of their own; rather, that mystical union communicates all Christ's merits to them (3.15.6). We mustn't underestimate the importance of this, for justification is "the sum of all piety." When this doctrine is lost, piety is lost.

Calvin's Roman Catholic opponents argued that "formed faith"—i.e., a love working faith or a faith working love—justifies. Calvin argues that this idea turns faith into a human performance and a kind of merit which depends as much on human free will as on divine grace. Faith becomes a good work. Advocates of this notion "filch something from God and turn it over to man." This runs directly contrary to Ephesians 2:10 ("For we are his workmanship, created in Christ Jesus unto good works, which God hath before ordained that we should walk in them"). "Since, therefore, no good comes forth from us except in so far as we have been regenerated, but our regeneration is entirely and without exception from God, there is no reason why we should claim an ounce of good works for ourselves" (3.15.7). The Roman doctrine discourages and disheartens consciences regarding God's kindness and favor, whereas the Reformation doctrine, making no appeal to our merits, cheers and comforts the hearts of believers (3.15.7).

Calvin urges us to build only on the foundation of Christ. "Let us not allow ourselves to be drawn even a finger's breadth from this sole foundation" (3.15.8). In being called to a life of cross-bearing and denying self, we are called to be obedient unto death, to labor for God's glory, to expend ourselves for His church, yet not without consolation (cf. 2 Cor. 4:8–10; 2 Tim. 2:11–12; Phil. 3:10–11) (3.15.8).

Chapter Sixteen: Refutation of the False Accusations by Which the Papists Try to Cast Odium upon This Doctrine

Justification and the Zeal for Good Works

The arrow that was continually aimed at the Reformation doctrine of justification by faith alone is that it does away with good works. The doctrine leads to a life lived in reckless immorality and makes the path to righteousness too easy.

Calvin responds to such arrows of criticism in this chapter. First he shows how the doctrine of free grace and the free remission of our sins through faith, not works, actually encourages godly conduct rather than subverting it. Calvin explains, "We dream neither of a faith devoid of good works nor of a justification that stands without them." Instead, "having admitted that faith and good works must cleave together, we still lodge justification in faith, not in works." To say "faith" is to say that we turn to Christ in whom all righteousness is found. "Why, then, are we justified by faith? Because by faith we grasp Christ's righteousness." By Christ's righteousness alone "we are reconciled to God" (3.16.1). As Calvin further explains, one cannot take hold of justification without simultaneously taking hold of sanctification. That Christ is our righteousness means that He is this for us altogether and comprehensively; He is our wisdom, our sanctification, and our redemption (cf. 1 Cor. 1:30). "Therefore Christ justifies no one whom he does not at the same time sanctify. These benefits are joined together by an everlasting and indissoluble bond, so that those whom he illumines by his wisdom, he redeems; those whom he redeems, he justifies; those whom he justifies, he sanctifies" (3.16.1).

It is important, however, not to miss how Calvin treats the relationship between justification and sanctification. The believer's union with Christ does not allow us to separate these blessings, though we may certainly differentiate them.

> Although we may distinguish them, Christ contains both of them inseparably in himself. Do you wish, then, to attain righteousness in Christ? You must first possess Christ; but you cannot possess him without being made partaker in his sanctification, because he cannot be divided into pieces [1 Cor. 1:13]. Since, therefore, it is solely by expending himself that the Lord gives us these benefits to enjoy, he bestows both of them at the same time, the one never without the other. Thus it is clear how true it is that we are justified not without works yet

not through works, since in our sharing in Christ, which justifies us, sanctification is just as much included as righteousness (3.16.1).

It is clear enough, then, our justification is a divine gift that God gives, and in giving it, He always gives the accompanying gift of sanctification and vice-versa.

Justification and the Right Motives for Good Works
In this line, Calvin refutes the snipe brought against the Reformation doctrine of justification from another angle as well, for he shows how the believer is subjectively encouraged to do good works because of the doctrine of justification by faith alone. The Roman error is egregious: "For first, in saying men will take no care to regulate their lives aright unless hope of reward is held out to them, they are completely in error. For if it is only a matter of men looking for reward when they serve God, and hiring or selling their labor to him, it is of little profit. God wills to be freely worshiped, freely loved. That worshiper, I say, he approves who, when all hope of receiving reward has been cut off, still ceases not to serve him" (3.16.2).

God's love is the spur that prods us and makes us press on in good works. The love of God—the love that first loved us—urges us forward in the new life He gives (1 John 4:19). This is why, being delivered from death and the life of sin, we can now live a new life, awaiting the hope to come (cf., e.g., Heb. 9:14; 10:29; Luke 1:74–75; Rom. 6:4–6; Col. 3:1–3; Titus 2:11–13; 1 Thess. 5:9; Eph. 5:8–9; 1 Thess. 4:7; Rom. 6:18; 2 Cor. 7:1; 1 Pet. 2:21) (3.16.2).

If God's love for us forms one motive for fastening good works to justification, our love for God forms another motive. Indeed, God's honor and mercy are motives for living a life surrendered and obedient to God. We love God in His goodness and grace. It is therefore mistaken to think that the most powerful exhortations to godliness are due to the promise of reward being held out to us. No, such exhortations derive their power "from the thought that our salvation stands upon no merit of ours but solely upon God's mercy" (see Rom. 12:1). It is utterly misguided to think, by stressing merits, persons will serve God freely and from love rather than slavishly and under coercion (3.16.3). To be sure, Scripture provides us with exhortations that promise reward (see Rom. 2:6–7; Matt. 16:27; 1 Cor. 3:8, 14–15; 2 Cor. 5:10, etc.). But such exhortations are not primary—and we shouldn't allow these to be our principal motivation for aiming to live in obedience to God.

Prompts and prods of future reward are of little value "unless we give prior place to the doctrine that we are justified by Christ's merit alone, which is grasped through faith, but by no merits of our own works, because no men can be fit for the pursuit of holiness save those who have first imbibed this doctrine" (3.16.3).

In addition to the above mentioned motives moving to good works, we need to remember Christ's sacrifice on the cross. While salvation is free for us, it wasn't so for Christ. He "dearly bought it at the cost of his most sacred blood, apart from which there was no ransom of sufficient worth to satisfy God's judgment" (3.16.4). This teaches us the nature of our predicament, the depth of our depravity, and why Christ alone is our hope. Here we are shown that we cannot live a life that makes Christ's atoning work unnecessary or even less necessary. Only His blood cleanses us of our foulness. If we fear God, how can we sin thoughtlessly and without remorse, or wallow in the mire, when the blood of Christ has been sprinkled for our purification? Reaching his conclusion, Calvin writes:

> Now it is plain which persons prefer to cheapen the forgiveness of sins, and which ones to prostitute the dignity of righteousness. They make believe that God is appeased by their wretched satisfactions, which are but dung [Phil 3:8]. We affirm that the guilt of sin is too heavy to be atoned for by such light trifles, that it is too grave an offense against God to be remitted by these worthless satisfactions, that this, then, is the prerogative of Christ's blood alone. They say that righteousness, if ever it fails, is restored and repaired by works of satisfaction. We count it too precious to be matched by any compensation of works; and therefore, to recover it, we must take refuge in God's mercy alone (3.16.4).

Chapter Seventeen: The Agreement of the Promises of the Law and of the Gospel

Orientation
With this chapter Calvin continues his discussion of justification and its relation to faith and works, especially the relationship between works and reward. In particular, Calvin wants to demonstrate that the doctrine of justification by faith alone does not stand in the way of (or discourage) works of godliness. Various objections continually come against this doctrine, how-

ever. Calvin regards this as a spiritual battle, not just a theological dispute. Indeed, "Satan, through his minions, tries to overthrow or weaken justification of faith."

Scholastic Objections Answered
In making his case for the role of works in the life of the believer, Calvin explains that justification does not negate works. On the contrary, the justified are to do good works and in doing them those works may be called good; but good works do not justify and we may not rely on them for justification. Neither may we appeal to our good works to "glory in them, or ascribe salvation to them" (3.17.1).

The key objection against the doctrine of justification by faith alone which occupies Calvin at this point has to do with the promises attached to the law. There are many texts that promise blessing if the law is honored and obeyed (cf. Deut. 7:12–13; 11:16; 30:15; Jer. 7:5–7). Calvin reminds readers that in fact the law condemns us unless we keep it perfectly (Deut. 27:26). The law utters down a curse on all human beings, for all have violated the law. What we need and what God gives to us in Christ is freedom from the law—that is, freedom from its sentence of damnation. This freedom is not a liberation from striving after holiness or living by the moral standard of the law. It is a "spiritual freedom," which consoles our "stricken and prostrate conscience, showing it to be free from the curse and condemnation with which the law pressed it down, bound and fettered" (3.17.1).

Calvin reminds us, too, that the promises attached to the law are null and void—unfulfilled—except that the gospel comes forth to do for us what we cannot do for ourselves. In the gospel God has intervened and fulfilled the conditions attached to the law. Out of His goodness, God provides the way. He refuses to leave to us even the smallest fragment of righteousness to perform. Instead, according to His loving-kindness, God supplies everything that is needed. He supplies it through Christ's fulfillment of all righteousness (3.17.2).

So what becomes of the promises attached to the law? Calvin offers this important explanation regarding the promises of the gospel standing in place of the conditional promises of the law:

> But when the promises of the gospel are substituted, which proclaim the free forgiveness of sins, these not only make us acceptable to God but render our works pleasing to him. And not only does the Lord adjudge them pleasing; he also extends to them the blessings which

under the covenant were owed to the observance of the law. I therefore admit that what the Lord has promised in his law to the keepers
of righteousness and holiness is paid to the works of believers, but in
this repayment we must always consider the reason that wins favor for
these works (3.17.3).

In fact, there are three reasons: (1) we, with our works, are viewed and
embraced in Christ, in whom our works are reconciled to God by faith alone,
certainly not by our works which are blameworthy; (2) God raises our works
to a place of honor, even attributing value to them, out of His fatherly generosity and loving-kindness; and (3) God pardons and forgives our works, "not
imputing the imperfection with which they are all so corrupted that they
would otherwise be reckoned as sins rather than virtues" (3.17.3).

Calvin explains that humans need "a double acceptance before God,"
which in fact God gives. First, we need divine acceptance since God finds
nothing in the natural man to move Him to mercy except his miserable
condition. God thus comes to humans as fallen, unlovable, and bereft of all
good, without any merits. "God's sole reason to receive man unto himself is
that he sees him utterly lost if left to himself, but because he does not will
him to be lost, he exercises his mercy in freeing him." This is the first sort of
acceptance, wherein God, solely from His own goodness, is moved to favor
man, who is utterly unworthy and absent righteousness (3.17.4). The second
acceptance comes after God's work of grace has been wrought in sinful humans. Being adopted and embraced as new creatures in Christ, God "cannot
fail to love and embrace the good things that he works in them through
his Spirit." God's acceptance of our works, however, is only because God
Himself is their source. Here Calvin again refers to the second justification
that believers enjoy, for God reckons our works "good" from His Fatherly
kindness by granting "pardon for those blemishes and spots which cleave to
them" (3.17.5). Indeed, the works of believers are incomplete, soiled with
sin and "redolent of the vices of the flesh." They are acceptable only in being
reckoned in Christ (3.17.5).

This doesn't disparage the believer's good works. Good works comport
with our covenantal obligation lest God's mercy be mocked and we pursue
wickedness instead of holiness. In fact, good works are our duty as living
within God's covenant fellowship. Only, this must not be misconstrued, for
"the covenant is from the outset drawn up as a free agreement, and perpetually remains such" (3.17.5).

The fulfillment of the Lord's mercy—the promises of the gospel—"does not depend upon believers' works." The promises of the law were after the order of: "Do this and live." They were conditioned on human performance. God fulfills His own gospel promises in His children. These promises depend upon the Lord. Such promises do not form the foundation for blessing, but serve as a pathway that urges us forward and along which God welcomes, protects, and strengthens us in the way of salvation. In this way we see how gospel promises function, which in no way undermines justification by faith alone. "Therefore if one seeks the first cause that opens for the saints the door of God's Kingdom, and hence gives them a permanent standing-ground in it, at once we answer: Because the Lord by his own mercy has adopted them once for all, and keeps them continually. But if the question is of the manner, we must proceed to regeneration and its fruits…" (3.17.6).

Sometimes the believer's observance of the law is referred to as righteousness. Calvin argues that this does not strictly apply, since righteousness through the law must be complete and perfect. Once more, righteousness cannot be obtained by our law-keeping, for in fact no one keeps it in this manner (3.17.7). More difficult is the matter where faith is counted as righteousness, i.e., the act of believing is viewed as a righteous deed. For example, Abraham's faith was reckoned to him as righteousness (Rom. 4:3; Gal. 3:6). This is faith righteousness. Opponents to free justification commandeer this idea in order to turn faith into a kind of work; then, it is argued, works form part of justification. Calvin points out that the matter is not that tidy. "It is one thing to discuss what value works have of themselves, another, to weigh in what place they are to be held after faith righteousness has been established" (3.17.8).

To clear up this misunderstanding, Calvin again defines justification: "the sinner, received into communion with Christ, is reconciled to God by his grace, while, cleansed by Christ's blood, he obtains forgiveness of sins, and clothed with Christ's righteousness as if it were his own, he stands confident before the heavenly judgment seat." Thus, now being found in Christ, with every stain and blot removed, God accounts the good works of believers righteous, i.e., He reckons them as righteousness (3.17.8). In Calvin's words, for the justified sinner, after

> forgiveness of sins is set forth, the good works that now follow are appraised otherwise than on their own merit. For everything imperfect in them is covered by Christ's perfection, every blemish or spot is cleansed away by his purity in order not to be brought in question at the divine judgment. Therefore, after the guilt of all transgressions

that hinder man from bringing forth anything pleasing to God has been blotted out, and after the fault of imperfection, which habitually defiles even good works, is buried, the good works done by believers are accounted righteous, or, what is the same thing, are reckoned as righteousness [Rom. 4:22] (3.17.8).

Faith righteousness must not be impugned. It should be beyond dispute that a person is not reckoned righteous from few works or manifold works. All our works may rightly be censured. We have no good work to offer to God that isn't besmirched with sin in some way or other. This should demonstrate that "faith righteousness," to which the Scripture refers from time to time, in no way mounts up to works of righteousness for justification; neither does such faith righteousness constitute a work that forms any part of our justification. How, asks Calvin, can one legitimately call such works righteous? "But if, of a certainty, it follows from justification of faith that works otherwise impure, unclean, half done, unworthy of God's sight, not to mention his love, are accounted righteousness, why do they by boasting of works righteousness try to destroy justification of faith, without whose existence they would boast of such righteousness in vain?" (3.17.9). In other words, if our works depend upon God's free justification in Christ through faith alone in order to be reckoned "good," it is absurd and indecent then to try to re-insert works into our justification (3.17.9).

Once more Calvin points us to his doctrine of double justification, wherein first the sinner is justified, and then the justified sinner is justified—that is, the works of the justified person are justified. "Therefore, as we ourselves, when we have been engrafted in Christ, are righteous in God's sight because our iniquities are covered by Christ's sinlessness, so our works are righteous and are thus regarded because whatever fault is otherwise in them is buried in Christ's purity, and is not charged to our account. Accordingly, we can deservedly say that by faith alone not only we ourselves but our works as well are justified" (3.17.10). Thus, even the good works believers do are accounted "good" by Christ's righteousness alone. This well answers the question of "faith righteousness."

Paul and James on Justification and Faith
At this point Calvin addresses the cavil that comes against the Reformation doctrine of justification by the appeal to James 2:21, 24. Rather than set Paul and James against one another—for the Spirit is not in conflict with Himself—Calvin observes that James "makes fun of the stupid assurance"

of those who openly manifest "their unbelief by neglecting and overlooking all the proper works of believers" (3.17.11).

Calvin sees his opponents falling into a "double fallacy: one in the word 'faith,' the other in the word 'justify.'" The faith that James calls 'dead' is clearly of a certain sort. "Obviously, if this faith contains nothing but a belief that there is a God, it is not strange if it does not justify!" For the nature of true faith is something different. Such faith justifies in that it binds us to Christ; thus, in being united to Him, we participate in His righteousness (3.17.11).

Likewise, James uses the word "justify" in a different sense than Paul's use of the term. James speaks of the "declaration" [or demonstration] of righteousness, not its "imputation." Notes Calvin, "It is as if he said: 'Those who by true faith are righteous prove their righteousness by obedience and good works, not by a bare and imaginary mask of faith'" (3.17.12). If James had used the word "justify" the way Paul does, then

> ...it would have been preposterous for him to quote Moses' statement: "Abraham believed God" [Gen. 15:6; James 2:23], etc. For this is the context: Abraham attained righteousness by works because at God's command he did not hesitate to sacrifice his son [James 2:21]. Thus is the Scripture fulfilled that says: "He believed God, and it was reckoned to him as righteousness" [James 2:23]. If it is absurd that an effect precedes its cause, either Moses testifies falsely in that place that faith was reckoned to Abraham as righteousness or, from that obedience which he manifested by offering Isaac, he did not merit righteousness. Abraham had been justified by his faith when Ishmael was as yet not conceived, who had already reached adolescence before Isaac was born. How, then, shall we say that he obtained righteousness by an obedience that followed long after? (3.17.12).

Paul and James labor with different aims, each addressing different problems. James fights against the empty show of faith, Paul against dependence upon works (3.17.12).

Calvin closes this chapter by stating and answering several more objections which are of the same order already examined. We will not trace out Calvin's discussion except to observe that when believers appeal to their works before God's tribunal, as the psalmist does more than once (Ps. 7:8; 17:1, 3; 18:20ff.; 26:10ff.), we must understand these statements in their context or circumstances: "Now this is twofold. For neither would they have a full investigation of themselves so as to be either condemned or acquitted

according to the character of their entire lives—rather they bring to judgment a special cause to be decided—nor do they claim righteousness for
themselves with reference to divine perfection but in comparison with evil
and wicked men" (3.17.14).

Calvin also rejects the idea of the believer's perfection in this life
(3.17.15).

Chapter Eighteen: Works Righteousness Is Wrongly Inferred from Reward

Calvin here returns to a topic he has discussed previously—that of reward.
Whereas earlier Calvin's concern was to show that reward is a matter of
grace, demonstrating that the believer's good works are without any merit,
here Calvin is concerned that believers understand the Christian life is not
without reward, though merit remains foreign to what reward means.

Although the Bible refers to reward in various passages (see, e.g., 2 Cor.
5:10; Rom. 2:9–10; John 5:29; and Matt. 25:34–35, 42, along with Prov.
12:14; 13:13; Isa. 3:11; Matt. 5:12; Luke 6:23; 1 Cor. 3:8; and Rom. 2:6),
none of these texts supports the notion of reward as one's due. Believers are
not the authors of their own salvation and salvation does not stem from
their own works (3.18.1).

In fact, "The use of the term 'reward' is no reason for us to suppose that
our works are the cause of our salvation." Salvation is not a matter of "servants' wages" but of a "sons' inheritance" (Eph. 1:18). In calling everlasting
glory an inheritance the Holy Spirit shows us that we are not the source
of such blessing. Abraham serves as a sterling example, for he is promised
seed that will bless all the nations of the earth. Then many years later, with
the fulfillment of God's promise, God calls him to sacrifice Isaac, the very
one who personified the promise fulfilled. Abraham obeys God and God
rewards him, saying, "because you have done this thing,…I will bless you
…and in your seed shall all the nations of the earth be blessed…." (Gen.
15:5; 17:1ff.; 18:18; and 22:3, 16–18). "Here clearly…the Lord rewards the
works of believers with the same benefits as he had given them before they
contemplated any works, as he does not yet have any reason to benefit them
except his own mercy" (3.18.2).

Reward, then, is of God's grace. God isn't mocking us when He rewards
our works, but we certainly aren't meriting the reward by our works. "[God]

wills that we be trained through good works to meditate upon the presentation or fruition, so to speak, of those things which he has promised, and to hasten through them to seek the blessed hope held out to us in heaven." This is why "the fruit of the promises is duly assigned to works, which bring us to the ripeness of that fruit" (3.18.3). The parable of the workers in the vineyard (Matt. 20:1ff.) is sufficient to disprove any notion of merit in our works (3.18.3). There is no correlation between merit and reward, for nothing "is clearer than that a reward is promised for good works to relieve the weakness of our flesh by some comfort but not to puff up our hearts with vainglory" (3.18.4).

That God promises to give His own "the crown of righteousness" (2 Tim. 4:8), is not according to our merits, but is, as Augustine says, according to God's grace. Divine grace precedes whatever righteousness we might venture to apportion in ourselves—the very grace that justifies the ungodly so that their works might be accounted righteous. Calvin then further elucidates Augustine's observation with these words: "How could [the Lord] impute righteousness to our works unless his compassion covered over whatever unrighteousness was in them? And how could he judge them worthy of reward save that he wiped out by his boundless kindness what in them deserves punishment?" As Augustine maintains, "the righteousness of good works depends upon the fact that God by pardon approves them" (3.18.5).

Calvin wants us to see that the Christian life is grounded in divine mercy. The treasures in heaven that await us reflect the very nature of the believer's desire, seeing that God's kindness precedes our works. Meanwhile, we do not labor in vain, or suffer for Christ's sake in vain. God pricks our sloth, encourages us with His promise, and blesses His own work of grace in our lives (3.18.6–7). "Let us always remember that this promise, like all others, would not bear fruit for us if the free covenant of his mercy had not gone before, upon which the whole assurance of our salvation depended" (3.18.7).

It is also mistaken, notes Calvin, to think that our works of love justify us or that justification is by love rather than by faith (cf. 1 Cor. 13:2ff.; Col. 3:14). This is altogether misguided, for neither love nor faith as virtues justify us. "The power of justifying, which faith possesses, does not lie in any worth of works." Rather, to affirm justification by faith alone is to say that we are justified by "God's mercy alone and Christ's merit, and faith, when it lays hold of justification, is said to justify." That is only to say that faith lays hold of Christ, in and by whom we are justified (3.18.8). Again, "We say that faith justifies, not because it merits righteousness for us by its own worth, but because it is an instrument whereby we obtain freely the righteousness of Christ" (3.18.8).

To be sure, if one seeks life and salvation by works, then the commandments must be kept for the attainment of the same (see Matt. 19:17). However, it is precisely this truth that drives us away from ourselves and into the arms of Christ. The righteous standard of God's commandments is not to be ignored—knowledge of it shows us that we stand on the brink of death. From God's righteousness as defined by the law, we see how far short we fall. We become aware that in order to obtain salvation our "refuge is in Christ" (3.18.9).

> To sum up, if we seek salvation in works, we must keep the commandments by which we are instructed unto perfect righteousness. But we must not stop here unless we wish to fail in mid-course, for none of us is capable of keeping the commandments. Therefore, since we are barred from law righteousness, we must betake ourselves to another help, that is, to faith in Christ (3.18.9).

Calvin closes this chapter by answering a particular objection, which one might think has some semblance of truth to it, namely, that if sin is imputed to us for unrighteousness, then, applying the law of contraries, good works must be imputed to us for righteousness. The error here is easy to expose.

> ...works righteousness is perfect obedience to the law. Therefore, you cannot be righteous according to works unless you unfailingly follow this straight line, so to speak, throughout life. The minute you turn aside from it, you slip into unrighteousness. From this it is apparent that righteousness does not come about from one or a few works but from an unwavering and unwearying observance of the divine will. But very different is the rule for judging unrighteousness. For a fornicator or thief is by one offense guilty of death because he has offended against God's majesty [see James 2:10–11].... Accordingly, it ought not to seem absurd when we say that death is the just payment for each several sin, for each one deserves God's just wrath and vengeance. But you would be a foolish reasoner if you concluded, on the contrary, that man can be reconciled to God by a single good work when by his many sins he deserves God's wrath (3.18.10).

Chapter Nineteen: Christian Freedom

The Importance of Christian Freedom
It may seem that Calvin has left behind the doctrine of justification in addressing Christian freedom. This is not the case. Calvin calls Christian freedom "an appendage of justification"; and in understanding freedom in Christ the believer comes to see the power of justification. Calvin calls Christian freedom "a thing of prime necessity, and apart from a knowledge of it consciences dare undertake almost nothing without doubting; they hesitate and recoil from many things; they constantly waver and are afraid" (3.19.1).

Calvin knows that the issue of Christian freedom makes tempers run hot. "Some, on the pretext of this freedom, shake off all obedience toward God and break out into unbridled license. Others disdain it, thinking that it takes away all moderation, order, and choice of things." So Calvin asks, "What should we do here, hedged about with such perplexities? Shall we say good-by to Christian freedom, thus cutting off occasion for such dangers?" Calvin refuses this path. He writes, "Unless this freedom be comprehended, neither Christ nor gospel truth, nor inner peace of soul, can be rightly known" (3.19.1).

The Three Parts of Christian Freedom
Christian freedom has three parts, for Calvin. The first part is freedom from the law—that is, the believer's conscience is not bound to the law. The law, on the one hand, leaves everyone under its verdict of condemnation. No person escapes its declaration of unrighteousness, followed by the negative sentence of accursedness. Christian freedom involves deliverance from guilt under the law, an escape from the law's accusing finger regarding our works. The believer's works have nothing to do with acceptance before God. We are free from the law's frown. We look to and embrace God's mercy in Christ; we turn from ourselves to Him—He is our righteousness. "If consciences wish to attain any certainty in this matter, they ought to give no place to the law" (3.19.2).

Yet, on the other hand, the law has not therefore become "superfluous for believers, since it does not stop teaching and exhorting and urging them to good, even though before God's judgment seat it has no place in their consciences" (3.19.2). The entire Christian life is a pursuit of godliness, says Calvin, and the law calls and arouses us to this pursuit. We are called to be sanctified (1 Thess. 4:3, 7; Eph. 1:4; 1 Thess. 4:3). Thus the law, for Christians, still bids them to obedience and a zeal for holiness. In their failure to live by the law's perfect standard, however, there is no despair or fear, for they are bonded to Christ who "surpasses all perfection of the law." He is their righteousness and acceptance with God, freeing them from the law's condemnation (3.19.2). Calvin points out that the entire argument of the epistle to the Galatians turns on this hinge. We aren't merely freed from certain Old Testament ceremonies in embracing Christ by faith; more than that, "through the cross of Christ" we are altogether set free from the law's condemnation and "may rest with assurance in Christ alone." This freedom deliverers us from unnecessary and obsolete obligations (3.19.3).

The second part of Christian liberty, says Calvin, depends on the first. This is the freedom to observe the law *willingly*—without necessity, constraint, or the law's yoke. This is the freedom to live in accord with the law, with a desire to do so, while being delivered from dread of the law and its threat of judgment. This is the difference between serving God as a servant versus serving our heavenly Father as a son (3.19.4–5). Joyous obedience marks this freedom. To be sure, the law demands perfection. We aren't perfect—even the works of believers are tainted and befouled by sin, needing the second justification of forgiveness. But in Christ we are liberated from the law's demand: do this and live. We are liberated, too, from the law's curse, its rigor. Instead, in Christ the law calls to us with "fatherly gentleness" (3.19.5). Calvin offers this summary, which helps us see what his conception of the Christian life is and isn't:

> Those bound by the yoke of the law are like servants assigned certain tasks for each day by their masters. These servants think they have accomplished nothing, and dare not appear before their masters unless they have fulfilled the exact measure of their tasks. But sons, who are more generously and candidly treated by their fathers, do not hesitate to offer them incomplete and half-done and even defective works, trusting that their obedience and readiness of mind will be accepted by their fathers, even though they have not quite achieved what their fathers intended. Such children ought we to be, firmly trusting that our services will be approved by our most merciful Father, however small, rude, and imperfect these may be. Thus also he assures us through the prophet: "I will spare them as a man spares his son who serves him" [Mal. 3:17]. The word "spare" is clearly here used in the sense of "to be indulgent or compassionately to overlook faults," while also mention is made of "service." And we need this assurance in no slight degree, for

without it we attempt everything in vain. For God considers that he is revered by no work of ours unless we truly do it in reverence toward him. But how can this be done amidst all this dread, where one doubts whether God is offended or honored by our works? (3.19.5).

God accepts our sin-stained works in Christ, being judged by faith alone (Heb. 11:2ff.; 11:17). Paul emphatically maintains that we are not under law but under grace (Rom. 6:12, 14). We are exhorted simultaneously to live holy lives, and assured of our emancipation from the law, to live by divine grace. Our works are not measured according to the strict rules of the law (3.19.6).

The third part of Christian liberty is our liberation before God concerning "things indifferent" (*adiaphora*), such that we are not bound to their observance or non-observance. Liberty with respect to things which are in themselves "indifferent" frees us from all superstition, despair, and anxiety concerning our use of them. Without this freedom, "our consciences will have no repose...." We will ever be vexed with scruples. As Calvin observes: "For when consciences once ensnare themselves, they enter a long and inextricable maze, not easy to get out of." He offers an illustration:

> If a man begins to doubt whether he may use linen for sheets, shirts, handkerchiefs, and napkins, he will afterward be uncertain also about hemp [a coarse fabric]; finally, doubt will even arise over tow [another kind of cheap fabric]. For he will turn over in his mind whether he can sup without napkins, or go without a handkerchief. If any man should consider daintier food unlawful, in the end he will not be at peace before God, when he eats either black bread or common victuals, while it occurs to him that he could sustain his body on even coarser foods. If he boggles at sweet wine, he will not with clear conscience drink even flat wine, and finally he will not dare touch water if sweeter and cleaner than other water. To sum up, he will come to the point of considering it wrong to step upon a straw across his path, as the saying goes (3.19.7).

Others examples Calvin alludes to are the unrestricted eating of meat, use of holidays, and the matter of vestments for the clergy. Tempers flare, passions are stirred, a weighty controversy ensues. The debate surrounds God's will for such things. Some despair and find themselves in "a pit of confusion." They don't know how to proceed. Others cast off fear of the Lord altogether and live by their own rules (3.19.7). Calvin takes us to Romans 14:14 ("I know, and am persuaded by the Lord Jesus, that *there is* nothing unclean of itself: but to him that esteemeth any thing to be unclean, to him *it is* unclean"). "With these words Paul subjects all outward things to our freedom" (3.19.8). Christian freedom does not lead us carelessly to dare all things in confidence. Christian freedom is moved by love for God and godly fear of Him.

"To sum up," says Calvin, "we see whither this freedom tends: namely, that we should use God's gifts for the purpose for which he gave them to us, with no scruple of conscience, no trouble of mind. With such confidence our minds will be at peace with him, and will recognize his liberality toward us. For here are included all ceremonies whose observance is optional, that our consciences may not be constrained by any necessity to observe them but may remember that by God's beneficence their use is for edification made subject to him" (3.19.8).

Abuses of Christian Freedom

For Calvin, "Christian freedom is, in all its parts, a spiritual thing" (3.19.9). It is open to abuse. It brings solace to troubled souls, whose consciences accuse them. Others turn liberty into license. Whether one is overly scrupulous or given to unbridled lust, Christian liberty directs us along a safer path. Calvin warns against indulging ourselves in luxury and extravagance in food, drink, apparel, dwelling-place, recreations, etc. To be sure, such things can be regarded as "things indifferent," says Calvin, "provided they are used indifferently." But this is rarely the case. Instead, these things are greedily coveted; we are puffed up by and boast of them. They are also squandered. Yes, these things are lawful in themselves but are "defiled by these vices" (3.19.9). So Calvin does not discourage us to make a right use of things, like finer wares and goods, which are part of God's good creation. Neither are we forbidden to enjoy ourselves with laughter, to accumulate possessions, or to delight in music. A warning, however, is in order. We must guard against our propensities: "Where there is plenty, to wallow in delights, to gorge oneself, to intoxicate mind and heart with present pleasures and be always panting after new ones...." Says Calvin, "such [behaviors] are very far removed from a lawful use of God's gifts" (3.19.9).

Another sort of abuse in the name of Christian freedom regards the weaker brother. Some put their freedom on display and use it "indiscriminately and unwisely." In doing so, they often offend others. Calvin reminds us that Christian freedom means the freedom to use something or not to use it. Abstaining is a use of freedom as well. While it is sometimes necessary to manifest our freedom in front of others, we must own this caution: not to harm the weak or abandon care of them. Scripture bids us not to make our brother stumble (3.19.10).

So what about "offenses"? Calvin offers this distinction: "Now I like that common distinction between an offense given and one received, inasmuch as it has the clear support of Scripture and properly expresses what is meant." When we conduct ourselves without consideration of others, we cause or give offense. This is blameworthy. Meanwhile, offense is received when a person "from ill will or malicious intent of mind" wrenches the conduct of another "into an occasion for offense." The one offended wickedly interprets the behavior of the other as offensive, unjustly so. This is rooted in a "bitter disposition and pharisaical pride" (3.19.11). Again Calvin points us to Romans 14:1ff. He also reminds us of Romans 15:1–2; 1 Corinthians 8:9; 10:25, 29, 32; Galatians 5:13. "Our freedom is not given against our feeble neighbors, for love makes us their servants in all things; rather it is given that, having peace with God in our hearts, we may also live at peace with men" (3.19.11).

But whom are we to consider the weaker brother? The ones to whom we seek not to *give offense*. And whom are we to regard as "Pharisees"? The ones who easily and deliberately *receive offense*. Calvin reminds us of the apostle Paul's diverse and proper use of freedom in circumcising Timothy in order to win the Jews and refusing to circumcise Titus in order to expose false brothers who were trying to impose a new bondage upon the church (Acts 16:3; Gal. 2:3–5; cf. 1 Cor. 9:19–22; 10:23–24). There are those who make unjust demands on others. Calvin offers this rule: "that we should use our freedom if it results in the edification of our neighbor, but if it does not help our neighbor, then we should forgo it" (3.19.12).

Of course, notes Calvin, all of this applies "to things intermediate and indifferent." Other things fall into a different class—things that are necessary to be done and may not be omitted. Freedom submits to love and love submits to faith. Christian freedom requires that we resist those who act intemperately and conduct themselves in a tumultuous manner; it also requires us to resist those who teach impiety with smooth tongues and a soft manner (3.19.13).

Christian Freedom in Relation to Traditions and the Civil Magistrate
Calvin brings his analysis of Christian freedom to a close by addressing human tradition and the civil government. Christian freedom means that

believers are liberated from human traditions. We can even say that believers are *not free* to place themselves under the bondage and yoke of human invention. They may not worship or serve God under human rules that are without biblical sanction and therefore without authority to bind the conscience (cf. 1 Pet. 1:18f.; Gal. 2:21; 5:1, 4) (3.19.14).

Christian freedom also applies to the civil sphere. Only, we must see that the temptation of many is to misuse this freedom and transform it into gross licentiousness, as if believers need not obey the civil authorities since they are under God's authority. To correct this error Calvin first distinguishes between two kingdoms or what he calls "a twofold government in man." The one government refers to the spiritual jurisdiction and is eternal; it pertains to the life to come. The other government refers to the political jurisdiction and is temporal; it pertains to the present life. The former teaches our conscience in piety and reverence for God; it deals with the life of the soul. The latter informs us about our duties toward humanity and citizenship that compose society; it deals with our physical needs and the laws needed to establish and safeguard civic life. The first, says Calvin, "resides in the inner mind"; the second "regulates only outward behavior." Thus the first is called "the spiritual kingdom"; the second is termed "the political kingdom." Having defined these two kingdoms, Calvin writes: "Now these two, as we have divided them, must always be examined separately; and while one is being considered, we must call away and turn aside the mind from thinking about the other." The divide that Calvin posits here resides in the fact that "there is in man, so to speak, two worlds, over which different kings and different laws have authority" (3.19.15).

Calvin's burden is to formulate his own version of the separation of church and state. He does not want the political sphere impinging on the ecclesiastical sphere. More importantly for his discussion of Christian freedom, as noted above, Calvin is concerned about the misapplication of Christian freedom to the political jurisdiction. He opposes the Libertines and others who, in the name of Christian freedom, argue that believers are free from obeying the civil authorities and living by the rules of society. This is entirely mistaken, says Calvin. Our freedom of conscience does not liberate us from submitting to the civil government and conforming our behavior to human laws in the civic domain (3.19.15). He will take up both civil laws and ecclesiastical polity later in the *Institutes*. Here he only wants to emphasize that freedom of conscience pertains to things indifferent, not to necessary things. Submission to civil authorities and living according to apt civil laws are necessary things; they are not indifferent. Conscience isn't free from all things. It must live before God, who is holy and righteous, in both jurisdictions of life. This means that if you were the last person on earth, you would still be subject to God's righteous rule regarding, say, wholesome speech. Writes Calvin, "My conscience is subject to the observance of this law, even if no man lived on earth. So he who conducts himself intemperately not only sins because he gives a bad example to his brothers but has a conscience bound by guilt before God" (3.19.16).

The civil authority, of course, may only bind outward conduct, not the heart. In this way, believers retain Christian liberty.

Questions for Reflection and Discussion

1. What is "merit" and what does it mean "to merit"? Why can neither believers nor unbelievers merit before God?

2. Why is Christ's merit the foundation of justification? What does this mean?

3. How does justification inspire rather than thwart good works, according to Calvin?

4. What is Calvin's way of distinguishing between justification and sanctification? Why is this important to do?

5. According to Calvin, what are the proper motives that should move us to do good works? What are improper motives?

6. Why can't salvation be found through the conditional promises of the law? How does the promise of the gospel differ from these conditional promises?

7. Following Calvin's analysis, how do Paul and James differ in their use of the terms "justification/justify" and the term "faith"? Why is the doctrine of justification destroyed when these differences in the use of language are not observed or recognized?

8. What are "rewards" for Calvin?

9. What is Christian freedom and what are its parts?

10. What is meant by "things indifferent"? Is there a sense in which nothing is indifferent?

11. What are the abuses of Christian freedom today?

12. How are Calvin's comments about "offense given" and "offense received" important and helpful for dealing with others? Give examples.

13. What is Calvin's doctrine of the "two kingdoms"? What is Calvin's doctrine of the separation of church and state? How does Christian freedom apply to the believer's relationship to the governing authorities?

14. How do matters of Christian liberty emerge in the church today? What are some areas in which there is no clear "right" or "wrong" as such? Do we make good use of this liberty? How?

≈ 16 ≈

Prayer

Chapter Twenty: Prayer, Which Is the Chief Exercise of Faith, and by Which We Daily Receive God's Benefits

Orientation

CALVIN HAS SHOWN that salvation is not from us or found within us. We only find life from God who has freely revealed Himself in Christ. "For in Christ he offers all happiness in place of our misery, all wealth in place of our neediness; in him he opens to us the heavenly treasures that our whole faith may contemplate his beloved Son, our whole expectation depend upon him, and our whole hope cleave to and rest in him" (3.20.1). Our faith rests thus completely on Christ. But "just as faith is born from the gospel, so through it our hearts are trained to call upon God's name [Rom. 10:14–17]" (3.20.1).

The Nature and Necessity of Prayer

It is by prayer that believers call upon the Lord. By means of prayer we dig up the treasures shown us in the gospel. Thus Calvin turns to a discussion on the necessity of prayer. In his view the importance of prayer is something words fail to explain. Prayer is the believer's stronghold (cf. Joel 2:32); and by it we call on God "to reveal himself as wholly present to us" (3.20.2).

A perennial question surrounding prayer concerns its necessity. Since God knows our needs already, isn't it silly to pray, as if God "should be stirred up by our prayers—as if he were drowsily blinking or even sleeping until he is aroused by our voice?" (3.20.3). But prayer isn't for God's sake (although we worship Him by our prayers) but for ours. In fact, Calvin offers six reasons why it is important for us to pray. First, prayer inspires zeal in the love and service we owe God. Second, it exposes our hearts to the Lord and teaches us to hide nothing from Him. Third, it gives opportunity for genuine expressions of gratitude to God. Fourth, prayer also helps us see God's hand in our lives as we contemplate how prayers have been answered and how God is kind to us. Fifth, we in turn can enjoy and value the blessings that come to us in answer to prayer. And, sixth, we see how God's providential hand guides our lives and how His promises never fail us (3.20.3).

Calvin reminds us that God neither slumbers nor sleeps (Ps. 121:4), for His eyes are upon the righteous (1 Pet. 3:12; Ps. 34:15) (3.20.3).

Rules for Prayer

But how ought we to pray? Calvin sets forth four rules.

First Rule: "that we be disposed in mind and heart as befits those who enter conversation with God." It is inappropriate that we pray without concentration. Wandering thoughts are irreverent. It is proper that our requests be moderate, seeking only what God allows. Thus, we remember that we need the Holy Spirit to guide our prayers (3.20.4–5).

Second Rule: "that in our petitions we ever sense our own insufficiency, and earnestly pondering how we need all that we seek, join with this prayer an earnest—nay, burning—desire to attain it." Therefore all perfunctory prayers and prayers offered merely out of a sense of duty dishonor God. God isn't appeased just because we pray. We can't find grace by this work. So let us pray in earnest at all times, and let us pray in repentance (3.20.6–7).

Third Rule: "that anyone who stands before God to pray, in his humility giving glory completely to God, abandon all thought of his own glory, cast off all notion of his own worth, in fine, put away all self-assurance—lest if we claim for ourselves anything, even the least bit, we should become vainly puffed up, and perish at his presence." Daniel, David, Isaiah, and Jeremiah represent biblical examples of self-abasement before God. Repentance and the seeking of forgiveness are the most important part of prayer. We plead for mercy and we pray specifically that God would release us from our present guilt and grant remission for every sin. We know God's cause is just. To the extent we are identified with that cause we know we are right, while our hope is only in God's mercy (3.20.8–10).

Fourth Rule: "that, thus cast down and overcome by true humility, we should be nonetheless encouraged to pray by a sure hope that our prayer will be answered." As we are taught by Jesus, "whatever you seek…, believe that you will receive it, and it will come to you" (Mark 11:24; also cf. Matt. 21:22). James instructs us to pray in faith without wavering (James

1:5–6). "To sum up, it is faith that obtains whatever is granted to prayer." It is impossible to call upon God sincerely except we embrace Him in His kindness and gentle mercy to us, both of which are revealed in the gospel (3.20.11). Prayer, then, ought to have the posture of trusting in God's favor and benevolent disposition toward us in spite of "our misery, destitution, and uncleanness" (3.20.12).

We should also remember that God commands us to pray and promises to bless us in the way of prayer. Both the divine imperative and the promised blessing ought to motivate us to pray (3.20.13). And when we pray let us do so confident of God's generosity, for we should never forget that "our prayers depend upon no merit of ours, but their whole worth and hope of fulfillment are grounded in God's promises, and depend upon them, so that they need no other support, nor do they look about up and down, hither and thither" (3.20.14). Rather than call upon God "deceitfully," Calvin calls us to pray with "sincerity of heart," in "dissatisfaction with ourselves," as well as in "humility" and "faith." As he also says, "a dauntless spirit of praying rightly accords with fear, reverence, and solicitude, and it is not absurd if God raises those who lie prostrate." We embrace God's "fatherly love," trusting in His "safekeeping" and promised assistance, while we abase ourselves before Him for our sins (3.20.14).

God's Graciousness and Our Prayers

Calvin next reminds us that God hearkens even to defective prayers, and provides Jotham and Samson as examples (cf. Judg. 9:20; 16:28). Calvin observes that God even answers prayers that do not always please Him. Nonetheless, we do better to follow the principles of prayer laid out for us in Scripture. If God sometimes answers the misconceived prayers of the ungodly because He is graciously disposed, all the more we should take consolation in knowing that this gives evidence "how easily entreated he is toward his elect when they come with true conversion to appease him" (3.20.15). In addition, when we face those situations in which the petitions of our prayers run contrary to God's eternal decree, Calvin reminds us of the words of Augustine: "How do the saints pray in faith when they seek from God what is against his decree? They pray according to his will, not that hidden and unchangeable will but the will that he inspires in them, that he may hearken to them in another way, as he wisely decides." Our prayers are "a mixture of faith and error," but God orders events such that our prayers "are not nullified" (3.20.15).

Calvin also notes the important place God's grace and forgiveness have relative to our prayers, for prayer is not a matter of simply following the four rules he has earlier set forth. We all fail to pray *rightly*; we all violate the rules to varying degrees. We should not give up trying to honor God in our prayers according to His due, for "God tolerates even our stammering and pardons our ignorance whenever something inadvertently escapes us; as indeed without this mercy there would be no freedom to pray." Our minds wander in prayer; and here too we need divine pardon. We often pray with apathy, with hands uplifted but with hearts still on the ground. We likewise can pray to God without a properly broken spirit or contrite heart. Again, we need a twofold pardon in this regard inasmuch as we know our many offenses but do not despise them as we ought. "Most of all," Calvin adds, "it is weakness or imperfection of faith that vitiates believers' prayers, unless God's mercy succor them; but no wonder God pardons this defect, since he often tests his own with sharp trials, as if he deliberately willed to snuff out their faith" (cf. Ps. 80:4; Lam. 3:8). In the trial of faith, our prayers are commingled with doubt. Thus Calvin observes that "there is no prayer which in justice God would not loathe if he did not overlook the spots with which all are sprinkled" (3.20.16).

God's forgiveness of our prayers is rooted in the intercession of Christ. The Scriptures bid us to pray in Jesus' name since He is our Mediator and Advocate (3.20.17), whereas prayers offered to saints dishonor Christ and strip Him of His Mediatorship (3.20.21–27). Indeed, Christ our Mediator is the risen and ascended One, who makes intercession for us in the heavenly presence of the Father (3.20.18). He alone is our way of access to God's throne of mercy. Even our intercessions for one another depend upon Christ's intercessory work (3.20.19). Christ is also our eternal and abiding Mediator. We are mistaken if we would conceive of His work of intercession having the character of a suppliant or a beggar pleading for God to be merciful to us. On the contrary, "he so appears before God's presence that the power of his death avails as an everlasting intercession in our behalf [cf. Rom. 8:34], yet in such a way that, having entered the heavenly sanctuary, even to the consummation of the ages [cf. Heb. 9:24ff.], he alone bears to God the petitions of the people, who stay far off in the outer court." We are members of Christ—He being our Head and we His body (3.20.20).

Christ, then, is our sole access to God's mercy and forgiveness. Calvin calls it "the height of stupidity, not to say madness, to be so intent on gaining access through the saints as to be led away from him, apart from whom no entry lies open to them." When we circumvent Christ we forget His love and regard Him as "insufficient or too severe." This dishonors and defrocks Him of His mediatorship, making "void the cross." Calvin aptly quotes Ambrose who writes that Christ "is our mouth, through which we speak to the Father; he is our eye, through which we see the Father; he is our right hand, through which we offer ourselves to the Father. Unless he intercedes, there is no intercourse with God either for us or for all saints." The prayers and merits of the dead may not be commingled with the merits of Christ lest we profane His intercessory work for us (3.20.21).

Calvin likewise contends against the superstitious veneration of the saints (3.20.22–26). This practice is neither commended by Scripture nor does it reckon with the reality that the departed saints are not engaged in earthly worries and cares as to lose their repose.

> Scripture, in the worship of God, sets the chief matter before us: how we should call upon him in prayer. Consequently, as he requires of us this duty of piety, holding all sacrifices secondary to it, to direct prayer to others involves manifest sacrilege.... Again, only out of faith is God pleased to be called upon, and he expressly bids that prayers be conformed to the measure of his Word. Finally, faith grounded upon the Word is the mother of right prayer; hence, as soon as it is deflected from the Word, prayer must needs be corrupted. But it has already been shown that...this honor is there claimed for God alone. What pertains to the office of intercession we also see is peculiar to Christ, and no prayer is pleasing to God unless this Mediator sanctifies it. Yet even if believers reciprocally offer prayers before God for the brethren, we have shown that this detracts nothing from Christ's unique intercession. For all together, relying upon this, commend both themselves and others to God. We have, moreover, taught that it is inappropriately applied to the dead, of whom we nowhere read that they have been bidden to pray for us. Scripture often urges us to do our duty by one another but has not one syllable of the dead. Indeed, James by joining these two exhortations—to confess our sins to one another, and to pray for one another [James 5:16]—tacitly excludes the dead (3.20.27).

Private and Public Prayer

Calvin next offers instruction about private and public prayers (3.20.28–33). Regarding private prayer, he observes that "there is such a close connection between petition and thanksgiving that they may conveniently be included under one name." As we implore the Lord with our requests and petitions "we pour out our desires before God, seeking both those things which make for the extension of his glory and the setting forth of his name, and those benefits which conduce to our own advantage." Meanwhile, as we offer our thanksgiving to the Lord "we celebrate with due praise his benefits toward us, and credit to his generosity every good that comes to us" (3.20.28). In this two-pronged dimension of prayer we acknowledge the Lord as "the author of all blessings." A curse therefore abides with those who place confidence in themselves, as if they are the masters of their own plans. On the contrary, prayer inspires a submissive love for God and cultivates in us a life of sacrificial service (3.20.28).

As for public prayer, Calvin sets forth a more elaborate discussion. Although public prayer is necessary, it is fraught with dangers. The church is urged to constant prayer, and this ought to take place according to the established polity which serves human convenience and is serviceable to all. All things are to be done "decently and in order" in the church's public gatherings for worship (1 Cor. 14:40). Should a church find it fitting to give itself to prayer more frequently and urgently because of a major need, this sharpened zeal is not to be discouraged (3.20.29).

Dangers must be noted, however. Constancy in prayer is not to give way to "vain repetition." "For Christ does not forbid us to persist in prayers, long, often, or with much feeling, but requires that we should not be confident in our ability to wrest something from God by beating upon his ears with a garrulous flow of talk, as if he could be persuaded as men are." Practitioners of hypocrisy are deluded by such games, as they are by ostentation—that is, praying in a manner as to impress others (cf. Matt. 6:5).

Those who seek to pray in an obedient manner discover that true prayer reaches its goal in laying our hearts before God—both in praise and petition. Since God is the searcher of hearts, prayer—the most apt expression of the heart—brings our hearts under God's care. This is what Christ means in instructing us to pray in secret, in the inner chamber, where we can be most transparent to God and pour out our hearts to Him. There we can find consolation in our Father's presence, free from "all our teeming cares." Christ Himself practiced and exemplified this in His earthly ministry. Thus we discover that private prayer nurtures our (participation in) public prayers. Lest we lightly regard public prayer, Calvin reminds us that the temple of the Lord is called the "house of prayer" (cf. Isa. 56:7; Matt. 21:13) (3.20.29).

Inasmuch as we are now God's living, spiritual temple, our prayers are "never ineffectual." And while we rightly gather in buildings to worship and pray, we must resist the notion that God dwells in temples made with hands (Isa. 66:1; Acts 7:48–49) (3.20.30).

In this connection Calvin also argues that our tongues must be employed in the exercise of prayer—both in speaking and singing. All such audible exercises in prayer must "spring from deep feeling of heart" (3.20.31). Paul bids us to sing with the spirit and with the mind, even as he urges us to teach and admonish one another with hymns, psalms, and spiritual songs (1 Cor. 14:15; Col. 3:16). Says Calvin, "in the first passage he teaches that we should sing with voice and heart; in the second he commends spiritual songs, by which the godly may mutually edify one another." As for songs, Calvin adds this caution: "We should be very careful that our ears be not more attentive to the melody than our minds to the spiritual meaning of the words" (3.20.32). Furthermore, whether our public prayers are expressed in speaking or singing, they must be in the language of the people. It is inappropriate to use a tongue foreign to the assembled worshipers, for prayer must seek "the edification of the whole church, which receives no benefit whatever from a sound not understood" (3.20.33).

The Lord's Prayer

From here Calvin embarks upon an exposition of the Lord's Prayer (3.20.34–48). We can only briefly touch upon each of the petitions. As a general observation, however, Calvin maintains that this prayer gives us "the form" or content that ought to characterize our prayers inasmuch as we are taught by God's own beloved Son (Matt. 6:9ff.; Luke 11:2ff.). Here the Lord shows us what is proper and profitable for us to request, displaying "all that he allows us to seek of him, all that is of benefit to us, all that we need ask." In this way we steer clear of praying for things that displease Him and prove unacceptable (3.20.34).

Of the six petitions of the Lord's Prayer, the first three "have been particularly assigned to God's glory, and this alone we ought to look to in them, without consideration of what is called our own advantage." The other three petitions "are concerned with the care of ourselves, and are especially assigned to those things which we should ask for our own benefit" (3.20.35).

On the threshold of this prayer we address God as "Father," which means we pray in Christ's name as children of adoption according to God's grace (3.20.36). That we are instructed to pray "*our* Father" encourages us to view God according to His compassion toward us, for He is the Father of

mercies and the God of all comfort (2 Cor. 1:3). The parable of the prodigal son likewise teaches us the abundance of God's mercy and love, as the
father of the prodigal embraces his wayward son with welcoming arms, not
even waiting for him to utter words of repentance. On the contrary, viewing him from a distance, the father runs to meet him and consoles his son
by immediately receiving him into his paternal favor (cf. Luke 15:11–32).
We need only cast ourselves on God's mercy to discover that He is the
"best and kindest of all fathers...." The Spirit is also given to us to bear testimony in our hearts that God is our Father, so that we cry, "Abba, Father"
(Gal. 4:6; Rom. 8:15).

This manner of addressing God also reminds us of the communion of
the saints and of "how a great feeling of brotherly love ought to be among
us," for we are all children of the heavenly Father by the same source of
divine mercy and His free liberality. He is the one Father common to us all
(Matt. 23:9). We must embrace all brothers and sisters in Christ, as members of His household, "with love and good will." Thus "all prayers ought to
be such as to look to that community which our Lord has established in his
Kingdom and his household" (3.20.38). This doesn't mean we aren't permitted to pray for our own needs, but even our individually focused prayers are
directed to a communal end (3.20.39).

That we address God as "our Father ... *in heaven*" teaches us that "God
is set beyond all place, so that when we would seek him we must rise above
all perception of body and soul." God is also lofty, being "above all chance of
either corruption or change." It also testifies of His sovereignty, for He "embraces and holds together the entire universe and controls it by his might."
Even more, "it is as if he had been said to be of infinite greatness or loftiness, of incomprehensible essence, of boundless might, and of everlasting
immortality" (3.20.40).

Calvin turns to the petitions of this prayer. The first petition is that
God's name may be hallowed. In summary Calvin states that

> we should wish God to have the honor he deserves; men should never
> speak or think of him without the highest reverence. To this is op-
> posed the profanity that has always been too common and even today
> is abroad in the world. Hence ... here we are bidden to request not
> only that God vindicate his sacred name of all contempt and dishonor
> but also that he subdue the whole race of mankind to reverence for it
> (3.20.41).

The second petition is that God's kingdom may come. Calvin offers this definition of the kingdom: "God reigns where men, both by denial of themselves and by contempt of the world and of earthly life, pledge themselves to his righteousness in order to aspire to a heavenly life." Calvin states that there are two parts to God's kingdom: "first, that God by the power of his Spirit correct all the desires of the flesh which by squadrons war against him; second, that he shape all our thoughts in obedience to his rule" (3.20.42). Included in this petition is a call for all to be surrendered to and shaped by the royal scepter of God's Word, and for God to humble the whole world. It calls, too, for God to spread and increase His church in all lands, and to bless His church with all things needed for its well-being wherever it exists. May God's kingdom come till the day "God will be all in all" (1 Cor. 15:28). For God's kingdom to come also requires that our own lives experience mortification of the flesh and that we bear the cross (3.20.42).

The third petition is that God's will may be done on earth as it is in heaven. This is an extension of the previous petition, for where God's healing and saving reign is being manifest we see His will being done on earth. Consequently, this is not a prayer regarding God's "secret will" or His will according to His sovereign decree, that is, His "incomprehensible plan." Instead, this prayer pertains to God's revealed will—"namely, that to which voluntary obedience corresponds—and for that reason, heaven is by name compared to earth, for the angels…willingly obey God, and are intent upon carrying out his commands [Ps. 103:20]." We pray to God that we—indeed, the whole earth—may be subject to His rule, such that all human conceit, impiety, and evil may be vanquished (3.20.43).

More personally, with this petition "we renounce the desires of our flesh; for whoever does not resign and submit his feelings to God opposes as much as he can God's will, since only what is corrupt comes forth from us." In this way we are called and shaped to deny ourselves so that God's will prevails in our lives. Even more, in renouncing our desires, we are asking God to create in us new minds and hearts (cf. Ps. 51:20), to indwell and govern us by the Spirit, and to learn to hate what God hates and love what God loves (3.20.43).

Each of the above mentioned petitions, forming a unit, have "God's glory alone" as their goal. In uttering these words we seek no advantage or blessing for ourselves, though blessings come to us in answer to such petitions. Further, although God does not need our petitions for these things to be accomplished in due time (and most certainly they will be accomplished), nonetheless, "we ought to desire and request them." Thereby we show ourselves to be zealous for God's honor as His servants and children (3.20.43).

The next three petitions, comprising the second part of this prayer, likewise form a unit; and here we take up matters that directly treat "our own affairs." This doesn't mean that we are no longer concerned with God's glory and turn selfishly to our own stingy interests. Rather, the difference is this: "God specifically claims the first three petitions and draws us wholly to himself to prove our piety in this way." After this, "he allows us to look after our own interests, yet under this limitation: that we seek nothing for ourselves without the intention that whatever benefits he confers upon us may show forth his glory, for nothing is more fitting than that we live and die to him [Rom. 14:7–9]" (3.20.44).

The fourth petition, *Give us this day our daily bread,* is not limited to the bread we eat; instead, it asks God to grant us all the basic things of which we have physical need. We ask God for food and clothing, to be sure, but also for everything that He "perceives to be beneficial to us, that we may eat our daily bread in peace." We entrust ourselves to God's providential care to feed, nourish, and keep us. We cast upon the Lord our cares for the body and its needs; and in faith we know that He gives greater things, "even salvation and eternal life." We are also taught in this petition that even bread comes to us as a divine gift; it is not ours by right (cf. Lev. 26:20; Deut. 8:17–18) (3.20.44).

The terms "today" and "daily" contained in this petition teach us to bridle our "uncontrolled desires for fleeting things, with which we commonly burn without measure, and to which other evils are added." With discernment Calvin adds, "For if a greater abundance is at hand, we vainly pour it out upon pleasure, delights, ostentation, and other sorts of excess." Therefore it is fitting for us to ask simply for what meets our needs from one day to another, knowing that our heavenly Father, who takes care of us on this day, will not fail to take care of us tomorrow. Even when we enjoy a profusion of such benefits, with cupboards packed full, we should still utter this prayer. Without the Lord's blessing such abundance will not bless us. This petition also teaches us to learn contentment and not pant "after countless things with unbridled desire." How easy it is for us actually to mock God in speaking this petition when we find our contentment in our stockpiles of such goods, with our hearts "carefree in their piled-up riches." On the one hand, we become angry if God gives us only *daily bread,* for our greed brims over for much more; on the other hand, we become ungrateful, and show ourselves as ingrates, because we regard such meager gifts from God unnecessary given that we have larger blessings within ourselves (3.20.44).

The fifth petition asks God to *forgive us our debts*. If the prior petition concerns our earthly life, this petition and the next concern our heavenly life—"the spiritual covenant that God has made for the salvation of his church...." Christ here "calls sins 'debts' because we owe penalty for them, and we could in no way satisfy it unless we were released by this forgiveness." The pardon is from "free mercy." No payment is exacted from us for our debts, for God makes "satisfaction to himself by his own mercy in Christ, who once for all gave himself as a ransom [cf. Rom. 3:24]" (3.20.45).

Calvin notes that it is a mistake to think that believers are delivered from praying this petition to God's throne of mercy. Believers pray for pardon, knowing that they have not yet put on perfection. In truth, being far from perfection, "believers are never divested of the vices of their flesh without always remaining liable to God's judgment." To conceive that we no longer need to pray for pardon fosters an incautious spirit of indolence in us, "diametrically opposed to God's mercy" (3.20.45).

The other part of this petition is that God might forgive us our debts *as we forgive our debtors*. That is, may God forgive us "as we spare and pardon all who have in any way injured us, either treating us unjustly in deed or insulting us in word." This doesn't mean we remit the guilt of others; instead, our forgiveness of others means that we willingly cast from our minds "wrath, hatred, desire for revenge, and willingly banish to oblivion the remembrance of injustice." If we ask God to forgive us while we harbor hatred in our hearts, while we plot revenge for a wrong, or conceive of doing harm to another to even the score, or while we fail to seek reconciliation with our foe, then "we entreat God not to forgive our sins." In fact, we ask God to do to us what we would do to others—exact revenge. The petition is clear: Lord, do not forgive us unless we forgive others. We should not, then, "seek forgiveness of sins from God unless we ourselves also forgive the offenses against us of all those who do or have done us ill." Not that the condition set forth here means that we merit or deserve God's forgiveness because we forgive others. "Rather, by this word the Lord intended partly to comfort the weakness of our faith." Christ adds the condition to this petition to assure us that God "has granted forgiveness of sins to us just as surely as we are aware of having forgiven others, provided our hearts have been emptied and purged of all hatred, envy, and vengeance." But the condition also serves as a warning to all persons who refuse to forgive others and foment discord and fury. Such persons do not bear the marks of God's children (3.20.45).

The sixth and last petition of the Lord's Prayer, *Lead us not into temptation, but deliver us from evil*, "corresponds," says Calvin, "to the promise that the law is to be engraved upon our hearts [Prov. 3:3; 2 Cor. 3:3], but because we obey God not without continual warfare and hard and trying struggles, here we seek to be equipped with such armor and defended with such protection that we may be able to win the victory." We need the Spirit's fortifying care "to soften our hearts within and to bend and direct them to obey God"; and we need the Spirit's aid "to render us invincible against both all the stratagems and all the violent assaults of Satan" (3.20.46). We are tempted in multiplex ways, whether in the shape of riches, power, and honor or in the form of poverty, disgrace, and contempt. In the former we forget God by becoming drunk with the sweets of worldly wealth or accomplishments; in the latter we reveal ourselves estranged from and bitter toward God in our despondency, losing our assurance and hope because of life's difficulties, disappointments, and afflictions. Either sort of temptation wages war against us. Thus we pray for deliverance, that "we may not be puffed up in prosperity or yet cast down in adversity" (3.20.46).

This petition, however, is not asking God to allow no temptation to come upon our path, for "we grow sluggish" unless we are tested. God, in fact, chastises His elect "by disgrace, poverty, tribulation, and other sorts of affliction." God and Satan have diverse aims in such testing—Satan to destroy us, God to sanctify us (cf. 1 Cor. 10:13; 2 Pet. 2:9). Truly, in our own strength we combat the devil in vain. Only in God's power can we find strength and stand fast. We must, then, cast off our weakness of flesh and depend upon the Spirit who indwells us (3.20.46).

Calvin also maintains that this package of petitions demonstrates that our prayers should be public, directed at the church's collective edification and the "advancement of the believers' fellowship." As for the conclusion of this prayer, *Thine is the Kingdom, and the power, and the glory, forever*, Calvin acknowledges a textual issue here, but argues that these words are appropriate and make a fitting conclusion, giving us a "firm and tranquil repose for our faith." The *Amen* expresses the confidence that "all things of this sort have already been brought to pass, and will surely be granted to us, since they have been promised by God, who cannot deceive" (3.20.47).

Practical Advice on Prayer

Having completed his exposition of the Lord's Prayer, Calvin turns to a few ancillary issues, as well as some practical matters. He asserts that this prayer provides the true and proper content of what we may lawfully ask of God (3.20.48). That does not mean however that "we are so bound by this form of prayer that we are not allowed to change it in either word or syllable." Scripture, of course, gives us many prayers. Though the words of these prayers are very different from those given to us in the Lord's Prayer, the sense is the same. Thus "no man should ask for, expect, or demand, anything at all except what is included, by way of summary, in this prayer…" (3.20.49).

Finally, in concluding his discussion on prayer Calvin urges believers to be regular in their life of prayer and to persevere in it (3.20.50–52).

Questions for Reflection and Discussion

1. Of the four rules on prayer Calvin sets forth, which one do you think is most often violated and why? Are there any other rules you would want to add to the list? Which of these rules most helps you to improve your prayer life?

2. Why must we pray in accord with God's revealed will? Why is this not inconsistent with God's hidden will?

3. How does the intercessory work of Christ comfort and encourage you to pray?

4. Why does prayer inspire a submissive love for God and cultivate in us a life of sacrificial service?

5. What do you judge to be the most common fault of much public prayer?

6. How do the first three petitions of the Lord's Prayer involve and interweave with one another? Why is this important for us to understand?

7. Why do prosperity and wealth, on the one hand, or poverty and scarcity

on the other, discourage or otherwise hinder us from praying sincerely the petition for "daily bread"?

8. Why is it so difficult to forgive those who have sinned against us? What forms the foundation of and motivation for our forgiveness of others?

9. Temptation comes to every believer; what are God's intentions in allowing temptations to afflict us versus Satan's motives? Explain.

10. In Calvin's discussion of prayer, what has helped you the most to pursue a devout life of prayer?

☞17☜

Predestination

Chapters 21–24 of Book Three

Chapter Twenty-one: Eternal Election, by Which God Has Predestined Some to Salvation, Others to Destruction

Orientation

CONTRARY TO POPULAR opinion, predestination is not the key to Calvin's theology, nor the key to his doctrine of salvation. It is, however, the key to his doctrine of grace. No other doctrine accents God's free mercy and unfathomable love better than divine election. Predestination demonstrates that God's goodness and justice originate in Himself, for He acts according to His own good pleasure. In saving sinners, God reveals that He brims with grace, for He loves the unlovable, saves His own from perdition, and ushers them to glory. In fact, being altogether gracious, God provides His Son as their Redeemer unto eternal life.

Calvin, in re-working his *Institutes* into a final edition, decided to place this doctrine near the end of the doctrine of salvation—probably for the pedagogical and spiritual advantages this placement presented for his readers. Having worked through the highpoints of the doctrine of salvation, Calvin turns to divine predestination as exhibit front and center of God's saving mercy—a doctrine that gives believers an impregnable security.

Calvin unpacks this doctrine first by setting forth some safeguards in treating predestination. Then he defines predestination, noting both its corporate and individual aspects. The next chapter presents the scriptural materials in support of the doctrine, followed by a chapter that takes up and responds to numerous objections against predestination. Finally, Calvin, in a separate chapter, considers the relation between predestination and preaching, or the call of the gospel, which confirms that election is God's sovereign choice, rooted and grounded in His love in Jesus Christ.

Two Errors in Treating Predestination

Calvin commences his presentation of the doctrine of predestination with an observation about preaching, namely, that the proclamation of the gospel does not reach out to all people, and those to whom the gospel is presented meets with a varied response. What accounts for these discrepancies? The answer that Calvin sets forth is grounded in God's own wisdom, inscrutable to us. "In actual fact, the covenant of life is not preached equally among all men, and among those to whom it is preached, it does not gain the same acceptance either constantly or in equal degree" (3.21.1). Moreover, "In this diversity the wonderful depth of God's judgment is made known. For there is no doubt that this variety also serves the decision of God's eternal election" (3.21.1). Calvin knows this "diversity" causes many brows to wrinkle, and some regard the question of divine predestination baffling, even disturbing and unhelpful to contemplate. Calvin views matters differently. In fact, he regards the doctrine of predestination to be of great use and benefit for the believer. "We shall never be clearly persuaded, as we ought to be, that our salvation flows from the wellspring of God's free mercy until we come to know his eternal election, which illumines God's grace by this contrast: that he does not indiscriminately adopt all into the hope of salvation but gives to some what he denies to others" (3.21.1).

Rather than resist this doctrine and entangle ourselves in unanswerable questions, we must, insists Calvin, see how this doctrine affords us "very sweet fruit" (3.21.1).

However, there are two dangers we must avoid as we approach the doctrine of election: (1) wanton curiosity, which renders the doctrine difficult and dangerous; and (2) anxious silence. Calvin acknowledges that predestination deals with the hidden, "sacred precincts of divine wisdom." Thus rather than try to penetrate the hidden things of God (which cannot be done), Calvin urges us to revere them. He implores believers to be instructed by what God has revealed in Scripture. "For we shall know that the moment we exceed the bounds of the Word, our course is outside the pathway and in darkness, and that there we must repeatedly wander, slip, and stumble" (3.21.2). Calvin bids us to adopt a certain "learned ignorance," a posture which calls us to stop trying to be wise when God sets an end to teaching (3.21.2–3).

Besides the danger of "wanton curiosity," Calvin equally challenges "anxious silence," that is, those who would silence the doctrine of predestination out of fear. The Word of God must rule, for it is "the school of the Holy Spirit, in which, as nothing is omitted that is both necessary and useful to know, so nothing is taught but what is expedient to know" (3.21.3). This is among the chief doctrines of the faith and must not be silenced. God has taught it to us and to ignore it is to reproach God (3.21.4).

Predestination Defined and Explained
But what is predestination? Calvin offers this definition: "We call predestination God's eternal decree, by which he compacted with himself what he willed to become of each man. For all are not created in equal condition; rather, eternal life is foreordained for some, eternal condemnation for others. Therefore, as any man has been created to one or the other of these ends, we speak of him as predestined to life or death" (3.21.5).

Here Calvin explains that predestination is not mere divine foreknowledge. He also notes that predestination, or divine election, has individual persons and also entire nations as its objects. For example, God elects Abraham, the individual man, and works His saving blessings in him. God also peculiarly chooses one people over another. There is a corporate election besides individual election. The ends might be different, but the sovereign act of God applies in both cases (3.21.5). However, unlike corporate election, individual election—that "more limited degree of election"—is an election "in which God's more special grace" comes to expression. Here we see that even among an elect nation, Israel, among the covenant seed of Abraham, God rejects some and elects others, such as Ishmael in the one case and Isaac in the other; similarly Esau and Jacob, Saul and David. "The very inequality of grace proves that it is free" (3.21.6). Calvin drives home this point:

> Although it is now sufficiently clear that God by his secret plan freely chooses whom he pleases, rejecting others, still his free election has been only half explained until we come to individual persons, to whom God not only offers salvation but so assigns it that the certainty of its effect is not in suspense or doubt. These are reckoned among the unique offspring mentioned by Paul [cf. Rom. 9:7–8; Gal. 3:16ff.]. The adoption was put in Abraham's hands. Nevertheless, because many of his descendants were cut off as rotten members, we must, in order that election may be effectual and truly enduring, ascend to the Head, in whom the Heavenly Father has gathered his elect together, and has joined them to himself by an indissoluble bond (3.21.7).

Calvin is careful to explain that we are not elect in Abraham, or saved in Abraham, but our election and salvation are in Christ (3.21.7). Corporate election, then, is not the same as the election in Christ to salvation, for "the general election of a people is not always firm and effectual: to those with whom God makes a covenant, he does not at once give the spirit of regeneration that would enable them to persevere in the covenant to the very end." "Outward change" is not the same as "inward grace." The covenant certainly possesses great value, for God continually gathers His church in this way. But the covenant is not intrinsically effectual unto salvation—divine election is according to God's unchangeable plan (3.21.7).

Election and Reprobation in Summary
Calvin offers this summary of his discussion of election and reprobation to this point:

> As Scripture, then, clearly shows, we say that God once established by his eternal and unchangeable plan those whom he long before determined once for all to receive unto salvation, and those whom, on the other hand, he would devote to destruction. We assert that, with respect to the elect, this plan was founded upon his freely given mercy, without regard to human worth; but by his just and irreprehensible but incomprehensible judgment he has barred the door of life to those whom he has given over to damnation (3.21.7).

Moreover, there are clear signs of one's election—that is, responding to the call of the gospel in faith, being forgiven and justified. But the reprobate remain shut off from the knowledge of God and the sanctification of the Spirit. Thus, while the elect are sealed in their election by God's call and justification—these being manifestations of their election—the reprobate are excluded from these gifts and consequently exhibit in themselves the judgment that awaits them (3.21.7).

Chapter Twenty-two: **Confirmation of This Doctrine from Scriptural Testimonies**

Orientation
Naturally Calvin is not oblivious to the objections that his doctrine of predestination elicits. However, he is sure of its scriptural validity. He thus sets for himself the task of presenting the scriptural witness for the doctrine he

explained in the previous chapter. First he distinguishes election from divine foreknowledge; then he responds to opponents while setting forth the meaning of some key biblical texts.

Election Is Not from Divine Foreknowledge of Merit

Calvin counters various objections to and misunderstandings of the doctrine of election. One of the most common notions is to conceive of election as based upon foreseen merit—as if God looks ahead into the future, sees who will be upright and repentant, who will respond in faith to the gospel, who will choose Him; and, then, on that basis God elects such persons (3.22.1).

Calvin replies to this view by pointing to Ephesians 1:4–5. This passage clearly and indisputably teaches that the elect are chosen in Christ to be blameless and holy, not that they were foreseen as such. The elect are chosen so that they become unblemished and sanctified, which means that election is not based on divine foreknowledge of human merits. Rather, election is grounded in God's own "good pleasure." Furthermore, God "purposed this in himself," which means "he considered nothing outside himself with which to be concerned in making his decree" (Eph. 1:9) (3.22.2–3). 2 Timothy 1:9 confirms this, as does Romans 9–11, John 6:44–45, John 13:18, and John 10:28–29. These texts show that God freely chooses His own and adopts them as His sons and daughters, and "the intrinsic cause of this is in himself, for he is content with his own secret good pleasure" (3.22.7).

Election and Reprobation Not Based on Works

Calvin next shows that neither election nor reprobation is based on works. He spends some time on Jacob's election because some argue that Jacob's election, with its attendant benefits, was not unto salvation or to "the inheritance of heaven." Calvin maintains that earthly symbols could serve as signs of Jacob's "spiritual election." Indeed, "Jacob…is chosen and distinguished from the rejected Esau by God's predestination, while not differing from him in merits" (cf. Rom. 9:15). Speaking more generally, Calvin asserts that there is never a reason residing in a person for God to be moved to extend His mercy to him or her, but God does extend mercy from Himself; He establishes salvation "in himself alone." It is folly for us to seek recourse in our merits and works. God foreknows not as an idle fellow in a watchtower but as the Author of the plan (Acts 2:23). God foreknows as He has purposed, not the other way around (cf. 1 Pet. 1:2) (3.22.6).

Calvin appeals to the church fathers, especially Augustine, in order to fortify his position (3.22.8), but he refuses to be drawn into subtleties that diminish glorying in and contemplating God's goodness in divine election (3.22.9). As for the universality of the call of the gospel and the particularity of saving election, Calvin points out that even in the broad scattering of the seed of the gospel, the gospel does not go forth to all equally, as manifest when Paul is forbidden by the Holy Spirit to preach the gospel in Asia, being directed to Macedonia instead. Such discrimination shows us that God "has the right to distribute this treasure to whom he pleases" (3.22.10). Further, Calvin asserts that "although the voice of the gospel addresses all in general, yet the gift of faith is rare." Indeed, inasmuch as "faith is a special gift, the ears are beaten upon in vain with outward preaching." Outward preaching refers to hearing the gospel without faith and therefore abiding in unbelief. Preaching by itself, or preaching without faith, apart from receiving the gospel in faith, does not make a person God's child. Faith is requisite. And faith is revealed in rebirth; rebirth is of God, even as faith is (John 1:12–13) (3.22.10).

Just as election is not based upon works of merit, reprobation is not grounded on sinful actions, faults, or debts. Predestination is not about works! Paul is emphatic in making this point in Romans 9. Referring to Jacob and Esau, twins, both seed of the covenant, both not yet born and prior to doing anything good or evil, the apostle teaches about them that "one was chosen, the other rejected." Says Calvin,

> This is to prove that the foundation of divine predestination is not in works. Then when [the apostle] raised the objection, whether God is unjust, he does not make use of what would have been the surest and clearest defense of his righteousness: that God recompensed Esau according to his own evil intention. Instead, he contents himself with a different solution, that the reprobate are raised up to the end that through them God's glory may be revealed. Finally, he adds the conclusion that "God has mercy upon whomever he wills, and he hardens whomever he wills" [Rom. 9:18]. Do we see how Paul attributes both to God's decision alone? If, then, we cannot determine a reason why he vouchsafes mercy to his own, except that it so pleases him, neither shall we have any reason for rejecting others, other than his will. For when it is said that God hardens or shows mercy to whom he wills, men are warned by this to seek no cause outside his will (3.22.11).

We see, then, that for Calvin, seeking to speak scripturally, election and reprobation both serve God's glory, according to His will (3.22.11).

Chapter Twenty-three: Refutation of the False Accusations with Which This Doctrine Has Always Been Unjustly Burdened

Orientation

With this chapter Calvin nuances and expands his expositions on reprobation, especially since some suppose to affirm election without reprobation. This leads to a consideration of a variety of charges directed against predestination. This is the most polemical of the four chapters Calvin writes in treating this topic. Specifically, he considers five objections that are raised against the doctrine of election and reprobation. Naturally, he seeks to offer what he considers to be scriptural answers or solutions to each of these protests.

Election without Reprobation?

There are those (mostly Lutherans) who embrace divine election but reject reprobation. Calvin believes that this view is untenable. Election is meaningless without reprobation. In his words, "election itself could not stand except as set over against reprobation" (3.23.1). This leads him to define reprobation in terms that have become familiar to the classical Reformed tradition, and yet in some ways stronger. He writes: "those whom God passes over [*praeterit*], he condemns [*reprobat*]; and this he does for no other reason than that he wills to exclude them from the inheritance which he predestines for his own children" (3.23.1). The severity of this statement promptly receives a defense: "And men's insolence is unbearable if it refuses to be bridled by God's Word, which treats of his incomprehensible plan that the angels themselves adore" (3.23.1). Will the clay contend with its potter? (Rom. 9:20). Further, Calvin reminds readers that the apostle shows how "hardening" is as much in God's hand as "showing mercy" (cf. Rom. 9:14ff.). Sober faith accepts this teaching about "God's secret plan" (3.23.1). It is futile to quarrel with God, especially since God has endured patiently with the vessels of wrath made for destruction, even as He has shown the riches of His glory to the vessels of mercy who are being saved for glory (Rom. 9:22–23). "Ultimate sovereignty" belongs to God's wrath and might in subjecting the rejected to destruction, and that according to His "secret plan." We act wickedly when we try to subject God's "deep judgments" to the powers of our puny minds. Indeed, the apostle teaches us that the Lord hardens whom He pleases (Rom. 9:18), which proves that "God's secret plan is the cause of hardening" (3.23.1).

Replying to Five Objections

Calvin next defends the doctrine of predestination against "venomous dogs" who "spew out more than one kind of venom against God" (3.23.2). This spewed venom comes in the form of five objections, which Calvin considers and answers individually.

• *First Objection: God Becomes a Tyrant.* One objection against Calvin's doctrine of predestination is that it turns God into a tyrant. Isn't it unfair of God to become "angry at his creatures who have not provoked him by any previous offense" (3.23.2)? This action is "more like the caprice of a tyrant than the lawful sentence of a judge" (3.23.2). Is one sentenced to eternal death solely by God's decision apart from the question of merit?

Calvin answers this objection by asserting that God's will is the "cause of all things that are." God's will itself is not caused by anything beyond itself—if it were, God would be bound to something beyond Himself, which is an unimaginable idea for Calvin. "For God's will is so much the highest rule of righteousness that whatever he wills, by the very fact that he wills it, must be considered righteous" (3.23.2). Further inquiry into the cause of God's will is wickedness. If we ask why God chooses some and not others the biblical answer, according to Calvin, is because God has *willed it.* If we probe deeper by asking, "Why has He so willed?" we inquire into the impossible, since nothing is higher than or found beyond the will of God. We may not peer into the secrets of God. As for the cry of "injustice," God defends Himself without our help, says Calvin. Besides, God isn't answerable to humans and humans are "incompetent" to judge God (3.23.2).

Calvin rejects the validity of the "tyranny" objection for other reasons as well. Since God does not condemn persons apart from their sin, Calvin insists that God is *just* toward the reprobate. As Calvin reasons: "if all whom the Lord predestines to death are by condition of nature subject to the judgment of death, of what injustice toward themselves may they complain?" (3.23.3). Like Augustine, Calvin maintains that humans, as descendants of Adam, are all drawn from a "corrupt mass," and therefore God commits no injustice in condemning them (cf. Book III.1-3). Whereas the reprobate are culpable for their *condemnation,* God is the ultimate cause or author of their *reprobation.* The sovereign choice of election and rejection are alike hidden in God Himself. Writes Calvin, we must "always at last return to the sole decision of God's will" (3.23.3–4).

If a person still wishes to object, Calvin invokes the apostle's rebuke in

Romans 9:20: "Who are you, O man, to argue with God?" Calvin sees this as no "subterfuge." With these words, the apostle shows that "the reason of divine righteousness is higher than man's standard can measure, or than man's slender wit can comprehend" (3.23.4).

Like Augustine before him, Calvin also appeals to Romans 11:33 for support: "Oh, the depth of the riches of the wisdom and knowledge of God! How unsearchable his judgments, and his paths beyond tracing out!" Reprobation, like election, is hidden in God's secret plan. To try to dig deeper into what is "unsearchable" is not only "madness" but "monstrous." The narrowness of our minds cannot grasp God's decree with Himself, for God does not temper the greatness of His works to our ignorance (3.23.4). Calvin agrees with Augustine: "Ignorance that believes is better than rash knowledge" (3.23.5). Why try to search out what is unsearchable? Why attempt to track down what is inscrutable? Reverent mystery is better than proud reason.

• *Second Objection: Sinners Excused.* Opponents of Calvin's doctrine charge that he excuses sinners since all guilt and responsibility are yanked from them. "Profane tongues chatter," to use Calvin's words, "why should God impute those things to men as sin, the necessity of which he has imposed by predestination?" (3.23.6).

Calvin counters with an appeal to Solomon: "God has made everything for himself, even the wicked for the evil day [Prov. 16:4]" (3.23.6). Thus we see that God's decree encompasses all things. And this decree, lest there be a misunderstanding, is not dependent upon divine foreknowledge but rather the reverse: divine foreknowledge is founded upon the divine decree (3.23.6). What this boils down to is that even the fall into sin is decreed by God. In that context, Calvin utters the infamous words: "The decree is dreadful indeed, I confess (*decretus quidem horribile, fateor*)." "Dreadful" in this case means to fill with awe. Calvin is saying, as it were: "The decree indeed fills one with awe, I confess." Notice the defense Calvin gives to those words: "Yet no one can deny that God foreknew what end man was to have before he created him, and consequently foreknew because he so ordained by his decree" (3.23.7).

Calvin goes even further. He rejects the distinction between God's "will" and "permission." Consequently, when some suggest that "although God permits the wicked to perish, He does not will it," they engage in futility. The distinction is useless in Calvin's mind. If God "permits" He *wills* to permit, which means God ordains what takes place—even the destruction of the wicked. For "the will of God is the necessity of all things," as Augustine taught. It is not as though, however, God's will is an unjust will. God acts justly and for His own glory. The wicked are worthily predestined to destruction (3.23.8). "Besides," as Calvin is careful to say, "their perdition depends upon the predestination of God in such a way that the cause and occasion of it are found in themselves" (3.23.8).

This goes back to Calvin's distinction between *reprobation*, which is God's sovereign and free choice apart from our works, and *condemnation*, which is God's just judgment on our sin. As Calvin never tires to repeat, "the ordinance of God…has its own equity—unknown, indeed, to us but very sure" (3.23.9). Hence, the reprobate are fully culpable in their sin and justly condemned.

• *Third Objection: Partiality in God.* Calvin's doctrine of predestination, however, faces another charge of injustice, namely, that his teaching means that God shows partiality toward persons, something which Scripture denies. Why does God in His work of election and reprobation distinguish between persons of indistinguishable merit? Calvin believes he finds the answer to this objection in the nature of God's mercy itself. Since grace is free, no one may make a demand upon it. When God chooses to bestow His mercy on one person and withhold it from another, He does so solely according to His free decision (3.23.10).

But isn't God's justice still biased, since in predestination He does not treat all sinners alike? If all are guilty, wouldn't equity demand that God condemn all alike? If God extends mercy apart from merit, shouldn't He extend His mercy to all equally? Calvin finds this objection founded upon a false conception. Since God is under no obligation to sinners, He is free to show Himself merciful and just. He need not renounce all judgment in order to show mercy, nor must He withhold mercy in order to judge all. If God were a debtor to humans, grace would cease to be grace (3.23.11). Calvin uses the example of a lender: "Because God metes out merited penalty to those whom he condemns but distributes unmerited grace to those whom he calls, he is freed of all accusation—like a lender, who has power of remitting payment to one, of exacting it from another" (3.23.11).

Calvin bids believers to remember that the Lord is merciful and just. God shows His mercy in giving to some what is undeserved; this is grace. In not giving His grace to all, He manifests His justice, which all deserve (3.23.11).

• *Fourth Objection: Apathetic Living.* Yet another objection states that this doctrine destroys all zeal for holiness or concern to lead a godly life, since God's decision preempts anything persons can do. When people hear that God has either appointed them to life or death, the irrepressible conclusion is that one's own personal conduct is irrelevant (3.23.12). Calvin states that this is an obvious caricature and even a form of lying, "for there are many swine that pollute the doctrine of predestination with their foul blasphemies, and by this pretext evade all admonitions and reproofs" (3.23.12). In fact, this doctrine does not make us jaded and careless but humble and cast down. We are taught "to tremble at [God's] judgment and esteem his mercy." Our election has as its end blamelessness and holiness, as Paul teaches in Ephesians 1:4, not vice and carelessness. This doctrine ought to "arouse" and "goad" us to holiness rather than indifference. Indeed, when a person endeavors to pursue an upright life, the pursuit itself is born of election (3.23.12).

• *Fifth Objection: Admonitions and Preaching Meaningless.* The fifth objection states that predestination renders admonition, and even the proclamation of the gospel, meaningless; even more, it overthrows all biblical exhortation to lead a godly life. Calvin holds up the apostle Paul as a clear rebuke of this charge. Paul proclaimed God's free election, yet he was not cold either in admonition or exhortation (3.23.13). Writes Calvin:

> To sum up, those moderately versed in Paul will, without long proof, understand how aptly he harmonizes those things which they pretend disagree. Christ commands us to believe in him. Yet when he says, "No one can come to me unless it has been granted him by my Father" [John 6:65], his statement is neither false nor contrary to his command. Let preaching, then, take its course that it may lead men to faith, and hold them fast in perseverance with continuing profit. And yet let not the knowledge of predestination be hindered, in order that those who obey may not be proud as of something of their own but may glory in the Lord (3.23.13).

In saying this Calvin is aware of the potential abuses to which the doctrine can be subjected. An imprudent pastor can preach predestination in an offensive manner. Augustine's words should be heeded: "If anyone addresses the people in this way: 'If you do not believe, the reason is that you have already been divinely destined for destruction,' he not only fosters sloth but also gives place to evil intention" (3.23.14). However, Calvin also emphasizes with

Augustine God's irresistible will which efficaciously works repentance and renewal, since the Holy Spirit works in human hearts through the admonition and exhortation of the Word of God. Therefore, the church must preach the gospel indiscriminately. As Augustine teaches: "For as we know not who belongs to the number of the predestined or who does not belong, we ought to be so minded as to *wish that all men be saved*" (3.23.14, italics added).

Chapter Twenty-four: Election is Confirmed by God's Call; Moreover, the Wicked Bring upon Themselves the Just Destruction to Which They Are Destined

Orientation

With chapter twenty-four Calvin seeks to clarify two aspects of his doctrine of predestination: (1) how election is confirmed by God's call; and (2) how God's justice is not impugned by condemning the reprobate. Hence, Calvin addresses the practical question about one's assurance of election. Practical questions do emerge: How do persons come to Christ? How can the elect be confirmed in their election? Isn't the nature of election itself—rooted in God's eternal decision—remote, hidden, and secret? How can persons know they are among God's chosen?

Election Confirmed through Faith or Inward Calling

Calvin explains that divine election, which is otherwise hidden from us, receives God's own attestation through the call of the gospel. Romans 8:29–30 reveals that election is not an entity that stands alone, but finds fruition in "calling" and "justification" (3.24.1). Indeed, God's chosen people only come to possess the great gift of salvation when they are "called" and "led to faith." Calling, then, when coupled with election, magnifies God's free mercy. Nothing demonstrates the graciousness of election more than this chain of salvation (3.24.1). As Acts 13:48 states: "Those who had been ordained to eternal life, believed." Humans as sinners are without ears to hear and eyes to see. The call of the gospel must be accompanied with the "inner call" of the Spirit, a gift given only to the elect (3.24.2).

Calvin repeatedly warns against making humans co-workers with God in the work of salvation, as if man ratifies divine election "by his consent" (3.24.3). Is human will superior to God's plan? We are not given the mere "ability" to believe, says Calvin, but we are given faith itself. Do we then place our faith in *our faith*? Calvin vehemently maintains that the believer will not find assurance in the hidden decree—just as he is convinced that the believer will not find assurance in him or herself. Thus he rejects the erroneous notion that our faith "ratifies" election. Hence the question: Wherein resides the confirmation of one's election? Calvin elucidates his position as follows:

> Indeed, that [election] is confirmed, with respect to us, is utterly plain; we have also already seen that the secret plan of God, which lay hidden, *is brought to light,* provided you understand by this language merely that what was unknown is now verified—sealed, as it were, with a seal. But it is false to say that election takes effect only after we have embraced the gospel, and takes it validity from this. We should indeed seek assurance of it from this; for if we try to penetrate to God's eternal ordination, that deep abyss will swallow us up (3.24.3, italics added).

Calvin thus contends that uncertainty takes place when people perversely seek "to flit about above the clouds" into God's secret plan. Since it is perverse to attempt to do that, Calvin seeks a saner path. Assurance must begin with the outward Word whereby God testifies of His secret grace (3.24.3).

For Calvin, "as it is wrong to make the force of election contingent upon faith in the gospel, by which we feel that it appertains to us, so we shall be following the best order if, in seeking the certainty of our election, we cling to those latter signs which are sure attestations of it" (3.24.4). The "latter signs" Calvin has in mind are the effectual gospel call and its consequent fruits of faith. To speculate on the question of one's status as elect or reprobate is to cast yourself "into the depths of a bottomless whirlpool to be swallowed up." It is to become entangled "in innumerable and inextricable snares." It is to bury yourself "in an abyss of sightless darkness" (3.24.4). Calvin uses the metaphor of the sea:

> Even though discussion about predestination is likened to a dangerous sea, still in traversing it, one finds safe and calm—I also add pleasant—sailing unless he willfully desire to endanger himself. For just as those engulf themselves in a deadly abyss who, to make their election more certain, investigate God's eternal plan apart from his Word, so those who rightly and duly examine it as it is contained in his Word reap the inestimable fruit of comfort. Let this, therefore, be the way of our inquiry: to begin with God's call, and to end with it (3.24.4).

In other words, what is your response to the gospel—faith or unbelief?

Inseparably linked to understanding the comfort of election is our *election in Christ*. In Christ we discover God's "fatherly mercy and kindly heart" (3.24.5). Christ alone "is the fountain of life, the anchor of salvation, and the heir of the Kingdom of Heaven." The elect are not chosen in themselves, but in Christ (cf. Eph. 1:4). Hence, assurance of election is not found in us or in the Father as such, but in His Son. "Christ…is the mirror wherein we must…contemplate our election" (3.24.5). Calvin uses this metaphor to remind us that Christ is the one in whom salvation is found. The promise of the gospel is sure: "whosoever believes in him will not perish" (John 3:16). Christ, as the "mirror" of election, reflects God's mercy of salvation for sinners. In him alone believers find solace and true security.

Perseverance—General and Special Calling

This leads Calvin into a discussion of perseverance. He recognizes that some persons who appear to belong to Christ slip from the faith and lead ungodly lives. Thus, "we are taught by this experience that call and faith are of little account unless perseverance be added; and this does not happen to all" (3.24.6).

Calvin appeals to a variety of biblical passages to make his point. The elect are "ever safe" because they have been made Christ's once for all (cf. John 6 & 10) (3.24.6). He preserves and keeps His own. John 17 teaches that the elect do not perish, only the son of perdition (3.24.7, 9). Similarly, 1 John 2:19 says, "They went out from us, but they were not of us; for if they had been of us, they would *no doubt* have continued with us." That is, some are illumined with the gospel "only for a time." This illumination or call comes through the proclamation of the gospel. Preaching, however, constitutes only the outward form of calling. Calvin thus distinguishes between a general call and a special call through the gospel. For example, Matthew 22:2–13, the parable of the wedding banquet, shows that the reprobate are temporarily mingled with the church, but eventually are unmasked and judged as when the man without the wedding garment is cast out (3.24.8). This text is readily understood when we recognize "two kinds of call":

> There is the general call, by which God invites all equally to himself through the outward preaching of the word—even those to whom he holds it out as a savor of death [cf. 2 Cor. 2:16], and as the occasion for severer condemnation. The other kind of call is special, which he deigns for the most part to give to the believers alone, while by the inward il-

lumination of his Spirit he causes the preached Word to dwell in their hearts (3.24.8).

The phrase "for the most part" is added because Calvin also sees God's special call reaching those who have a temporary sort of faith: "Sometimes... he communicates it also to those whom he enlightens only for a time, and whom afterwards, in just punishment for their ingratitude, he abandons and smites with greater blindness" (3.24.8). Meanwhile, the elect are indistinguishable from the reprobate until called, i.e., experiencing regeneration and coming to faith (3.24.10–11).

In opposition to Martin Bucer, Calvin's one time colleague in Strasbourg, there is no "seed of election" sown in the elect from birth, which then produces an inclination of piety and fear of God. After all, notes Calvin, we are all sons of wrath before regeneration (cf. Eph. 2:1–3). Moreover, there are numerous examples of believers who prior to faith wallowed in "abominable and execrable sins," e.g., Rahab the harlot. The elect do not possess a *tendency* to godliness (see 3.24.10–11).

Justice toward the Reprobate

From this discussion an objection emerges from another angle. If God effectually calls the elect unto salvation, what of the others whom God has "created for dishonor in life and destruction in death?" (3.24.12). How do they come to their end? Calvin writes that God "sometimes deprives them of the capacity to hear his word; at other times he, rather, blinds and stuns them by the preaching of it" (3.24.12). Calvin cites the example of the four thousand years of ignorance among the Gentiles before the gospel of Christ was published to them. God is the supreme judge who justly "leaves in blindness" whom He will. Calvin offers the following example:

> If the same sermon is preached, say, to a hundred people, twenty receive it with the ready obedience of faith, while the rest hold it valueless, or laugh, or hiss, or loathe it. If anyone should reply that this diversity arises out of their malice and perverseness, I still will not be satisfied, because the nature of the former would be occupied with the same malice if God did not correct it by his goodness. Therefore, we shall always be confused unless Paul's question comes to mind: Who distinguishes you? [1 Cor. 4:7]. By this he means that some excel others not by their own virtue but by God's grace alone (3.24.12).

The distinguishing effect is according to God's sovereign choice (3.24.13).

Furthermore, sometimes the Lord even wills to increase the blindness of the reprobate through the preaching of the gospel, e.g., the sending of Moses to Pharaoh and Ezekiel to the rebellious Israelites. Christ Himself deliberately preached in parables lest perchance the people turn and be healed. Although in the preaching of the gospel there is "always enough light to convict the conscience of the wicked," and although the reprobate may readily infer their guilt if they look inside themselves, conviction of conscience is one thing, conversion quite another (3.24.13; 3.23.3–4, 8).

Calvin is unyielding in ascribing this difference among people to God's immutable plan. He recognizes that human wickedness plays a role. But "wickedness" alone is not the Scriptural answer. For the reprobate "have been given over to this depravity because they have been raised up by the just but inscrutable judgment of God to show forth his glory in their condemnation" (3.24.14). Eli's sons, for example, were stubbornly wicked men, but God left them in their stubbornness since his "immutable decree had once for all destined them to destruction" (3.24.14).

Such strong statements, Calvin knows, do not go unchallenged or without complaint. Some of Calvin's opponents object that Calvin gives us a God who "with unbridled power abuses his miserable creatures for his cruel amusement" (3.24.14). But, says Calvin, we know that the wicked are *justly* condemned. If we are unable to fully understand the reason for God's distinguishing selection of people, let us be willing to offer an admission of ignorance concerning God's great wisdom.

Calvin's Exegesis of the Universalistic Texts

Calvin also discusses the so-called universalistic texts, such as Ezekiel 33:11, where it says: "God does not will the death of the wicked but wills that the wicked turn back and live"; 1 Timothy 2:3–4: God "wills all men to be saved"; and 2 Peter 3:9: "God does not will that any should perish but that he should receive all to repentance." Do such passages teach the opposite of Calvin's position? (3.24.15–16).

Calvin responds to each text in turn. He believes that these texts present more serious difficulties for his opponents than for himself, and that their interpretation of these texts meets with contradictions. For example, with regard to Ezekiel 33:11 Calvin asks: if God was happy and desirous of saving all men, why didn't He send the gospel of repentance to those who apparently would have been more receptive to it rather than to those who coldly despised it? Didn't Jesus say that the preaching of the gospel and the miracles performed in Judea would have accomplished more in the cities of Nineveh and Sodom? (3.24.16). "If God wills that all be saved, how does it come to pass that he does not open the door of repentance to the miserable men who would be better prepared to receive grace?" (3.24.15).

Calvin believes his opponents go astray when they make God's will oppose "his eternal plan, by which he has distinguished the elect from the reprobate" (3.24.15). The proper understanding of this text, according to Calvin, is that God is ready to forgive the sinner upon conversion. God thus desires repentance over death. But the invitation to repentance does not meet with the same effect in the hearts of all; for some obey, others do not. Believers are, therefore, comforted by seeing God's readiness to pardon, and the wicked are made to see the gravity of their sin when they refuse to repent (3.24.15).

Taking up 1 Timothy 2:3–4, Calvin asks: "How did it happen that God deprived many people of the light of his gospel while others enjoyed it?" (3.24.16). The gospel is not equally broadcast to all, nor explained with the same clarity. Hence, what does it mean that God wills all persons to be saved? The context shows that God has not closed the door of salvation to any order of persons; rather, "he has so poured out his mercy that he would have none without it" (3.24.16). The apostle had urged Timothy to bring prayers to God for governing authorities, but since it seemed silly to pray for a generally hopeless class of men—kings and rulers who often viciously opposed the kingdom of God, by way of explanation it is added: "This is acceptable to God, who wills all men to be saved" (3.24.16). No class of persons is excluded.

Calvin recognizes the kind of questions 2 Peter 3:9 may elicit, for the apostle writes that God is "not willing that any should perish, but that all should come to repentance." For Calvin, this text shows "the means of obtaining salvation," which is repentance. Repentance (or conversion), however, is in God's hand. He cites Ezekiel 36:26, which indicates that God is the giver of new hearts and the remover of stony hearts. Since conversion is God's work, Calvin asks: Has God converted all? Do all have new hearts? No one "approaches God unless God anticipates him." "Indeed," writes Calvin, "unless the same God who urges all to repentance with his own voice also drew the elect to himself by the secret moving of his spirit, Jeremiah would not have said: 'Convert me, O Lord, and I will be converted...For when thou didst convert me, I repented' [Jer. 31:18–19, cf. Vg]" (3.24.16). Thus, on the one hand, God is ready to pardon the repentant since it is the means by which sinners embrace salvation; on the other hand, repentance itself is God's gift.

The challenge the universalistic texts presents for Calvin is whether God wills what is against His inviolable decree. Does God on the one hand desire the salvation of all men, but on the other hand decree only the salvation of some? Does God have a "double will"?

Calvin sees no inconsistency. The universality of the gospel call agrees perfectly with God's ordination from eternity to save and to condemn, since the gospel offer is tied to faith. Where faith is absent the offer of salvation is null and void; the promise of salvation is abolished. The promise of redemption merely means that God's "mercy is extended to all, provided they seek after it and implore it. But only those whom he has illumined do this. And he illumines those whom he has predestined to salvation" (3.24.17).

At this point Calvin faces this question: Why doesn't God accomplish the salvation of all His creatures according to His love? Does God hate anything He has made? Calvin's reply is that God does not hate His creatures. However, since the reprobate are without His Spirit and "can bring forth nothing but reason for cursing," they are hateful to God (3.24.17). It is not unjust of God, according to Calvin, to forsake those who previously of themselves have incurred guilt and earned His wrath. He bids us to consider God's work of election through the call of the gospel, and points out that redemptive history displays the work of God's sovereign action when the Lord "bound himself to one people, to be their Father" and "picked a small number of these, like a flower." The sovereignty and good pleasure of God's choice is irrefutable (3.24.17). Thus Calvin offers one final word of caution for proponents of both sides of the predestination debate:

> Now when many notions are adduced on both sides, let this be our conclusion: to tremble with Paul at so deep a mystery; but, if froward tongues clamor, not to be ashamed of this exclamation of his: 'Who are you, O man, to argue with God?' [Rom. 9:20 p.]. For as Augustine truly contends, they who measure divine justice by the standard of human justice are acting perversely (3.24.17).

Observations

For Calvin, the very nature of predestination—with God's discriminating choice cutting a path through humanity—elicits deep humility and reverence for God. Believers burst forth in praise. God's sovereign discrimination between elect and reprobate obliterates every notion of merit, unmasks human incapacity, and reveals the sovereign nature of divine mercy. Consequently, the doctrine moves believers to praise and worship. For Calvin, rather than reprobation serving to dampen the good news of grace, quite the opposite, seeing reprobation next to election enhances the reason for worship and humble thanksgiving to God.

Thanksgiving, however, is not apart from the assurance of divine election in Christ. Calvin calls Christ the mirror of election. Christ, however, is not an abstract Christ! Repeatedly Calvin points the believer back to Christ through *the written Word* of God. The manifestation of God's grace in Christ is through the revelation of God given in the Scriptures. Hence, for Calvin, the hiddenness of election was not a particularly relevant issue, since God's electing grace is revealed in the gospel. Only the imprudent and impious attempt to bypass the inscripturated revelation. What we should not miss is that though one's election is hidden in God's decree, it is brought to light, verified and sealed, when one embraces the gospel by faith. Moreover, for Calvin, the believer's assurance, which begins with God's call and which looks to the fruits of faith, is not anthropologically oriented (as if the believer looks to himself) but Christologically focused; the believer looks to Christ. This means that we can know our election truly and certainly, but indirectly. Election precedes one's faith, but by faith one's election is discerned.

For Calvin, most objections to this doctrine find an answer in humble submission to and faith in God's Word. Calvin firmly believes that he surmounts the obstacle of "injustice" the way Scripture does, namely, in the unashamed confession *of faith* that *God is just.* Only unbelief questions God's justice; and only unbelief questions sovereign predestination. Calvin, therefore, is determined to embrace both doctrines passionately. He bids his readers to an admission of ignorance rather than to accuse God in His dealings with humanity. Calvin is convinced that his *faith*-apologetic for predestination is scripturally valid and constitutes the final answer to all opponents. Indeed, Calvin is content to leave unresolved what he believes Scripture does not resolve. For him, this requires deep humility, or piety, and is integral to true knowledge of God. Hence predestination, despite its accompanying difficulties, is a doctrine confessed with *learned ignorance.* He calls us to "adore" God's ways "reverently" rather than "cross-examine" them.

Questions for Reflection and Discussion

1. Calvinism is often identified with and reduced to the doctrine of pre-destination. Is this accurate and is it fair? What do you think best characterizes Calvin's theology and Reformed theology? Do we exercise a proper "learned ignorance" regarding this doctrine?

2. Given what Calvin says about Abraham and Christ, why is it a mistake simply to equate covenant with election? What is the difference? How does God use the covenant to fulfill His elective purposes?

3. Look up Romans 9:10–16; Ephesians 1:5, 11–12; John 6:44, 64–65. How do these texts show that both election and reprobation are according to God's "good pleasure"? How does Calvin make this point?

4. What are the most common objections you have confronted regarding the doctrine of predestination? Why is it often difficult to persuade people of the biblical necessity of this doctrine?

5. Have you ever worried whether you were non-elect or reprobate, or doubted whether you were among the elect? Have you worried that a loved one or good friend is reprobate? Why is it a mistake to make this judgment about others? How does Calvin's instruction console us?

6. What does it mean that "Christ is the mirror wherein we must contemplate our election"? Why is it important?

7. Given the biblical testimony about election, why do so many people still "argue with God"?

8. Calvin bids us to view our election from the revealed will of God given to us in the gospel, that is, in Scripture. How is this done? What are the marks of a Christian? (cf. Belgic Confession, art. 29).

9. Is the doctrine of election "sweet fruit" for you, bringing consolation and strength to your faith? Explain.

10. How does divine election, more than any other doctrine, place the spotlight on God's grace?

11. What role, if any, do the believer's works play for him or her to have assurance of salvation? See Heidelberg Catechism, Q/A 86 and Belgic Confession, art. 24.

☙ 18 ☙

Future Glory

Chapter 25 of Book Three

Chapter Twenty-five: The Final Resurrection

Orientation

SOMETIMES IT SEEMS that we have obtained no blessing from Christ's victorious work of redemption. Although we have passed from death into life (John 5:24) and have become fellow citizens of the saints and members of God's household (Eph. 2:19), we soon discover that we still need to place our hope in God's promises. This brings Calvin to a consideration of the final resurrection. Our final restoration—including our bodily resurrection—brings about the fulfillment of all God's promises to us. In this chapter Calvin not only discusses the resurrection of the body, but also what coincides with this startling manifestation of God's power—namely, judgment day and the final states of those in Christ and those without Christ.

The Hope for Resurrection

Believers await the fullness of all that Christ has won for them. Since they do not yet possess perfection, they must be vigilant. Calvin states that "whatever has so far been explained concerning our salvation calls for minds lifted up to heaven, so that 'we may love Christ, whom we have not seen, and believing in him may rejoice with unutterable and exalted joy' until, as Peter declares, we receive 'the outcome of our faith' [1 Peter 1:8–9]" (3.25.1). This is our resurrection hope. We need this hope because "above and below us, before us and behind, violent temptations besiege us, which our minds would be quite unable to sustain, were they not freed of earthly things and bound to the heavenly life, which appears to be far away. Accordingly, he alone has fully profited in the gospel who has accustomed himself to continual meditation upon the blessed resurrection" (3.25.1).

Indeed, as Plato rightly said, man's highest good is union with God. We know that this is true, for Paul lays before us that very goal, to which he strives, laboring on until he attains it (see Phil. 3:8). The whole creation longs for renewal (Rom. 8:19–23). Our redemption and resurrection have already and entirely been obtained for us, but we await the application of the same to be completed in us (3.25.2).

Believers thus await the resurrection of the body with hope, having as an example and proof Christ's resurrection. His resurrection is the prototype for ours—and this is no small matter. The apostle argues that if Christ is not raised, then our faith is vain and mythical (cf. 1 Cor. 15:13ff.). Thus we must carefully attend to this topic; in fact, Calvin's treatment of it seeks to show believers that "when they have received Christ, the Author of perfect salvation," they may "rise up higher" and know "that he is clothed in heavenly immortality and glory so that the whole body may be conformed to the Head." Of course, it is difficult to believe that rotted corpses can be raised up to new life. But "Scripture provides two helps by which faith may overcome this great obstacle: one in the parallel of Christ's resurrection; the other in the omnipotence of God" (3.25.3).

Christ's resurrection is the divine pledge for the certainty of our own. We are joined to Christ and may not conceive of ourselves apart from Him. Christ died *for us* and His resurrection is victory, guaranteeing our own victorious resurrection from the dead. What is begun in the Head must be brought to completion in all His members. "Now, that our fellowship with Christ in the blessed resurrection may not be doubtful, in order that we may be content with this pledge, Paul plainly declares that Christ is seated in heaven [cf. Eph. 1:20], and will come on the Last Day as judge to conform our lowly, inglorious body to his glorious body" (Phil. 3:20–21; also see Col. 3:4; Rom. 8:11). Christ conquers death so that we may be His "companions in the life to come" (3.25.3).

Scriptural Testimony of Resurrection

Scorners, naturally, rail at this doctrine and regard the Gospels' accounts of the resurrection as fairy tales. Proofs of Christ's resurrection are said to be weak and wholly inadequate to persuade. Frightened women and fearful disciples hardly count as robust witnesses to such an event! Calvin counters that if we carefully examine the manifold witness of Scripture regarding

Christ's resurrection, we detect that, though the beginnings show weakness, "by God's wonderful providence all this was so governed that they who had just been overwhelmed with fright," that is, the very ones who came "to the tomb partly by love of Christ and zeal for piety, partly by their un-belief," that these very ones "might not only be eyewitnesses of the matter but might hear from the angels the same thing that they beheld with their eyes." Christ's resurrection was made known, for the most part, to those who loved Him, not those who despised Him. Moreover, when the biblical materials are studied and the circumstances surrounding the resurrection explored, "To discredit so many authentic evidences is not only disbelief but a depraved and even insane obstinacy" (3.25.3).

Since God is omnipotent, it is not beyond His power to accomplish such a feat. Resurrection from the dead is not something too hard for God to accomplish. His "boundless might" forms the foundation for such "an incalculable miracle." All things are subject to Christ's power (cf. Phil. 3:21). If we refuse to render the glory due God's power, we will not be persuaded of the resurrection. Even the Old Testament, however, testifies of hope in the resurrection (see Isa. 26:19; Ps. 68:20; Job 19:25–27). The vision of the valley of dry bones—bones that come to life by the power of God through His Word and Spirit—well bears witness to this confidence (Ezek. 37:1–10). Christ also bears witness of hope in resurrection, confident of its truth (John 5:28–29). Paul confirms this hope as well (cf. 2 Tim. 1:12; 4:8; 2 Thess. 1:6–8, 10) (3.25.4).

Defective Views of Resurrection

Of course, many persons have denied the resurrection from the dead and have raised various objections against it. Specifically, Calvin addresses the objections adduced by Atheists, Sadducees, Chiliasts, Universalists, Annihi-lationists, Manicheans, as well as other defective views (3.25.5–8). Among these defective views is the notion that the resurrection body will not be the same body with which we were clothed in this life. Calvin calls this a mon-strous error, and he cites numerous Scriptural passages that demonstrate that the selfsame body that was subject to death is resurrected and ushered into its perfection, being cleansed and set free from all that is unworthy of glory (cf. 2 Cor. 7:1; 5:10; 4:11; 1 Thess. 5:23; 1 Cor. 3:16; 6:15, 20; 1 Tim. 2:8; Rom. 12:1; 1 Cor. 15:53; Acts 17:32; Matt. 10:28; John 5:28–29; 2:19; Matt. 27:52) (3.25.7). In fact, to posit the necessity that believers be given *wholly other* bodies from those which went down into the grave of corruption is born of "sheer unbelief." Against this idea, Scripture repeatedly affirms the sanctity of the body (cf. Col. 2:12; Rom. 6:13, 19; 8:11; 1 Cor. 6:13–20; Phil. 3:20–21; John 6:39). Even our burial rites function to teach us that new life is prepared for the bodies we place in the ground. The Bible reminds us that sleep—which refers to the body—can be a metaphor for death (1 Cor. 15:6, 18; 1 Thess. 4:14–16). The word "cemetery," Calvin reminds us, means "sleeping place" (3.25.8).

Glorification in Resurrection

From here Calvin takes up the perfection of resurrection—that is, what is different about our resurrected bodies over against the bodies that were subject to curse and decay? Calvin offers an expansive explanation from 1 Corinthians 15:

> First, we must hold, as I have indicated, that as to substance we shall be raised again in the same flesh we now bear, but that the quality will be different. So it was that, when the same flesh of Christ which had been offered as a sacrifice was raised up, it yet excelled in other gifts as if it had become utterly different. This Paul asserts through familiar examples [1 Cor. 15:39]. For just as the substance of human and animal flesh is the same, but not the quality [v. 39], and all stars are of the same material, but differ in their brilliance [v. 41], so he teaches that, although we shall retain the substance of our bodies, there will be a change [vs. 51–52], that its condition may be far more excellent. Therefore, that we may be raised, the corruptible body will not perish or vanish, but, having laid aside corruption, will put on incorruption [vs. 53–54] (3.25.8).

Meanwhile, Scripture also teaches that some will not experience the death of the body, but, at Christ's return, will be changed in a moment, in the twinkling of an eye (cf. 1 Cor. 15:51–53). For this reason it will not be necessary that there exist "an interval of time between death and the beginning of the second life" in order for this change to take place. At the blast of the trumpet the dead will be raised imperishable, while the living will be suddenly changed along with them in order to participate in the same glory that awaits all God's sons and daughters (cf. 1 Thess. 4:15–16) (3.25.8).

Awaiting Resurrection

Truly, the righteous will be raised to glory, but the wicked will be raised to damnation (John 5:29; Matt. 25:32) (3.25.9). This is why believers await the day when death is swallowed up in victory (cf. Isa. 25:8; Hos. 13:14; 1 Cor. 15:54–55). Calvin calls us to meditate upon the future glory that awaits us. "Let us always have in mind the eternal happiness, the goal of resurrection—a happiness of whose excellence the minutest part would scarce be told if all were said that the tongues of all men can say." This is an important part of our present struggle as believers inasmuch as the promised joy that we will one day know is in this life "wrapped in obscurities." Although we are God's children, it requires faith if we would be assured that this is true. We do not yet behold this glory face to face; we do not yet see Christ glorified—that is, as He is (cf. 1 Cor. 13:12; 1 John 3:2) (3.25.10). Calvin amplifies on this theme:

> If the Lord will share his glory, power, and righteousness with the elect—nay, will give himself to be enjoyed by them and, what is more excellent, will somehow make them to become one with himself, let us remember that every sort of happiness is included under this benefit. And…let us…acknowledge that, if our mental capacity be compared with the height of this mystery, we still remain at the very lowest roots. In this matter, we must all the more, then, keep sobriety, lest forgetful of our limitations we should soar aloft with the greatest boldness, and be overcome by the brightness of the heavenly glory (3.25.10).

Calvin has elaborated on this theme at length earlier in his *Institutes*, in chapter nine of Book Three, treating meditation upon the future life.

Next Calvin briefly treats the varying degrees of glory for the saints. "We should regard as above all controversy the teaching of Scripture that, just as God, variously distributing his gifts to the saints in this world, beams upon them unequally, so there will not be an equal measure of glory in heaven, where God shall crown his own gifts" (3.25.10).

Many speculative questions emerge about the future state and the nature of its glory, and we do well, says Calvin, to guard ourselves against such alluring speculations wherein we are pleased with our own opinions and are drawn more and more deeply into a labyrinth that does not edify. Instead, we must learn to be satisfied in our ignorance—that is, "satisfied with the 'mirror' and its 'dimness' until we see him face to face [1 Cor. 13:12]." The sad part of this spectacle of human speculation is that most people are overly curious about what heavenly glory will be like but care little about how they can actually go to heaven. "Almost all are lazy and loath to do battle, while already picturing to themselves imaginary victories" (3.25.11).

The Destiny of the Unsaved

God's elect shall be received into indescribable glory (3.25.10), while the reprobate are subject to torments that no words adequately convey (3.25.12). This is why Scripture makes figurative use of physical things to express "the gravity of God's vengeance against the wicked..." (cf. Matt. 8:12; 22:13; 3:12; Mark 9:43; Isa. 66:24). The horrors depicted to us are "intended to confound all our senses with dread..." (3.25.12), which in turn ought to fix our attention on the wretched state one experiences in being cut off entirely from fellowship with God. Even more, these horrors express what it means to have God as your enemy, so that His sovereign power is brought to bear against you, with no escape from it (3.25.12).

> For first, his displeasure is like a raging fire, devouring and engulfing everything it touches. Secondly, all creatures so serve him in the execution of his judgment that they to whom the Lord will openly show his wrath will feel heaven, earth, sea, living beings, and all that exists aflame, as it were, with dire anger against them, and armed to destroy them. Accordingly, it was no insignificant thing that the apostle declared when he said that the faithless "shall suffer the punishment of eternal destruction, excluded from the presence of the Lord and from the glory of his might" [2 Thess. 1:9 p.]. And whenever through physical metaphors the prophets strike us with fear, although they employ no exaggeration to match our sluggishness, they still mingle with their message foreshadowings of the coming judgment, in the sun, the moon, and the whole fabric of the universe [Matt. 24:29, etc.]. Consequently, unhappy consciences find no rest from being troubled and tossed by a terrible whirlwind, from feeling that they are being torn asunder by a hostile Deity, pierced and lanced by deadly darts, quaking at God's lightning bolt, and being crushed by the weight of his hand—so that it would be more bearable to go down into any bottomless depths and chasms than to stand for a moment in these terrors (3.25.12).

And just how horrific are these terrors? Just what does it mean to have God as your unceasing and eternal foe? Calvin points to Psalm 90 in order to offer one biblical answer to such a question, for the Psalmist tells us that by a mere glance God "scatters and brings to nought all mortal men" (Ps. 90:7–11). The Psalmist also shows us that the worshipers of God are urged on in their struggle, "burdened with the cross," and inspired to press on until God is all in all (cf. Ps. 90:12–17; 1 Cor. 15:28) (3.25.12).

Questions for Reflection and Discussion

1. Calvin says that until we meditate on the future life and the blessing of our resurrection to come we will not fully profit in the gospel. Do we meditate on the future life? What distracts us from this meditation?

2. If Christ did not rise from the dead, how would that change the way you live your life now? Since Christ did rise from the dead, how should you be living your life today?

3. Why does God's omnipotence make resurrection non-controversial, though still startling and amazing?

4. How does Christ's resurrection strengthen hope in our own resurrection?

5. What is annihilationism? How does it fit with naturalism and a worldview in which chance reigns?

6. How might meditation upon the life to come strengthen our obedience and walk of faith in this life? How might meditation on the future life be misapplied and harmful to the Christian life?

7. What roles do the realities of heaven and hell have for your life of devotion, obedience, and piety?

8. Many North Americans believe in mandatory heaven for everyone, except for notorious villains—Adolf Hitler, Joseph Stalin, Jeffrey Dahmer, and other heinous criminals. How can we present the scriptural doctrine of hell to a skeptical and secular general public that wants to console itself that hell doesn't exist? How might we, without sounding glib or smug, help people to understand that God is just, and without Christ a person is under God's wrath?

Institutes of the Christian Religion

Book Four

The External Means or Aids by Which God Invites
Us into the Society of Christ and Holds Us Therein

≈ 19 ≈

The Church of Christ

Chapter One: The True Church with Which as Mother of All the Godly We Must Keep Unity

Orientation

IT MIGHT BE helpful for us to take note of the title of Book Four of the *Institutes*: "The external means or aids by which God invites us into the society of Christ and hold us therein." This brings us to the doctrine of the church. For Calvin, it is not enough to simply have faith in Christ. We are too weak, slothful, ignorant, and fickle to grow in faith or to remain faithful on our own. We don't have the capacity to advance in godliness without outward aids. In order to assist us, the Lord deposited the treasure of the gospel in the church. "He instituted 'pastors and teachers' [Eph. 4:11] through whose lips he might teach his own; he furnished them with authority; finally, he omitted nothing that might make for holy agreement of faith and for right order" (4.1.1). To the church was given sacraments, as well, to foster and strengthen faith, and draw believers closer to their Savior.

Calvin thus proposes in Book Four to discuss the church, its government, orders, and power; then to delve into the sacraments; and finally, to examine the relationship between church and state.

The Nature of the Church

For Calvin the church is our spiritual mother, "into whose bosom God is pleased to gather his sons, not only that they may be nourished by her help and ministry as long as they are infants and children, but also that they may be guided by her motherly care until they mature and at last reach the goal of faith" (4.1.1).

In the Apostles' Creed we do not say we believe *in* the church. We confess that we believe "a holy catholic church." Here we refer "not only to the visible church but also to all God's elect, in whose number are also included the dead" (4.1.2).

> For [God] alone 'knows who are his' [2 Tim. 2:19], and, as Paul says, encloses them under his seal [Eph. 1:13], except that they bear his insignia by which they may be distinguished from the reprobate. But because a small and contemptible number are hidden in a huge multitude and a few grains of wheat are covered by a pile of chaff, we must leave to God alone the knowledge of his church, whose foundation is his secret election (4.1.2).

"The Church is called 'catholic,' or 'universal,' because there could not be two or three churches unless Christ be torn asunder [cf. 1 Cor. 1:13]— which cannot happen! But all the elect are so united in Christ that they are dependent on one Head.... They are made truly one since they live together in one faith, hope, and love, and in the same Spirit of God" (4.1.2).

The phrase, "the communion of the saints," very well expresses what the church is, states Calvin. We are called to keep brotherly agreement with all God's people, and ought to submit ourselves to the church's authority. We are called to unity and fellowship since we are under the one Head, Christ (4.1.3).

As noted above, the church is the mother of believers. The maternity of the church is important in Calvin's thinking.

> For there is no other way to enter into life unless this mother conceive us in her womb, give us birth, nourish us at her breast, and lastly, unless she keep us under her care and guidance until, putting off mortal flesh, we become like the angels [Matt. 22:30]. Our weakness does not allow us to be dismissed from her school until we have been pupils all our lives. Furthermore, away from her bosom one cannot hope for any forgiveness of sins or any salvation, as Isaiah [Isa. 37:32] and Joel [Joel 2:32] testify [cf. also Ezk. 13:9] (4.1.4).

God therefore places us under the education of the church, so that we might grow up to maturity. That is why He gave the gift of apostles, prophets, evangelists, pastors, and teachers, for the equipping of the saints [Eph. 4:10–13]. The Lord is pleased to use ordinary means (such as human lips) to accomplish His extraordinary work of salvation.

For some, this seems too mundane and ordinary. They believe that the sacred Word is compromised and its authority "dragged down by the base-ness of the men" when it must be taught. Calvin's reply is pointed: such persons "disclose their own ungratefulness," for God "deigns to consecrate to himself the mouths and tongues of men in order that his voice may re-sound in them" (4.1.5).

It is true, notes Calvin, that "many are led either by pride, dislike, or rivalry to the conviction that they can profit enough from private reading and meditation; hence they despise public assemblies and deem preaching superfluous." But these fellows are self-deceived and bewitched with foul delusions. They despise God's ordering of our faith as revealed in the Scrip-ture. Yet, observes Calvin, even more detestable than this attitude which won't submit to human word and ministry "is that of the apostates who have a passion for splitting churches, in effect driving the sheep from their fold and casting them into the jaws of wolves. We must hold to what we have quoted from Paul—that the church is built up solely by outward preaching, and that the saints are held together by one bond only: that with common accord, through learning and advancement, they keep the church order es-tablished by God [cf. Eph. 4:12]" (4.1.5).

Calvin is careful to point out that while God is pleased to use means (like human agents) and ordained instruments (Word and sacraments) to establish and nurture us in faith, nonetheless, God alone remains the au-thor of our faith and brings it to fruition. That means God is the "author of preaching, joining his Spirit with it," and He promises to bestow blessings from it. In saying this, we must also acknowledge God's freedom to separate Himself from "outward helps," so that He rightly claims for Himself alone both "the beginnings of faith and its entire course" (4.1.6).

The Church as Visible and Invisible
The Scriptures speak of the church in a twofold manner, as invisible and as visible. Sometimes the word "church" refers to all those who are the truly adopted children of God, the elect. Other times the word refers to the vis-ible manifestation of those on earth who profess an allegiance to Christ. "In this church are mingled many hypocrites who have nothing of Christ but the name and outward appearance." What is important for us to see is this: "Just as we must believe... that the former church, invisible to us, is visible to the eyes of God alone, so we are commanded to revere and keep communion with the latter, which is called 'church' in respect to men" (4.1.7).

We must not be rash but cautious in how we handle this reality. Sometimes those who belong to the church seem "utterly lost and quite beyond hope," yet God calls them back according to His goodness. Others, however, who seem invulnerable and solid in their faith "often fall." We cannot penetrate into God's secret predestination. Of the visible members of the church, wearing God's badge of ownership through baptism, He alone sees "the ones who are unfeignedly holy and will persevere to the very end [Matt. 24:13]—the ultimate point of salvation" (4.1.8). Meanwhile, it is not God's intention that we doubt His promises or our salvation, as such. Therefore, God "accommodated himself to our capacity." That is, as believers God calls us to exercise "a certain charitable judgment whereby we recognize as members of the church those who, by confession of faith, by example of life, and by partaking of the sacraments, profess the same God and Christ with us" (4.1.8).

Discerning the True Church and Not Separating from It

Laying out this groundwork, Calvin takes up a practical question: How can one find a true church? He offers this answer: "Wherever we see the Word of God purely preached and heard, and the sacraments administered according to Christ's institution, there, it is not to be doubted, a church of God exists [cf. Eph. 2:20]." Such things are not without fruit. "But that we may clearly grasp the sum of this matter, we must proceed by the following steps: the church universal is a multitude gathered from all nations; it is divided and dispersed in separate places, but agrees on the one truth of divine doctrine, and is bound by the bond of the same religion. Under it are thus included individual churches, disposed in towns and villages according to human need, so that each rightly has the name and authority of the church" (4.1.9).

This brings Calvin to take up the matter of schism, which he calls a sin. For Calvin, where a church manifests the true marks, even though defective, it is not to be forsaken. As he states: "For the Lord esteems the communion of his church so highly that he counts as a traitor and apostate from Christianity anyone who arrogantly leaves any Christian society, provided it cherishes the true ministry of Word and sacraments" (4.1.10). The church is called in Scripture "the pillar and ground of the truth" and "the house of God" (1 Tim. 3:15). It is Christ's body and bride (Eph. 1:23, 5:27). "From this it follows," argues Calvin,

> that separation from the church is the denial of God and Christ. Hence, we must even more avoid so wicked a separation. For when with all our might we are attempting the overthrow of God's truth, we deserve to

have him hurl the whole thunderbolt of his wrath to crush us. Nor can any more atrocious crime be conceived than for us by sacrilegious disloyalty to violate the marriage that the only-begotten Son of God deigned to contract with us (4.1.10).

Consequently,

in order that the title 'church' may not deceive us, every congregation that claims the name 'church' must be tested by this standard as by a touchstone. If in Word and sacraments it has the order approved by the Lord, it will not deceive; let us, then, confidently pay to it the honor due to churches. But again, if, devoid of Word and sacraments, it advertises the name of church, we must just as scrupulously beware such deceits, as we must avoid rashness and pride on the other side (4.1.11).

Even when a church otherwise "swarms with many faults," if the preaching of the gospel resides there, we must not reject it. For example,

some fault may creep into the administration of either doctrine or sacraments, but this ought not to estrange us from communion with the church. For not all the articles of true doctrine are of the same sort. Some are so necessary to know that they should be certain and unquestioned by all men as the proper principles of religion. Such are: God is one; Christ is God and the Son of God; our salvation rests in God's mercy; and the like. Among the churches there are other articles of doctrine disputed which still do not break the unity of faith (4.1.12).

A difference of opinion over non-essential matters is no basis of schism among believers.

Calvin also notes that scandal in the church does not constitute a basis for leaving it. To those who object and insist that the church is holy, Calvin bids them to realize that the church, composed of saints, is mingled with hypocrites. Consider the parable in which Christ compares the church to a net into which all kinds of fish are gathered, yet the fish are not sorted until laid out on the shore (Matt. 13:47–58). Likewise, consider the field of the wheat and the tares (Matt. 13:24–30). Calvin writes, "if the Lord declares that the church is to labor under this evil—to be weighed down with the mixture of the wicked—until the Day of Judgment, they are vainly seeking a church besmirched with no blemish" (4.1.13).

Calvin would have us consider the errors within the church at Corinth. This church was rent asunder with quarrels, divisions, and factions. An evil deed is openly approved which even pagans detest. The name of Paul is defamed. Some mock the resurrection of the dead, to the destruction of the whole gospel. God's free gifts are abused, serving self-centered ambition rather than love. Order and decency are compromised. In summary, disobedience infected this body of believers on all sides. Yet Calvin asks, does the apostle seek to separate himself from them? Does he cast them out of Christ's kingdom? Does he utter down thunderbolts of anathema? "He not only does nothing of the sort; he even recognizes and proclaims them to be the church of Christ and the communion of saints [1 Cor. 1:2]" (4.1.14). Similarly, consider the churches of Galatia, all but deserters of the gospel. Yet they too are still reckoned as Christ's body.

The question of schism stands in relation to the question of church discipline. Calvin is aware that discipline is not always carried out with the care and frequency Scripture demands. The Lord calls the church to vigilance in this regard. "But," as Calvin notes, "because pastors are not always zealously on the watch, and are also sometimes more lenient than they should be, or are hindered from being able to exercise the severity they would like, the result is that even the openly wicked are not always removed from the company of the saints." Calvin continues: "This I admit to be a fault and I do not intend to excuse it, since Paul sharply rebukes it in the Corinthians. But even if the church be slack in its duty, still each and every individual has not the right at once to take upon himself the decision to separate" (4.1.15).

Good men can possess an ill-advised zeal for righteousness. A false opinion of holiness, along with pride and arrogance, then gives birth to an over-scrupulousness. As standard-bearers such individuals show contempt for all while being puffed up that they are better than others. We may not forget that we are called to mutual forbearance. Scripture bids us to correct our brother's vices and errors with more moderate means, while doing all things in love and preserving the unity of peace.

The church must be on guard against those who hanker for divisions in Christ's body. They are puffed up with pride, mad with obstinacy, and deceitful in their slanders. They tread a path that slopes toward destruction (4.1.16).

The church manifests itself as defective in holiness, for its sanctification is not yet complete. "The church is holy, then, in the sense that it is daily advancing and is not yet perfect: it makes progress from day to day but has not yet reached its goal of holiness…" (4.1.17). The prophets serve as examples to us, for even when the church could rightly be likened to Sodom and Gomorrah (Isa. 1:10), they "did not because of this establish new churches for themselves, or erect new altars on which to perform separate sacrifices." In fact, "Nothing...kept them from creating a schism save their zeal to maintain unity." We are quite mistaken if we "withdraw at once from the communion of the church just because the morals of all do not meet our standard or even square with the profession of Christian faith" (4.1.18).

Christ and the apostles also serve as examples for us in this regard. Citing various passages, Calvin reaches this conclusion: "Let the following two points...stand firm. First, he who voluntarily deserts the outward communion of the church (where the Word of God is preached and the sacraments are administered) is without excuse. Secondly, neither the vices of the few nor the vices of the many in any way prevent us from duly professing our faith there in ceremonies ordained by God" (4.1.19). When persons give in to a surly spirit, requiring the church to be free of blemish if they are to be part of its membership and life, not only is a false perfection imposed on the church in this life but the forgiveness of sins has also been abandoned. Baptism, the sign of initiation into the society of God's people, is, we must remember, a sign of washing, for "entrance into God's family is not open to us unless we first are cleansed of our filth by his goodness" (4.1.20).

The Function of the Church

Thus, if the *nature* of the church is best characterized by the phrase "the communion of the saints," the *function* of the church is best described as "the forgiveness of sins." These belong together. As Calvin notes: "Not only does the Lord through forgiveness of sins receive and adopt us once for all into the church, but through the same means he preserves and protects us there." "Consequently, we must firmly believe that by God's generosity, mediated by Christ's merit, through the sanctification of the Spirit, sins have been and are daily pardoned to us who have been received and engrafted into the body of the church" (4.1.21).

Indeed, the church is the arena of God's covenantal mercy and the sphere where God's forgiveness is found (4.1.22). God imparts the blessing of forgiveness to us in giving the church certain "keys" (cf. Matt.16:19; 18:18; John 20:23; 2 Cor. 5:18, 20). In the administration of these keys by presbyters or bishops to the consciences of God's people, the church is strengthened in the assurance of divine pardon and mercy. All members of the church need its admonition (4.1.22). This leads Calvin to offer three noteworthy observations:

First, however great the holiness in which God's children excel, they still—so long as they dwell in mortal bodies—remain unable to stand before God without forgiveness of sins. Secondly, this benefit so belongs to the church that we cannot enjoy it unless we abide in communion with the church. Thirdly, it is dispensed to us through the ministers and pastors of the church, either by the preaching of the gospel or by the administration of the sacraments; and herein chiefly stands out the power of the keys, which the Lord has conferred upon the society of believers. Accordingly, let each one of us count it his own duty to seek forgiveness of sins only where the Lord has placed it (4.1.22).

Every believer, then, must continually confess his or her sins, and take assurance that God promises to pardon (4.1.23). Such grace was granted to God's people in the Old Testament, who lived under the law. God ever shows Himself to be ready and willing to forgive our transgressions (4.1.24–25). Obviously, this same grace is applied to believers who live under the new covenant. "Let us not doubt that the Heavenly Father's clemency flows forth to us much more abundantly, rather than it is cut off or curtailed" (4.1.26). The New Testament shows us the long reach of God's pardon extended to churches guilty of heinous sins (cf. e.g., Gal. 1:6; 3:1; 4:9; 2 Cor. 12:21). Calvin reminds us that the order of the clauses in the Apostles' Creed teaches us "that continual grace for sins remains in Christ's church." God first establishes His church, then He extends to His people what they will continually need, the forgiveness of sins (4.1.27).

An interesting question that Calvin takes up here is whether only unconscious sins are forgivable. In other words, if someone voluntarily and thereby deliberately sins against God's law, are such crimes pardonable? Calvin notes that the Levitical stipulations laid out different sorts of sacrifices that address this type of issue (see Lev. 6:1ff.; 4:1ff.). That alone shows us that God's mercy extends to the transgressions we deliberately commit. Truly, "what depravity it is not to grant any expiation for voluntary sin!" Christ's sacrifice was offered for those sins, too. We must remember the pardon granted to David for his deliberate crimes (see 2 Sam. 11), as well as the sins mentioned in Corinth and the fall and restoration of Peter (see 1 Cor. 5; Matt. 26:74; John 21:15–17) (4.1.28). We should also remember, says Calvin, that the church is not to be too rigorous in exercising the keys of pardon and condemnation, for Scripture teaches us not to overwhelm the person under such discipline with sorrow (2 Cor. 2:7) (4.1.29).

Chapter Two: A Comparison of the False and the True Church

Orientation

With chapter two Calvin takes up the issue of the true and false church. Calvin is concerned that we not wrongly divide the church or withdraw ourselves from it, even if beset with certain kinds of errors. The false church may, however, in no manner command our allegiance. As we noted earlier, the papacy, as manifest in Calvin's day, claimed to be the only true manifestation of the body of Christ on earth. Their arrogance, pretension, and blindness found a forerunner in the Jews of the Old Testament.

The True Church Distinguished from the False Church

Calvin reiterates the importance of the Word and sacraments as perpetual tokens "by which to distinguish the church." "That is, wherever the ministry remains whole and uncorrupted, no moral faults or diseases prevent it from bearing the name 'church.' Secondly, it is not so weakened by trivial errors as not to be esteemed lawful" (4.2.1). The Roman Catholic Church, however, posits and exhibits a different standard for making the claim that it alone is the true church of Christ on earth. In place of the ministry of the Word of God it has established a perverse government for ruling the church which partly extinguishes the pure light of the gospel and partly chokes it. In place of the Lord's Supper it has introduced the foulest sacrilege of the Mass. Divine worship has been deformed by the introduction of "a diverse and unbearable mass of superstitions." Sound doctrine has been wholly covered over and driven away (4.2.2). In addition, like the Jews in the age of the prophets, the Roman church boasts in externals and appearances (cf. Jer. 7:4), but forgets that without obedience to God's Word all such boasts are idle and vain (4.2.3).

Calvin contravenes Rome's claims. The church isn't founded on blood, tradition, or ancestry. It is founded upon the Word of God.

> Therefore, although [the papists] put forward Temple, priesthood, and the rest of the outward shows, this empty glitter which blinds the eyes of the simple ought not to move us a whit to grant that the church exists where God's Word is not found. For this is the abiding mark with which our Lord has sealed his own: 'Everyone who is of the truth hears my voice' [John 18:37; also cf. 10:4–5, 14, 27] (4.2.4).

Christ's kingdom cannot possibly exist where the scepter of His Word does not reign (4.2.4).

Calvin, having warned his readers against the sin of schism, briefly addresses the charge that the papists laid at his and the other Reformers's feet, namely that they are guilty of breaking the unity of faith and tearing Christ's bride asunder. Calvin denies the charge of heresy and schism, for he and his fellows do not teach false doctrine and they have not broken the bond of fellowship in Christ (4.2.5). On the contrary, true communion in the church, writes Calvin, is held together by two bonds: (1) agreement in sound doctrine; and (2) brotherly love. Heretics corrupt true faith by false doctrine; schismatics break bonds of fellowship, though a common faith is confessed. The Reformed movement in the church is guilty neither of heresy nor schism. Those shoes really belong on the feet of the papacy (4.2.5). As Calvin chastises: "Now let them go and shout that we who have withdrawn from their church are heretics, since the sole cause of our separation is that they could in no way bear the pure profession of truth.... [I]t is clear that we have been cast out, and we are ready to show that this happened for Christ's sake..." (4.2.6).

As for the Roman Catholic Church as it existed under the Pope at that time, Calvin likens it to ancient Israel in her wayward journey and idolatrous corruption. To be sure, "The true church existed among the Jews and Israelites when they kept the laws of the covenant." Indeed, they were a people who fell away from God by degrees. What is important to see, and what advocates of the papacy must see, is that the papacy is now as "corrupt and debased" as the Jews were in the days of Jeroboam. The chief sin is that of idolatry, for that principal bond of communion, the Mass, is also their "greatest sacrilege" (4.2.7–9).

The Necessity of Leaving the False Church

If Calvin warns against the sin of schism, he also acknowledges the necessity of leaving the false church. As we saw, he likens the Roman church to ancient Israel under Jeroboam, for religion among the papists is as "corrupt and debased" as it was during that time, polluted with idolatry and sacrilege. Calvin therefore writes, "if anyone recognizes the present congregations—contaminated with idolatry, superstition, and ungodly doctrine—as churches (in full communion of which a Christian man must stand—even to the point of agreeing in doctrine), he will gravely err. For if they are churches, the power of the keys is in their hands; but the keys have an indissoluble bond with the

Word, which has been destroyed from among them" (4.2.10). This means that although Rome is a false church, vestiges of the church remain under the papacy. The constancy of God's goodness hasn't been wholly obliterated by their treachery, for the Lord maintains baptism there, a witness to the covenant of grace; consecrated by His own mouth, it retains its force despite the impiety of men. Moreover, by His own providence God has caused other vestiges to remain, that the church might not utterly die. God has not allowed the Roman church to be destroyed to the foundations or leveled to the ground, but it does remain a half-demolished building (4.2.11).

Yet these vestiges do not constitute or render the church of Rome a true church. Calvin writes, "when we categorically deny to the papists the title of *the* church, we do not for this reason impugn the existence of churches among them. Rather, we are only contending about the true and lawful constitution of the church, required in the communion not only of the sacraments ... but also especially of doctrine" (4.2.12). Indeed, churches do exist which remain subject to the tyranny of the Roman pontiff. "But," Calvin notes,

> these [the pope] has profaned by his sacrilegious impiety, afflicted by his inhuman domination, corrupted and well-nigh killed by his evil and deadly doctrines, which are like poisoned drinks. In them Christ lies hidden, half buried, the gospel overthrown, piety scattered, the worship of God nearly wiped out. In them, briefly, everything is so confused that there we see the face of Babylon rather than that of the Holy City of God (4.2.12).

Thus, by way of summary, Calvin calls these churches "to the extent that the Lord wonderfully preserves in them a remnant of his people, however woefully dispersed and scattered, and to the extent that some marks of the church remain...." Yet, in his judgment, *the marks* of the church are so lacking that neither any of their congregations nor their whole body constitutes a *lawful form* of the church (4.2.12).

Questions for Reflection and Discussion

1. It is noteworthy that the church, in its final, glorified state, consists (not surprisingly) only of God's elect. How does this fact help us understand the unity of the church and the current struggle of the church?

2. What constitutes the communion or fellowship of the church? In the face of so much fracturing and splits among churches today, what does the confession of "a holy catholic church" and "the communion of the saints" mean? Explain how this can still be a meaningful confession for the church today. How can saints strive for better and more visible communion with one another before a watching world?

3. How is the church your spiritual mother? The Belgic Confession, art. 28, says that "there is no salvation outside [the church]"; similarly, the Westminster Confession of Faith (XXV.ii), says, regarding the visible church, that "there is no ordinary possibility of salvation" outside of it. What do these statements mean, and why is the church not to be slighted or ignored with respect to our walk of faith and salvation? Why is the maternity of the church and the necessity of membership in it not a Roman Catholic idea?

4. Why is preaching so important in the public assembly and not to be neglected?

5. In what way has modern media evangelism (radio, TV, CDs, DVDs, celebrity preachers, etc.) contributed to the neglect of public assembly and/or a propensity toward private meditation? Can anything be done about it?

6. Why is it necessary to affirm (even dangerous to deny) the distinction between the church as visible and invisible? What abuses and errors emerge when this distinction is denied? Or misapplied?

7. How does Calvin's discussion on schism play out in our modern ecclesiastical quarrels and divisions? Do churches split too easily today? What seems to be the direction of Calvin's analysis?

8. Why, for Calvin, is submission to God's Word the key to church unity?

9. Why do we need to walk in the fellowship of the church in order to enjoy the forgiveness of sins?

10. Why is the distinction between the true and false church so important to understand and apply in our modern North American, ecclesiastical "melting pot"?

11. What are the marks of the true church? (See Belgic Confession, art. 29.) Do these marks apply to churches that are not "easy to recognize" as false?

❧ 20 ❧

The Church's Officebearers and
Ecclesiastical Power

Chapters 3–13 of Book Four

Chapter Three: The Doctors and Ministers of the Church,
Their Election and Office

Orientation

IF THE PAPACY corrupts the church, how ought the church of Christ to be ordered and governed? Calvin's answer centers upon Christ Himself. "He alone should rule and reign in the church as well as have authority or pre-eminence in it, and this authority should be exercised and administered by his Word alone. Nevertheless, because he does not dwell among us in visible presence [Matt. 26:11], we have said that he uses the ministry of men to declare openly his will to us by mouth, as a sort of delegated work, not by transferring to them his right and honor, but only that through their mouths he may do his own work—just as a workman uses a tool to do his work" (4.3.1).

Offices in the Church

Christ appoints His own ambassadors (2 Cor. 5:20), hiding heavenly treasures in earthen vessels (2 Cor. 4:7). This ministry of the gospel through human agents is for our benefit. It teaches us humility to submit ourselves to the Word preached through weak men like ourselves. It fosters mutual love by uniting the church around the teaching of one mouth. It is also a knot that keeps unity, the chief sinew by which believers are joined together in one body (cf. Eph. 4:4–16). For

> through ministers to whom he has entrusted this office and has conferred the grace to carry it out, he dispenses and distributes his gifts to the church; and he shows himself as though present by manifesting the power of his Spirit in this his institution, that it be not vain or

idle. Thus the renewal of the saints is accomplished; thus the body of Christ is built-up.... For neither the light and heat of the sun, nor food and drink, are so necessary to nourish and sustain the present life as the apostolic and pastoral office is necessary to preserve the church on earth (4.3.2).

The importance and dignity, even necessity, of the preaching office is well-attested in Scripture and commended in many ways (cf. Isa. 52:7; Matt. 5:13–14; Luke 10:16; Acts 10:3–6; 9:6). In fact, the ministry of the gospel for the church's well-being must never be minimized, "since it is the administration of the Spirit and of righteousness and of eternal life [2 Cor. 4:6; 3:9]" (4.3.3).

Having noted the centrality of the ministry of the Word, Calvin turns to discuss the offices of apostle, prophet, evangelist, pastor, and teacher. Whereas the first three offices are temporary, the last two are permanent (cf. 4.3.4–5). Calvin believed that the government of the church was administered by Jesus Christ, the Head of the church, and that He should have all authority and pre-eminence in it. The "Ecclesiastical Ordinances," which set forth the ecclesiastical polity for the church of Geneva, specify that Christ instituted four offices: pastors, doctors, elders, and deacons, in order that the church may be well ordered and maintained.

Calvin expounds particularly upon the pastoral office and its duties. Pastors are to preach the Word of God, engage in private admonition and instruction, administer the sacraments, and, with the elders, exercise discipline over the flock under their care. Moreover, pastors ought to keep themselves to their own domain of responsibility. Each should be assigned his own congregation. This isn't to say that a pastor bound to one church cannot come to aid other churches should some disturbances occur which require his presence, or should his advice be sought concerning some obscure matter. Nevertheless, each pastor should not intrude upon the province of another, but respect the limits of his duties (4.3.6–7).

Doctors, or teachers, are to instruct the faithful in true doctrine, so that the purity of the gospel isn't corrupted either by ignorance or by contrary opinions. They are to equip the church to maintain the apostolic faith and to defend it from injury by the failure of the pastors (4.3.4).

Calvin also offers an exposition of the office of presbyter (elder or overseer) and of deacon. The office of elder discovers its primary responsibility in the censure of morals and exercise of discipline. The office of deacon finds its primary expression in the care of the poor. Calvin sees two distinct types of deacons. The one type distributes alms; the other cares for the poor and sick. Widows should be involved in this work of mercy. The one type of deacon thus has a responsibility of administration, the other the responsibility of caring (4.3.6–9).

Calvin concludes this chapter with a discussion of the calling, authorization, and ordination of ministers (cf. 4.3.10–16). He believes that those who are called to be ministers of the Word must receive the consent or support of the people. "We therefore hold that this call of a minister is lawful according to the Word of God, when those who seemed fit are created by the consent and approval of the people; moreover, that other pastors ought to preside over the election in order that the multitude may not go wrong either through fickleness, through evil intentions, or through disorder" (4.3.15).

Chapter Four: The Condition of the Ancient Church, and the Kind of Government in Use before the Papacy

In chapters four through seven Calvin takes up an extended polemic against the Roman church. In chapter four Calvin sets forth a detailed historical narrative regarding the government of the church, particularly as it developed through the centuries. He shows how the respective offices underwent both refinement and enlargement, depending on circumstances, and what the government of the church looked like before the papacy gained the ascendency and came to dominate the life of the church. This survey is intended to give the reader a picture of the ancient church's practice of church government before the papacy gained the field.

Chapter Five: The Ancient Form of Government Was Completely Overthrown by the Tyranny of the Papacy

Chapters five through seven take up the rise, nature, and corruption of the Roman papacy. In chapter five Calvin argues that the papacy brought tyranny into the life of the church, since it overthrew the biblical stipulations regarding who may hold church office and how such persons should be appointed to the same. Meanwhile, the relations between church and state were compromised and various monstrous abuses were introduced, including benefices. The morals of the clergy devolved completely, being thoroughly corrupted. Calvin lays out the abuses and scandals in detail.

Chapter Six: The Primacy of the Roman See

Chapter six describes at length "the capstone" of the whole corrupt nature of the Roman hierarchical system and its abuses, namely the papacy. Here Calvin takes up the Roman Catholic claim of apostolic succession from Peter, the displacement of Christ as Head of the church by a human head, i.e., the Pope, and argues that Christ's headship cannot be transferred to another. While the Roman church was indeed honored in ancient times, it did not constitute the center of Christianity and the unity of the church did not depend upon or require a universal bishop over all.

Chapter Seven: The Origin and Growth of the Roman Papacy until It Raised Itself to Such a Height that the Freedom of the Church Was Oppressed, and All Restraint Overthrown

This chapter traces the rather modest position occupied by Rome in the early history of the church (seen for example at the councils of Nicaea and Ephesus) to an ever increasing place of importance and status, to outright usurpation. Naturally, in telling this story, Calvin explains how the authority of the Roman bishop was undergoing change and gaining supremacy. As the Roman bishop came to have first place, decay in the church set in until the time of Bernard of Clairvaux. The present-day papacy (i.e., the papacy in Calvin's day) is even more corrupt. Calvin maintains that the Pope has apostatized from the faith and his reign is the kingdom of Antichrist.

Chapter Eight: The Power of the Church with Respect to Articles of Faith; and How in the Papacy, with Unbridled License, the Church Has Been Led to Corrupt All Purity of Doctrine

Orientation

With this chapter Calvin begins his extended analysis of the power or authority of the church. He distinguishes between three types of ecclesiastical power: first, a doctrinal power, which means the church may rightly define doctrine and declare its faith against error (chapters 8–9); second, a legislative power, i.e., the authority to establish polity for its well-ordered governance (chapter 10); and third, a jurisdictional authority, which has to do with the power of church discipline (chapter 11).

Centrality of the Word

As Calvin explains at the outset of this chapter, the doctrinal power of the church has two parts: (1) "authority to lay down articles of faith," and (2) "authority to explain them." This does not mean that the church or its ministers has any right to displace Christ's authority in the church. "He alone is the schoolmaster of the church" (4.8.1).

Moreover, we need to remember that the authority granted to the church in this regard is granted to "the ministry," i.e., to the Word administered, not to the persons who serve as ministers. The ministers must speak "from the Lord's mouth." There resides their authority, and without this they forfeit proper authority (4.8.2). This sort of authority can be traced out in Scripture in the office of the prophets in the Old Testament and the apostles in the New Testament (4.8.3–6). Definitively this is manifest in Christ, the Word in the flesh (4.8.7).

The firm principle that may not be abandoned, however, is this: "No other word is to be held as the Word of God, and given place as such in the church, than what is contained first in the Law and the Prophets, then in the writings of the apostles; and the only authorized way of teaching in the church is by the prescription and standard of his Word" (4.8.8). Practically speaking, this means that pastors exercise a kind of sovereign power when they faithfully adhere to and administer the Word, so that

> they may dare boldly to do all things by God's Word; may compel all worldly power, glory, wisdom, and exaltation to yield to and obey his majesty; supported by his power, may command all from the highest even to the last; may build up Christ's household and cast down Satan's; may feed the sheep and drive away the wolves; may instruct and exhort the teachable; may accuse, rebuke, and subdue the rebellious and stubborn; may bind and loose; finally, if need be, may launch thunderbolts and lightnings; but do all things in God's Word (4.8.9).

Conversely, let us not doubt but observe this universal rule: "God deprives men of the capacity to put forth new doctrine in order that he alone may be our schoolmaster in spiritual doctrine as he alone is true [Rom. 3:4] who can neither lie nor deceive" (4.8.9).

In the remainder of this chapter Calvin disputes and refutes the Roman claim of doctrinal infallibility (sec. 10–16). The key point of dispute between the papacy and the Reformers is that the former, says Calvin, locates "the authority of the church outside of God's Word"; but the latter insists "that it be attached to the Word, and do not allow it to be separated from it" (4.8.13).

Chapter Nine: Councils and Their Authority

In this chapter Calvin gives attention to church councils and the decrees they issue. In short form, he sanctions their use and necessity but denies that they are infallible. It is sufficient for our purpose to offer a few quotations from Calvin in order to demonstrate his position. First, we must properly esteem the ancient councils without granting to them an unassailable character, for there are true councils and false councils (4.9.1–2). Second, we must exercise discrimination with regard to pastors, for the truth is not always nurtured in their bosom. The truth always opposes error, and thus the truth stands against councils that err (4.9.4–6). Third, it is easily demonstrated that councils are not definitive as such or infallible inasmuch as they contradict one another (4.9.9–11). Fourth, for Calvin, we must test all spirits, all decisions of councils—even when they are lawfully called—by "the standard of God's Word in order to determine whether or not they are from God" (4.9.12). Thus, Calvin is led to this conclusion:

> We indeed willingly concede, if any discussion arises over doctrine, that the best and surest remedy is for a synod of true bishops to be convened, where the doctrine at issue may be examined. Such a definition, upon which the pastors of the church in common, invoking Christ's Spirit, agree, will have much more weight than if each one, having conceived it separately at home, should teach it to people, or if a few private individuals should compose it. Then, when the bishops are assembled, they can more conveniently deliberate in common what they ought to teach and in what form, lest diversity breed offense. Thirdly, Paul prescribes this method in distinguishing doctrines. For when he assigns the distinguishing of doctrines to the separate churches [cf. 1 Cor. 14:29], he shows what should be the order of procedure in more

serious cases—namely, that the churches should take common cog-
nizance among themselves. And the very feeling of piety so instructs
us that, if anyone disturb the church with a strange doctrine, and the
matter reach the point that there is danger of greater dissension, the
churches should first assemble, examine the question put, and finally,
after due discussion, bring forth a definition derived from Scripture
which would remove all doubt from the people and stop the mouths of
wicked and greedy men from daring to go any further (4.9.13).

Chapter Ten: The Power of Making Laws, in Which the Pope, with His Supporters, Has Exercised upon Souls the Most Savage Tyranny and Butchery

Orientation
Calvin now takes up the second part of church power (or authority), namely
whether the church has the power to make laws that bind consciences.
Rome, for its part, maintains that the church may legitimately impose such
laws. From this practice, says Calvin, has "arisen innumerable human traditions"—traditions that function as "so many nets to ensnare miserable
souls." The key question is "how God is to be duly worshiped according to
the rule laid down by him, and how the spiritual freedom which looks to
God may remain unimpaired for us" (4.10.1).

Ecclesiastical Laws and the Abuse of Conscience
Calvin opposes the establishment of human traditions that make rules apart
from God's Word and are enforced with penalties if not followed. Of course,
Calvin is not against "holy and useful church institutions, which provide
for the preservation of discipline or honesty or peace." Specifically, Calvin
contends against the displacement of Christ as the one King of His church,
who governs us by one law of freedom, "the holy Word of the gospel," the
grace He obtained for us (4.10.1).

Rome, however, enslaves human consciences by erecting various ecclesiastical constitutions and requirements that are imposed upon the church's
members, with the result that false scruples are laid upon souls, binding
them inwardly before God, and making the performance of these requirements necessary for salvation (4.10.2).

Calvin unpacks this issue by first examining the nature of the human conscience; indeed, what is the conscience? Calvin offers this explanation: "When men have an awareness of divine judgment adjoined to them as a witness which does not let them hide their sins but arraigns them as guilty before the judgment seat—this awareness is called 'conscience.'" (4.10.3). Conscience pursues us with the verdict of guilty. Moreover, conscience relates to God, so that we have a "good conscience" when before God we have an "inward uprightness of heart." This means that if one were the last human being alive on earth, what he or she thinks, says, and does, is still subject to the law of God and the observance of this law. We can sin before God and our conscience even when no one else is aware of our transgression. But Calvin is also concerned that we see that some things are "intrinsically indifferent." In this case the apostle shows us that the way in which we handle such things pertains to others and their scruples. While our conscience remains free, theirs is not, and so we act as not to give offense to them (see 1 Cor. 10:28–29) (4.10.4).

As for human laws, "If they were passed to lay scruples upon us, as if the observance of these laws were necessary of itself, we say that something unlawful is laid upon conscience." Why? Because "our consciences do not have to do with men but with God alone." The magistrate, though he may impose laws of outward conduct to which we must submit, may not impose laws that inwardly govern our souls, namely "the worship of God and the spiritual rule of right living." Further, "human law, whether made by magistrate or by church, even though they have to be observed (I speak of good and just laws), still do not of themselves bind the conscience." Other laws, however, are of a different sort, for they "prescribe a new form for worshiping God, and impose necessity even in matters that are free" (4.10.5). In short, the church has no right to command the obligatory observance of laws or rules which have been conceived "apart from God's Word" (4.10.6). We may not transfer to human beings what belongs to God—to rule us by the authority of His Word (4.10.7).

> The whole case rests upon this: if God is the sole lawgiver, men are not permitted to usurp this honor. Consequently, we ought at the same time to keep in mind these two reasons already mentioned why the Lord claims this for himself alone. The first is that we should have in his will the perfect rule of all righteousness and holiness, and thus in knowing him possess the perfect knowledge of the good life. The second is that he alone (when we seek the way to worship him aright and

fitly) has authority over our souls, him we ought to obey, and upon his will we ought to wait (4.10.8).

Calvin offers an extended analysis of and polemic against the Roman constitutions (4.10.9–18). We merely note that Calvin would have us follow a simple prescription in order to escape the imposition of these human traditions in our service of God, namely, with respect to such traditions we recognize

> ...that they are all laws apart from God's Word, laws made by men, either to prescribe the manner of worshiping God or to bind consciences by scruples, as if they were making rules about things necessary for salvation. If other faults be added to one or both of these—that they obscure by their multitude the clarity of the gospel, that they are in no sense constructive but are useless and trifling occupations rather than true exercises of piety, that they are calculated for sordid and base gain, that they are too difficult to observe, that they are befouled with shameful superstitions—these will help us to comprehend how much evil these constitutions contain (4.10.16).

Calvin next analyzes the rise of various "rites" and practices which are without biblical pedigree (4.10.19–22). This is followed by a scriptural analysis of the issue, wherein Calvin demonstrates the Bible's condemnation of human inventions in worship and human traditions that supercede and trump God's Word (4.10.23–26). The last sections of this chapter (4.10.27–32) present the biblical standard for the right ordering or government of the church and its worship, where the principles of decency, good order, love, and liberty of conscience are honored and followed. Thus in this section Calvin seeks to present the legitimate exercise of church power vis-à-vis ecclesiastical rules or polity.

The Necessity of Ecclesiastical Polity

Calvin does not advocate the "erasure of all the laws by which the order of the church is shaped" (4.10.27). To sort through the legitimate and illegitimate imposition of ecclesiastical rules, Calvin observes that every form of human association needs "some form of organization" in order to foster peace and maintain concord. The interests of decency must be honored as well. These principles certainly apply to the life of the church. Scripture even dictates the same, "Let all things be done decently and in order" (1 Cor. 14:40). In view of the diversity of human customs and the like, the apostle sets forth a rule that can be implemented by all everywhere—a rule that sanctions the addition of observances that form a bond of union if order is to be maintained and decorum followed—that is, an agreed upon polity. Here Calvin immediately adds a caution: that these observances or policies must not be considered "necessary for salvation" and thus "bind consciences by scruples"; likewise, these rules must not be "associated with the worship of God, and piety thus be lodged in them" (4.10.27).

Calvin provides examples of polity of this sort—for example, that set hours be established for public prayers, sermons, and sacraments; that public worship have set times, places, the singing together of hymns, fixed days for celebration of the sacraments, and the like. "Especially are there those things which maintain discipline, such as catechizing, church censures, excommunication, fasting, and whatever can be referred to the same list" (4.10.29).

Lest he be misunderstood, Calvin presents an additional principle, namely that we may approve "only those human constitutions which are founded upon God's authority, drawn from Scripture, and, therefore, wholly divine" (4.10.30). Calvin presents posture at public prayer as an example of how to apply these principles. Clearly, God's Word sanctions, say, kneeling for such prayers. But kneeling is not so necessary that it becomes a matter of salvation. Scripture also allows other postures for prayer. Here a diversity of practice is permitted, says Calvin, depending on circumstances, customs, what gives rise to decorum and good order, as well as issues of necessity that must be respected, etc. The church, then, ought to require what leads to edification, safeguarding its freedom to accommodate itself to customs of each nation and age. Calvin opposes rashly charging into innovation without sufficient cause. Instead, he says this rule should apply, that love judge what may hurt or build up, for "if we let love be our guide" on these kinds of matters, "all will be safe" (4.10.30). Calvin also believes that the observances imposed should be few and edifying (4.10.32).

Chapter Eleven: The Jurisdiction of the Church and Its Abuse as Seen in the Papacy

Orientation
The third aspect of ecclesiastical power or authority, and the most important, is the power of discipline—specifically, that jurisdiction of the church's power pertaining to "the discipline of morals." The church needs "a spiritual

polity." Calvin observes, "For this purpose courts of judgment were established in the church from the beginning to deal with the censure of morals, to investigate vices, and to be charged with the exercise of the office of the keys" (cf. Matt. 18) (4.11.1).

Binding and Loosing

Calvin is very careful to distinguish the binding and loosing of Matthew 16 from that of Matthew 18. The first text deals with the preaching of the gospel, the official ministry of the Word; and at root here

> Christ has testified that in the preaching of the gospel the apostles have no part save that of ministry; that it was he himself who would speak and promise all things through their lips as his instruments. Accordingly, he has testified that the forgiveness of sins which they preached was the true promise of God; the damnation which they pronounced, the sure judgment of God. This testimony, moreover, was given to all ages, and remains firm, to make all men certain and sure that the word of the gospel, whatever man may preach it, is the very sentence of God, published at the supreme judgment seat, written in the Book of Life, ratified, firm and fixed, in heaven. We conclude that in those passages the power of the keys is simply the preaching of the gospel, and that with regard to men it is not so much power as ministry. For Christ has not given this power actually to men, but to his Word, of which he has made men ministers (4.11.1).

Matthew 18, by contrast, deals with the power of binding and loosing with respect to church discipline. Hence, Matthew 18 is not to be directly identified with Matthew 16; rather, it must be understood a bit differently, says Calvin, although there are connections between the two texts. He begins with their similarities and then explains their differences.

> Both are alike in this first respect: each is a general statement; in both is always the same power of binding and loosing (that is, through God's Word), the same command, the same promise. But they differ in this respect: the first passage is particularly concerned with the preaching which the ministers of the Word execute; the latter applies to the discipline of excommunication which is entrusted to the church. But the church binds him whom it excommunicates—not that it casts him into everlasting ruin and despair, but because it condemns his life and morals, and already warns him of his condemnation unless he should repent. It looses him whom it receives into communion, for it makes

him a sharer of the unity which it has in Christ Jesus. Therefore, that no one may stubbornly despise the judgment of the church, or think it immaterial that he has been condemned by the vote of the believers, the Lord testifies that such judgment by believers is nothing but the proclamation of his own sentence, and that whatever they have done on earth is ratified in heaven. For they have the Word of God with which to condemn the perverse; they have the Word with which to receive the repentant into grace. They cannot err or disagree with God's judgment, for they judge solely according to God's law, which is no uncertain or earthly opinion but God's holy will and heavenly oracle (4.11.2).

In exercising this sort of authority, unlike the state, the church does not have the power of the sword and it may not compel by force. Thus, the power of the church and of the magistrate are quite distinct. Calvin shows how in the case of a drunk the state has its punishments for such a person, while the church's care and discipline is very different toward that individual (4.11.3).

The Aim of Church Discipline
The aim of ecclesiastical discipline is "that offense be resisted, and any scandal that has arisen be wiped out." Here we must be careful to impose only a spiritual sort of correction and that discipline be administered by a lawful assembly, not by a single man. Excommunication is "the severest punishment of the church, the final thunderbolt," and is to be used "only in necessity." With the public proclamation of the gospel, private admonition is to be applied in order to correct those wayward in doctrine or in life. Before the extreme remedy of excommunication is exercised, however, the church has "the right to bar from the communion of the Lord's Supper those who cannot be received without profaning this great mystery." God's children, then, are subject to "censures to chastise their vices" (4.11.5).

Sadly, various abuses crept into the church regarding ecclesiastical discipline (see 4.11.6–10). The papacy even came to usurp worldly powers (see 4.11.11–16). Calvin traces out these themes, concluding with the reminder that "the church does not have the power to coerce" and must not seek such power for itself inasmuch as "it is the duty of godly kings and princes to sustain religion by laws, edicts, and judgments" (4.11.16).

Chapter Twelve: The Discipline of the Church:
Its Chief Use in Censures and Excommunication

Orientation

As we have seen, Calvin distinguishes between three types of ecclesiastical power or authority: doctrinal (chapters 8–9), legislative (chapter 10), and jurisdictional (chapter 11). Closely related with the last of these is a disciplinary authority, a discussion that Calvin began in chapter eleven, and concerning which he now offers a fuller treatment.

The Benefits of Ecclesiastical Discipline

Whereas the Anabaptists tended toward "perfectionism," Calvin maintains that there is no such thing as an ideal human community on earth, composed of completely righteous and saintly people. Hence emerges the necessity of discipline within the church. Discipline aids believers in sanctification as we crucify the flesh and get ready for the final resurrection. Moreover, it also protects the dignity of Christ and His church (4.12.1).

Consider what would happen if every professing believer were allowed to do whatever he or she pleases. Yet, argues Calvin, what is to prevent it "if to the preaching of doctrine there were not added private admonitions, corrections, and other aids of the sort that sustain doctrine and do not let it remain idle"? "Therefore, discipline is like a bridle to restrain and tame those who rage against the doctrine of Christ; or like a spur to arouse those of little inclination; and also sometimes like a father's rod to chastise mildly and with the gentleness of Christ's Spirit those who have more seriously lapsed" (4.12.1).

Steps of Ecclesiastical Discipline

Calvin next presents the stages of church discipline, following the order presented in Matthew 18 (4.12.2), which has to do with "secret faults." Calvin is therefore concerned that we distinguish private sins from public ones. "Of the former, Christ says to every individual: 'Reprove him, between you and him alone' [Matt. 18:15]." Meanwhile, "Paul says to Timothy of open sins: 'Rebuke them in the presence of all, so that the rest may stand in fear' [1 Tim. 5:20]." Thus the order established is clear: "to proceed in correcting secret sins according to the steps laid down by Christ; but in open sins, if the offense is indeed public, to proceed at once to solemn rebuke by the church" (4.12.3).

Calvin also reminds us to distinguish sins that may be characterized as "faults" and sins that are "crimes or shameful acts." It is the church's responsibility to exclude from its fellowship manifest adulterers, fornicators, thieves, robbers, seditious persons, perjurers, false witnesses, and the rest of this sort, as well as the insolent who, when duly admonished of their lighter vices, mock God and His judgment. In doing so, the church is merely pronouncing the Lord's own sentence, not imposing something of its own apart from Him (4.12.4).

"In such corrections and excommunication, the church has three ends in view." He says that the first end "is that they who lead a filthy and infamous life may not be called Christians, to the dishonor of God...." As for the second purpose, it "is that the good be not corrupted by the constant company of the wicked, as commonly happens...." Finally, regarding the third purpose, it "is that those overcome by shame for their baseness begin to repent" (4.12.5). We see therefore three dimensions to the church's practice of discipline: (1) to honor God—the doxological (theological) reason; (2) to keep the church pure—the purgative (ecclesiological) reason; and (3) to lead to repentance and amendment of life—the curative (soteriological) reason.

Calvin treats the various ways church discipline should be handled. Returning to his distinction between sins as faults and sins as crimes, he says that a "great severity is not to be used in lighter sins, but verbal chastisement is enough—and that mild and fatherly—which should not harden or confuse the sinner, but bring him back to himself, that he may rejoice rather than be sad that he has been corrected." However, with regard to "shameful acts," these "need to be chastised with a harsher remedy." Mere words are likely not sufficient; he should be barred from the Supper "until he gives assurance of his repentance" (4.12.6).

Discipline applies to all, none are exempt from it (4.12.7). In its exercise, though, a rule of moderation must apply in the performance of discipline, requiring "gentleness" from the whole body of Christ (4.12.8–9). It is also important to remember that the extreme remedy of excommunication is not a declaration of "everlasting ruin and damnation"; rather, it is a verdict of damnation so long as that person remains unrepentant. It is corrective in nature. Excommunication, then, is not an "anathema." An anathema is a verdict of condemnation without pardon (4.12.10). Again, Calvin warns the church away from an excessive or an extremely rigorous manner in the practice of ecclesiastical discipline. Such abuses must be avoided (4.12.11), for we can see the harmful nature of severity in the practices of the Dona-

tists and the Anabaptists (4.12.12). We do better to follow the wisdom of
Augustine (4.12.13).

Fasting

Interestingly, Calvin addresses the subject of fasting at this point—both
private and public fasting—for fasting is part of discipline. As Calvin states:
"The remaining part of discipline, which is not properly contained within
the power of the keys, is where pastors, according to the need of the times,
should exhort the people either to fasting or to solemn supplications, or
to other acts of humility, repentance, and faith—of which the time, the
manner, and the form are not prescribed by God's Word, but left to the
judgment of the church" (4.12.14). More specifically, Calvin believes that
the church should be called to fasting in times of great need, struggle, or
perplexity. He believes that fasting "is a holy ordinance and one salutary for
all ages," and that it is right for pastors to urge "the people to public fasting
and extraordinary prayers" (4.12.14).

As for the purpose of holy and lawful fasting, it has three objectives:
"We use it either [1] to weaken and subdue the flesh that it may not act
wantonly, or [2] that we may be better prepared for prayers and holy medi-
tations, or [3] that it may be a testimony of our self-abasement before God
when we wish to confess our guilt before him" (4.12.15). As for the first
objective, comments Calvin, it refers to private fasting; the second objective
is common to both private and public fasting; and the last is likewise common to both. What is key to fasting is the motive of the heart, for when the
inward heart is sincere, outward practice follows (4.12.15).

Fasting and prayer are often paired together, particularly when fasting
is a sign of self-abasement before God. The purpose of fasting in this regard
is principally to render ourselves "more eager and unencumbered for prayer"
(4.12.16). "Again, if either pestilence, or famine, or war begins to rage, or
if any disaster seems to threaten any district and people—then also it is
the duty of the pastors to urge the church to fasting, in order that by sup-
plication the Lord's wrath may be averted" (4.12.17). Calvin denies that
such a practice of fasting and like activities were abrogated with the coming
of Christ; rather, it still helps to stir believers "in order that they may not
provoke God more and more by their excessive confidence and negligence,
when they are chastised by his lashes" (4.12.17).

In order to avoid error or misconceptions about the nature of fasting,
Calvin offers this extended definition and explanation:

For here we do not understand it simply as restraint and abstemiousness [abstinence] in food, but as something else. Throughout its course, the life of the godly indeed ought to be tempered with frugality and sobriety, so that as far as possible it bears some resemblance to a fast. But, in addition, there is another sort of fasting, temporary in character, when we withdraw something from the normal regimen of living, either for one day or for a definite time, and pledge ourselves to a tighter and more severe restraint in diet than ordinarily. This consists in three things: in time, in quality of foods, and in smallness of quantity. By time, I mean that we should carry out those acts of fasting for the sake of which that fast is appointed.... Quality consists in that all elegance should be absent, and that, content with common and baser foods, we should not whet our palate with delicacies. The rule of quantity in this is that we should eat more sparingly and lightly than is our custom; only for need, not also for pleasure (4.12.18).

Calvin concludes this chapter by warning us of the danger of superstition and notions of merit that get associated with fasting, as well as hypocrisy in fasting and its observance during the season of Lent (4.12.19–21). This is followed by an extensive evaluation and critique of priestly celibacy (4.12.22–28).

We need to remember that Calvin did not make discipline one of the marks of the true church. For him, it appears, discipline belongs essentially to the church's organization and well-being, not to its definition and being.

Chapter Thirteen: Vows; and How Everyone Rashly Taking Them Has Miserably Entangled Himself

In this chapter (we will forego any lengthy analysis of it), Calvin first examines vows in general (4.13.1–7); then he looks at monastic vows in particular, especially the vow of celibacy (4.13.8–21). Calvin presents guidelines by which we can examine when and how and for what end a vow can be made acceptable to God. He also treats the misuse of the taking of vows, along with the weaknesses and abuses within monasticism and the vows imposed in its structures.

Questions for Reflection and Discussion

1. Do you view the centrality of preaching as indispensable? What tends to displace preaching as the centerpiece of worship today—that is, as the one "essential" for the church's worship?

2. What do you think of Calvin's view that there are two types of deacons? Does this allow the proper use of women's gifts in the church?

3. Calvin isn't only concerned that we see the authority of God's Word for His church, but also that we see the centrality of the *ministry of the Word* by pastors and teachers/doctors. In that light, why aren't private Bible reading and personal devotions sufficient?

4. Why, given Calvin's stated views, is the form of church government known as congregationalism open to serious abuses or even a dangerous practice?

5. How do we avoid being under the tyranny of the weaker brother's over-scrupulous conscience? How do we sort out the call not to give offense to the weaker brother and the need for the weaker brother to become stronger?

6. The Westminster Confession of Faith (I.vi), agreeing with Calvin, says that "The whole counsel of God concerning all things necessary for his own glory, man's salvation, faith and life, is either expressly set down in Scripture, or *by good and necessary consequence may be deduced from Scripture...*" (italics added). How does this statement help us avoid biblicism in constructing a polity for the life of the church? How does this also help the enterprise called "theology"?

7. Why is a strictly scriptural form of church polity—i.e., a polity derived directly from prescriptions in the Bible—impractical and unhelpful for the life of the church today, especially as the church exists in very diverse and varied cultural circumstances? Even if one were to compose a polity consisting only of direct quotations of biblical prescriptions, why would that not be enough in order to put such a polity into practice?

8. Why is the power of the church discipline in *the Word of God*, not in the eldership as such?

9. If a person has been excommunicated, why does he or she become an object of the church's evangelistic efforts?

10. What are the principles Calvin sets forth in the exercise of discipline? Why are they important to remember?

❧ 21 ❧

The Sacraments

Chapter 14 of Book Four

Chapter Fourteen: The Sacraments

Orientation

DURING THE PERIOD of the Protestant Reformation the doctrine of the sacraments was hotly contested. For Calvin, the sacraments play an important role for the well-being of our faith, for they prop up and strengthen faith.

Calvin's discussion of the sacraments can be divided into two parts: part one—the sacraments in general (4.14.1–6), followed by an examination of two types of opponents: (a) those who undervalue the sacraments, and err in defect (4.14.7–18); and (b) those who overvalue the sacraments, and err in excess (4.14.14–17); and part two—sacraments in particular (4.14.18–26).

The Sacraments in General

• *Sacraments Defined.* Calvin begins with a definition of sacrament, which, with preaching, is an additional aid to our faith. A sacrament "is an outward sign by which the Lord seals on our consciences the promises of his good will toward us in order to sustain the weakness of our faith; and we in turn attest our piety toward him in the presence of the Lord and of his angels and before men." He also offers a briefer definition: "it is a testimony of divine grace toward us, confirmed by an outward sign, with mutual attestation of our piety toward him." Or, as Augustine, said: it is "'a visible sign of a sacred thing,' or 'a visible form of an invisible grace'" (4.14.1).

After explaining the derivation of the word "sacrament" (4.14.2), Calvin explains his definition. Sacraments are never without preceding promise, which means sacraments come after the promise. They function as a kind of appendix to the promise; they serve to make the promise more evident to us, and so in a sense "ratify" it. God uses sacraments because we are weak, ignorant, and dull. There is nothing wrong with God's Word of promise! The problem rests with us—we are feeble of faith and need to be propped up on all sides. And so God condescends to us and gives us "a mirror" by which we can see "spiritual things." Because we are corporeal and spiritual beings (souls engrafted into bodies), God imparts spiritual things to us under visible ones. "Not that the gifts set before us in the sacraments are bestowed with the natures of the things, but that they have been marked with this signification by God" (4.14.3).

This means that the sacraments do not naturally point to what they are commandeered to signify. Bread and wine do not naturally signify Christ's body and blood. God, by his Word, gives them this signification for us. The Word always precedes sacrament (4.14.4), but the sacraments do not only signify something, they also function as "seals." Sacraments may be likened to seals attached to official government documents. They confirm and seal what is written therein. Calvin appeals to Romans 4:11, where Paul expressly argues that "Abraham's circumcision was not for his justification but for the seal of that covenant by faith in which he had already been justified." The promise, then, is sealed by sacraments, which in turn fortifies faith. Sacraments bring a dimension to strengthening faith that is not manifest in the Word, namely, that over and above the Word they represent God's promises for us "as painted in a picture from life." They enable us to view something visually that points us beyond themselves, so they lift us up to the devout contemplation of "those lofty mysteries which lie hidden in the sacraments" (4.14.5).

More specifically, the sacraments are visible signs and seals of God's "covenant" promises; thus, they are "tokens" of the covenant. Covenants are ratified by signs, though they are composed by words. "The sacraments, therefore, are exercises which make us more certain of the trustworthiness of God's Word. And because we are of flesh, they are shown us under things of flesh, to instruct us according to our dull capacity, and to lead us by the hand as tutors lead children." Sacraments fortify the Word (4.14.6). We can also call sacraments, says Calvin, "the pillars of our faith." Our faith rests upon the foundation of God's Word, but the foundation is strengthened by pillars, and so our faith is likewise more secure when sacraments are added. Or, again, sacraments may also be likened to mirrors which reflect God's grace back to us (4.14.6).

• *The Sacraments Undervalued.* Next Calvin turns to expose the error of those who undervalue the sacraments. In contesting false views, Calvin brings clarity to his own position, for he shows us that sacraments do not contain the power of instrumentality in themselves; rather, they are instruments *of the Holy Spirit,* and the Holy Spirit is *the agent* in both the Word and the sacraments.

Calvin opposes those who deny that sacraments are means of grace. The objection is raised that since sacraments do not bless all who partake of them—indeed, many remain unsaved or unconverted by them—it is mistaken to regard them as *means of grace* and to ascribe much value to them. Calvin replies to this objection by noting that the same sort of protest could be directed against God's Word, the very gospel, which is spoken into the ears of unbelievers. Nonetheless, that unbelievers scorn the gospel does not negate the more fundamental truth of the gospel, namely, that it is God's chosen means to save sinners. By way of analogy, we may think of a prince who issues a decree for the benefit of his subjects, even presenting official documents, signed and sealed, which guarantee the promises issued; but some of the citizens, for their part, spurn, reject, or ignore the prince's decree, in spite of the pledge with royal signature. None of this undermines the value of the prince's actions for those who accept and heed his pledge. The despicable conduct of some doesn't negate the value and benefit of the sign and seal of the prince's promise. "It is therefore certain that the Lord offers us mercy and the pledge of his grace both in his Sacred Word and in his sacraments. But it is understood only by those who take Word and sacraments with sure faith, just as Christ is offered and held forth by the Father to all unto salvation, yet not all acknowledge and receive him." Concerning believers Paul uses the language of Galatians. 3:27 and 1 Corinthians 12:12–13, but to hypocrites, to those without faith, the sacraments remain "cold and empty figures." Be that as it may, for Calvin, "sacraments are truly named the testimonies of God's grace and are like seals of the good will that he feels toward us, which by attesting that good will to us, sustain, nourish, confirm, and increase our faith." Sacraments help dispel our unbelief (cf. Mark 9:24) (4.14.7).

Sacraments, however, are not efficacious in themselves, just as the Word isn't efficacious in itself. Grace is pledged and offered in the Word and sacraments, but without "sure faith" they come to naught. Only when the Word and the sacraments are "believed" are they effective (4.14.7).

Calvin is also careful to stipulate a certain order to faith and its confirmation: "For first, the Lord teaches and instructs us by his Word. Secondly, he confirms it by the sacraments. Finally, he illumines our minds by the light of his Holy Spirit and opens our hearts for the Word and sacraments to enter in, which would otherwise only strike our ears and appear before our eyes, but not at all affect us within" (4.14.8). Both Word and sacrament, then, do not possess a power in themselves to produce faith or strengthen it, for the agent who is the author of these blessings, using Word and sacrament, is the Holy Spirit alone.

Indeed, the sacraments are used as instruments of the Holy Spirit and their specific ministry is for "the confirmation and increase of faith." Again, no secret force is to be found in them as such; rather, God has instituted them for the purpose of building up our faith through the ministry of the Spirit. And so, "the sacraments properly fulfill their office only when the Spirit, that inward teacher, comes to them, by whose power alone hearts are penetrated and affections moved and our souls opened for the sacraments to enter in. If the Spirit be lacking, the sacraments can accomplish nothing more in our minds [*mentibus*] than the splendor of the sun shining upon blind eyes, or a voice sounding in deaf ears" (4.14.9). Sacraments are worthless without the Spirit."

Both Word and sacrament, for Calvin, are ineffectual without this prior work of the Spirit. Calvin, with all the Reformed, refuses any notion of *ex opere operato* (from the act done). Sacraments do not automatically effect or bestow the thing signified by them. The Spirit's operations remain God's sovereign prerogative. "Therefore, I make such a division between Spirit and sacraments that the power to act rests with the former [the Spirit], and the ministry alone is left to the latter [the sacraments]—a ministry empty and trifling, apart from the action of the Spirit, but charged with great effect when the Spirit works within and manifests his power." In other words, the power belongs completely to the Spirit, and a servant-role belongs to the sacraments—an empty and frivolous servant-role, unless the Spirit acts. Eyes are designed (or naturally endowed) for seeing; similarly, the ears for hearing. Our hearts, too, are designed for God, but need to be supernaturally endowed, and that by God's special grace to us. Eyes need sunlight to see. Ears need sound in order to ear. Even so, our hearts (*anima*) need the Holy Spirit in order to believe. In short, "the sacraments profit not a whit without the power of the Holy Spirit…" (4.14.9).

Since faith is a divine gift, it will never do to ascribe to a creaturely thing the increase and confirmation of faith. The Spirit is the "sole author" of faith; He prepares our hearts and minds to benefit from the sacraments. One does not learn unless he or she has a teachable disposition. The Word of God beats a person's ears in vain and the sacraments strike the eyes in vain unless the Holy

Spirit softens our stubbornness of heart, illumines our minds, and inclines us to obey the Lord. Thus, "the Spirit transmits those outward words and sacraments from our ears to our soul." So the sacraments benefit us, strengthening our faith, when the Spirit engraves in our minds the sign and seal of the sacrament—the confirmation of God's favor and love toward us (4.14.10).

The Word is likewise impotent without the Spirit. Consider the parable of the sower (Matt. 13:3–23; Luke 8:5–15). The Word is without effect upon those who are stiff-necked; and it remains barren as though cast upon sand. However, when the Spirit works, the Word is not without fruit. The Spirit abides as agent; the Word and the human preaching of the Word abide as instruments of His power, "ordained by himself for the unfolding of his spiritual graces" (4.14.11). Calvin therefore beats this drum with consistency and passion: no power resides in creatures. Yet "God uses means and instruments which he himself sees to be expedient, that all things may serve his glory...." And so God uses the sacraments to nourish our faith, whose function is to place His promises before our eyes, and to serve as guarantees of those promises. As instruments of God, the glory may not be applied to them; neither may we place our confidence in them. Rather, from them we lift our faith to Him who is the author of the sacraments. We do not place our faith in sacraments, but our faith, by means of the sacraments, ought to rise up to God's throne of grace (4.14.12).

Meanwhile, let us not forget that the word *sacramentum* "signifies the solemn oath that the soldier took to the commander when he entered military service." So we likewise profess to Christ our allegiance and serve Him under this ensign. But more importantly, it is God's pledge to us that He will be our God and we shall be His people (2 Cor. 6:16; Ezek. 37:27). Thus, sacraments are first God's pledge to us; secondly, our pledge to God (4.14.13).

• *The Sacraments Overvalued.* Having defended the importance of the sacraments against those who would undervalue them, Calvin turns to address those who overvalue them—the former, we might say, err in defect, the latter err in excess.

Calvin thus now attacks a magical view of the sacraments—specifically the notion that the sacraments possess some secret powers. The Roman Catholics, for example, taught that the sacraments confer grace, provided we place no obstacle in their way. Calvin regards this as a diabolical error, for it promises righteousness apart from faith and deceives persons to their everlasting ruin. Moreover, it derives righteousness from the sacraments themselves; and misguided persons look to them superstitiously as having a power in themselves. But, says Calvin, sacraments are empty things without the divine promises that precede them. Indeed, the sacraments no less threaten wrath where faith is absent than they promise blessing where faith is present. Sacraments, then, do not offer a different or additional blessing than that which is given to us by God's Word and received in true faith. Besides, the assurance of salvation does not require the sacraments, "as if justification consisted in it." No, justification is "lodged in Christ alone," and this is conveyed to us in both the Word and the sacraments (4.14.14).

This brings Calvin, following Augustine, to distinguish between "the sign" and "the thing signified," or in his language, between "a sacrament" and "the matter of the sacrament." These are not "so linked that they cannot be separated"; and what is more, even in the union that exists between them, "the matter [the thing signified] must always be distinguished from the sign, that we may not transfer to the one what belongs to the other." Calvin quotes Augustine, who writes, "In the elect alone the sacraments effect what they represent." The power of the sacraments, God's grace, is not bestowed commonly to all—that is, to all those who are recipients of the sacramental signs. For some receive the sacraments unto life, others unto death. Those who receive the sacraments unto life receive "the matter of the sacraments," that is, the thing signified, namely Christ and all His benefits. Those who receive the sacraments unto death receive only the sign of the sacrament, without the thing signified, for if they received Christ (the matter of the sacrament), they would not be faithless and dead. Genuine eating at the Lord's Supper, for example, is not an outward eating with the teeth merely; but eating with the heart. Without faith the sacrament is "empty of truth" (4.14.15).

Calvin elaborates upon the above discussion: "I say that Christ is the matter or (if you prefer) the substance of all the sacraments; for in him they have all their firmness, and they do not promise anything apart from him." Again, the sacraments do not confer blessing *ex opere operato* (from the work performed). Sacraments do not have within themselves an operative power. Without faith, the sacraments are devoid of blessing—that is, their effectiveness may not be separated from faith; but when conjoined to faith they strengthen faith. This does not mean, however, that the force and truth of the sacraments are voided or nullified by unbelief, as if dependent upon the condition and choice of the recipients. It is only to say, with Augustine, that those who receive carnally—the sacraments being spiritual and representing the thing signified—do not obtain the reality in the sacrament. Augustine bids us neither to receive the signs as empty of content nor to focus upon the visible signs as ends in themselves, failing to lift our minds [*mentes*] to heaven and to Christ, for Christ by the Holy Spirit confers grace to us, not the signs as such. Indeed, the Spirit "makes us partakers in Christ," using the outward signs as aids pointing us to Christ. If the signs fail, however, to direct us to Christ, they become encumbrances and "their whole worth is shamefully destroyed" (4.14.16).

In this light Calvin comes to sum up the true office of the sacraments— namely that they have "the same office as the Word of God: to offer grace and set forth Christ to us, and in him the treasures of heavenly grace" (4.14.17). "But," as Calvin adds, "they avail and profit nothing unless received in faith. As with wine or oil or some other liquid, no matter how much you pour out, it will flow away and disappear unless the mouth of the vessel to receive it is open; moreover, the vessel will be splashed over on the outside, but will still remain void and empty" (4.14.17). To those without faith, the church's labor to minister the Word and the sacraments may be likened to trying to pour wine into a corked bottle; the bottle remains unfilled. Faith is the vessel by which the bottle is, as it were, opened so that we receive the blessings of the Word and sacraments—and faith, Calvin knows, is a divine gift (4.14.17).

The sacraments, then, do not—repeat, do not—possess a hidden power to confer grace to sinners "of themselves." Calvin rejects the Roman Catholic doctrine of *opus operatum* (act performed) or what is known as *ex opera operatum* (from the work performed)—the idea that sacraments confer grace irrespective of whether the recipients possess faith (4.14.17, 26). No, unless the Holy Spirit accompanies them, they have no benefit to us, though they don't cease to attest and certify God's promises of favor. It belongs to the Holy Spirit to open minds and hearts and "make us receptive to this testimony" (4.14.17). "The Holy Spirit (whom the sacraments do not bring indiscriminately to all men but whom the Lord exclusively bestows on his own people) is he who brings the graces of God with him, gives a place for the sacraments among us, and makes them bear fruit" (4.14.17). This means that the sacraments do not contain a hidden power to "confer the graces of the Holy Spirit upon us." Rather, sacraments testify and confirm God's grace, but cannot in themselves impart grace to those who receive them. The sacraments therefore are not magic.

Moreover, the sacraments do not bestow something that God otherwise does not give. On the contrary, the sacraments serve as tokens and guarantees of God's covenant promises previously spoken to us (4.14.17).

Thus we see that Calvin distinguishes the sacraments in their outward ministry from the Spirit's inner operation of blessing. God does not relinquish His power to outward symbols. Though the sacraments are instruments God uses, "these detract nothing from his original activity." Forgiveness and our justification, along with the Spirit's power, are not enclosed in earthly elements. God remains the agent of what sacraments picture and promise to us. In short, without the inner operation of God's invisible grace in us, nothing is gained by the outward visible sacraments (4.14.17).

This concludes Calvin's discussion of the theology of the sacraments in general. Next he considers the sacraments in particular.

The Sacraments in Particular
Calvin notes that the idea of sacrament extends to "all those signs which God has ever enjoined upon men to render them more certain and confident of the truth of his promises"—whether he made use of natural things or miracles. Examples are "the Tree of life" and the rainbow. "These, Adam and Noah regarded as sacraments." "Because they had a mark engraved upon them by God's Word…they were proofs and seals of his covenants." (Here we see that Calvin hints at a pre-fall covenant.) God can use ordinary elements (trees and rainbows), and by His Word make them into sacraments. He can also make miracles (like a smoking fire pot or Gideon's fleece, the sundial casting a shadow in a backward direction) function as sacraments (4.14.18).

If the above are peculiar or extraordinary sacraments, Calvin proceeds to discuss what he terms ordinary sacraments—that is, the sacraments God ordained for ordinary use in His church. Ceremonies accompany these signs. Together, the sign and ceremony in the sacraments, serve as God's testimony of grace, where He leagues Himself with us, and we in turn pledge ourselves to purity and holiness of life. There is a "mutual agreement" between God and ourselves (4.14.19).

The ordinary sacraments that God ordains for His church vary from one period of redemptive history to another. In the Old Testament circumcision (along with purifications and sacrifices) was established as a sacrament until it was abrogated by the two sacraments of the Christian church, namely baptism and the Lord's Supper. These sacraments seal the divine promises to us, which have Christ as their content. The Old Testament sacraments foreshadowed Christ as promised to us, while the New Testament sacraments attest to Him as the One already given and revealed (4.14.20). Circumcision, then, along with the requisite washings and sacrifices, pointed to Christ to come (4.14.21), but baptism and the Eucharist more fully present Christ to us.

> For baptism attests to us that we have been cleansed and washed; the Eucharistic Supper, that we have been redeemed. In water, washing is represented; in blood, satisfaction. These two are found in Christ "…who," as John says, "came in water and blood" [1 John 5:6]; that is, to wash and to redeem. The Spirit of God is also witness of this. Indeed, "there are three witnesses in one: the water, the blood, and the Spirit" [1 John 5:8 p.]. In the water and the blood we have testimony of cleansing and redemption. But the Spirit, the primary witness, makes us certain of such testimony (4.14.22).

At this point Calvin detours to respond to the impious doctrine of the Schoolmen (i.e., the medieval scholastic theologians) who falsely established a gross discontinuity between the sacraments of the Old Testament and the New Testament. No, says Calvin, for the Old Testament fathers ate the same spiritual food as we, and that food was Christ Himself (1 Cor. 10:3). The covenant (of grace) is singular—and Christ is at the center and forms the content of this covenant in both the old dispensation and the new (4.14.23). In both dispensations, whether dealing with circumcision or baptism, there is a distinction between mere external or outward ceremony and inward cleansing and change. To be sure, old shadows must give way to the new reality—but the old shadows were not false (4.14.24). Promise and fulfillment, the shadow and reality, do not indicate falsehood and truth. The promise, in the form of shadows, is truth—truth in the form of shadows. The fulfillment, the reality having arrived, is truth as the fulfilled promise. The "mode of signification" changes, not the truth of the thing. Thus Calvin offers this summary reply to objections: "The whole matter comes to this: first, all the pomp of ceremonies which was in the law of Moses, unless it be directed to Christ, is a fleeting and worthless thing; secondly, they looked to Christ in such a way that, when he was at length revealed in the flesh, they had their fulfillment; lastly, it was fitting that they should be abrogated by his coming, just as shadows vanish in the clear light of the sun" (4.14.25).

Calvin appeals to Augustine for aid and support, who argues that although the signs differ from the Old to the New Testament, the thing signified remained the same—though, Calvin admits, the New Testament sacraments offer a clearer and brighter, that is, a richer and fuller, testimony to Christ in their signification (4.14.26).

Questions for Reflection and Discussion

1. Explain how baptism and the Lord's Supper each function as a mirror that reflects God's grace back to us. Why is this important?

2. Why isn't there much interest in the sacraments today among many evangelical and Reformed churches? Some churches neglect one or both sacraments. Are sacraments worthless? What can be done so that we do not undervalue them?

3. Why is the doctrine of *ex opera operatum* a danger to true faith?

4. If the undervaluation of the sacraments is one error, the overvaluation of the sacraments is the other. What traditions in Christianity overvalue the sacrament or rite of baptism? How? What traditions in Christianity overvalue the Lord's Supper and how does this affect the Christian life?

5. How does Calvin's definition and explanation of what sacraments are, how they function, and the role of the Holy Spirit in them help you to better appreciate and properly value the role of the sacraments in your life as a believer?

6. Some evangelicals deny that there are any such things as sacraments—visible signs of invisible grace—and they deny that these so-called sacraments are official channels through which God works His gracious blessings in us, especially the strengthening of our faith; instead, they speak of "ordinances" that Christ has established which we are obliged to obey. Explain how viewing baptism and the Supper as mere commandments—ordinances—to be obeyed rather than as sacraments to be exercised and used affects our faith and Christian walk.

∽ 22 ∽

Christian Baptism

Chapters 15–16 of Book Four

Chapter Fifteen: Baptism

Orientation

FOR CALVIN, THE sacrament of baptism "is the sign of initiation by which we are received into the society of the church, in order that, engrafted in Christ, we may be reckoned among God's children" (4.15.1). God has given us the sacrament of baptism "to serve our faith before him" and "to serve our confession before men" (4.15.1).

Baptism Serves Our Faith before God

• *The Benefits of Baptism.* Baptism benefits us in three ways: (1) it testifies to forgiveness, that is, our being washed in Christ's blood; (2) it shows us our death and new life in Christ; and (3) it assures us of our union with Christ so that we partake of all His blessings. Calvin explores each of these benefits in turn.

First, says Calvin, baptism serves as "a token and proof of our cleansing; or (better to explain what I mean) it is like a sealed document to confirm to us that all our sins are so abolished, remitted, and effaced that they can never come to his sight, be recalled, or charged against us" (4.15.1). Unquestionably, baptism is linked with the idea of the remission of sins (Matt. 28:19; Acts 2:28). Hence, baptism is more than a public testimony of our faith in Christ. It is God's testimony to us regarding the remission of our sins. In saying this Calvin does not want us to think that the water of baptism—the water itself—cleanses us from sin. Indeed, the act of baptism does not save us. Baptism functions in a different way—that is, baptism promises us no other purification than through the sprinkling of Christ's blood, which is represented by means of water from the resemblance to cleansing and washing…. Thus, the surest argument to refute the self-deception of those who attribute everything to the power of the water can be sought in the meaning of baptism itself, which draws us away, not only from the visible element which meets our eyes, but from all other means, that it may fasten our minds upon Christ alone (4.15.2).

Baptism serves to fortify our faith. When we stumble and fall into sin, coming to despair and turmoil, our baptism reminds us that "we are once for all washed and purged for our whole life" (4.15.3). Truly, baptism is God's testimony of mercy to us; and this mercy extends to us throughout our lives. "Therefore, as often as we fall away, we ought to recall the memory of our baptism and fortify our mind with it, that we may always be sure and confident of the forgiveness of sins." The consolation afforded to us through baptism is not to make us careless or profane; rather, baptism offers to a person who is genuinely despairing and troubled in conscience ("sinners who groan") a visible witness of the invisible grace of God's mercy in Christ—the washing away of our sins (4.15.3). We mustn't treat baptism as if it regenerates us or grants a "first regeneration" that can subsequently be lost. Baptism does not function apart from the preaching of the Word and the call to faith. But precisely in the struggle of faith we may look to our baptism to be strengthened in the sufficiency of Christ's sacrifice for us. In short, baptism reminds and assures us that we receive the remission of all our sins in the blood of Christ (4.15.4).

The second benefit that baptism brings to us is the testimony of death and rebirth, "for it shows us our mortification in Christ, and new life in him. Indeed (as the apostle says), 'we have been baptized into his death,' 'buried with him into death, … that we may walk in newness of life' [Rom. 6:3–4]" (4.15.5). Through baptism "Christ makes us sharers in his death, that we may be engrafted in it" (Rom. 6:5). The baptized, engrafted into Christ, in the act of faith, "truly feel the effective working of Christ's death in the mortification of their flesh, together with the working of his resurrection in the vivification of the Spirit" (Rom. 6:8). In this manner death and renewal are potently portrayed and promised to us in baptism (4.15.5).

The third benefit that baptism grants us is that we are participants in all the good gifts that Christ bestows. Writes Calvin, "Lastly, our faith receives from baptism the advantage of its sure testimony to us that we are not only engrafted into the death and life of Christ, but so united to Christ himself that we become sharers in all his blessings. For he dedicated and sanctified baptism in his own body [Matt. 3:13] in order that he might have it in common with us as the firmest bond of the union and fellowship which he has deigned to form with us" (4.15.6). In baptism, we put on Christ (Gal. 3:26–27). Scripture tells us that the apostles baptized "with a baptism of repentance unto forgiveness of sins" [Acts 2:38, 41]—"meaning by the word 'repentance' such regeneration; and by 'forgiveness of sins,' cleansing." All of which, however, take place through the work of the triune Name, since we are baptized into the name of the Father, and of the Son, and of the Holy Spirit—indeed, the Father is the cause, the Son the matter, and the Holy Spirit the effect of our rebirth and renewal (4.15.6).

• *Baptism Performed by John the Baptist.* Calvin next takes a brief detour to consider the question of John's baptism. That is, was the baptism performed by John the Baptist the same baptism later performed by the apostles? Calvin argues that the former is one and the same as the latter. "John and the apostles agreed on one doctrine: both baptized to repentance, both to forgiveness of sins, both into the name of Christ, from whom repentance and forgiveness of sins came" (4.15.7). The only difference is that John baptized in the name of the One who was yet to accomplish His saving ministry on earth, while the apostles baptized in the name of the One who had finished His saving ministry on earth (4.15.7).

In answer to the objection that John's baptism is with water, whereas the baptism that is to come will be with the Holy Spirit and with fire, Calvin offers this reply: "John did not mean to distinguish one sort of baptism from another, but he compared his person with that of Christ—that he was a minister of water, but Christ the giver of the Holy Spirit; and that this power would be declared by a visible miracle on the day when he would send the Holy Spirit to the apostles under tongues of fire [Acts 2:3]."

In baptism, the human agents administer the outward sign, but Christ administers the inward grace. Although the human agents who administer the water of baptism vary, "Christ alone presides" (4.15.8).

• *Baptism Symbolized in the Old Testament.* Next Calvin demonstrates how the meaning of baptism is symbolized or foreshadowed already in the Old Testament. Indeed, mortification and washing were portrayed in Israel's salvation through the Red Sea, for they were "baptized in the cloud and in the sea" (1 Cor. 10:2). Israel's passage through the Red Sea on dry ground was their passing from death to life (Exod. 14:21), even as the cloud symbolized God's presence and their sanctification or cleansing (Num. 9:15; Exod. 13:21) (4.15.9).

• *Baptism and Original Sin.* From here Calvin considers the question concerning what baptism actually effects in us. Calvin argues that it is altogether mistaken to think that baptism removes original sin—that is, that depravity of nature which we inherited from Adam and with which we are born, rendering us guilty before God and inclined to every sort of evil. Similarly, it is mistaken to think that baptism renders us delivered and restored to Adam's original state of righteousness (4.15.10). Calvin believes this issue requires attention.

> As we are vitiated and corrupted in all parts of our nature, we are held rightly condemned on account of such corruption alone and convicted before God, to whom nothing is acceptable but righteousness, innocence, and purity. Even infants bear their condemnation with them from their mother's womb; for, though they have not yet brought forth the fruits of their own iniquity, they have the seed enclosed within themselves. Indeed, their whole nature is a seed of sin; thus it cannot but be hateful and abominable to God. Through baptism, believers are assured that this condemnation has been removed and withdrawn from them, since...the Lord promises us by this sign that full and complete remission has been made, both of the guilt that should have been imputed to us, and of the punishment that we ought to have undergone because of the guilt. They also lay hold on righteousness, but such righteousness as the people of God can obtain in this life, that is, by imputation only, since the Lord of his own mercy considers them righteous and innocent (4.15.10).

This is the first key point Calvin wishes to make regarding baptism's effect. It does not vanquish original sin. Believers remain under the burden and taint of sin, but not sin's guilt. But even this point requires clarification. Calvin therefore makes another key point pertaining to this matter. Regarding the corruption of our nature inherited from Adam, i.e., original sin, Calvin says that

> ...this perversity never ceases in us, but continually bears new fruits—what we have previously described as "works of the flesh" [Gal. 5:19]—just as a glowing furnace continually emits flame and sparks, or

a spring ceaselessly gives forth water.... Baptism indeed promises to us the drowning of our Pharaoh [Ex. 14:28] and the mortification of our sin, but not so that it no longer exists or gives us trouble, but only that it may not overcome us. For so long as we live cooped up in the prison of our body, traces of sin will dwell in us; but if we faithfully hold fast to the promise given us by God in baptism, they shall not dominate or rule (4.15.11).

Here we see that Calvin distinguishes between the state and condition of persons in Adam and persons in Christ, of persons who are not able not to sin and persons who are, by the Holy Spirit, able not to sin—that is, enabled not to be altogether dominated and ruled by sin. In this way the depravity of nature that a believer struggles against may be distinguished from an unbeliever's depravity—the former possess the Holy Spirit so that "traces of sin" dwell in us but sin does not "overcome" us; the latter are without any sanctifying grace, sin is their master and reigns in them, only held in check by the non-saving, restraining work of God.

All this is confirmed from Romans 7. The apostle points us to the depravity that afflicts a regenerated person—namely himself. "He therefore says that he has a perpetual conflict with the vestiges of his flesh, and that he is held bound in miserable bondage, so that he cannot consecrate himself wholly to obedience to the divine law [Rom. 7:18-23]." The cry of wretchedness and deliverance is met by the assurance of pardon and condemnation overcome (Rom. 7:24; 8:1). "There he teaches that those whom the Lord has once received into grace, engrafts into the communion of his Christ, and adopts into the society of the church through baptism (even though they are besieged by sin and still carry sin about in themselves)—are absolved of guilt and condemnation" (4.15.12).

Baptism Serves Our Faith before the World

As earlier noted, baptism on the one hand serves our faith before God; but on the other hand it serves our confession before others. Having examined this first aspect of baptism, Calvin now turns to consider the second aspect—that baptism is a token of our confession before the world. "It is the mark by which we publicly profess that we wish to be reckoned God's people; by which we testify that we agree in worshiping the same God, in one religion with all Christians; by which finally we openly affirm our faith" (4.15.13). Baptism, therefore, should be a public event. Believers wear the badge of Christ by means of baptism, identifying themselves as His. Baptism also calls us "to live harmoniously with all believers in complete agreement of faith and love" (4.15.15).

• *The Right Use of Baptism.* Inasmuch as baptism serves to arouse, nourish, and confirm our faith, "it is to be received as from the hand of the Author himself." God speaks to us through this sign; God purifies us and washes away our sins; God makes us sharers in Christ's death and weakens Satan's sway in our lives; and God brings us into union with Himself, as we put on Christ, and are therefore reckoned as His children. "These things, I say, he performs for our soul within as truly and surely as we see our body outwardly cleansed, submerged, and surrounded with water." This fits with the function of sacraments—spiritual things are depicted for us through physical things. Not that the spiritual reality is conveyed or "bound and enclosed" in the sacrament of baptism—conferring on us this reality by its power. Rather, the Lord gives us an attestation of His will toward us by this outward sign, namely, "that he is pleased to lavish all these things upon us." This is not a subterfuge or a "mere appearance only"; on the contrary, by means of the outward sign God "leads us to the present reality and effectively performs what it symbolizes" (4.15.14).

Baptism doesn't impart the reality to which it points, but it does assure us of the reality to which it points. This is important to say since some mistakenly conceive of baptism as possessing a power that imparts forgiveness and rebirth. It is not Calvin's aim, however, to create a false divide between the sign and the reality or truth of what is signified. "But from this sacrament, as from all others, we obtain only as much as we receive in faith." Accordingly, "If we lack faith, this will be evidence of our ungratefulness, which renders us chargeable before God, because we have not believed the promise given there" (4.15.15).

Baptism does not depend on the merit of the administrator for it to have validity, for even in the case of an unworthy or godless minister performing the baptism, God's hand is the true instrument. Baptism is of God (4.15.16).

Moreover, baptism is not invalidated—or only validated—upon our believing reception and acknowledgment of it. "That promise, since it was of God, ever remained fixed and firm and trustworthy." God is true even if people are liars.

We therefore confess that for that time baptism benefited us not at all, inasmuch as the promise offered us in it—without which baptism is nothing—lay neglected. Now when by God's grace, we begin to repent, we accuse our blindness and hardness of heart—we who were for so long ungrateful toward his goodness. But we believe that the promise itself did not vanish. Rather, we consider that God through baptism promises us forgiveness of sins, and he will doubtless fulfill his promise for all believers. This promise was offered to us in baptism; therefore, let us embrace it by faith. Indeed, on account of our unfaithfulness it lay long buried from us; now, therefore, let us receive it through faith (4.15.17).

This is also why we never need to perform rebaptisms (4.15.18).

• *Issues surrounding Baptism.* As for the "mode" or "method" of baptism, Calvin offers these words: "But whether the person being baptized should be wholly immersed, and whether thrice or once, whether he should only be sprinkled with poured water—these details are of no importance, but ought to be optional to churches according to the diversity of countries. Yet the word 'baptize' means to immerse, and it is clear that the rite of immersion was observed in the ancient church" (4.15.19).

Private individuals may not assume the right to perform baptisms, not even in so-called cases of emergency. Baptism, like the Lord's Supper, belongs to the church and each sacrament is to be administered by those ordained to that office. As for so-called emergencies, say, lest one die before being baptized, this reveals a gross misconception about baptism's import. For we do not baptize persons in order they may participate in the covenant promise of God; rather, because such persons participate in that covenant promise, we baptize them (4.15.20). Nor are baptisms to be performed by women (4.15.21). Baptism is to be administered by the church, not by those unauthorized. Private baptism is improper. No emergency baptism is necessary either.

To those who would argue that rather than omit baptism it is better to administer it, even if no officiant is available, Calvin makes this observation: "Infants are not barred from the Kingdom of Heaven just because they happen to depart the present life before they have been immersed in water.... From this it follows that the children of believers are baptized not in order that they who were previously strangers to the church may then for the first time become children of God, but rather that, because by the blessing of the promise they already belonged to the body of Christ, they are received into the church with this solemn sign" (4.15.22). We must not neglect baptism, but neither should we panic and administer it without the church.

Chapter Sixteen: Infant Baptism Best Accords with Christ's Institution and the Nature of the Sign

Orientation

With this chapter Calvin takes up a defense of infant baptism against certain "frantic spirits" and their "mad ravings" (4.16.1). Calvin presents a very comprehensive argument in support of infant baptism, the salient features of which we will attempt to trace out.

Similarities and Differences of Baptism and Circumcision

After reviewing the meaning of baptism (4.16.2), Calvin turns to the similarity and dissimilarity of baptism and circumcision. Since baptism has as its primary import the "forgiveness of sins" or "cleansing," we must not miss the clear connection or continuity between circumcision in the Old Testament and baptism in the New Testament. The promise is the same in both testaments, namely, "that of God's fatherly favor, of forgiveness of sins, and of eternal life." The dissimilarity between them is in externals only; "there is no difference in the inner mystery" (4.16.4). It is beyond dispute that circumcision was administered to covenant infants—not merely as something permitted but "as something owed to them." Likewise baptism is owed to covenant infants as well. God doesn't offer empty promises; He doesn't mock us "with mere trickery," as if what is symbolized in baptism is without foundation in reality. To that end, "if the covenant remains firm and steadfast, it applies no less today to the children of Christians than under the Old Testament it pertained to the infants of the Jews" (4.16.5). We must face this truth: if the children participated in "the thing signified," we may not bar them from the sign that points to it (4.16.5). Only outward ceremony distinguishes baptism from circumcision, not the spiritual reality to which both point, for they both point to the same promises of forgiveness and renewal.

The Covenant Promise and Baptism

As for the covenant, we know that this is still in force today and applies to Christians even as it applied to the Jewish people in the Old Testament. The holy seed and heirs of the covenant in the former age (Ezra 9:2; Isa. 6:13) have become the holy seed and heirs of these covenant promises in the new epoch of Jesus Christ's coming (1 Cor. 7:14). "The covenant is common, and the reason for confirming it is common. Only the manner of confirmation is different—what was circumcision for them was replaced for us by baptism" (4.16.6).

The covenant promise of God's mercy does not shrink with Christ's coming; rather, it is enlarged. Jesus said that the kingdom of heaven belongs to infants (Matt. 19:13–15). If the reality of the kingdom belongs to them, why should the "sign" of that kingdom be denied them? (4.16.7). Furthermore, observes Calvin, while it is true that we nowhere find mention made of infant baptism in the New Testament, there is no good reason to rashly conclude that infants were excluded from "household" baptisms, although admittedly household baptisms did not necessarily include them (4.16.8).

The Benefits of Infant Baptism

But what practical benefit presents itself in the practice of infant baptism? Some judge the practice superfluous. Calvin maintains that genuine benefits are present for both the parents bringing their children to be baptized and for the children that are baptized. He explains:

> For God's sign, communicated to a child as by an impressed seal, confirms the promise given to the pious parent, and declares it to be ratified that the Lord will be God not only to him but to his seed; and that he wills to manifest his goodness and grace not only to him but to his descendants even to the thousandth generation [Ex. 20:6]. God's boundless generosity, in showing itself there, first gives men ample occasion to proclaim his glory, then floods godly hearts with uncommon happiness, which quickens men to a deeper love of their kind Father, as they see his concern on their behalf for their posterity (4.16.9).

Children need the same props and helps as adults, i.e., they need the symbols God offers us to move them to "surer confidence" in His promises. God shows them that a seal of their adoption was granted to them before they were old enough to acknowledge God as their heavenly Father (4.16.9).

Answering Objections to Infant Baptism

Some opponents of infant baptism (the Anabaptists) remain unconvinced by the analogy between circumcision and baptism—that is, that the sacrament of baptism now has replaced the rite of circumcision (4.16.10). Not surprisingly, Calvin appeals to Colossians 2:11–12. Believers are the circumcision of Christ, for they were buried with Christ in baptism. Asks Calvin, "What do these words mean, except that the fulfillment and truth of baptism are also the truth and fulfillment of circumcision, since they signify one and the same thing?" (4.16.11).

Still the objection is raised that while Abraham's offspring was at one time traced according to bloodlines, now it is traced by faith in Christ. While there is truth in such a comment, says Calvin, if what is being intimated is that God never promised Abraham's physical descendants His spiritual blessings, this must be completely rejected as error (4.16.12). The symbols differ between circumcision and baptism, but the meaning is the same. The promise to Abraham carries through to the New Testament, finding its fulfillment in Christ (4.16.13). It is false to say that the covenant under Abraham is null and void and no longer applicable. It cannot be made void by unbelief (cf. Rom. 9:6ff.; chapter 11), for although the freedom of God's election stands, God builds us up and displays His mercy to us through the signs and seals of circumcision in the Old Testament and of baptism in the New Testament (4.16.14–15).

More weighty, perhaps, is the objection that inasmuch as infants are incapable of faith, they are not the proper recipients of baptism. This too is wholly mistaken, says Calvin. Christ commands that children of the covenant, though unconscious of their fall in Adam and of God's mercy towards them, be brought to Him (Matt. 19:14), since He is the source of life and salvation also for them. "Therefore to quicken them he makes them partakers in himself." The opponents of infant baptism, however, unlike Christ, abandon them to identify with Adam in guilt and depravity and God's wrath (4.16.17).

Of course, they might try to argue that such children, for now, escape the sentence of death that rests upon Adam and his descendants until they reach an age of accountability. Such a claim has no support from Scripture, however. Scripture testifies to the opposite effect: they are under wrath unless in communion with Christ (cf. Rom. 5:12ff.; 1 Cor. 15:22; Eph. 2:3; Ps. 51:5; 1 Cor. 15:50). Just as infants can perish at a tender age, they can likewise be the objects of God's work of regeneration at a tender age. Obviously, if they are to be saved they must be "previously regenerated by the Lord." "For if they bear with them an inborn corruption from their mother's womb, they must be cleansed of it before they can be admitted into God's Kingdom, for nothing polluted or defiled may enter there [Rev. 21:27]." Again, "If they are born sinners...either they remain unpleasing and hateful to God, or they must be justified." Thus sanctification in the mother's womb, though rare, is not impossible or beyond God's power (Luke 1:15) (4.16.17).

Truly, "Christ was sanctified from earliest infancy in order that he might sanctify in himself his elect from every age without distinction." This merely demonstrates that "the age of infancy is not utterly averse to sanctification." For Calvin, it is "incontrovertible that no one of the elect is called from the present life before being sanctified and regenerated by the Spirit of God" (4.16.18).

Only, the objection is further pressed, that since faith is necessary to salvation, and since faith is acquired through hearing the gospel preached, infants, being incapable of the hearing and of faith wrought by it, cannot be the proper candidates for baptism (cf. Rom. 10:17). Calvin acknowledges that infants are indeed incapable of the way of salvation specified by the apostle in Romans 10. To be sure, that is the ordinary arrangement and common method God uses to bring His people to faith and salvation. Yet this doesn't forbid God to grant to a child that death snatches away in infancy some part of His saving grace, or a tiny spark of it, which, then, represents an extraordinary "illumination of the Spirit apart from the medium of preaching" (4.16.19).

Still, the objection is "more stoutly" urged, for baptism is a sacrament of repentance and faith—again acts which infants cannot perform. Such darts, says Calvin, "are aimed more at God than at us," since circumcision is also "a sign of repentance [Jer. 4:4; 9:25; cf. Deut. 10:16; 30:6]." Yet infants were circumcised in the Old Testament though incapable of performing an act of repentance. Obviously, though such infants could not understand the meaning of their circumcision when first administered to them, with maturity the meaning of their circumcision—a mortification of their corrupt nature, a turning in repentance to God as an expression of this dying away—is embraced and put into practice. This applies to the sacrament of baptism administered to covenant infants as well. They "are baptized into future repentance and faith, and even though these have not yet been formed in them, the seed of both lies hidden within them by the secret working of the Spirit" (4.16.20).

Practical Questions surrounding Infant Baptism

This brings Calvin to emphasize the point that in infant baptism we need not expect an immediate effectiveness to be manifest except that the sacrament confirms and ratifies the covenant of grace. In due time, the remaining significance of baptism will show itself as God intends. Accordingly, some of God's elect children, being baptized, depart this life prior to manifesting the marks of faith, God "renews them by the power, incomprehensible to us, of his Spirit, in whatever way he alone foresees will be expedient." Others, however, grow to maturity and their baptism serves to fire them "with greater zeal for renewal" and they can meditate on the meaning of their baptism throughout their lives (4.16.21).

Baptism comforts us. We are all born sinners. We all need forgiveness, being poisoned and sinful from our mother's wombs. God's mercy of pardon extends to infants. Therefore the sign of that favor, promised to them, should be given to them. As recipients of God's forgiveness (the reality and the superior thing), infants are entitled to the sign (the much inferior thing) (4.16.22).

Naturally, those biblical texts that call adults to faith and repentance do not apply to infants who are not of "fit age" to respond to exhortation of this sort (4.16.23). Let us not forget that while Abraham received the promise, then believed, and lastly received the sign of circumcision, with Isaac the order was different. Isaac received the promise, then was circumcised, and lastly believed. This varied response exists among believers today as well (4.16.24). We see, then, that although Abraham received the sign of the covenant after believing, his son Isaac received it as an infant prior to faith. This is because God came to Abraham when he was already an adult and called him to faith. Isaac participates by the stipulations of the divine promise, and so as an infant receives the sign of that promise. Says Calvin, "Those who embrace faith in Christ as grown men, since they were previously strangers to the covenant, are not to be given the badge of baptism unless they first have faith and repentance, which alone can give access to the society of the covenant. But those infants who derive their origin from Christians, as they have been born directly into the inheritance of the covenant, and are expected by God, are thus to be received into baptism" (16.24).

Calvin takes time to consider a number of texts that opponents of infant baptism appeal to in an effort to rebut the practice of infant baptism. Among them is John 3:5, wherein Jesus says that unless a man is born again of water and the Spirit, he cannot enter into the kingdom of God. "Water and the Spirit," says Calvin, simply refers to the Spirit who regenerates and gives life. It is to receive "that power of the Spirit, which does in the soul what water does in the body" (4.16.25).

It is also quite mistaken to maintain that all persons who have not been baptized perish. Some press the necessity of baptism to such an extreme as to teach that believing persons who are snatched away by death prior to undergoing baptism are, in spite of their faith, consigned to eternal death. Calvin refutes this notion by citing John 5:24, which aptly states that those who believe have passed from death into life (4.16.26).

Some raise an objection by appealing to Jesus' words of great commission in Matthew 28:19, where the command given to the apostles is first that they make disciples, then baptize those who are committed to the Lord. Similarly, Mark 16:16 couples faith with baptism. Consequently, preaching must precede baptizing, and believing comes before baptism. But this is to quibble over the order of words, says Calvin. The ministry of the Word is of first order in such texts; and infants, clearly, are not in view or the object of attention, but ministry to those who are mature and can respond to the exhortations of the gospel (4.16.27–28).

Opponents also assert that Jesus' baptism, being administered to Him in adulthood, shows that infant baptism is invalid. The misuse of Scripture evident in such reasoning hardly deserves a reply. It is on the level of saying that infants should not be allowed to eat since they cannot work with their own hands (cf. 2 Thess. 3:10). Jesus' baptism coincided with His ministry of the gospel and embarking upon His work to teach and offer Himself as the Lamb of God (4.16.29).

Baptism and the Lord's Supper

Another argument to which Calvin responds concerns the relationship between the sacraments of baptism and the Lord's Supper. If children are barred from the Supper, they should likewise be barred from baptism. Calvin explains that the two sacraments are not identical. "For if we consider the peculiar character of baptism, surely it is an entrance and a sort of initiation into the church, through which we are numbered among God's people: a sign of our spiritual regeneration, through which we are reborn as children of God." The Supper, however, has a different focus. It "is given to older persons who, having passed tender infancy, can now take solid food." The Supper is specifically for those who can discern the body and blood of the Lord, and can examine their own conscience, etc. (1 Cor. 11:25–29). For this reason there is a very great difference between the two signs, just as circumcision was administered to infants but the Passover was given only to those who were old enough to inquire into its meaning (Exod. 12:26) (4.16.30).

Calvin presents another twenty objections to infant baptism set forth by Servetus, to which he offers rather pithy or otherwise taciturn replies, which we need not explore (4.16.31). In all such contentiousness and disputes over infant baptism, we must beware of Satan's devices to despoil the church of the "assurance and spiritual joy" to be derived from this practice and diminish the splendor of God's goodness. Indeed, how wonderful to contemplate that God is the heavenly Father of our children and they are under His care. Let us therefore "offer our infants to him, for he gives them a place among those of his family and household, that is, the members of the church" (4.16.32).

Questions for Reflection and Discussion

1. Do you view your baptism as a source of assurance of God's forgiveness? Have you been taught to regard and use baptism that way?

2. How can we better embrace and apply the second and third benefits of baptism that Calvin mentions—that is, seeing our baptism as death and resurrection, as dying to the old self and coming to life in the new self?

3. Why is it important to keep the unity between John's baptism and the baptism instituted by Jesus in the name of the Father, and of the Son, and of the Holy Spirit? (Hint: Consider the significance of Jesus' baptism for our baptism.)

4. Given Calvin's argument in this chapter, should Christians regard themselves as "totally depraved" or should they use other language to describe their ongoing battle with sin? (See Heidelberg Catechism, Q/As 8, 32, 43, 45, 49, 62, 86, 88–91, 114, 115; Westminster Confession, IX.iv; XIII. i–iii; XV.i–ii; XVI.ii–vi.)

5. Do you regard your baptism as a public profession of faith? How can we use it this way?

6. What does it mean to improve your baptism? (See Belgic Confession, art. 34; Westminster Larger Catechism, Q/A 167.)

7. In light of Calvin's teaching, how should devout parents regard their children who depart this life at a tender age—as lost? as saved? or with uncertainty about their status? (See Canons of Dort, I.17; Westminster Confession of Faith, X.iii.)

8. Have you ever heard of "private baptisms"? What about private celebrations of the Lord's Supper? What is wrong with each of these practices?

9. In your own words, trace out Calvin's argument for infant baptism. What are its key features?

10. Do you think parents take seriously enough the promises of God signified and sealed to their children in baptism? Likewise, do the children take these promises seriously enough? Why is this a challenge for us and what can we do to remedy the problem?

11. Is it helpful or harmful to think of baptism planting a seed of faith and repentance in a covenant child, awaiting the marks of life? What are the implications of affirming and of opposing this idea?

12. How might a Baptist (or any opponent of the baptism of small children) try to escape the force of Calvin's arguments favoring infant baptism?

13. How do proponents of "child communion" use the practice of infant baptism to garner support for that view? Why doesn't Calvin agree with making the Lord's Supper available to infants or small children?

∽ 23 ∾

The Lord's Supper

Chapters 17–19 of Book Four

Chapter Seventeen: The Sacred Supper of Christ, and What It Brings to Us

Orientation

CALVIN OBSERVES THAT with baptism, God regenerates us, engrafts us into the body of Christ, the church, and makes us His own by adoption. As a faithful Father, He also supplies us with that spiritual food we need to be sustained and preserved in the new life into which He has begotten us by His Word. To assure believers of His abiding grace and mercy, God, through His Son, ordained another sacrament in the church, the Lord's Supper. Calvin calls this Supper "a spiritual banquet, wherein Christ attests himself to be the life-giving bread, upon which our souls feed unto true and blessed immortality [John 6:51]" (4.17.1).

This is a "high mystery" that we very much need to know. Calvin offers some summary statements in an effort to cut through the tangle of arguments and misunderstandings that plague the doctrine of the Lord's Supper.

Preliminary Definitions and Observations

"First, the signs are bread and wine, which represent for us the invisible food that we receive from the flesh and blood of Christ." What is that invisible food we need? "Now Christ is the only food of our soul, and therefore our Heavenly Father invites us to Christ, that, refreshed by partaking of him, we may repeatedly gather strength until we shall have reached heavenly immortality" (4.17.1).

The mystery of Christ's secret union with believers, though incomprehensible, is shown to us through visible signs of bread and wine, which are the tokens and guarantees of our salvation in Christ's blood. God strengthens us in the way of faith by confirming to us the fact that the Lord's body was once for all sacrificed for our sakes, and we may "feed upon it, and by feeding feel in ourselves the working of that unique sacrifice...." Likewise, Christ's blood has been shed for our sakes and is now "our perpetual drink" (4.17.1).

Just as bread and wine sustain physical life, so our souls are fed by partaking of Christ. Calvin calls this a "mystical blessing." Believers receive great assurance and delight in this sacrament, because by means of it we commune of Christ and His sacrifice for us. Indeed, they may dare assure themselves that eternal life is theirs, for they are absolved of the guilt of their sins—the guilt Christ took upon Himself (4.17.2).

Calvin's doctrine of the Lord's Supper is unique in what has come to be called the "spiritual presence" of Christ in the sacrament. By bidding us to eat, says Calvin, as when Christ says, "Take, eat, drink: this is my body, which is given for you; this is my blood, which is shed for forgiveness of sins," Christ "indicates that it is ours; by declaring that his body is given for us and his blood shed for us, he teaches that both are not so much his as ours" (4.17.3). Calvin offers this important and helpful elaboration on the analogy between physical and spiritual things:

> Thus, when bread is given as a symbol of Christ's body, we must at once grasp this comparison: as bread nourishes, sustains, and keeps the life of our body, so Christ's body is the only food to invigorate and enliven our soul. When we see wine set forth as a symbol of blood, we must reflect on the benefits which wine imparts to the body, and so realize that the same are spiritually imparted to us by Christ's blood. These benefits are to nourish, refresh, strengthen, and gladden (4.17.3).

Calvin wants us to grasp the meaning of the promise of the Lord's Supper considering the chief function of this sacrament is "to seal and confirm that promise by which [Christ] testifies that his flesh is food indeed and his blood is drink [John 6:56], which feed us unto eternal life [John 6:55]." The Supper, then, "sends us to the cross of Christ, where that promise was indeed performed and in all respects fulfilled" (4.17.4). If Christ took on our human mortality, as seen in the cross, by this Supper He shows us that we partake of His immortality, for He bore our curse but imbues us with His blessing (4.17.4).

The Role of Faith

But how is all this applied to us? Calvin here points to the centrality of faith in the partaking of this sacrament, for we participate by faith. Through the gospel (that is, through the ministry of the gospel), "but more clearly through the Sacred Supper," Christ offers us Himself and all the blessings that are His—all of which we receive by faith (4.17.5). In this connection, Calvin is concerned to guard against two mistakes: (1) to have such little regard for the signs that they are divorced from the mysteries to which they are appointed; and (2) to extol the signs so immoderately that they obscure the mysteries they signify. That is, Calvin is concerned, on the one hand, that we not under-identify the relationship between the signs—the bread and wine—from the thing signified—Christ's body and blood unto our redemption; and on the other hand, that we not over-identify these, so that the signs are regarded as themselves the body and blood of Christ.

This issue also relates to "the mode" of partaking of Christ. Some (Zwingli) think that to partake of Christ is merely to believe in Him. "But," writes Calvin, "it seems to me that Christ meant to teach something more definite, and more elevated…[in John 6:26ff.]"—namely, "that we are quickened by the true partaking of him; and he has therefore designated this partaking by the words 'eating' and 'drinking,' in order that no one should think that the life that we receive from him is received by mere knowledge. As it is not the seeing but the eating of bread that suffices to feed the body, so the soul must truly and deeply become partaker of Christ that it may be quickened to spiritual life by his power" (4.17.5). Of course, eating is by way of faith, but "we eat Christ's flesh in believing, because it is made ours by faith, and…this eating is the result and effect of faith." As Calvin also says, in partaking of Christ, "his life passes into us and is made ours—just as bread when taken as food imparts vigor to the body" (4.17.5).

The Undervaluation of the Supper

Meanwhile, some undervalue the sacrament of the Lord's Supper, turning it into a mere profession of faith; or still others maintain that in the Supper we partake of the Holy Spirit alone but not of Christ's flesh and blood. This great mystery is dishonored with such notions, for truly our minds cannot reach up to grasp it, nor our tongues to express it (4.17.6–7).

Calvin insists that we do not reduce the Lord's Supper to our cognitive memory, for we truly, by the Holy Spirit, partake of the body and blood of Christ in this sacrament. The flesh of Christ, of course, does not of itself have the power to quicken us (4.17.8–9), but it is the food that is imparted to nurture our new life. Calvin summarizes his staked out position as follows: "our souls are fed by the flesh and blood of Christ in the same way that bread and wine keep and sustain physical life. For the analogy of the sign applies only if souls find their nourishment in Christ—which cannot happen unless Christ truly grows into one with us, and refreshes us by the eating of his flesh and the drinking of his blood" (4.17.10).

Calvin continues: "Even though it seems unbelievable that Christ's flesh, separated from us by such great distance, penetrates to us, so that it becomes our food, let us remember how far the secret power of the Holy Spirit towers above all our senses, and how foolish it is to wish to measure his immeasurableness by our measure. What, then, our mind does not comprehend, let faith conceive: that the Spirit truly unites things separated in space" (4.17.10). Then follows another critical passage for understanding his view: "Now, that sacred partaking of his flesh and blood, by which Christ pours his life into us, as if it penetrated into our bones and marrow, he also testifies and seals in the Supper—not by presenting a vain and empty sign, but by manifesting there the effectiveness of his Spirit to fulfill what he promises. And truly he offers and shows the reality there signified to all who sit at that spiritual banquet, although it is received with benefit by believers alone, who accept such great generosity with true faith and gratefulness of heart" (4.17.10).

The Overvaluation of the Supper

It is important that we grasp the two aspects of the sacrament: the physical signs, and the things invisible, the spiritual truth. But we might better grasp this under three headings: "the signification, the matter that depends upon it, and the power or effect that follows from both." Calvin expands on this: "The signification is contained in the promises, which are, so to speak, implicit in the sign. I call Christ with his death and resurrection the matter, or substance. But by effect I understand redemption, righteousness, sanctification, and eternal life, and all the other benefits Christ gives to us" (4.17.11).

Fortified with this conceptual apparatus, Calvin next turns his guns against those who overvalue this sacrament. He specifically has in mind the Schoolmen who posited the doctrine of transubstantiation (cf. 4.17.11–17). Calvin, for his part, wants nothing to do with a "fictitious transubstantiation," but neither will he allow us to reduce the Supper to a "memorial." Transubstantiation teaches the spatial or local presence of Christ at the

Lord's Supper—that is, the bread and wine are converted into the body and blood of Christ while remaining veiled under the form of bread and wine.

The Nature of Christ's Presence at the Supper

Calvin argues that Christ's presence at the Table isn't because He corporeally—i.e., physically—comes down to us under the cover of bread and wine; rather, His presence is known when we lift up our minds to heaven. For "if we are lifted up to heaven with our eyes and minds, to seek Christ there in the glory of his Kingdom, as the symbols invite us to him in his wholeness, so under the symbol of bread we shall be fed by his body, under the symbol of wine we shall separately drink his blood, to enjoy him at last in his wholeness" (4.17.18). The Spirit is the agent that bridges the gap between Christ in heaven and His people on earth. "In short, [Christ] feeds his people with his own body, the communion of which he bestows upon them by the power of his Spirit" (4.17.18).

Calvin knows that his own position, often called the true spiritual presence of Christ, cannot be adequately expressed. What is essential is that we maintain the following: that there is a "true and substantial partaking of the body and blood of the Lord," and that this "is shown to believers under the sacred symbols of the Supper," and, further, that we understand in partaking of the bread and wine we receive Christ's body and blood, indeed, we receive and enjoy "the thing itself"—His body and blood sacrificially and redemptively—not merely by imagination or memory or understanding of the mind, but by the Holy Spirit in our partaking of the bread and wine (4.17.19).

The summary offered above constitutes the heart of Calvin's teaching on the Lord's Supper. We need not explore every avenue of his discussion that follows, wherein he takes up various topics and debated issues (cf. 4.17.20–29). We do note that Calvin spends some pages distinguishing his doctrine from the doctrine of ubiquity, advocated by the Lutherans, which comes to expression in their doctrine of consubstantiation (cf. 4.17.30–31). We also note that Calvin is aware that his doctrine of the Supper remains mysterious in some respects, which leads him to bid us not to despair if we do not fully understand how we feed upon Christ in eating bread and drinking wine. Surely the mystery is too lofty for us, says Calvin. "I rather experience than understand it" (4.17.32). But the work of this union between Christ and ourselves is effectuated by the Holy Spirit; indeed, "it is through his incomprehensible power that we come to partake of Christ's flesh and blood" (4.17.33). This is what

Calvin means by the spiritual partaking of Christ. Christ is not enclosed in bread and wine. "For us the manner is spiritual because the secret power of the Spirit is the bond of our union with Christ." Christ is the substance or the matter or the thing signified in the Supper (4.17.33)

Calvin also rejects the notion that by the very act of partaking we are blessed. In fact, faith is necessary; and faith is a divine gift which is not bestowed on all. Calvin endorses and quotes the words of Augustine, "In the elect alone do the sacraments effect what they symbolize." The wicked partake of the Lord's Supper to their detriment and condemnation (4.17.34). For this reason we must ever guard against superstition in treating this sacrament (cf. 4.17.35–37). Likewise, we do well to see that this sacrament reaches its purpose in serving our faith before God, for our faith is exercised and strengthened in the remembrance of Christ's death—that death that is our life. We are encouraged and exhorted to charity and peace, and to practice concord with other members of the church. We are also called to purity, holiness of life, and devotion to the Lord. The church is called to unity in this way (4.17.37–38).

God's Word and Self-examination

Calvin bids us to remember that the Lord's Supper cannot exist apart from the Word. "For whatever benefits may come to us from the Supper requires the Word: whether we are to be confirmed in faith, or exercised in confession, or aroused to duty, there is need of preaching" (4.17.39). Preaching may not be subjugated by the sacrament. Indeed, the gospel calls us to examine ourselves before we partake of the Supper (1 Cor. 11:28). The nature of this self-examination Calvin describes in this way:

> that each man descend into himself, and ponder with himself whether he rests with inward assurance of heart upon the salvation purchased by Christ; whether he acknowledges it by confession of mouth; then, whether he aspires to the imitation of Christ with the zeal of innocence and holiness; whether, after Christ's example, he is prepared to give himself for his brethren and to communicate himself to those with whom he shares Christ in common; whether, as he is counted a member of Christ, he in turn so holds all his brethren as members of his body; whether he desires to cherish, protect, and help them as his own members. Not that these duties both of faith and love can now be made perfect in us, but that we should endeavor and aspire with all our heart toward this end in order that we may day by day increase our faith once begun (4.17.40).

This spiritual food, however, becomes a deadly poison for those who eat and drink unworthily. Worthiness is measured not by perfection but by the One who makes us worthy in the way of faith, manifest in contrition and confession, and love. Hence, faith and love are necessary, not perfection (4.17.39–41). Says Calvin, "this is the worthiness—the best and only kind we can bring to God—to offer our vileness and (so to speak) our unworthiness to him so that his mercy may make us worthy of him; to despair in ourselves so that we may be comforted in him; to abase ourselves so that we may be lifted up by him; to accuse ourselves so that we may be justified by him; moreover, to aspire to that unity which he commends to us in his Supper; and, as he makes all of us one in himself, to desire one soul, one heart, one tongue for us all" (4.17.42).

The Right Manner of Celebrating the Supper
As to the manner in which the Supper should be celebrated—especially to liberate it from all sorts of superstitions and a pile of ceremonies—Calvin sets forth the following, urging that the Supper be very often celebrated or "at least once a week":

> First, then, it should begin with public prayers. After this a sermon should be given. Then, when bread and wine have been placed on the Table, the minister should repeat the words of institution of the Supper. Next, he should recite the promises which were left to us in it; at the same time, he should excommunicate all who are debarred from it by the Lord's prohibition. Afterward, he should pray that the Lord, with the kindness wherewith he has bestowed this sacred food upon us, also teach and form us to receive it with faith and thankfulness of heart, and, inasmuch as we are not so of ourselves, by his mercy make us worthy of such a feast. But here either psalms should be sung, or something be read, and in becoming order the believers should partake of the most holy banquet, the ministers breaking the bread and giving the cup. When the Supper is finished, there should be an exhortation to sincere faith and confession of faith, to love and behavior worthy of Christians. At the last, thanks should be given, and praises sung to God. When these things are ended, the church should be dismissed in peace (4.17.43).

Calvin, as noted above, bids us to celebrate the Supper frequently. Indeed, he goes so far as to urge that no meeting of the church should take place without the presence of "the Word, prayers, partaking of the Supper, and almsgiving" (4.17.44–45). This practice was urged against the custom in his day of infrequent communion, that is, the practice of partaking "once a year" (4.17.46).

To be condemned is not only the practice of infrequent communion, but the practice of withdrawing the cup from the laity, Calvin concludes (4.17.47–50).

Chapter Eighteen: The Papal Mass, a Sacrilege by Which Christ's Supper Was Not Only Profaned but Annihilated

Orientation

This chapter is wholly polemical in nature. The heart of the argument centers upon the Roman Catholic claim that the Mass is not, strictly speaking, a re-sacrifice of Christ; rather, it is just an extension or continuation or application of the sacrifice of Christ on the cross, being of one fabric with it. Calvin carefully rebuts this claim.

Calvin regards the sacrifice of the Mass a frightful abomination, a defiling of Christ's Sacred Supper, a device of Satan that erases from human memory the truth, "a most pestilential error" whereby a priest offers up Christ as an expiatory victim so that we can be reconciled to God (4.18.1). Calvin sets forth five functions or consequences of the Mass, i.e., errors that undermine what Christ intended in instituting the Lord's Supper.

The Errors of the Mass

First, the Mass is an unbearable blasphemy, for it dishonors Christ our only high priest. Indeed, we don't need other priests or other sacrifices. Scripture clearly presents Christ to us as our eternal high priest (Heb. 5:6, 10; 7:17; 9:11; 10:21; Ps. 110:4; Gen. 14:18). This mystery was prefigured in Melchizedek. Christ is an eternal priest after the order of that priesthood. Christ therefore needs no partners, for there is none greater than He (Heb. 7:7, 17–19) (4.18.2).

Second, the Mass suppresses and buries the cross and Passion of Christ. This error is encapsulated in the erection of "the altar," for in that act Christ's cross is overthrown. If Christ offered Himself for our eternal redemption (Heb. 9:12), there is no place for any further sacrificial work. To perform another offering of Christ is to impugn His cross and render it without sufficient power to save. No repetition of His sacrifice is necessary—the very attempt negates it (cf. Heb. 9:26; 10:10, 14, 18; John 19:30). Moreover, Christ's sacrifice does not need new oblations in order to apply or ratify it unto us (cf. 1 Cor. 5:7–8) (4.18.3).

Third, the Mass wipes out the true and unique death of Christ and drives it from human memory. Inasmuch as "the confirmation of a testament depends upon the death of the testator," Christ's death is the confirmation of the covenant of grace, for He gives us forgiveness of sins and eternal righteousness (Heb. 9:15–17). The Mass, however, is nothing other than "a new and wholly different testament," for individual masses promise new forgiveness of sins, new bestowal of righteousness. Calvin admits that Rome does not intend some of the consequences of its doctrine; nevertheless, its doctrine sinks into absurdities contrary to Scripture—for example, their claim that the Mass is a bloodless sacrifice when a sacrifice requires the shedding of blood for cleansing (cf. Heb. 9:22) (4.18.5).

Fourth, the Mass robs us of the benefit that comes from Christ's death while causing us not to recognize or ponder that death as intended in the Lord's Supper. This is seen in the idea of our offering Christ to the Father in the Mass, whereby we are then said to obtain the forgiveness of sins and to participate in Christ's Passion. This turns Christ's Passion into *one example* of redemption. We are to remember Christ's sacrifice on the cross, not offer Him anew (4.18.6).

Fifth, the Mass has taken away, destroyed, and abolished the Sacred Supper that Christ instituted for our blessing. Whereas the Lord's Supper is to be received with thanksgiving, "the sacrifice of the Mass is represented as paying a price to God," which in turn accomplishes satisfaction and imparts forgiveness. The Lord's Supper promises us that we are continually revived and forgiven; but the Mass declares that we need new forgiveness. The Supper is for the public testimony and fellowship or communion of the gathered church; but the sacrifice of the Mass dissolves and breaks apart that community of faith, for priests constantly perform private masses (4.18.7).

The Rise of the Sacrifice of the Mass
Calvin next explains the origin of the Mass, that is, how the practice of the ancient church mutated into the Roman sacrilege—the principal error coming when the idea of the church's sacrifice to God was transformed into a sacrifice made for us. We need to remember that in connection with the Lord's Supper sacrifice originally referred to the sacrifice of praise and reverence, the offering of our gifts to God. But Rome changed that sacrifice

into an offering for sin, a sacrifice of propitiation and expiation, a re-sacrifice of Christ for divine appeasement and forgiveness in order to recover God's favor. Rome even allowed masses to be sold, so that persons could purchase an oblation of Christ to appease God's wrath (4.18.8–17). Indeed, this devolution is an abomination, says Calvin.

> Offered in a golden cup, it has so inebriated all kings and peoples of the earth, from highest to lowest, and has so stricken them with drowsiness and dizziness, that, more stupid than brute beasts, they have steered the whole vessel of their salvation into this one deadly whirlpool. Surely, Satan never prepared a stronger engine to besiege and capture Christ's Kingdom. This is the Helen for whom the enemies of truth today do battle with so much rage, fury, and cruelty—a Helen indeed, with whom they so defile themselves in spiritual fornication, the most abominable of all (4.18.18).

Calvin says that the Mass, "from root to top, swarms with every sort of impiety, blasphemy, idolatry, and sacrilege" (4.18.18).

The church thus contends to preserve the purity of the sacraments against every sort of superstition and error, but also to maintain the number of the sacraments, for there are only two Christ instituted for our use: baptism and the Lord's Supper (cf. 4.18.19–20). Rome insists that there are seven. Calvin gives himself to this question in the next chapter.

Chapter Nineteen: The Five Other Ceremonies, Falsely Termed Sacraments; Although Commonly Considered Sacraments Hitherto, They are Proved Not to Be Such, and Their Real Nature Is Shown

Orientation

Rome believes that there are seven sacraments: first, the sacraments of Christian initiation: baptism, confirmation, and the Eucharist; then the sacraments of healing: penance and extreme unction (i.e., the anointing of the sick); and, last, the sacraments at the service of communion: holy orders and matrimony.

Since he has already dealt with baptism and the Supper, Calvin here considers the five other ceremonies which the Roman Catholic Church regard as sacraments. In fact, if Rome did not call these rites "sacraments," much of the controversy would vanish. But in calling these five ceremonies or rites sacraments—visible forms of invisible grace, means of grace, vessels of the Holy Spirit for the nurture of our salvation—the genuine sacraments are compromised (4.19.1).

Our aim here is merely to present a few of Calvin's comments regarding each of these ceremonies.

Assessing the Five Ceremonies Wrongly Called Sacraments

Confirmation—a public profession of faith—is a necessary and commendable rite, but it is not a sacrament. That is, contrary to Rome's claim, confirmation does not confer the Holy Spirit to us for an increase of God's grace. Sadly, Rome has lifted up this rite to have an importance that supercedes baptism, and also has dressed it up with superfluous ceremony that has no biblical warrant (4.19.2–13). As Calvin says, quoting Augustine, "This is the first law of a minister, to do nothing without a command" from Scripture (4.19.5). Calvin calls the church to catechize all who need it, especially covenant youth, and when they come of age to have them recite the articles of faith in front of the whole church. This will make otherwise lazy parents more diligent to assist in the training of their children at home lest they suffer embarrassment at church; and it will promote unity of faith and thwart the temptation to embrace strange doctrines (4.19.13).

Penance (i.e., the biblical doctrine of repentance) is also misconstrued and perverted in Roman teaching and practice. Calvin has treated penance earlier in the *Institutes* (see 3.3–5); here he traces how the scriptural call to repentance and forgiveness devolved into the private confessional, priestly absolution, and the mandate to perform various acts of penance for the attainment of forgiveness. Truly, a whole theology is woven into Rome's doctrine of penance. Again, Calvin's chief complaint is that penance is not a sacrament. Moreover, baptism is the sacrament of repentance (see Mark 1:4; Luke 3:3) (4.19.14–17).

Extreme unction, or anointing the sick with oil (see James 5:14–15), is likewise not a sacrament, says Calvin. The passage from James, at best, presents a mandate regarding care for the sick. The oil of anointing, however, was never an instrument, only a symbol, of healing (4.19.18–21).

The alleged sacrament of holy orders, like the other alleged sacraments, takes rites, mandates, and gifts, which are biblically prescribed, and names them with the wrong word. That the Lord has given to His church ecclesiastical offices is not in dispute, though Rome has complicated matters in having seven ranks of clergy without biblical sanction, besides dressing everything up with all sorts of unwarranted ceremony and pomp. In addition, Rome has ceased to follow the simple order and pattern presented in the New Testament regarding the church offices (see 4.19.22–33). Calvin concludes by saying that "there is no sacrament of God except where a ceremony is shown joined to a promise, or rather, except where a promise is seen in a ceremony. In this rite one finds not even one syllable of any definite promise; hence, it would be fruitless to seek a ceremony to confirm the promise. Again, one reads of no ceremony ordained by God among those which they use. Therefore, there cannot be any sacrament" (4.19.33).

Finally, marriage, or matrimony, is ordained by God and to be esteemed by all (Gen. 2:21–24; Matt. 19:4ff.; Eph. 5:28), but it too is not a sacrament. Although a good and holy ordinance of God, marriage is no more a sacrament than is farming, building, cobbling, or barbering, which are also good and holy ordinances of God. However, inasmuch as the marriage bond is a symbol of the bond between Christ and His church, it is argued that marriage is a sacrament (Eph. 5:28). This misapplies the apostle's words, which were directed to husbands to love their wives as Christ loves His bride, the church. Moreover, Rome is inconsistent in teaching that matrimony is a sacrament, a means of grace to bless and save, and then forbidding priests to make use of this "sacrament." Although it seems commendable to esteem marriage as a sacrament, doing so has led to all sorts of abuses and oppressive rules, which do not have biblical sanction (4.19.34–37).

Questions for Reflection and Discussion

1. What are the "tokens" of the Lord's Supper? What are the "guarantees" given to us in the Supper?

2. What does Calvin mean by saying that Christ is "food for the soul"?

3. Why is the Supper of no effect without faith? What is the faith necessary for the Supper to be effectual to us?

4. Why is Calvin concerned to say that the Supper doesn't present us with a vain and empty sign? What would make the Supper a vain and empty sign?

5. What is meant by the distinction between "the sign" and "the thing signified" or "the symbol" and "the truth" of the sacrament?

6. Has Calvin convinced you that when you celebrate the Lord's Supper you must lift up your mind to heaven? Or, do you strive to bring Christ down to earth in an act of mental cognition?

7. How does Calvin's view on the "spiritual presence" of Christ at the Lord's Supper differ from the memorial view? Which of these views is more commonly embraced by Reformed and Presbyterian believers today?

8. What is the Lutheran doctrine of "ubiquity"? What is the Lutheran doctrine of consubstantiation? How do these doctrines fit together?

9. What is the "union" in communion? That is, what is it to be united to Christ and to one another as members of Christ in the Supper? How, according to Calvin, does this take place?

10. How are you helped by Calvin's view regarding self-examination before coming to the Lord's Table?

11. Would it be harmful or helpful to celebrate the Lord's Supper as often as Calvin suggests? Defend your answer.

12. Is the Mass an accursed idolatry (see Heidelberg Catechism Q/A 80)? Explain why Calvin and the catechism call it this. Why do some Protestants today want to abandon this language about the Roman Mass?

13. Calvin rightly rejects calling the five ceremonies treated in this chapter sacraments. How should we regard each of these ceremonies and how should they function in the Christian life?

14. The sacraments, along with the preaching of the Word, are means of grace. The Westminster Standards regard prayer also as a means of grace. Is prayer a means of grace in your view?

❧ 24 ❧

The Duties of the Civil Magistrate

Chapter 20 of Book Four

Chapter Twenty: Civil Government

Orientation

CALVIN HAS TOUCHED upon the role of the civil authorities in discussing ecclesiastical power, for the authority of the church and the authority of the magistrate occupy distinct realms and exercise different sorts of inducements and punishments. Moreover, whereas the church is principally concerned to assist believers in their faith and address what resides in the inward person unto eternal life, the state concerns itself with the outward person, and with a citizen's conformity to the rules of society for temporal life (see 4.11.1, 2–4).

Calvin first introduced the distinction between "a twofold government in man" in his treatment of Christian liberty. There he explained that one aspect of this government is "spiritual," which deals with the conscience being instructed in the ways of piety and reverence for God, while the other aspect is "political," and has to do with persons being taught their duties toward humanity, i.e., the laws for citizens in the maintenance of society (3.19.15). This is the difference between the spiritual and the temporal jurisdictions. The one may be called the spiritual, the other the civil kingdom. These kingdoms are "completely distinct" (3.19.15; cf. 4.20.1).

The Necessity of Civil Government

Calvin now returns to this discussion in the last chapter of the *Institutes*, treating the responsibility and calling of the civil authority—which is to say, he treats that which "pertains only to the establishment of civil justice and outward morality" (4.20.1). This chapter begins with a brief defense of the legitimacy of the state, wherein Calvin argues for the necessity, dignity, and role of the civil government. Then follows a lengthy exposition of the duties of the magistrate and various issues that need clarification in how believers are to view and submit themselves to civil authorities.

The twin evils that afflict a right conception of the state are, on the one hand, to disregard and dishonor the civil authority; and, on the other hand, to grant too much power to the state, allowing civil authorities to overthrow the rule of God Himself. "Unless both these evils are checked, purity of faith will perish." For this reason Calvin seeks a middle path wherein the legitimacy of civil power is recognized but also properly circumscribed. Indeed, God shows Himself to be loving toward us in providing for human life through the civil magistrate; and this in turn should move us to pursue piety zealously as an expression of our gratitude to the Lord (4.20.1).

Calvin argues that the kingdom of Christ is not enclosed "within the elements of this world." This means that Christ's spiritual kingdom does not reside in things pertaining to civil privileges, such as whether a believer lives under the bondage of slavery or as a free person. It is not important "what your condition among men may be or under what nation's laws you live, since the Kingdom of Christ does not at all consist in these things" (4.20.1).

Certain fanatics (Calvin appears to have in mind certain Anabaptists and Libertines) propagate the error of "unbridled license." That is, they claim that their freedom in Christ, and with it their new citizenship in Christ's heavenly kingdom, liberates them from the concerns of this life, arguing that it is beneath Christian persons to occupy themselves with the affairs of this world.

Calvin responds to this notion by distinguishing between the spiritual government of the church, which already now manifests "certain beginnings of the Heavenly Kingdom," providing "a certain forecast of an immortal and incorruptible blessedness," and the civil government of the magistrate, which is a calling that pertains to human society in this temporal life. Calvin, however, is jealous to emphasize that these two governments both come from God and are "not at variance" with one another, though their tasks are distinct (4.20.2). In fact, the task of the state is not in doubt for Calvin. He maintains that the civil government has the duty "to cherish and protect the outward worship of God, to defend sound doctrine of piety and the position of the church, to adjust our life to the society of men, to form our social behavior to civil righteousness, to reconcile us with one another, and to promote general peace and tranquility" (4.20.2).

Until Christ's return, such government is necessary for human life to proceed under any kind of order. Believers, to be sure, are on a pilgrimage—this world is not their "true fatherland." And this pilgrimage requires the "helps" of the civil authority. "Our adversaries claim that there ought to be such great perfection in the church of God that its government should suffice for law." Calvin refuses to ascribe such perfection to the church in this life. In reply he asserts that it is foolish to think that such perfection can be found among people. Can the church play cop? "For since the insolence of evil men is so great, their wickedness so stubborn, that it can scarcely be restrained by extremely severe laws, what do we expect them to do if they see that their depravity can go scot-free—when no power can force them to cease from doing evil?" (4.20.2).

The importance of civil government is not to be underestimated for Calvin.

> Its function among men is no less than that of bread, water, sun, and air; indeed, its place of honor is far more excellent. For it does not merely see to it, as all these serve to do, that men breathe, eat, drink, and are kept warm, even though it surely embraces all these activities when it provides for their living together. It does not, I repeat, look to this only, but also prevents idolatry, sacrilege against God's name, blasphemies against his truth, and other public offenses against religion from arising and spreading among the people; it prevents the public peace from being disturbed; it provides that each man may keep his property safe and sound; that men may carry on blameless intercourse among themselves; that honesty and modesty may be preserved among men. In short, it provides that a public manifestation of religion may exist among Christians, and that humanity be maintained among men (4.20.3).

In order to clarify his own staked-out position regarding the duties of the civil magistrate, Calvin divides his discussion into three parts: (1) the office of the magistrate itself, the protector and guardian of the laws, including the nature of this office and the extent of its power as a calling from God; (2) the laws by which the magistrate is to govern, specifically, the laws by which a *Christian* magistrate must govern; and (3) the people who are governed by the laws of the magistrate and the obedience they owe, including how these laws benefit them (4.20.3).

The Office of the Magistrate

For Calvin, the office of the magistrate is ordained by God, having a mandate from God, and is invested with divine authority. The civil government functions as God's representative, acting, so to speak, as His vicegerents. Calvin cites various texts, but perhaps the most decisive text is Romans 13:1–4. The state, God's own instrument for the governance of human life in this world, has a calling from God; and believers must acknowledge it and submit themselves lawfully to it. What is beyond dispute, for Calvin, is that the civil authority, possessing such a calling from God, takes on "the most sacred and by far the most honorable of all callings in the whole life of mortal men" (4.20.4).

We may not be propagators of anarchy; quite the opposite, we must pray for our rulers (1 Tim. 2:2) (4.20.5). Meanwhile, magistrates, acting as God's deputies, must be faithful and just in fulfilling the duties of their office. They must be upright, prudent, gentle, and sober in the exercise of their authority. They must regard themselves, for in fact they are, "ordained ministers of divine justice." "To sum up, if they remember that they are vicars of God, they should watch with all care, earnestness, and diligence, to represent in themselves to men some image of divine providence, protection, goodness, benevolence, and justice." Indeed, like all ministers of God, they will have to render an account to the Lord. In wronging those they govern, they insult God Himself (4.20.6).

As for those who rail against the legitimacy and holy calling of the civil authorities, they actually revile God and dishonor Him. Our duty to submit to the authorities that God has placed over us does not merely apply to upstanding and just governments, but also to unjust and coercive governments. For "among magistrates themselves, although there is a variety of forms, there is no difference in this respect, that we must regard all of them as ordained of God." There is no power except from God (Rom. 13:1; also see Prov. 8:15; 24:21; and 1 Pet. 2:17) (4.20.7).

In light of the above, it is not surprising that Calvin does not think that only one form of government is legitimate; and it is not his interest to debate what might be the best form of government in any particular place or time. Actually, circumstances largely dictate how we might attempt an answer to such questions. Speaking abstractly, Calvin believes that a form of aristocracy or "a system compounded of aristocracy and democracy" constitutes the best form of government. Monarchy is ever under the obstacle of the monarch's own inability to exercise self-control. It is therefore "safer and more bearable" when there is a plurality of leaders to govern us, to assist one another, to teach and admonish each other, and for there to be checks and balances to restrain willfulness (4.20.8).

This portrait of aristocracy, bordering on democracy, is depicted for us in Israel's early history (see Exod. 18:13-26; Deut. 1:9-17). Calvin freely admits "that no kind of government is more happy than one where freedom is regulated with becoming moderation and is properly established on a durable basis"; and so he also reckons "most happy [are] those permitted to enjoy this state; and," says Calvin, "if they stoutly and constantly labor to preserve and retain it, they are doing nothing alien to this office" (4.20.8). Magistrates should labor to preserve this sort of freedom. And we are not free to revolt against the government that God has appointed, for in His divine providence God "has wisely arranged that various countries should be ruled by various kinds of governments." In other words, it is mistaken to think that one form of government is most apropos in all times, in all places, among all peoples. God has purposely not so arranged things. Consequently, "it is our duty to show ourselves compliant and obedient to whomever he sets over the places where we live" (4.20.8).

Calvin strongly maintains that the civil magistrate has the duty to enforce laws that protect true religion and the welfare of the citizens in general—thus both tables of the Mosaic law are to be honored. In order to enforce the second table of the law—i.e., the welfare of citizens in general—the state is to protect and vindicate "public innocence, modesty, decency, and tranquility," as well as focusing particularly upon providing for "the common safety and peace of all" (4.20.9). The state is armed with the sword in order to prevent criminals and other lawbreakers from disturbing the public peace and harming others, and punishes them when they do so. Reward and punishment are instruments that the state uses to promote public safety, for the civil authorities must repress violence and punish misdeeds (4.20.9).

The enforcement of punishments and penalties against law-breakers is not incompatible with the standards of godliness. For example, although Christians are commanded not to kill (Exod. 20:13), and the church may not wield the sword in order to defend or propagate the gospel, the civil authorities may shed the blood of murderers in order to inflict punishment equal to the crime and to protect others (see Rom. 13:4). The magistrate is also called to exercise such power with restraint and justice. Calvin knows rulers easily slide into abuses. "For I am not one either to favor undue cruelty or think that a fair judgment can be pronounced unless clemency...is always present—clemency...the chief gift of princes." The just magistrate pays due attention to both, "lest by excessive severity he either harm more than heal;

or, by superstitious affectation of clemency, fall into the cruelest gentleness, if he should…abandon many to their destruction" (4.20.10).

In exercising the sword, the state also has the right and the duty to wage war—this is just an extension of protecting the tranquility of the citizens under its charge. "Therefore, both natural equity and the nature of the office dictate that princes must be armed not only to restrain the misdeeds of private individuals by judicial punishment, but also to defend by war the dominions entrusted to their safekeeping, if at any time they are under enemy attack." Such wars are lawful (4.20.11). But even the waging of war requires the exercise of restraint, and that it be pursued justly (4.20.12).

At this point Calvin turns his attention to the right of civil authorities to levy taxes and the like, in order "to meet the public expenses of their office." Although the civil authorities may legitimately use public revenues in order to establish appropriate facilities and private dwellings in keeping with the dignity of their office, they do not have permission to indulge themselves with "waste and expensive luxury" (4.20.13).

In summary, we see that Calvin conceived of the civil government as having a twofold purpose: (1) to secure a safe environment for the gospel to flourish, and (2) to maintain order and civilization as a restraining effect upon human rebellion. The magistrate is a gift from God, bestowed upon mankind in consequence of the fall. We are called to hold the magistrate in high esteem, since he is called from God. Indeed, the magistrate possesses the "most honorable of all callings." Romans 13 clearly indicates that the governing authorities represent God's authority over us. Rebellion against the magistrate is rebellion against God.

The Laws of the Magistrate

Having commented on the necessity of civil government and its principal duties, Calvin next considers the second major topic of this chapter—the laws by which a *Christian* magistrate is to govern. We must remember that the magistrate itself is subject to God's law and the written code of human law.

For Calvin, the laws and the magistrate stand together—"the law is a silent magistrate; the magistrate, a living law" (4.20.14). But this does not mean we are to turn to the laws of Moses in an effort to re-establish the Old Testament theocracy. Calvin views such efforts as dangerous and misguided. "Let all men consider how perilous and seditious this notion is; it will be enough for me to have proved it false and foolish" (4.20.14).

First, Calvin distinguishes between the moral, ceremonial, and judicial laws of Moses in order to discern what laws still apply to us and what laws do not. "The moral law...is contained under two heads, one of which simply commands us to worship God with pure faith and piety; the other, to embrace men with sincere affection." This law abides eternally and is prescribed for all. As for the ceremonial law, it served for "the tutelage of the Jews, with which it seemed good to the Lord to train this people...in their childhood, until the fullness of time should come...." Finally, regarding the judicial law, they were given to the Jews for civil government, "imparting certain formulas of equity and justice," for the promotion of peace and the ordering of their life together. Both the ceremonial and judicial laws have been abrogated or taken away without abandoning what is needful for the ordering of society, for the moral law, which sets forth God's eternal law, gives us the precepts of love and justice in order to make laws for the ordering of public life (4.20.15). In fact, "every nation," says Calvin, "is left free to make such laws as it foresees to be profitable for itself." But, he adds, such laws "must be in conformity to that perpetual rule of love, so that they indeed vary in form but have the same purpose" (4.20.15).

Says Calvin, all laws have two elements that we must attend to—namely (1) the constitution of the law, which depends upon varying and changing circumstances; and (2) the equity on which the constitution of the law is founded, that is, that unchanging and constant foundation which must be maintained and which must be the aim of any law imposed. Accordingly, when we come to think of the equity, we are dealing with what is natural and unchanging. This means that what is called the moral law as given by Moses is in fact "nothing else than a testimony of natural law and of that conscience which God has engraved upon the minds of men" (4.20.16). In other words, equity does not vary or change according to time, place, culture, or circumstances, for it must govern all laws that are established, and such laws so constituted can and may vary or change according to time, place, culture, and circumstances.

Calvin provides some examples. We examine just one. God's moral law forbids stealing. The judicial laws under Moses imposed certain punishments (Exod. 22:1-4). The laws of other nations impose other sorts of penalties, with varying degrees of severity. But stealing is universally forbidden. "Yet we see how, with such diversity, all laws tend to the same end." They pronounce punishment upon misdeeds that "God's eternal law has condemned, namely, murder, theft, adultery, and false witness," while the penalties meted out differ. This is as it should be, says Calvin, for place and circumstance dictate that severer punishments be imposed in certain lands for the preservation of order and to discourage further disregard for law. Some nations are more inclined to this vice or that. Such vices therefore require harsher penalties in order to more sharply inhibit and discourage them. Again, this is as it should be, notes Calvin; and it is utterly mistaken to think that the judicial laws of Moses should be followed and put in force everywhere (4.20.16).

The Duties of the People Governed by the Magistrate

The last major topic of this chapter concerns the people who are governed by the civil authorities—which brings Calvin to the question of Christians making use of the law courts. He counsels us to do so without hatred and revenge. It is a mistake to think that believers may not seek justice from the courts at all; but it is also a mistake to become litigious and pursue lawsuits from spite or a vindictive spirit, which reveals a lack of charity for others (4.20.17). For this reason believers must examine their motives in all litigious matters. For Calvin, this principle best serves us: "that a lawsuit, however just, can never be rightly prosecuted by any man, unless he treats his adversary with the same love and good will as if the business under controversy were already amicably settled and composed" (4.20.18).

It is therefore a mistake to condemn all legal disagreements, which require the courts for resolution (4.20.19). But in pursuing justice we must "utterly recoil from any desire to retaliate" or to pay back (4.20.20). For the apostle Paul condemns "an immoderate rage for litigation in the church...." The gospel is disgraced by the quarrels of believers which require the courts to resolve. We must consider how it is better to yield our own right rather than land ourselves in court against a brother, concerning whom we will find it hard not to harbor feelings of discord and hatred. "To sum up,...love will give every man the best counsel. Everything undertaken apart from love and all disputes that go beyond it, we regard as incontrovertibly unjust and impious" (4.20.21).

The last issue Calvin addresses regarding civil government is whether we must submit ourselves to unjust rulers. It is easy to be submissive to godly and just rulers. But what about those who clearly disregard God's standard of justice? Calvin bids us, as noted earlier, to respect and reverence civil authorities, and this as an expression of love and reverence for God. The nature of the office demands this from us (4.20.22). Even more, the magistrate is due our obedience, which includes heeding the laws imposed, paying taxes, etc. (4.20.23); and this applies also to the unjust magistrate. We must admit, says Calvin, that civil rulers often manifest undesirable traits. That does not give us license to disrespect or disobey them (4.20.24).

Calvin bids us to look carefully at God's Word, for therein we are taught that we are subject not only to the governing authorities who lead well and uprightly, but we must also submit ourselves to those who perform their office wickedly and ineptly. Even the unjust ruler is ordained of God. Although the man might be a disgrace, the office he holds still deserves our esteem (4.20.25).

The book of Daniel serves as a primary exhibit of this truth. Although Nebuchadnezzar was dishonorable, he reigned by God's ordination, and Daniel rendered this king the honor due his office (also see 1 Sam. 8:11–17; Jer. 27; Jer. 29:7; 1 Sam. 24:6, 9–11) (4.20.26–28). For our part, it is not our place to vindicate justice against a cruel ruler; rather, we must leave that to God. We must look after our own duties and responsibilities. We should examine our own misdeeds and sins, realizing that an irreligious or disgraceful ruler can be a divine punishment against us, and we may need to suffer under God's correction (cf. Dan. 9:7). Humility restrains impatience. "Let us then also call this thought to mind, that it is not for us to remedy such evils; that only this remains, to implore the Lord's help, in whose hand are the hearts of kings, and the changing of kingdoms [Prov. 21:1 p.]" (4.20.29).

We see, then, for Calvin, citizens owe obedience to the magistrate. In this respect, Calvin is an anti-revolutionary. He teaches that even if we live under Turks, tyrants, or other cruel oppression we may not revolt (cf. 1 Pet. 2:13). However, there is an exception. A duly appointed lesser magistrate is called to protect his subjects from a cruel Monarch. If a lesser magistrate calls his subjects to arms against, say, the King of France, they must comply (4.20.30–31). Moreover, we must disobey the magistrate in order not to disobey God. Daniel 6:22–23 is the key text Calvin cites in this connection. In obeying civil authorities we may never be led away from obedience to God. When a choice must be made between obeying God or human beings, we must with Peter choose to obey God (Acts 5:29) (4.20.32). Thus, civil disobedience is permissible, for Calvin, only in a very limited scope: (1) lesser magistrates must protect their citizens; (2) when civil rulers demand from us that which is contrary to God's moral law, we must obey God.

This brings to a close Calvin's discussion of the civil magistrate, which also brings us to the end of Calvin's *Institutes of the Christian Religion.*

We conclude this summary analysis of Calvin's *Institutes* with the words he used to end his great work: *LAUS DEO*, that is: *GOD BE PRAISED!*

Questions for Reflection and Discussion

1. Calvin mentions two errors that people fall into regarding the civil authorities—either to dishonor them and to regard them as having little value, or to over inflate their importance and allow them too much power and authority over human affairs. Toward which of these errors do our churches or many Reformed believers today tend with respect to this issue? Why? Do modern Christians show the kind of respect for the governing authorities that Calvin advocates?

2. Why is it mistaken to think, as Calvin suggests, that Christians should have no concern with the affairs of this life—especially civil affairs?

3. Do you think Calvin is right in what he describes as the functions of the state? How does his view differ from our common, North American conceptions of the duties of the state?

4. Explain why you agree or disagree with the statement that the calling of the civil magistrate is the most sacred and honorable of all callings in this life.

5. In view of Calvin's firm stance that civil authorities are to be obeyed, can modern revolutions be defended as just?

6. Some Christians maintain that they are under no obligation to pay taxes to the secular state. Would Calvin agree with that view? Explain Calvin's reasoning on this issue.

7. Modern day theonomists argue that the Mosaic civil laws are still applicable today, and ought to be imposed in the civil sphere. Calvin explicitly rejects this view. Explain why Calvin regards that view as dangerous.

8. What does Calvin mean by natural law? Why is it important? And how does it function even in non-Christian societies?

9. What might be some modern day examples of needing to disobey the state in order to obey God?

10. What have you learned in this summary of Calvin's theology that has most benefited you?

Selected Bibliography

Battles, Ford Lewis, and John Walchenbach. *Analysis of the Institutes of the Christian Religion*. Grand Rapids: Baker Book House, 1980.

Calvin, John. *Calvin's New Testament Commentaries*. Edited by David W. Torrance and Thomas F. Torrance. 12 vols. Grand Rapids: Eerdmans, 1963–1974.

_____. *Commentaries of John Calvin*. 46 vols. Edinburgh: Calvin Translation Society, 1844–55. Reprint, Grand Rapids: Baker Book House, 1979.

_____. *Institutes of the Christian Religion* (1559). 2 vols. Ed. John T. McNeill. Translated by Ford Lewis Battles. Library of Christian Classics. Philadelphia: The Westminster Press, 1960.

_____. *Institutes of the Christian Religion* (1559). 2 vols. Translated by Henry Beveridge. Reprint, Grand Rapids: Eerdmans, 1966.

_____. *Institutes of the Christian Religion* (1559). 2 vols. Translated by John Allen. Reprint, Grand Rapids: Eerdmans, 1949.

_____. *The Institutes of the Christian Religion*. Edited by Tony Lane and Hilary Osborne. Grand Rapids: Baker Book House, 1987.

Chung, Sung Wook, editor. *John Calvin and Evangelical Theology: Legacy and Prospect*. Louisville: Westminster John Knox Press, 2009.

Cottret, Bernard. *Calvin: A Biography*. Translated by M. Wallace McDonald. Grand Rapids: Eerdmans, 2000. de Greef, W. *The Writings of John Calvin: An Introductory Guide*. Translated by Lyle D. Bierma. Grand Rapids: Baker Books, 1993.

Dowey, Edward A. Jr. *The Knowledge of God in Calvin's Theology*, 3rd ed. Grand Rapids: Eerdmans, 1994.

Gordon, Bruce. *Calvin*. New Haven: Yale University Press, 2009.

Hall, David W. and Peter A. Lillback, eds. *Theological Guide to Calvin's Institutes: Essays and Analysis.* The Calvin 500 Series. Phillipsburg, NJ: P&R Publishing, 2008.

Helm, Paul. *John Calvin's Ideas.* Oxford: Oxford University Press, 2004.

Klooster, Fred H. *Calvin's Doctrine of Predestination.* 2nd ed. Grand Rapids: Baker Book House, 1977.

Lane, Anthony L. *A Reader's Guide to Calvin's Institutes.* Grand Rapids: Baker Academic, 2009.

McGrath, Alister E. *A Life of John Calvin.* Oxford: Basil Blackwell, 1990.

McKim, Donaald K., ed. *The Cambridge Companion to John Calvin.* Cambridge: Cambridge University Press, 2004.

Muller, Richard A. *The Unaccommodated Calvin: Studies in the Foundation of a Theological Tradition.* New York: Oxford University Press, 2000.

Niesel, Wilhelm. *The Theology of Calvin.* Translated by Harold Knight. Reprint, Grand Rapids: Baker Book House, 1980.

Parker, T. H. L. *Calvin: An Introduction to His Thought.* Louisville: Westminster/ John Knox Press, 1995.

_____. *John Calvin: A Biography.* Philadelphia: The Westminster Press, 1975.

Partee, Charles. *The Theology of John Calvin.* Louisville: Westminster John Knox Press, 2008.

Schreiner, Susan. *The Theater of His Glory: Nature and the Natural Order in the Thought of John Calvin.* Reprint, Grand Rapids: Baker Academic, 1995.

Selderhuis, Herman J. *John Calvin: A Pilgrim's Life.* Translated by Albert Gootjes. Downers Grove, IL: IVP Academic, 2009.

Selderhuis, Herman J., ed. *The Calvin Handbook.* Translated by Henry J. Baron, Judith J. Guder, Randi H. Lundell, and Gerrit W. Sheeres. Grand Rapids: Eerdmans, 2009.

Steinmetz, David. *Calvin in Context.* New York: Oxford University Press, 1995.

Torrance, Thomas F. *Calvin's Doctrine of Man.* London: Lutterworth Press, 1949.

_____. *The Hermeneutics of John Calvin.* Edinburgh: Scottish Academic Press, 1988.

Venema, Cornelis P. *Accepted and Renewed in Christ: The "Twofold Grace of God" and the Interpretation of Calvin's Theology.* Reformed Historical Theology, vol. 2. Edited by Herman J. Selderhuis, et al. Gottingen: Vandenhoeck & Ruprecht, 2007.

Wallace, Ronald S. *Calvin's Doctrine of the Christian Life*. Reprint, Tyler, TX: Geneva Divinity School Press, 1982.

_____. *Calvin's Doctrine of the Word and Sacrament*. 1953; reprint, Tyler, TX: Geneva Divinity School Press, 1982.

_____. *Calvin, Geneva, and the Reformation: A Study of Calvin as Social Worker, Churchman, Pastor and Theologian*. Grand Rapids: Baker Book House, 1988.

Wendel, François. *Calvin: Origins and Development of His Religious Thought*. Translated by Philip Mairet. Reprint, Durham, South Carolina: The Labyrinth Press, 1987.

Zachman, Randall C., ed. *John Calvin and Roman Catholicism: Critique and Engagement, Then and Now*. Grand Rapids: Baker Academic, 2008.

_____. *John Calvin as Teacher, Pastor, and Theologian: The Shape of His Writings and Thought*. Grand Rapids: Baker Academic, 2006.